Old Testament Priests
and the New Priest

Studies in Scripture

Board of Editors

OLD TESTAMENT PRIESTS and the NEW PRIEST

According to the New Testament

ALBERT VANHOYE, SJ

Translated by
J. Bernard Orchard, OSB

ST. BEDE'S PUBLICATIONS
Petersham, Massachusetts

Originally published in French under the title
Prêtres Anciens, Prêtre Nouveau, selon le Nouveau Testament
© 1980 by Editions du Seuil

Copyright © 1986 by St. Bede's Publications
All Rights Reserved
PRINTED IN THE UNITED STATES OF AMERICA
5 4 3 2 1

Imprimi Potest Maurice Gilbert, SJ
                  Rector, Institute Biblique
Imprimatur   Giovanni Canestri
                  Titular Archbishop of Monterano

Rome, 19 May 1980

The *Imprimi Potest* and *Imprimatur* are official declarations that a book or pamphlet is free of doctrinal and moral error. No implication is contained therein that those granting the *Imprimi Potest* and *Imprimatur* agree with the content, opinions or statements expressed.

LIBRARY OF CONGRESS CATALOGING IN PUBLICATION DATA

Vanhoye, Albert.
  Old Testament priests and the new priest.

  Translation of: Prêtres anciens, prêtre nouveau selon le Nouveau Testament.
  Bibliography: p.
  Includes index.
  1. Priesthood—Biblical teaching. 2. Bible. N.T.—Criticism, interpretation, etc. 3. Jesus Christ—Priesthood. 4. Priests, Jewish.
5. Priesthood, Universal. I. Title.
BS2545.P69V3613 1986   262'.1   85-2171
ISBN 0-932506-38-0

Contents

Translator's Foreword

The translator wishes to acknowledge with gratitude not only the personal interest of Father Vanhoye himself, who has carefully read and approved the text, but also the extensive help he has received from Moira B. Mathieson, the editor of the English edition, particularly in checking the accuracy of the translation and improving the flow of the language.

He also wishes to acknowledge the generous help and support for the whole project received from Msgr. Richard Malone and the Office of the Committee on Doctrine of the National Conference of Catholic Bishops.

Last, but not least, he wishes to thank the publishers, St. Bede's Publications, for their patient cooperation and helpfulness.

J. B. Orchard, OSB

Ealing Abbey

Abbreviations of Scientific Periodicals and Reviews

Bib	Biblica, Rome
BZ	Biblische Zeitschrift, Paderborn
MuTZ	Munchener Theologische Zeitschrift, Munich
NRT	Nouvelle Revue theologique, Tournai
NTS	New Testament Studies, Cambridge
NT	Novum Testamentum, Leiden
RB	Revue biblique, Gabalda, Paris
RHPR	Revue d'Histoire et de Philosophie religieuses, Strasbourg
RSPT	Revue des Sciences philosophiques et theologiques, Vrin, Paris
RSR	Recherches de Science religieuse, Paris
RQum	Revue de Qumran, Letouzey et Ane, Paris
RThom	Revue thomiste, Toulouse/Brussels
Sal	Salesianum, Turin
SvExAb	Svensk Exegetisk Arsbok, Uppsala
TWNT	Theologisches Worterbuch zum Neuen Testament, Stuttgart, 1933-1979
TZ	Theologische Zeitschrift, Basle
VD	Verbum Domini, Rome
ZNW	Zeitschrift fur die neutestamentliche Wissenschaft und die Kunde der alteren Kirche, Berlin
ZTK	Zeitschrift fur Theologie und Kirche, Tubingen

Abbreviations of The Books of The Bible

Ac	Acts of the Apostles
Am	Amos
Bar	Baruch
1 Ch	1 Chronicles
2 Ch	2 Chronicles
1 Cor	1 Corinthians
2 Cor	2 Corinthians

Col	Colossians
Dn	Daniel
Dt	Deuteronomy
Ep	Ephesians
Ex	Exodus
Ez	Ezechiel
Ezr	Ezra
Gal	Galatians
Gn	Genesis
Hag	Haggai
Heb	Hebrews
Hos	Hosea
Is	Isaiah
Jb	Job
Jam	James
Jdt	Judith
Jg	Judges
Jn	John
1 Jn	1 John
2 Jn	2 John
3 Jn	3 John
Jer	Jeremiah
1 Kg	1 Kings
2 Kg	2 Kings
3 Kg	Greek translation of 1 Kings
Lk	Luke
Lev	Leviticus
1 Mac	1 Maccabees
2 Mac	2 Maccabees
Mk	Mark
Mic	Micah
Ml	Malachi
Mt	Matthew
Num	Numbers
Neh	Nehemiah
1 Pet	1 Peter
Ph	Philippians
Pr	Proverbs

Ps	Psalms
Qoh	Ecclesiastes (Koheleth)
Rev	Revelation
Rom	Romans
1 Sam	1 Samuel
2 Sam	2 Samuel
Sir	Ecclesiasticus (Sirac)
1 Thess	1 Thessalonians
1 Tim	1 Timothy
2 Tim	2 Timothy
Tit	Titus
Wis	Wisdom
Zech	Zechariah
Zeph	Sophonias (Zephaniah)

Abbreviations of Non-Biblical Works Cited

DamD	Ecrit de Damas (Hebrew ms. related to 1QS).
De opif. mundi	Philon of Alexandria, *De opificio mundi* (on the creation of the world)
Leg. Alleg.	Philon of Alexandria, *Legum Allegoriae* (allegorical commentary on the Law of Moses)
4 M	4th Book of the Maccabees
1 QS	Rule (*seder*) of the community, found in grotto 1 at Qumran.
1QSa	Appendix A to 1 QS
1QpHab	Commentary (*pesher*) of Habbakuk, found in grotto 1 of Qumran.
Test. Judah	Testament of Judah (in: The Testaments of the 12 Patriarchs)
Test. Levi	Testament of Levi
Test. Reuben	Testament of Reuben
Test. Simeon	Testament of Simeon

Introduction

By promising a comparison between "Old Testament Priests" and "New Priest," the title of this book clearly alludes to the passionate debates that have caused tensions and divisions among Christians in recent years. In particular, the opponents of the "new priests" and the "new liturgy" have drawn the public's attention to themselves by organizing traditionalist ceremonies and even going so far as to occupy one church or another by force. On a different and less disturbing level, the question of the priesthood has given rise to a number of discussions that are far from over. The vocabulary of the priesthood, which the Church had been using peacefully for centuries, has suddenly met with strong objections from many sides. Some think that there is no sense in talking about priesthood in a secularized world. Others feel that, by insisting on priesthood, the Church has brought about an unjustifiable return to the ritualistic aspect of the Old Testament and so has forsaken the authentic message of the Gospel. Because the notion of priesthood is tied to that of sacrifice, the virulent critics who have recently attacked the sacrificial concept of religion have also, as a direct consequence, radically depreciated the priesthood. Moreover, certain teachings of the last Council have revived or created other problems. In restoring the doctrine of the common priesthood of all the faithful to a place of honor, Vatican II shattered the existing notion by which, more or less consciously, the monopoly of the priesthood in the Catholic Church was assigned to the clergy. Some then went from the one extreme to the other. If all the faithful are priests by virtue of their baptism, it is no longer clear, they say, what ordination can add in the way of priesthood to those who receive it. Many wonder if there is really room to speak of "priestly ordination" or of a ministerial "priesthood." Would it not be better to say simply "ordination to the ministry" and "ordained ministers"?

The questions therefore are many and thorny. In this book they are not treated on the level either of current events or of systematic theology, but as the title specifies, "according to the New Testament"; that is to say, by carrying out an exegesis of the New Testament texts that speak of priests and of priesthood. It is easily understood that a study of this kind is of fundamental importance for those who are not content with *a priori* ideas or subjective impressions. Before discussing the place that should or should not be given to the priesthood and to sacrifice in the faith and life of the Church, it is advisable first to examine closely what the New Testament writings say on these subjects.

We must immediately make it clear, in this regard, that for Christians in the first century the question of the priesthood was a distinct issue from that of ministries in the Church. The subsequent evolution of Christian terminology has closely linked the two ideas, but it was not so at the beginning. One of the problems to be faced is precisely to discern the reasons for this evolution and to discuss its legitimacy.

Serious works have already been published on the ministries in the earliest years of the Church. One of the most recent and most remarkable preceded the present volume in the series "Parole de Dieu" under the title *Le Ministère et les ministères selon le Nouveau Testament* (no. 10 in the series). Far from making a study on the priesthood such as the present one superfluous, this book on the ministry rather confirms its usefulness, for it ends with an explicit avowal of a vacuum in this regard: "Throughout this work there has been practically no question of priests and very little of priesthood" (p. 474). The subject therefore remains to be treated. It is necessary to return to the New Testament to see what place the reality of the priesthood occupies there and how it understands the priest. Do the writings of the New Testament speak much about priests and the priesthood, or do they speak of them only rarely? Do they do so with sympathy, indifference or hostility? Are they content to reflect the ideas of that time or do they develop a new understanding? How is this understanding defined? All these points, and above all the last two, call for precise and methodical research.

A first inventory reveals that the New Testament contains three series of texts about the priesthood. In a first series, the vocabulary of the priesthood is used only in connection with Jewish priests and high priests, or—in one case only—in connection with pagan priests. In a second series, whose texts are all found together in a single writing, the Epistle to the Hebrews, Christ himself is proclaimed, with great insistence, priest and high priest, and a comparison is made between his priesthood and the old priesthood. Finally, in some other texts which make up a third series, priesthood is attributed to Christians. This breakdown commands the overall plan of this book, whose eleven chapters fall into three main sections. The first shows how the problem of the priesthood was posed by the first Christians. The Gospel catechesis, which evoked and nourished their faith, did not treat this question explicitly, rather, it showed the role that the Jewish priests and high priests had played in the course of the life of Jesus, a role of increasingly unmistakable opposition. Another source of reflection also influenced the thinking of the Christians: the Old Testament. This pointed in another direction by its witness to the fact that cultic institutions centered on the Temple and in particular on the priesthood held a primary place in the life of the people of God. Between these two components of revelation, then, one would have perceived a dissonance at first rather than harmonious accord. Was there not a deadlock here? Certainly, the difficulties were great, but the elements of a solution gradually began to appear as soon as they started to explore in greater depth certain fundamental ideas in the Old Testament, certain aspects of the mystery of Jesus and certain realities of the Christian life.

Finally, the Christians arrived at a discovery that struck them with the irresistible force of light: it was in the very person of Christ Jesus that the old priesthood had found its fulfillment. There was no need to look elsewhere. This triumphant conviction, which rings through the Epistle to the Hebrews and is there supported by a proper demonstration, furnishes the matter for the second part of the present work, obviously the most important. Jesus Christ is High Priest. He has offered a sacrifice. How are we to take doctrines of this kind? Are they to be bitterly contested because they express a "sacrificial reading of the Passion," and so to be denounced (with Rene Girard) as "the most paradoxical and colossal misunderstanding in all history"? Before passing such a judgment, it is surely right, in good method, to analyze carefully the texts themselves and to allow oneself to be guided by them, instead of hastily projecting preconceived ideas upon them. For then the reader will understand that the author of the Epistle, enlightened by the mystery of Christ, has freed the expressions he has used from their negative or defective elements and has given them a new fullness of meaning. His concept of the priesthood and of sacrifice can in no way be reduced to the ancient schemas. Indeed it transforms them utterly and makes them shine forth in all directions by opening them to all the human and spiritual richness of the existence of Christ. For this reason, his understanding throws a vivid light on humanity in its concrete reality, both in people's personal relations with God and in their fellowship with one another. Far from constituting "a deplorable regression," the proclamation of the priesthood of Christ represents a forward step for the faith and imparts a new impetus to Christian life. Expressing in a clearer way the profound significance of the intervention of Christ, this understanding of the priesthood simultaneously promotes the unfolding of the vital dynamism that emerges from it. Christ the High Priest causes humanity's paths to emerge into the light of God; he alone can free human existence and give it all its true dimensions.

When it describes the Christian transformation of human existence, the Epistle to the Hebrews does not say that believers become priests. It reserves the title of priest for Christ alone. But two other writings of the New Testament, the First Letter of Peter and Revelation, do attribute priestly dignity to Christians themselves. They express another point of view about the reality of the priesthood, to which the third and last part of this book is devoted. Here too it is necessary to distinguish between completely different interpretations. Are we to understand that each believer becomes a priest individually and enjoys a sort of religious autarchy or, instead, that the priesthood is exercised communally by the entire Church, thanks to its constitution as a priestly people? Is it correct, as a recent article has maintained, that "the significance of the priestly vocabulary is negative, its intention being only to prohibit distinctions between the level of priesthood of Christians"? Or should one recognize that there is no sign whatever of a negative intention in the texts and that these seek only to give a positive vision of the Christian ideal? If we are to be able to decide between the opposing theses or to escape in some other way from the dilemma, nothing can replace a first-hand study of the disputed texts.

The present work is the result of a study of this kind. The method followed is that of exegetical research. One does not begin therefore either from *a priori* definitions or from previously established positions. Nor does one claim to deal with all the questions. But one sets out to listen to the New Testament and to be guided by its texts toward a progressive discovery of the profound meaning of the priesthood.[1] Instead of directly proposing solutions to the various problems as they arise, this book instead invites the reader to an overall reflection, which could result in changing the very way of looking at the problems.

Note

[1]The reader who, on reading the title, is puzzled by the use of the singular in "New Priest," will find the explanation in Part Two: "Jesus Christ. New Priest"; see Ch. IX, Conclusion and Final Reflections, c and d.

PART ONE

Old Testament Priests
and
the Christian Faith

CHAPTER I

The Old Testament Priesthood in the First Christian Traditions

The simplest way to approach the question of the priesthood in the New Testament is undoubtedly to go through the Gospels, observing what the traditions reported there have to say about priests. One can, in this way, gradually put oneself in the place of the first Christians, who were formed by these traditions and took part in developing them and passing them on. Our intention is not to pass the Gospels through the sieve of historical criticism, but simply to gather their testimony on this particular point in order to understand better the situation of the Church in the time of the apostles. The observations that may be made do not all point in the same direction. But their very diversity is instructive.

1. Priests in the Gospels

In the Gospels the word "priest" (*hiereus*) is never applied either to Jesus or to his disciples, but always designates the Jewish priests, who are presented in different ways depending on the case in question.

The first person to appear in the Gospel of Luke is a priest, Zechariah, and Luke shows him exercising his priestly duties. The description is insistent. Luke recalls the organization of the Jewish priesthood, its division into a number of "classes," each of which in turn performed its duties:[1]

> Zechariah, when his class's turn came, performed his priestly duties before God; he was designated by lot, according to the custom of the priesthood, to enter into the sanctuary of the Lord and burn incense there. (Lk 1:8-9)[2]

The account clearly shows the privilege of the priest and the different status of the people. The priest is authorized to "enter the sanctuary of the Lord" in order to carry out there the ceremonies of public worship; the crowd of faithful, on the other hand, must remain "outside" and can only "pray" (Lk 1:10). When it happens that the priest is delayed in some unusual way in the sanctuary, nobody can go in to see what has happened; they must be content to remain outside and be patient (Lk 1:21). In the above description one does not sense the slightest intention of criticising the priestly institution. On the contrary, Luke recognizes that the Jewish priests perform their functions "before God" and he reports that the liturgical ceremony was the occasion of a divine manifestation: "an angel of the Lord appeared to him, standing at the right of the altar of incense"; Zechariah had "seen a vision in the sanctuary" (Lk 1:11, 22). It all amounts to a positive appreciation of the public worship celebrated by the Jewish priests in the Temple of Jerusalem.

However, the episode that immediately follows—the annunciation to Mary—shows that the temple worship cannot be given an exclusive value in the relationship with God. Indeed, this second episode does not take place in a consecrated place, but in an obscure village which none the less has been chosen for a divine manifestation more important than the first. The angel does not address himself to a priest but to a simple young girl, and she shows herself better disposed than the priest to welcome the word of God (compare Lk 1:45 with 1:20).

There is no further mention of priests in the remainder of the Infancy Narratives. Their intervention must, of course, be presumed when the child Jesus was presented in the Temple at Jerusalem, because reference is made here to a sacrifice and the Law states that the turtle doves or pigeons must be brought to "the priest" for offering.[3] But the Gospel does not think it necessary to record this detail. Nor does it mention the priests when the boy Jesus is found in the Temple. One might ask whether the "masters" in whose midst Jesus had taken his place were not Jewish priests. According to Malachi, "The lips of the priest should guard knowledge; it is from his mouth that instruction should be sought."[4] At the time of Jesus, however, it seems that the priests had given up this part of their task. In any case, the Gospel does not give us any further information on the subject.

In the course of the public life of Jesus, priests are not often mentioned. The Fourth Gospel only speaks of them once and that is before Jesus has come on the scene. The occasion is that of a commission of inquiry sent by the authorities to inquire about the status of John the Baptist: "the Jews sent priests and Levites from Jerusalem to ask him,

'Who are you?' " (Jn 1:19). The preaching of John the Baptist was concerned with the realm of relationships with God. It was normal for priests to be appointed to verify that he was in agreement with the traditional religion. John the Baptist was urging his audience to be baptised. As a rite of purification, baptism came under the jurisdiction of the Jewish priests, who were responsible for regulating ritual purity. One is therefore not surprised to hear them ask, "Why are you baptizing?" (Jn 1:25). The evangelist reports the replies of the Baptist, because they are an announcement of the arrival of the Christ, but he is not interested in the reaction of the priests. In his account, their only function is to elicit the witness of John, which directs everyone's attention toward "the one who is to come after him," Jesus (Jn 1:29-30).

In the first three Gospels, Jesus himself sometimes speaks of priests. The tradition common to the Synoptics contains two texts where he mentions them. The first time is when he commands a leper whom he has healed to go and show himself to the priest and to make a ritual offering:

> "Mind you say nothing to anyone, but go and show yourself to the priest and make the offering for your healing prescribed by Moses as evidence of your recovery." (Mk 1:44)

Jesus is thus inviting the leper to comply with the Jewish Law, which made the priests responsible for the sanitary supervision of lepers (Lev 13-14). This particular function, which seems strange to us today, was based on their understanding of leprosy: it was considered to be a kind of impurity rather than merely a disease. In reference to this affliction one did not speak of a cure but of "purification."[5] Being "impure," lepers could not join in religious celebrations, for which ritual purity was required. The priest, who was in charge of worship, had to assure the ritual purity of the worshippers and in particular to verify the possible cure of lepers.

In this Gospel episode, Jesus recognizes the jurisdiction of the Jewish priest in this matter, and gives the ritual offerings prescribed by the Law their proper place as offerings which were to pass through the hands of the priest. Nevertheless, Jesus' attitude is not simply one of submission; by touching the leper Jesus has broken the letter of the law of purity, which forbade this contact, but at the same time he has fulfilled the spirit of this law, because by this act he has made the leper pure. In this way Jesus has shown himself superior to the Law, which was incapable of curing the leper, and superior to the priest, whose role was limited to checking the leper's condition.

In addition to this episode, common to all three Synoptic Gospels, Luke relates another, which though different in more than one way nevertheless involves a similar command and allows interesting comparisons. Jesus orders ten lepers who implore his mercy: "Go and show yourselves to the priests." The lepers obey him and on the way find themselves "cleansed."[6] Here Jesus' submission to the Law appears at first to be even greater: he does not touch the lepers but sends them at once to the priests for judgment. As the story continues, however, the perspective is reversed, because the emphasis shifts to the attitude of the healed leper who, finding himself cured, retraces his steps to glorify God and to thank Jesus. A word from Jesus underlines that it was in fact proper to come back to him in order to give glory to God. Again, Jesus proves his superiority to the priest, not only in restoring purity, but also in establishing a relationship with God. For though the normal way of giving thanks to God was to go to the priest, in this instance it consisted in coming back to Jesus.

The second text of the common tradition in which Jesus speaks of priests occurs in the context of a controversy. Jesus replies to the Pharisees who were criticizing his disciples for not perfectly respecting the Sabbath, by recalling the example of David, who, driven by hunger one day "went into the House of God when Abiathar was high priest, and ate the loaves of offering which *only the priests* are allowed to eat."[7] Jesus uses the episode related in 1 Sam 21:2-7 to show that the precepts, or rather the prohibitions regarding ritual worship do not have absolute value. Scripture itself bears witness that in certain circumstances they may be broken. The privileges of the Jewish priests are not inviolable.

To this statement the Gospel of Matthew immediately adds another and still more significant one. Jesus supports his argument: "Or again have you not read in the Law that on the Sabbath day the *Temple priests* break the Sabbath rest without being blamed for it?" (Mt 12:5). The allusion seems to refer to the activity of the priests in the Temple on the Sabbath, activity which conflicts with the prohibition of all work on that day. Leviticus, for example, commands that the Loaves of Proposition are to be carried into the sanctuary on the Sabbath itself (Lev 24:8), and the Book of Numbers not only does not demand that the works required for the offering of the ritual sacrifices should cease, but even prescribes supplementary sacrifices (Num 28:9-10). The Gospel text argues from these undeniable facts to state an extremely strong antithesis. It emphasizes that the priests, *sacred persons (hiereis)*, in the Temple, a *sacred place (hieron)*, "profane," that is to say, violate the sacred character of the *Sabbath, the sacred time.* It would be difficult to find stronger words. And all this is done in conformity with the Law and therefore does not constitute a sin. By speaking in this way the evangelist is pointing out the relative value of the "sacred," which the priests serve, or rather, he is rejecting the traditional notion of "sacred," for the "sacred" is normally presented as a reality that is absolutely inviolable for any reason whatever. The argument is most clever because it is based on what the priests themselves do in obedience to liturgical law.

To end the argument, the Gospel then cites the divine proclamation announced by the prophet Hosea: "What I want is mercy not sacrifice" (Hos 6:6). The word "sacrifice" refers here to the ritual offerings performed by the priests in the Temple. God prefers works of mercy to this sacred worship; an attitude of openness to persons to a formalistic religion. This is a fundamental evangelical option, which however is not entirely new, since it is explicitly situated in the line of the preaching of the prophets.

Only one other Gospel text features a priest: the Parable of the Good Samaritan. This parable, which is found only in Luke (10:30-37), certainly does the priesthood no credit. The priest, who happens to pass along the road and sees the injured man lying there, is completely unconcerned about his fate. His attitude contrasts with that of the Samaritan, who is moved by his plight, approaches him and takes care of him. No polemical comment underlines the contrast, but the intention of the text is sufficiently clear and it exactly matches that of Matthew: the Samaritan has "practised mercy," the priest has not. Commentators observe that the priest's attitude was probably dictated by his concern to obey the law of purity, which instructed him not to risk contact with a dead man, unless it should be a very close relative (Lev 21:1-2). Jesus, by implication, refuses to be constrained by these limitations and he invites everyone to get very close to whoever is in need. The ritual preoccupations of the priests must give way to the dynamism of a generous love. This was also recognized by a scribe in the Gospel of Mark, without, however, mentioning the priests. In stating his agreement with an answer given by Jesus, he declares that, in effect, to love God with all one's heart and to love one's neighbor as oneself "is better than all holocausts and sacrifices" (Mk 12:33).

The first stage of our inquiry therefore concludes with a twofold observation: on the one hand, the Gospels recognize the prerogatives of the Jewish priests and show no systematic opposition to them; on the other hand, they relativize their role by refusing to give primordial importance to ritual worship. In his preaching and in his conduct, Jesus further insists on other points.

2. The High Priests in the Gospels

The Gospels speak not only of priests (*hiereis*), but also—and much more often—of high priests (*archiereis*).[8] These were persons who were more representative of the priestly class. The title "high priest" appears sometimes in the singular, "the high priest," without further specification; at other times in the plural, also without explanation. These different usages reflect a situation which is known from other sources and which it is useful to recall briefly before considering the Gospel texts.

In the singular, the title refers to the person situated at the summit of the priestly hierarchy, the successor of Aaron, but also of the priest-kings who had exercised power in Judea after the victory of the Maccabees. In fact, it was only in the time of the Maccabees that the title *archiereus* was introduced into the religious vocabulary of the Jews. A king of Antioch conferred it at that time on one of the brothers of Judas (1 Mac 10:20). It continued to be used and the high priest continued to be recognized as having political as well as religious authority.

The plural, "high priests," is never used in the Old Testament, but in the first century of our era the historian Josephus uses it in the same way as the Gospels. No ancient text precisely defines its meaning among the Jews. The contexts in which it is used show that it referred to what we would call the "religious authorities." These included—in addition to the high priest himself and, eventually, his still-living predecessors—the provost of the Temple, the assistant high priest, the head of the priestly class which provided the liturgical service, the heads of the temple departments and, finally, the temple treasurers. In the first century, it seems that the majority of these positions of authority were monopolized by four families who formed the priestly aristocracy of Jerusalem.[9]

If one studies the tradition common to the Synoptic Gospels, one must read far into the texts before coming across the first mention of the high priests, but the context is then most significant: it occurs in the first prediction of the Passion. After having solicited Peter's profession of faith at Caesarea Philippi, "Jesus began to show to his disciples that he had to go up to Jerusalem and to suffer greatly from the elders, *the high priests*, and the scribes, and to be put to death and on the third day to rise again."[10] In addition to the verb "to suffer" Mark and Luke use the verb "to be rejected," in which one recognizes an allusion to the verse in Ps 118 which is quoted later in the Gospels: "The stone which the builders *rejected* has become the keystone of the structure."[11]

The text foretelling the Passion is clearly of prime importance in the unfolding of the Gospel narrative. It invites several comments, the most striking of which is that the high priests are presented here as responsible for the sufferings of Jesus. Jesus will have to "suffer [in Greek *pathein*, from which the name of the Passion, *pathema*, comes] greatly at the hands of the high priests." It is in connection with the Passion that the high priests come into the Gospel picture. After this first prediction of the sufferings of Christ, they will reappear very often in the Synoptic Gospels and it will always be in connection with the Passion. One will find them again in the third prediction of the Passion, then in the course of an interrogation which anticipates the trial of Jesus, and finally in an attempt to arrest him, in the plot against Jesus and in the deal concluded with Judas.[12] In the account of the Passion, the high priests are mentioned no less than 15 times in Matthew and Mark. Luke, with his more peaceful character, is content to mention them eight times. The Gospels then reveal a very strong clash, an unyielding conflict between the high priests and Jesus.

The second comment: in this conflict the high priests are presented rather as authorities (*archai*) than as priests (*hiereis*). The prediction of the Passion does not speak of them separately, but puts them together with two other groups which, with them, made up the Sanhedrin. It is this body, in full session, with its "elders" (*presbyteroi*), "high priests" (*archiereis*) and scribes (*grammateis*), which will subject Jesus to his Passion. The verb "to reject," added in Mark and Luke, accentuates the aspect of authority. By an official judgment, the "builders" will decide that Jesus is a stone to be rejected, unfit for the construction of the house of God.

The perspective of opposition that was expressed in the first fore-telling of the Passion recurs regularly in the other passages of the Gospels which feature the high priests. They are spoken of several times together with the two other groups of the Sanhedrin.[13] In other instances we find only the high priests and the scribes or the high priests and the elders;[14] only very rarely are the two other groups mentioned without the high priests (Mt 26:57). The general rule is that they are named and given prominence; they are nearly always listed in first position. Finally, in some cases they are mentioned without the others.[15]

The presence of the high priests in the first rank of the leaders of the Jewish nation certainly indicates that, for the nation itself, authority existed not only on the political level, but in an inseparable way on both the political and religious levels. The fact that, in the account of the Passion, the high priests are sometimes named without the other members of the Sanhedrin tends to accentuate their share of responsibility and to underline the religious dimension of the trial.

The high priests alone are mentioned in this way by Matthew and Mark in the episode that sets the Passion in motion: the treachery of Judas. Judas goes off to find the high priests and makes his ignoble bargain: "What will you give me and I will deliver him up to you?" (Mt 26:14). They eagerly accept. Their part in the arrest of Jesus is thus decisive. In the parallel passage, Luke couples them with the "officers of the guard" (*strategoi*), which does not really take it out of the area of priestly control, because the temple guard was in fact entrusted to the priests and Levites.

After the Jewish trial, which took place before the Sanhedrin in full session, Matthew relates an episode which illustrates the sinister conclusion of the treacherous affair (Mt 27:3-10), and here again the priests are in the forefront. It is true that "the elders" are also mentioned at the beginning of the story, but when Judas gets rid of his silver pieces by throwing them down, the account speaks only of the high priests. They pick up the silver and decide what to do with it. This circumstance corresponds with the logic of the situation, for the story notes that Judas had thrown the money down in the "sanctuary" (*naos*), that is to say, not just in the courts or the porticos of the Temple (*hieron*), where all the faithful could come, but in the sacred building to which only the priests had access. One therefore understands why the elders do not take any action at this point, but leave everything to the high priests. Judas' action is not meaningless: it establishes a link between the sanctuary of the Old Covenant and the treason money, a logical link since the money had been given to Judas by the high priests, the guardians of the sanctuary. Other Gospel texts have the same meaning: they affirm a relationship between the sanctuary made by the hand of man and the Passion of Christ. The high priests, however, do not wish to see this relationship. They refuse to put the treason money into the treasury of the Temple (Mt 27:6-7). They use it to buy a field, thus inscribing their crime on the soil of Israel.

Several Gospel texts draw attention to the role played by the high priests during the trial before Pilate. They are the ones who heap accusations on Jesus. Mark does not speak of anyone else, Matthew links "the elders" with them and Luke, "the crowds."[16] We find them again before Herod, supported this time by the scribes (Lk 23:10). According to Mark, who is more precise on this point than Matthew, Pilate had noted that "the *high priests* had betrayed Jesus through jealousy." When Pilate proposes to free "the king of the Jews," the high priests are the ones who "incited the crowds that he should rather liberate Barabbas for them" (Mk 15:9-11). Matthew again associates them with "the elders" (Mt 27:20). Once the sentence has been passed and executed, we find the high priests on Calvary mocking the Crucified. Even the death of Jesus does not make them let go: they make it their business to keep him in his tomb "by sealing it with a stone and setting a guard over it." They will make every effort to suppress by false rumors the announcement of the Resurrection.[17] It is clear then that the Gospel tradition has recorded an implacable opposition to Jesus on the part of the priestly authorities.

To complete the picture, we must now consider the instances where the Gospel tradition speaks of *the* high priest, in the singular. In these texts one never sees him presiding over worship ceremonies. In every case, it is his authority functions that are in question. This authority of the high priest stands out first of all in the account in St. Matthew of the actions taken against Jesus: indeed, it is "in the palace of the high priest" that the members of the Sanhedrin meet some days before the Passover, to find a way "to arrest Jesus by cunning and to put him to death" (Mt 26:3). Again, it is in the palace of the high priest that Matthew and Mark place the night session of the Sanhedrin.[18]

The stand taken by the high priest in the course of this session confirms and aggravates the observations already made concerning the relations between the Jewish priesthood and Jesus. For it is clearly the high priest who directs the course of the trial. He rises to his feet after the witnesses have testified and proceeds with the questioning himself. The confrontation then reaches its climax. The high priest stands before Jesus like a judge. Matthew underlines the dramatic solemnity of this confrontation more than the other Synoptics. The high priest appeals to the power of the living God to force Jesus to answer. Jesus confidently complies with this command; he observes that the very words of the high priest have described his position as the Son of God and he predicts the decisive manifestation of this dignity. The opposition then becomes total: the high priest tears his garments, cries blasphemy and incites to the condemnation.[19]

This scene does not take place in the context of a religious service but in the context of the exercise of power. The high priest is not in the Temple; he is surrounded by the members of the Sanhedrin. His actions are not cultic but juridical: he hears witnesses, he interrogates, he passes judgment.

However, the elements preserved by the Gospel tradition show how the points of view have merged. The interrogation could have been directed toward political offences: attempted rebellion, a plot to seize power. Instead, it is centered on the Messianic claim: "Are you the Messiah?"[20] Now, for the Jews, the importance of the Messiah was in the religious rather than in the political sphere. One is therefore not surprised to see the high priest emphasizing the religious aspect, that is, the privileged relationship between the Messiah and God. In the end, only this aspect will be used in the charge and condemnation: Jesus is found guilty of "blasphemy"; this is the main accusation which, from the Jewish authorities' point of view, required his death.[21] The high priest and the Sanhedrin are not posing as guarantors of the political order, but as defenders of the Law of God.

The testimony of the Fourth Gospel does not differ greatly from that of the Synoptics on the point that concerns us. Like the Synoptics, John confirms the attitude of opposition taken by the high priests against Jesus. The difference is that this attitude appears sooner, well before the week of the Passion. John reports that at the time of a Feast of Tabernacles, because they were worried by the success of Jesus, "the *high priests* and the Pharisees together sent temple guards to arrest him" (Jn 7:32). The attempt did not succeed (Jn 7:45-46). The difference in chronology compared to the Synoptics is due to the fact that the Fourth Gospel does not follow the schematic arrangement adopted by the others. The Synoptics speak of only one journey made by Jesus to Jerusalem and situate it just before the events of Holy Week. John, on the other hand, takes note of several such journeys, which allows him to show that the hostility of the high priests toward Jesus had begun very early.

The conflict becomes sharper as the last Passover nears. High priests and Pharisees then get together to ward off the danger that Jesus represents. They decide to have him killed. They give orders for his denunciation in order to be able to arrest him.[22] In fact, they take an active part in his arrest: the band led by Judas to capture Jesus included "guards supplied by the high priests and the Pharisees" (Jn 18:3).

In all these texts one notes a peculiarity of the Johannine tradition: the high priests are regularly associated with the Pharisees.[23] In the Synoptics, as we have seen, the grouping is different: the high priests are associated with other members of the Sanhedrin, the scribes and the elders, two categories that the Johannine tradition completely ignores.[24] The association of the high priests with the Pharisees makes their opposition to Jesus still clearer, for the Gospel tradition as a whole shows the Pharisees as the bitter enemies of Jesus.

After Jesus' arrest, however, the Pharisees are not mentioned again by the evangelist, so that the high priests are the sole protagonists in the struggle against him. They play a decisive role in the course of the Roman trial. Pilate himself emphasizes this strange fact in a statement made to Jesus: "It is your own people and the *high priests* who have handed you over to me. What have you done?" (Jn 18:35). Later, when Pilate tries to pardon the prisoner, it is the high priests who, with their servants, cry out: "Crucify him, crucify him." To Pilate's objection: "Shall I crucify your king?" they are the ones who reply: "We have no king but Caesar," and who ensure that Jesus will be handed over to them to be crucified. When he has been crucified, they again are the ones who make it their business to demand a rectification of the motive of condemnation affixed to the cross.[25] Thus, the hostility of the high priests toward Jesus has a special prominence in the Fourth Gospel.

In this context, John does not fail to make clear also the position taken by the most qualified member of the group, the high priest (in the singular). During the discussion that ended in the decision that

Jesus should die, the evangelist reports that it was "Caiaphas, the high priest of that year," who made the decision, saying to his colleagues:

"You don't understand anything. You don't realize that it is much better for one man to die for the people than for the whole nation to perish." (Jn 11:49-50)

These cynical words clinched the debate. Their formulation reveals the dominant part taken by the high priest in the conspiracy against Jesus. The rest "understand nothing." It is he who points out the direction to be taken. He displays a political realism devoid of all scruple. His responsibility is overwhelming. In the remainder of the story, other details will recall this: at the time of Jesus' arrest, John notes in passing the presence of "the servant of the high priest," and even gives his name (Jn 18:10); then before the trial begins, he mentions again the statement pronounced by Caiaphas (Jn 18:13).

The evangelist might well have contented himself with this aspect of the affair, and by underlining the deadly opposition of the high priest to Jesus, have deduced the total break in the relations between the high priest and God. It is significant that he did not draw this conclusion. With paradoxical boldness, John on the contrary affirms the continuance of a positive aspect of the priesthood. In the Machiavellian statement of Caiaphas, he recognizes, in spite of everything, a prophetic value, the root of which he sees in the priestly dignity of the speaker. Caiaphas "did not say it of himself, but as the high priest of that year he was prophesying" (Jn 11:51). His words carried two very different meanings; they expressed at the same time a criminal human calculation and a divine plan of redemption. The relationships between the high priest and Christ are, at the same moment, revealed to be surprisingly complex. We must not forget this.

Furthermore, a complexity of another kind appears in John's account. The title of "high priest" in the singular seems to refer to two different persons: to Annas, in the account of the interrogation, and to Caiaphas in other passages.[26] In order to resolve this apparent confusion, different exegetes have proposed different solutions, but there is room for thinking that the text of the Gospel reflects the real situation: Caiaphas was the high priest in office; but Annas, the former high priest, whom the Romans had deposed, had retained his prestige and authority and was also called "the high priest."[27] This historical detail is not of great importance for our topic.

3. **Priests and High Priests in the Acts of the Apostles**

This is a suitable place to add the testimony of the Acts of the Apostles to that of the Gospels. Acts describes in more detail the situation in the Christian community in its beginnings and allows us to see what the relations were between this community and the Jewish priesthood. After the Resurrection of Christ, a number of possibilities existed: reconciliation and harmonious relations, renewed tensions and conflicts, or even mutual unawareness. In what direction did events in fact unfold?

On the part of the Christians, we do not see any desire to break with the Jewish priesthood. Luke shows the Apostles, after the Ascension of Jesus, "continually present in the Temple praising God" (Lk 24:53), and in the time following Pentecost, the entire Christian community adopts the same attitude: "Day after day they assiduously came together in the Temple" (Ac 2:46).

On the part of the Jewish priests, Luke relates that there was a strong trend favorable to the Christian faith: "the number of the disciples continued to grow considerably in Jerusalem and *a great crowd of priests obeyed the faith*" (Ac 6:7).

Another attitude, however, also came to light. In the first text which speaks of it (Ac 4:1), one is not quite certain whether Luke attributes it to the "priests" or to the "high priests," for the manuscripts are divided between these two titles. Immediately afterwards, however, the question is clarified: it concerns the high priests in the exercise of their authority (Ac 4:6). Their attitude is one of opposition. The reason given at first is not a matter of worship but of doctrine: they are vexed to see the Apostles "teaching the people and proclaiming the resurrection of the dead in the person of Jesus." At the same time as the priests or the high priests, Luke also speaks of the "captain of the temple guard and the Sadducees." It is to the latter that he attaches more directly the motive expressed: "The Sadducees, of course, maintain that there is no resurrection."[28] The high priests and the captain of the temple guard support them with their authority and proceed to arrest Peter and John (Ac 4:3).

On the next day, it is the Sanhedrin in full session that comes together to decide the fate of the two Apostles. Luke first mentions briefly "the leaders, the elders, the scribes," and then specifies further for the high priests: "Annas, the high priest, Caiaphas, John, Alexander and all the members of the high-priestly family." This insistence attracts attention. It does not, however, stand out in the rest of the account: when Peter begins to speak, he does not specifically mention the high priests, but says simply: "Leaders of the people and elders . . . ," which puts the debate in a context of authority rather than in the sphere of the sacred. From this moment on the position taken by the high priest and by the assembly of high priests will be one of greater and greater hostility toward the Apostles of Jesus and the Christian community.[29] The high priest has the Apostles arrested and imprisoned, proceeds to interrogate them and reproaches them violently. It is again the "high priest" who questions Stephen before his martyrdom (Ac 7:1). When Saul wants to set about persecuting the Church, it is to the high priest that he goes to obtain the necessary authority.[30] When he sets out for Damascus, his plan is to arrest the Christians there and "to bring them in chains before the high priests" (Ac 9:21). Later Saul, having become the Apostle Paul, suffers in his turn the hostility of the high priest Ananias and of the whole group of high priests who, supported by the elders, do their utmost to extract the condemnation of the Apostle from the Roman governor.[31]

When Paul appears before the Sanhedrin, Luke relates a revealing incident. Paul, subjected to much vexation, protests vigorously and describes the one who has given the order to mistreat him as a "whitewashed wall." When he is told that it was "the high priest of God," Paul excuses himself by saying: "I did not know that he is a high priest" and he adds: "It is indeed written: You shall not abuse the ruler of your people" (Ac 23:1-5). The interesting point for our study is that instead of considering the *consecration* of the high priest, as the remark of the bystanders would have suggested to him ("It is the *high priest of God* whom you are insulting"), Paul simply underlines the *authority* of the person ("a ruler of your people"), by citing a precept of the Bible concerning the respect due to the "rulers" (Ex 22:27). The change of emphasis is obvious. It undoubtedly reflects the situation at the time, which stressed the power of the high priest more than his priestly role, but it also allows us to glimpse a significant stand being taken.

All this supports what may have been observed throughout this chapter: that the narrative writings of the New Testament never show the Jewish high priests in the exercise of their cultic functions.[32] What is given emphasis is their authority rather than their priesthood; they are "important personages" i.e. "high" more than they are "priests." It was not possible, however, to separate the two aspects entirely, for the high priests were recognized as being the religious leaders of the people of God. It followed from this that the Christians were in an extremely embarrassing situation. The Gospel narratives, which say little about Jewish priests and much about the high priests, result inevitably in giving the priesthood an unfavorable image. And yet it could not be denied that the priesthood constituted one of the fundamental institutions of the Old Testament. How could the Christian Church claim to be faithful to the totality of biblical revelation and to possess in Christ its definitive fulfillment, if it found itself in a negative relationship with regard to this fundamental institution of the people of God?

Notes

[1]Cf. 1.Ch 24:7-18; 28:13, 21; 2 Ch 31:2.

[2]This text is full of specific terms from the priestly and ritual vocabulary: *hiereus* (priest), *hierateia* (priestly function), *hierateuein* (to exercise the functions of a priest) and also *naos* (sanctuary), *thymiazein* (to burn incense), *thymiama* (the offering of incense) and *thysiasterion* (altar).

[3]Lk 2:24; cf. Lev 12:8; Num 6:10.

[4]Mal 2:7. The Greek word used in Lk 2:46 is *didaskalos:* "teacher," "master." In the Gospels, this title is habitually reserved for Jesus. The only exceptions are: Lk 2:46, 3:12 (John the Baptist); John 3:10 (Nicodemus).

[5]Where the Greek text says "purify me," "be purified" and "purification," certain modern texts use "heal me," "be healed," and "healing," thus preventing the reader from grasping the internal logic of the story.

[6]Lk 17:12-14.

[7]Mk 2:26; cf. Mt 12:4; Lk 6:4.

[8]*Hiereus* appears only 11 times in the Gospels (Mt 3; Mk 2; Lk 5; Jn 1). *Archiereus* is used 83 times (Mt 25; Mk 22; Lk 15; Jn 21).

[9]For more information, see J. Jeremias, *Jerusalem in the Time of Jesus*, SCM Press, London, 1969, or in *Theological Dictionary of the New Testament*, the articles *hiereus* (vol. III, 1938, G. Schrenk, pp. 270-272), and *synedrion* (vol. VII, 1964, E. Lohse, p. 864).

[10]Mk 16:21; cf. Mk 8:31; Lk 9:22. In the traditions specific to each of the Synoptic Gospels, the title of high priest appears on only one occasion before this first mention in common. In Mk 2:26 and Lk 3:2 it concerns a simple chronology. In Mt 2:4-6, the

infancy narrative, the high priests appear once in company with the scribes, as experts in the Scriptures.

[11]Ps 118:22; cf. Mt 21:42; Mk 12:10; Lk 20:17.

[12]For these various episodes, common to the three Synoptic Gospels, cf. Mt 20:18; 21:23; 21:45; 26:3; 26:14 and parallels.

[13]In Mt 27:41; Mk 11:27; 14:43, 53; 15:1; Lk 20:1; (22:66).

[14]"High priests and scribes": Mt 2:4; 20:18; 21:15; Mk 10:33; 11:18; 14:1; 15:31; Lk 19:47; 20:19; 22:2; 23:10. In Luke 20:19 the scribes are mentioned first. "High priests and elders": Mt 21:23; 26:3, 47; 27:1, 3, 12, 20; (28:12).

[15]"High priests": Mt 26:14; 27:6; 28:11; Mk 14:10; 15:3, 10, 11; Lk 23:4; Jn 12:10; 18:35; 19:15, 21. The scribes are sometimes spoken of alone in the first part of the Synoptic Gospels; the same is true of the elders.

[16]Mk 15:3; Mt 27:12; Lk 23:4f.

[17]Mk 15:31; Mt 27:41,66; 28:11-15.

[18]Mt 26:57; Mk 14:53; cf. Lk 22:54.

[19]Mt 26:63-66; Mk 14:61-64.

[20]Mt 26:63; Mk 14:61; Lk 22:67.

[21]Mt 26:65; Mk 14:64.

[22]Jn 11:47-53, 57.

[23]In the Synoptics, the grouping "high priests and Pharisees" is found only in Mt 21:45 and 27:72.

[24]The word "scribe" (grammateus) does not occur in the Fourth Gospel, except in 8:3, in the passage on the adulterous woman, which does not belong to the Johannine tradition. And one finds the word "elder" (presbyteros) only in Jn 8:9, where it is used, moreover, in the non-technical sense of "older."

[25]Jn 19:6, 15-17, 21.

[26]Jn 18:19, 22 and 11:49-51; 18:13, 24.

[27]Cf. Lk 3:2; Acts 4:6.

[28]Cf. Ac 23:8; Lk 20:27-40 parallels.

[29]For the high priest, cf. Ac 5:17, 21, 27-28; 9:1; 24:1; for the high priests, cf. Ac 5:24; 9:14, 21; 25:2, 15.

[30]Ac 9:1f; 22:5; 26:10.

[31]Ac 23:2; 24:1; 25:2,15.

[32]The only text which speaks of priestly functions in the Temple at Jerusalem is that already discussed at the beginning of this chapter. It concerns a priest and not a high priest (Lk 1:8-10). In another connection, Ac 14:11-18 shows a priest preparing to offer a sacrifice, but this refers to a pagan priest.

CHAPTER II

The Complex Reality of the Old Testament Priesthood

To understand exactly the problem facing the Christian faith, it is necessary to have a clear idea of the context in which it was born. How did the institution of the priesthood appear in the eyes of Christ's contemporaries? What were the functions of the Old Testament priest? What was expected of him? What does the long biblical tradition have to say about him? It is not possible here to treat all the details of this subject, which would require another book; it will be sufficient to trace its main lines, taking care to observe in what direction priesthood was evolving.[1]

1. The Name

The word *hiereus*, which we have found in the Gospels, was chosen by the Greek translators of the Bible to render the Hebrew *kohen*, a very common word in the Old Testament. It signifies persons charged with religious functions. It is used for pagan priests as well as for Israelite priests. The first person to whom the Bible gives the title of *kohen* is Melchizedek, king of a town in Palestine in the time of Abraham; the second is an Egyptian priest in the time of Joseph. The beginning of the Book of Exodus speaks of a Midianite priest, whose son-in-law Moses became.[2] It is only after the exodus from Egypt that the Bible introduces us to Israelite priests, but these then have a prominent place, especially in Leviticus, where the title *kohen* recurs as often as 55 times in a single chapter (Lev 13).

The Greek word *hiereus* is connected by its origin with the notion of the "sacred" *(hieros)*; the priest is the man of the "sacred." The primitive sense of the Hebrew word *kohen* is less easy to discern. Some relate it to an Akkadian word, *kanu*, which can have the sense of "bowing." The *kohen* is then the one who bows before the divinity, the one who adores. Others, on the contrary, prefer a verbal root that means "to stand up" *(kun)* and see in the *kohen* one who "stands up in the presence of God," as a text of Deuteronomy (10:8) says of the tribe of Levi, although it uses another verb. A. Cody criticizes both these hypotheses[3] and proposes instead an etymology based on a root attested in Syriac and which expresses the idea of prosperity. The *kohen*, the Old Testament priest, is the one who procures prosperity; he is the man of "blessings." This view is very positive, not lacking in appeal and it must be acknowledged that it is quite biblical.[4]

2. Powers of the Priesthood

More relevant than the etymology of the word are the actual faculties belonging to the office that help to define the meaning of an institution. The biblical texts show that the powers of the *kohen* cover a very wide area. The *kohen* may be viewed as the man of the sanctuary, the one who has the right to touch the sacred objects and who is admitted into the presence of God, as the man charged with offering the sacrifices, or again as the one who utters oracles and who gives blessings and decides questions of ritual purity.

Which was the most characteristic, among so many diverse powers? Discussion is possible on this point, because the role of the Old Testament priest varied over the centuries. Some authors insist on his sacrificial function, to the point of always rendering the word *kohen* in the writings of the Old Testament and the word *hiereus* in the New Testament as "sacrificer." They translate *archiereus* as "supreme sacrificer" instead of "high priest." But this is a unilateral fixation which does not correspond with the rich diversity of the Old Testament concept. According to Cody, the most characteristic trait of the priesthood was not the offering of sacrifices—for other persons also exercised this function—but the close relationship with a sanctuary. Before the epoch of the Israelite monarchy, the Old Testament priest was, above all else, the man of a sanctuary and his principal role was to utter oracles.[5]

a) *The oracular function*

The oracular function of the Old Testament priest astonishes us today, all the more because it was done by some kind of casting of lots. In any difficult situation, people would go to consult the priest, who then had to determine what should be done, by making use of the "Urim" and "Thummim." This is the first function that we see attributed to the priest in the very ancient text of the blessing given to Levi. Moses, before his death,[6] says over Levi:

Give to Levi the Urim,
and the Thummim to thy gracious one. (Dt 33:8)

What exactly were the Urim and Thummim? Wands? Small stones? Knuckle-bones? We do not know exactly, but the biblical narratives indicate that they were in any case sacred objects which the priest used for drawing lots and deciding in this way the solution of difficult cases.

The following is the clearest text about them that one can reconstruct from the ancient versions.[7] In order to discover the cause of a desperate situation, Saul questions the Lord and says to him:

O Lord, God of Israel, if the fault is mine or my son Jonathan's, give *Urim*; if the fault is thy people's, give *Thummim*. (1 Sam 14:41)

Several similar consultations are recorded in the story of David. When tracked down by Saul and when in the grasp of the Amalekites, David has recourse to the priest Abiathar to consult the Lord on the tactics to be adopted.[8]

The least that one can say is that such practices hardly seem reasonable to us. In fact they correspond to a very primitive level of religiosity, closer to superstition than to an authentic spiritual life. We would be mistaken, however, if we felt nothing but scorn for them because, all things considered, they indicate the early stage of a basic spiritual attitude: the search for the will of God. The faithful manifested a sincere desire to "know the ways of the Lord" and to follow them, when he submitted to the mediation of the priest in "consulting the Lord." At the root of this desire we can discern a profound religious conviction: they were persuaded that human existence could not find its proper orientation without a positive relationship with God. The manner of the consultation is a secondary aspect. It is more significant that the oracle did not function automatically. The answer might not be forthcoming; this was the case in the episode in the story of Saul. Then it was necessary to look for the reason for the silence and to find out if one was properly disposed to receive an answer from God.

The oracular function of the Old Testament priests underwent an evolution that manifests an advance in the religious consciousness. The present wording of the blessing given to Levi bears witness to this. After the sentence about the Urim and Thummim, a later insertion can be discerned (the text changes unexpectedly from the singular to the plural), and the function of the priests is no longer to draw lots but to teach:

> Yes, they have kept your word and adhere to your covenant.
> They shall teach your customs to Jacob and your Law to Israel. (Dt 33:9b-10)

Here we see another way of discovering the will of God and relating mankind's existence to him, a less external way and one that has more respect for the human person. The priests were entrusted with the task of transmitting the "instruction" that came from God; at the beginning they did it occasionally and in special cases,[9] particularly in cultic matters. Later they did it in a more systematic way and the sum total of divine instructions was entrusted to them: "They teach . . . thy Law to Israel." According to Deuteronomy, Moses had handed the roll of the Law to the Levites for them to keep in the Ark of the Covenant and he had commanded the priests and the elders to "proclaim this Law in the ears of the whole of Israel."[10] After the return from the Exile, a verse of Malachi recalls that

> the lips of the priest are to preserve knowledge
> and it is from his mouth that instruction is to be sought;
> he is the messenger of the Lord of Hosts. (Mal 2:7)

The juridical competence attributed to the priests is attached to this function. Deuteronomy declares that it is for them "to pronounce on every dispute and on every act of violence." In particular, they are to intervene in cases that are difficult to resolve, such as those where there is no witness to a serious offence.[11]

Their position of authority was still admitted in the time of Christ, at least to some extent. One finds this confirmed in the texts of Qumran. In each of the sect's communities, the Damascus Document requires that "there should not be lacking a man, who is a priest instructed in the Book of Meditation; and all must obey his orders."[12] However, it does envision the case where the priest was not an "expert in all these matters" and then makes provision for a replacement. In fact, in the time following the Exile, the teaching of the Law was no longer the monopoly of the priests, the class of scribes and doctors of the Law, which was open to laymen, having begun to supplant them in this field.[13] The priests were beginning to limit their activity more and more to the worship ceremonies within the Temple.

b) *Men of the sanctuary*

The priests were now beginning to appear more exclusively as the men of the sanctuary. The link between priesthood and sanctuary is universally attested. "The priest is chosen and installed for the service of a sanctuary"[14] and no one else is authorized to take charge of it. In the time of the Exodus,

> Moses, Aaron and his sons had charge of the sanctuary in the name of the children of Israel. Any layman who encroached was to be put to death. (Num 3:38)

When a sanctuary is founded, a priest is consecrated to provide its cult. Thus it was with Micah in the time of the Judges, with the men of Kiriath-Yearim in the time of Samuel, and with Jeroboam after the division of the kingdom.[15]

With regard to the sanctuaries, the Old Testament reveals one of the clearest cases of historical evolution. At the very beginning, it was accepted that there should be a great diversity of holy places. The traditions relating to Abraham already mention several, that of Sichem, that of Bethel, that of Beersheba,[16] which will appear in other pages of the Bible. Other traditions speak of the sanctuary of Shilo, that of Gabaon, and that of Dan.[17] When David captured Jerusalem, he had the Ark of the Covenant brought there in order to give his new capital religious prestige (2 Sam 6). Later, when there was a plague, David hoped to bring about its end by constructing an altar on a site acquired for this purpose (24:18-25). In this way, a new holy place was established in addition to all the others. It was there that Solomon built the Temple of Jerusalem,[18] a sanctuary that immediately assumed great importance because its position in the royal city assured it a central role in the official worship. By degrees a tendency developed to claim for it not merely dominance but exclusiveness. The two kings, Hezekiah and Josiah, conscientiously set about reforming the Israelites' worship in this direction. Josiah in particular undertook the elimination of all the other sanctuaries from his kingdom: "He took away all the priests from the towns of Judah and he destroyed the high places where these priests had sacrificed" (2 Kg 23:8). A text of Deuteronomy supported this policy:

> Take care not to offer your holocausts in all the holy places that you see. It is only in the place chosen by the Lord in one of your tribes that you should offer holocausts. (Dt 12:13-14)[19]

This was done after the Exile. The uniqueness of the sanctuary had become a profound exigency of religious sentiment.[20] It was fitting for the unique God to have a unique sanctuary. /

c) *Sacrifice*

In the sanctuary the priests perform cultic ceremonies, the most important of which is sacrifice. Speaking to God about the priests of Israel, the blessing of Moses says of them:

> They are the ones who cause the smoke to rise up to your nostrils and they lay the holocaust on your altar. (Dt 33:10)

A twofold evolution is to be noted in this matter: on the one hand a more and more marked emphasis on the privilege of the priests, and on the other an increasing insistence on the expiatory aspect of the sacrifices.

Originally, the right to offer sacrifices was not the exclusive prerogative of the priests. Abraham, who was not a priest, offered holocausts to God; Jacob consecrated pillars, and we see him offering a sacrifice and inviting his kinsmen to it.[21] In the time of the Judges we read that the father of Samson offered a kid as a holocaust (Jg 13:19). According to the books of Samuel and Kings, David and Solomon offered solemn sacrifices.[22] Little by little, however, the offering of sacrifices was reserved to the priests and a text in Chronicles relates that King Uzziah had been punished by God for having dared to offer incense on the altar of incense.[23] This privilege of the priests can be considered as one among several cases of social specialization. We can, however, note certain differences. What led to reserving the duty of offering the sacrifices as a priestly role was not so much the quest for a better organization of work as the sense of the holiness of God. For an offering presented to God to have some chance of being acceptable, it was necessary that the offerer himself should not be repugnant to the divine holiness, but on the contrary he should be impregnated with it, in harmony with it—in a word, consecrated. As the priest was precisely a person consecrated to God and permitted to enter into relationship with him, it seemed obvious that he should be the one through whom sacrifices should be made.

Another aspect of the evolution of sacrificial worship concerns the importance attributed to expiatory sacrifices, ones offered to obtain pardon for offences committed. It would seem that before the Exile these did not play much part in the Israelite religion. Some authors even wonder if they took place at all. Holocausts and communion sacrifices were most important. But by degrees the expiatory sacrifices acquired greater importance, above all when "great national calamities had given the people a more lively sense of their guilt"[24] and had led them to realize better the necessity for sanctity imposed on every servant of God.

d) *Ritual purity*

Since the priest was in charge of offering the sacrifices in the name of the community, he had to take care that no one would participate in the worship who was not in a state of *ritual purity*. The presence of an "impure" man could only displease God and provoke the rejection of the offerings. The priests, therefore, had the duty of

converting the children of Israel from their impurities, lest they die as a result of them by desecrating my Dwelling which is in their midst. (Lev 15:31)

This preoccupation was shown in a particularly vivid way in connection with leprosy, the most dreaded impurity. As soon as a possible symptom appeared, the person who was presumed to be infected had to go to the priest, who would check the symptom. Leviticus gives very detailed instructions on this matter (Lev 13). After a thorough examination, it was the priest's duty to pronounce the diagnosis: he declared the patient to be either "impure" or "pure," as the case might be, at the same time either forbidding or permitting him to participate in the worship of Yahweh. If a leper was cured, it was obviously the priest who had to make the necessary verification—the Gospel stories respect this regulation—and the priest then began long ceremonies of "purification" (Lev 14). For other cases of ritual impurity, "lustral water" was used, prepared by mixing in it the ashes of a cow that had been sacrificed. Here again, it was the priest who performed the necessary rites.[25]

e) *Blessing*

In addition to this rather negative role concerning impurity, the priest had another very positive role, which was expressed in the blessing. He had the function of "blessing the people with the Name," as Sirac says (Sir 45:15/19). "To bless with the Name" means to bless by pronouncing the revealed Name. The Book of Numbers describes exactly in this sense the way in which the priests are "to bless the children of Israel." The benediction formula repeats the name of the Lord three times, and after having pronounced it himself, God concludes:

> In this way let them impose my Name on the children of Israel. (Num 6:27)

To put the name of God upon someone is to establish a personal relationship between God and that person. The benediction is therefore nothing other than effecting a lifegiving relationship with God. The people of Israel were to understand that the divine blessing is the fundamental condition on which the true success of human existence depends. Without a harmonious relationship with God, human life can neither find its rightful meaning nor attain its full development. But the divine blessing imparts everywhere peace and fruitfulness, because the relationship with God is the most decisive element in every situation and in all reality.

How did the priestly blessing of the Old Testament evolve? We know that the Israelites experienced an ever-increasing respect for the revealed Name and that the fear of profaning it finally led to their being forbidden to pronounce it. The rabbinic texts provide evidence of progressive limitations being imposed on the priests' blessing. They specify that the priests were not authorized to pronounce the revealed Name outside the Temple, but had to use another designation of God,[26] and that even in the solemn ceremonies of the Temple, the high priest had to take care not to pronounce the Name out loud; he was barely to murmur it, to "swallow" it. "Rabbi Tarphon used to say: I was keeping my place among the priests, my brothers; I strained my ears toward the high priest and I heard him 'swallow' [the Name] in the midst of the chants of the priests."[27]

On this point as on the preceding ones an ever-growing awareness of the holiness of God is revealed.

3. The Internal Dynamism of the Old Testament Priestly Worship

a) *Idea of holiness*

In effect, the whole organization of the Old Testament priestly worship was based on the idea of holiness, and on the conviction that it was necessary to be holy in order to approach God. But holiness was perceived at that time in a way that differs from our current conception. As we understand it, holiness is almost synonymous with moral perfection; it suggests an assortment of eminent virtues. In the process of canonization, the first stage consists in finding out if the person who died in the "odor of sanctity" had really attained "heroicity" in the practice of Christian virtues. The ancient mentality did not think of tying sanctity to perfection. For the ancients, "holy" was not the opposite of "imperfect" but of "profane." Sanctity or holiness defines above all the very being of God. It belongs properly to him alone. "Holy, holy, holy is the Lord Sabaoth" proclaim the seraphim in the vision of the prophet Isaiah (Is 6:3). Their acclamation expresses the authentic religious experience, the one that gives the true knowledge of God. God is not perceived here as a great abstract principle, necessary to account for the existence of the universe, but as an extremely powerful and moving presence, which simultaneously arouses in people's hearts both wonder and fear, unrestrained gratitude and the desire to hide. Man perceives a terrifying difference of quality between the explosive force of the life of God and the fragility of his own existence, and recognizes his unworthiness to enter into relationship with the Thrice Holy.

A radical transformation is necessary and this transformation is understood to be the passage from the profane level of ordinary existence to the holy or sacred level, which is the one which corresponds to relationship with God. To attain it, one does not rely on moral effort, for this leaves man in his own world. One relies on a divine action of separation and elevation, by which the distance between mankind and God will be overcome, at least to some degree, and the qualitative difference diminished. This is what is called sanctification or consecration. The specific problem of religious aspiration is the problem of sanctification. It is, indeed, a matter of entering into communication with God. Since God is holy, in order to get into relationship with him without injury, one must find a way to be made holy.

b) *Ritual solution*
Old Testament cult proposed a ritual solution as answer to this problem, or more precisely a system of ritual separations, whose dominant element was the institution of the priesthood.

People in general assuredly cannot claim to possess the holiness required to stand before God. "All the nations are as nothing before him; for him they are nothingness and emptiness" (Is 40:17). A people is then "set apart," it is "sanctified" in order to enter into relationship with God. It hears it said:

You are a people consecrated to the Lord your God. It is you whom the Lord your God has chosen as his own people, from among all the nations on the face of the earth. (Dt 7:6)

God promises to this people the dignity of the priesthood:

I will hold you as a kingdom of priests and a consecrated nation. (Ex 19:6)

The exact interpretation of this promise has triggered discussion,[28] but what is certain is that it concerns a privileged position with respect to other nations. The viewpoint is that of a special belonging to God, an incomparable privilege: "Among the peoples I will hold you as my own" (19:5). Nothing in the text or the context suggests a function of mediation for the benefit of other peoples. The idea that Israel would mediate in favor of the Gentiles is indeed found in the Bible, beginning with the book of Genesis, with its declaration that blessing will come to the nations through the descendants of Abraham (Gen 22:18). The same theme is developed by the Prophets, who foretell that Israel's glory will radiate throughout the world. But the link between this vocation of Israel and the priesthood of the people is never expressed in the Bible. The only other text which takes up the priestly promise of Exodus is situated in the same perspective and in a still clearer manner: far from saying that Israel will exercise the priesthood in the service of the nations, it underlines the contrast between the glorious position of the Israelites, who will be called "priests of the Lord," "ministers of our God," and the humiliation of the foreigners who will see themselves enslaved and exploited by Israel: "Strangers will come to pasture your flocks, men from elsewhere will become your laborers and vine-dressers . . . . You will consume the riches of the nations and you will deck yourselves out in their opulence" (Is 61:5-6).

Another limitation of these two texts should be noted: neither claims to describe a real-life situation. They both appear as promises of a marvelous future. According to the Book of Exodus, the realization of the promise was to depend on the obedience of Israel to God and its fidelity to the Covenant. But the Old Testament declares many times that this condition has never been fulfilled (Dt 9:7; Jer 7:25-26). It follows logically, therefore, that the priesthood promised to the people remained, so far as the Old Testament is concerned, an ideal never attained.

Nevertheless, at least the first step was taken toward the fulfillment of the divine plan. God "has set the people of Israel apart from all the nations," and so it is henceforth bound to respect this separation. Israel no longer has the right to mix with the pagans, and that is why it receives a whole series of precepts that create barriers around it, in particular the laws regarding clean and unclean foods. In imposing them, God declares: "You have been sanctified and you have been made holy, for I am holy; do not become unclean" (Lev 11:44).

In spite of this first sanctification, the people of Israel as a whole are not fit to face the immediate proximity of God. If they were to approach him, they would be wiped out by the devouring fire of the divine holiness.[29] And so a tribe is chosen, the tribe of Levi, to be more directly consecrated to the service of the sanctuary. Within this tribe, one single family receives a special consecration and is entrusted with the priesthood.[30] The members of this family are segregated from the people in order to be introduced into the sphere of the "sacred" and to be entrusted with the worship. They will be priests. Their "sanctification" is described in detail in the Law of Moses (Ex 29). It is brought about by means of symbolical ceremonies: a ritual bath to purify from contacts with the profane world, an anointing which instills holiness, sacred vestments which express their belonging to God, sacrifices of expiation and of consecration. The holiness gained in this way had to be conserved and preserved thereafter by means of the observance of detailed precepts: not to touch anything unclean or impure, not to approach a corpse, not even to go into mourning, etc. (Lev 21). The priests had to take care not to fall back into the profane world, for this would make them unfit to present themselves before God.

The priest's encounter with God requires even further rites of separation. One does not encounter God just anywhere, or at any time, or in any manner, but only in a holy place at a specific moment and in the performance of particular sacred gestures. The holy place is the sanctuary, a place separated from profane space and reserved for worship. Only the priests have access to it, and even they cannot go everywhere in the holy place: the holiest area is forbidden to them; it is open only to a single person, the high priest, and to him on one day only, the Day of Atonement (Lev 16).

Just as the holy place is separated from the profane area, so the holy days are separated from the times of profane occupations and the liturgical rites are separated from ordinary activities. As we have seen, sacrifice holds the first place among these rites. It is only by means of sacrifice that the high priest can approach God. To sacrifice a victim is, as the word indicates, to make it sacred.

Why, then, do the priests need to present sacrifices in order to reach God? The reason is simple and is to be found in the purest logic of ritual sanctification. Sacrifice is necessary as the final stage of separation from the profane world. The priest himself, in other words, cannot completely realize this separation in his own person. Despite all the ceremonies of his consecration, he remains a terrestrial being and does not pass into the divine world. He must therefore choose another creature, capable of achieving this passage. The ritual commands him to choose an animal of a particular species, while taking care to see that it is without any defect. This animal will be completely removed from the profane world, for it will be immolated and offered on the altar of the Temple. Consumed by the sacred fire of the altar, it will mount up to heaven and be transformed into "perfume of a pleasing odor,"[31] or, in another symbol, its blood will be sprinkled over the "Mercy Seat" as a gesture for reaching God himself.[32]

Old Testament cult was then a system of sanctification based on a series of ritual separations. To lift oneself up toward the most holy God, one erected a kind of pyramid which, starting from the multitude of the nations and taking as successive steps a people set apart, a chosen tribe, a privileged family, finally culminating in a single consecrated man, the priest, and, beyond him, in an animal offered up in sacrifice.

After this ascending series of separations, it was clearly hoped that there would be a descending movement in the form of blessings. If the sacrifice was worthy of God, it was bound to be accepted. The priest who offered it then secured the divine favor and the people whom the priest represented found themselves in a right relationship with God.

c) *Function of the priesthood*

Thanks to this simple dynamic scheme, the function of the priesthood is made clear; it becomes possible to establish a certain order among the activities of the priests, for their multiplicity otherwise would appear quite disparate. The *central element* is the favorable acceptance obtained before God. The priest is primarily the man of the sanctuary. If he is not accepted by God, he is a useless person. To become pleasing to God, he undergoes all the ritual requirements which separate him from the profane world and he is also responsible for seeing that the people maintain themselves in a state of purity or "cleanness." In the series of *ascending elements* which culminate in the entrance of the priest into the sanctuary, the decisive part is played by the sacrifice, which establishes contact with God. If the relationship has been broken, the sacrifice re-establishes it. In other instances, it actualizes the contact in the manner required by the concrete situation, whether it be a daily offering or a festive celebration, a joyful thanksgiving or a humble petition, and so on.

The other functions of the priest correspond to the *descending movement* and appear as the beneficent consequences of the contact realized: once admitted into the presence of God, the priest procures pardon for sin and the end of calamities for the people, he receives the divine oracles which indicate what is to be done to solve life's problems, and finally he can also pass on the blessings which assure success, peace and fruitfulness for all.

d) *Mediation*

It is easy to see that the sum total of all this activity answers a profound aspiration: the desire to live in communion. The role of the priest is to open to the people the possibility of communion with God and communion with all humanity, since the one necessarily involves the other. In other words, priesthood is to be defined as an undertaking of mediation. One is therefore not surprised to find de Vaux insisting on this point at the conclusion of his treatise on the priesthood in the Old Testament.[33]

Indeed, close attention is necessary if this aspect is to be perceived and its importance recognized. At first sight there seems to be a more striking feature that is consequently expressed more directly and more frequently in the Old Testament texts. At first glance, the most striking thing about the priesthood is its privilege of approaching God. The priest's honor consists in "exercising the priesthood of God." (Ex 28:1-4) His sacred vestments make him almost a celestial being. The ceremonies of worship transport him into the divine world. To define the priest, therefore, one instinctively stops at his role in worship: the priest is a "man who serves the Godhead at the altar."[34]

But to stop here is in fact to miss the most specific element of the priesthood, namely, the exercise of mediation. The ability to approach God possessed by the priest is not a privilege that he may selfishly enjoy; it makes him the official intermediary for contact with God. It is to him that one turns to present offerings and requests to God; after which, it is his duty to communicate the divine wisdom and graces to the people. He thus puts the people into personal relationship with God. Nothing could be more important.

The attention given to the relationships between persons constitutes, in effect, the most characteristic—and the most invaluable—contribution of biblical revelation. From this point of view we may note how it differs from Greek philosophy. In attempting to understand the world, the first Greek thinkers looked for an impersonal principle to explain it. They were interested in the "elements" of matter and in the "reasons" for beings. The Bible has not gone in this direction, but has always remained attentive to persons and their relationships. In this respect it is in harmony with an important feature of modern thought, which insists on the relational aspect of reality and, in the first place, of man himself. Psychology, psychoanalysis, sociology, ethnology and anthropology reveal more and more that interpersonal relationships are constitutive of the human being. No man exists in isolation, for each individual becomes a human person in virtue of a whole network of relationships with others. The progressive conquest of the external world is itself only possible by means of manifold interpersonal relationships.

In their effort to find their proper place in the world, men are led to take note of a more fundamental relationship, one that is at the root of their existence and gives it all its vitality. All other relationships depend on it. The Bible's only purpose is to illuminate fully this primordial relationship and to bring it to its flowering. We refer to the relationship with God. Man is a religious creature and nothing in his life is more important than his encounter with God. Often this search is a kind of "groping" (Ac 17:27) and it can take very different paths. But when the search ends, man realizes that he has rejoined the source of his being and that, thanks to his relationship with God, he has discovered his true dignity.

This relationship is distinguished from all others by its universal openness. It cannot be restricted to a particular sector of existence. It is the basis of everything and whoever opens himself to it must therefore be willing to be completely invaded by it, in order to be made entirely alive. So radical a requirement naturally arouses instinctive resistance, whether conscious or unconscious, and three kinds of attitudes may be observed. The first, completely negative, consists in an absolute rejection of the perspective as soon as it has been glimpsed. The second, which seems to be positive, is in fact as we shall see, another form of rejection. Only the third is truly coherent; it is characterized by the institution of the priesthood.

The first attitude finds its expression—and its condemnation—in Psalm 14: "The fool says to himself, 'There is no God.' " (Ps 14:1).[35] To escape more easily from the profound demands of the relationship with God, the first step is to question the importance of this relationship: "the Lord can do neither good nor evil" (Zeph 1:12), and from there one goes on to deny even the existence of God. The religious dimension of human existence is thus violently repressed. A simple solution, but one with devastating results. In his letter to the Romans (1:18-32) Paul realistically describes the disastrous consequences of the refusal to relate to God. All man's other relationships suffer the repercussions; they are falsified and perverted. The worst alienation for a man occurs when he shuts himself up in his own limited world. He then suffocates and struggles convulsively. To live completely, a man must frankly accept the religious dimension of his being and permit his relationship with God to give life to all his other relationships.

At first sight, the second attitude takes the opposite direction. While atheistic humanism claims to develop all human relationships but rejects the most fundamental one, religious individualism—the second attitude—expressly admits that fundamental relationship: mankind is to be open to a relationship with God. However, he conceives this relationship in a narrow way. He restricts it to the individual's psychological life and does not allow it to affect other relationships. Religion is to be a private affair, a secret intimacy between the soul and God. This attitude shows itself in many forms and becomes visible in many areas. St. John condemns a particularly shocking form, which consists in claiming to love God while shutting one's heart to others. The judgment of the Apostle is unambiguous: "If anyone says, I love God, and yet detests his brother, he is a liar" (1 Jn 4:20). When maintained at the expense of other relationships, this relationship with God cannot be authentic, for it would then be simultaneously accepted and rejected. Its specific character, as we have said, is that of being the fundamental relationship, the one that constitutes the basis of all the others and which has to exercise a decisive influence over them all. To cut it off from other relationships is to prevent it from being what it is.

It is therefore essential to look for a way to avoid both "the drama of atheistic humanism" and the falsehood of religious individualism. Man's entire existence must be open to life-giving relationships with God in order to realize fully the human vocation. Such is the third attitude, which finds its expression in the institution of the priesthood. Those who adopt this solution are necessarily beyond atheism, because the priest is explicitly charged with establishing a relationship with God. At the same time, religious individualism is avoided, since the priesthood is a social function. The priest represents the entire community and it is in the name of the community that he strives to enter into relationship with God. The different functions which the Old Testament attributes to him show that the relationship with God is accepted to its full extent, as the basis of all existence. When they put their gifts and sacrifices into the priest's hands, the people are acknowledging that everything comes to them from God and that everything must return to God.[36] In asking the priest for oracles and instructions, the people are acknowledging that the light of God is necessary to find the right path amid the perplexities of life and are disposing themselves to follow the "ways of the Lord." When they receive the priest's blessing, they are opening themselves to the universal radiance of a positive relationship with God and are attesting that without it there is no true reality. And all this they do as a society, by coming together to form a community.

The mediation of the priest appears, therefore, as a function of the highest importance for the realization of the human vocation.

e) *The final stage in the evolution of the Old Testament priesthood*

In what way was the mediation of the priest understood and lived out at the end of the long evolution reflected in the Old Testament? In the conclusion of his work, A. Cody underscores the ever-increasing emphasis on the necessity for "holiness," and, as he specifies, "sacral, ritual holiness rather than ethical or moral holiness."[37] What resulted was a God relationship with ever more stringent boundaries.

In the earliest times, the existence of numerous sanctuaries in the land of Israel and the validity of several lines of priesthood were recognized. Eventually, only one legitimate sanctuary was recognized, the Temple in Jerusalem; all the others were abominated as if they were pagan temples. The suppression of the "high places" had created problems for the priests who had formerly been responsible for the worship there, but this mattered little; the priesthood had been unified and established as a hierarchy in function of its relationship with the unique sanctuary.

In connection with sacrifices in the liturgy, the question of atonement, which answered more directly to the interest in "holiness," had taken the predominant place. The most important of all the sacrifices were those offered on the day of Kippur, the solemn Day of Atonement. They formed, as it were, the culmination of the liturgical celebrations of the whole year. Their characteristic was that they presented the most impressive union of ritual separations and limitations, which attested to the extreme difficulty of entering into relationship with the most holy God.

The ceremony of the Great Atonement took place only once a year and it was the sole occasion on which the priestly cult could, in some degree, achieve a direct contact with God. In fact, the holiest area of the Temple, the place of the divine presence, could be entered only in the course of this liturgy. Moreover, even on this day, access remained extremely limited. Only one person was qualified for this dangerous undertaking—the high priest. And he was bound to perform many preliminary rites, as necessary precautions.[38] When he entered into the Holy of Holies he brought with him the blood of sacrificed animals and sprinkled it on the Mercy Seat, which was considered the throne of God. In this way the sacrifice of the Great Atonement made contact with God. No other sacrifice throughout the entire year shared this privilege. The blood of other victims was never introduced into the Holy of Holies or sprinkled on the Mercy Seat. The liturgy of Kippur therefore constituted the sole and decisive point of fulfillment of the priestly system of the Old Testament: the sacred place, the sacred time, the sacred person, the sacred action, everything here prescribed in detail.

This final stage of the religious evolution of the Old Testament calls for several observations. First of all, one may well be astonished at such insistence on segregation, when the objective was to establish a service of mediation. However, it is sufficient to analyze the notion of mediation to realize that there is no inconsistency here. On the contrary, mediation normally involves some sort of segregation. One of the functions of a mediator is to place himself between the two parties in order to prevent a direct contact that might have disastrous consequences. That is why, for example, Joab acts as mediator between David and Absalom at a time when Absalom, the guilty son, cannot appear in person before his father without risking condemnation (2 Sam 14). It is surely better to have good relations, even though indirect, than to provoke irritation by obstinately seeking to make a direct contact that is not desired.

In the case of the Old Testament priesthood, the whole question will be to discover if the system of ritual segregation obtained a positive result, that is to say, if it facilitated the establishment of good relationships between the people and God. It is clear that the result of the priestly mediation depended on the value of the unique annual contact with God that it attempted to establish. If this contact was authentic and positive, the undertaking had succeeded and its success justified all the scaffolding which made it possible. On the opposite supposition, it would have to be acknowledged that the system as a whole has failed. It is not without reason, therefore, that the Epistle to the Hebrews centers its attention on the liturgy of Kippur when it is evaluating the Old Testament priesthood.

Finally, we may note a further historical consequence of the evolution that we have been discussing. Because the priestly worship of the Old Testament was attached exclusively to a single sanctuary, the destruction of this sanctuary in the year 70 A.D. meant the suppression of the priestly cult. Since that date the Jewish people have had neither temple nor altar, and have ceased to offer the sacrifices prescribed by the Law of Moses. The sacrificial liturgy of Kippur is no longer celebrated; it is only commemorated. The mediation of the high priest is no longer exercised.

Notes

[1]Readers wishing to investigate the question further have some excellent works at their disposal, in particular R. de Vaux, *Les Institutions de l'Ancien Testament*, v.II, Cerf, 1960 [English edition entitled *Ancient Israel, Its Life and Institutions*, 1961]; A. Cody, *A History of Old Testament Priesthood*, Rome, 1969. These two works provide a bibliography on the subject: de Vaux, *op. cit.* pp. 446-450; Cody, *op. cit.* pp. xvi-xxvii.

[2]Melchizedek: Gen 14:18; the Egyptian priest: Gen 41:45, 50; 46:20; the Midianite priest: Ex 2:16; 3:1.

[3]Cody, *op. cit.*, pp. 26-29.

[4]Cf. Num 6:22-27; Dt 28:3-12.

[5]Cody, *op. cit.*, p. 29; cf. de Vaux, *op. cit.*, pp. 199-200.

[6]Dt 33:1, 8.

[7]The Hebrew Bible in this place offers a text that is obviously incomplete.

[8]1 Sam 23:9; 30:7.

[9]Cf. Hag 2:11-13; Zech 7:3.

[10]Dt 31:9-13, 26.

[11]Dt 21:1-9; Num 5:11-31.

[12]DamD XIII,2-7: cf. 1QS VI, 3-4; 1QSa III, 22-25.

[13]As de Vaux noted, *op. cit.*, pp. 207-208 [English ed., p. 355.]

[14]*Ibid.*, p. 199 [English ed., p. 348.]

[15]Cf. Jg 17:5-13; 1 Sam 7:1; 1 Kg 12:31f.

[16]Gen 12:6-8; 13:3f; 21:33.

[17]1 Sam 1:3; 2 Sam 21:6; 1 Kg 3:4; Jg 18:31; 1 Kg 12:30.

[18]Cf. 1 Chr 22; 2 Chr 3:1.

[19]Cf. Dt 12:2-17.

[20]Cf. Jn 4:20. Outside Judea, however, we know of the existence of two Jewish temples, both in Egypt: that of Elephantine, which is confirmed by Aramean papyri of the 5th century B.C., and that of Leontopolis, founded about 160 B.C. and destroyed by the Romans in 73 A.D. Moreover, the Samaritans had a temple on Mt. Garizim. Cf. de Vaux, *op. cit.*, pp. 186-191 [English ed., pp. 339-343.]

[21]Gen 22:13; 28:18; 31:54; 35:14.

[22]2 Sam 6:13, 17f; 24:25; 1 Kg 3:4, 15; 8:5, 62-64; 9:25.

[23]2 Chr 26:16-20.

[24]de Vaux, *op. cit.*, p. 344 [English ed., pp. 453-454.]

[25]Num 19:1-10; 31:23; Heb 9:13.

[26]Cf. Bonsirven, J., *Textes rabbiniques*, Rome, 1954, no. 225 (see Num 6:23).

[27]*Ibid.*, no. 894 and no. 1583. *The Jerusalem Bible*, in a note on Sir 50:20, affirms that "the Feast of the Atonement was the only occasion on which the ineffable Name was pronounced over the people in the form of a blessing." This affirmation is without foundation. There is reason for thinking that the text of Sir 50:20 is not referring to the Feast of the Atonement but to the daily liturgy of the holocaust; cf. Fearghail, F.O., "Sir 50: 5-21: Yom Kippur or the Daily Whole Offering," *Bib* 59 (1978), pp. 301-316, n. 12.

[28]This point will be taken up in Chapter X, 1.

[29]Cf. Ex. 19:12; 33:3.

[30]Cf. Num 3:12; 8:5-22; Ex 28:1.

[31]Cf. Gen 8:20f; Lev 1:9, 17f.

[32]Lev 4:6, 17; 16:14, 15.

[33]de Vaux, op. cit., p. 201-211. [English ed., pp. 349-357.]

[34]von Baudissin, W.W., Die Geschichte des alttestamentlichen Priesterthums, Leipzig, 1889, p. 269; quoted by Cody, op. cit., p. 11.

[35]Cf. Ps 10:4; 36:2.

[36]Cf. Dt 26:9-10.

[37]Cody, op. cit., p. 191.

[38]Lev 16:2, 14.

CHAPTER III

The Priesthood, A Thorny Question
for the First Christians

The investigation in Chapter I of the place held by priests and high priests in the narrative writings of the New Testament concluded with ambiguous results: on the one hand, there was Jesus' recognition of the ritual role of the Jewish priests; on the other hand, there was proof of the avowed hostility of the high priests, first against Jesus, and then against his disciples. But this hostility itself was susceptible to several interpretations: was it to be attributed to the priesthood of the high priests or to their position of authority? Moreover, how were the Christians to respond to this existential situation? How would they define their relationships with the priesthood? What would their faith in Christ contribute in this area?

1. The Importance of the Jewish Priesthood in the Time of the New Testament

These questions could not be avoided. They were posed with urgency because of the prominent role played by the priesthood in the faith and life of the Jewish people at that time. The historical evolution that we have just observed, in the direction of an ever greater insistence on separations and on the "holiness" required, might have resulted in the Jewish priesthood being cut off from the rest of the nation. But paradoxically enough, the opposite can be shown to have occurred. The influence of the priesthood had gradually increased and the priestly hierarchy had acquired more extensive power and authority.

a) *In the Bible*
This state of affairs is clearly seen in the Bible itself. For proof, it is enough to compare the two successive presentations of the sacred

history that we find in the Books of Samuel and Kings on the one hand, and in those of Chronicles on the other. The facts related are the same; but the Books of Chronicles, which date from after the Exile, give much more space to worship and the priesthood. The whole history of the reign of David is explicitly oriented toward the construction of the Temple and contains long chapters on the organization of the priesthood (1 Chr 23-26), for which one can find no equivalent in the Books of Samuel, composed much earlier. The events of the succeeding reigns are dealt with from the same point of view: the Chronicler keeps his attention directed toward the legitimate priesthood, toward the elimination of the "high places" and the reform of worship.

The final version of the Pentateuch reflects similar preoccupations. It is generally acknowledged that it is the work of the priestly circles, and this very fact is itself indicative of the influence they had already acquired. One finds there the importance given to cultic institutions. In the Book of Exodus, immediately after the short account of the conclusion of the Covenant (Ex 24), the priestly editor inserts a very long series of regulations concerning the sanctuary and the priesthood (Ex 25-31). After the sin of Israel and the renewal of the Covenant (Ex 32-34), he again goes back to this abundant material to relate in detail the execution of the commands that had been given (Ex 35-40). The elaboration is in fact continued beyond the end of the Book, for it is continued in Leviticus with the laws regarding sacrifices, ritual purity, the holiness of the priesthood, and the feasts.[1] The Book of Numbers, in its turn, gives predominant importance to the Levites and to the priests, and defends the privileges of Aaron with extreme vigor.[2] Indeed, the priestly tradition sets the tone from the very first page of Genesis, because it provides the first account of the creation[3] and the framework of the Pentateuch as a whole. The authority attributed to the priesthood in the period following the Exile is thus evident.

b) *After the return from the Exile*

In fact, as we also know from other sources, after the return from the Exile the high priest began to play a more important role in the national life of the Jews. The repatriated group had first been organized under the authority of Zerubbabel, the descendant of David, aided and assisted by the high priest, Joshua. The oracles of the prophet Haggai witness to this situation by the fact that they are addressed to Zerubbabel in the first place or that they frequently mention him alone.[4] But later Zerubbabel disappeared without, it seems, leaving a successor, so that the high priest found himself in sole charge of public affairs. In the version that we have of a prophecy of Zechariah (6:11), the "crown" is attributed to Joshua. The exegetes believe that in the earlier version of the text the "crown" was intended for Zerubbabel and that the text was later altered in view of a change in the historical situation: the power had passed into the hands of the high priest.

In the wording of the prophecies of Haggai and Zechariah we should also note an innovation which underlines the importance then assumed by the priesthood: the two prophets make systematic use of the title "high priest," that is to say, of the Hebrew noun *kohén* followed by the adjective "great" (*gadol*). To translate this expression, the Septuagint does not use the Greek title *archiereus*, but prefers the literal translation *ho hiereus ho megas*, "the priest who is the great one."[5] According to de Vaux, the title was then new; its occasional appearance in some texts dating before the Exile would be due to a later modification of these texts.[6] In any case, the systematic employment of this title does not appear until after the Exile and it corresponds to an increase in power.

In the following centuries, the evolution continued in the same direction. The high priest added the exercise of political power, according to the degree to which the Jewish nation possessed it, to his authority in religious affairs. By way of eulogizing the high priest of his time, Sirac praises him not only for having restored the Temple and for having celebrated magnificent liturgies, but also for having fortified the city to enable it to resist a siege (Sir 50:4). This eulogy applies to Simon II, the son of Onias II, who lived at the end of the third century B.C. Thirty years or so later, the persecution of Antiochus Epiphanes was threatening to destroy the religious life of the people of God; it was a priestly family, the Hasmoneans, who then organized armed resistance and led the people to victory. The Jews won their political and religious autonomy. It was at this time, as is well known, that their high priest received the title *archiereus* (1 Mac 10:20).

Of the two aspects expressed by this title, that of authority (*arche*) was especially visible in the circumstances of the period. It was a matter not only of authority in the field of worship and the religious life, but also and above all of political and military power. The phrase that follows the mention of the new title, after saying that "Jonathan put on the sacred vestments," immediately adds that he "gathered troops and manufactured many weapons" (1 Mac 10:21). A little later, the narrative relates that he was named "general of the army and governor." Jonathan was succeeded by his brother Simon, who won fresh military victories and led the country to independence. "In the year 170 the yoke of the Gentiles was removed from Israel and the people began to write on their acts and contracts: In the first year of Simon, eminent *high priest, general of the army* and chief of the Jews" (1 Mac 13:41-42).

The priestly dynasty of the Hasmoneans kept itself in power through various vicissitudes until the time of Herod, whose reign began in 37 B.C. The political power of the high priest was then reduced to a secondary level, but it did not disappear. Even when the Roman Empire made Judea into one of its procuratorial provinces, the high priest continued to be the highest authority of the Jewish nation. He presided over the Sanhedrin, whose competence as a regional power the Romans acknowledged.

c) *Religious authority and political power*

This, therefore, is the situation reflected in the accounts of the Gospels and of the Acts of the Apostles. At that time it was impossible, when speaking of the high priests, to separate the aspect of religious authority from that of political power. They were inextricably intertwined. This amalgam greatly complicated for the first Christians the question of the relationships between their faith in Christ and the Jewish priesthood. A break had occurred, a tragic break which had reached final expression in the condemnation of Jesus and in his execution. But the problem was to discover the conclusions to be drawn from this break. Were the Christians in their turn bound to break with the priestly institution? Were they to introduce a distinction between priesthood and political authority, or reject them both? But was it legitimate to condemn an institution of such importance in the life of the people of God? Was it possible to forget that, whatever the wrongs committed by its representatives, this institution had been founded on the Word of God and guaranteed by an impressive collection of biblical texts?

2. The Expectation of a Great High Priest in Messianic Times

This last question reveals the most fundamental aspect of the problem, namely its relationship to the fulfillment of the Scriptures. From this point of view, the disillusionments provoked by the political behavior of the high priests[7] could neither monopolize the attention nor lead to a final verdict. These dissatisfactions could not sanction the condemnation of the institution of the priesthood, but were meant rather to serve to revive the hope of a renewed priesthood, for this was God's promise.

a) *Prophetic texts*
The prophets of Israel had not refrained from criticizing the priests of their own era and the too often formalistic worship they celebrated in the Temple.[8] But far from questioning the institution of the priesthood itself, they had proclaimed its perpetual durability and the renewal of worship and of the priesthood in the Last Days. A prophetic oracle is found both in Isaiah (2:1-5) and in Micah (4:1-3) predicting that "in the last days" [so translated in the Septuagint] the mountain of the Lord and the House of God [that is to say, the Temple of Jerusalem] would be raised above the hills and that "the nations would flow to it." The Book of Ezekiel concludes with a magnificent vision of the future Temple and it lays down the duties and functions of the priests. Jeremiah, who had been bold enough to foretell the destruction of the Temple, had nonetheless declared on God's authority that the Levitical priests would never lack successors to offer sacrifices.[9] For his part, the prophet Malachi, while sharply berating the negligence of the priests (Mal 2:1-9), does not remain at this negative level, but proclaims that the Lord "will enter into his sanctuary" and

he will purify the sons of Levi and will refine them like gold and silver, and they will become for the Lord persons who will present the offering as it ought to be. Then the offering of Judah and Jerusalem will be pleasing to the Lord as in the days of old. (Mal 3:3-4)

Already in the First Book of Samuel a mysterious "man of God" had uttered a promise of God which would be often referred to:

I will raise up for myself a faithful priest, who will behave according to my heart and according to my desire; I will assure to him a lasting house and he will walk always before my Anointed One. (1 Sam 2:35)

Shortly before the Christian era, Sirac recalled with insistence that the priesthood of Aaron had been guaranteed by an eternal pact.[10]

b) *Qumran and other writings*
A renewal of the priesthood was then quite naturally included in references to the fulfillment of the plan of God promised for Messianic times. This is attested by several Jewish writings dating to around the Christian era. They show that not all the aspirations of the Jews in the time of Jesus were concentrated on the expectation of a royal Messiah. This was held with hesitancy for a long time, but the matter has become more evident since the discovery of the Qumran manuscripts.

There is in fact a text in the Rule of the Community that explicitly refers to the coming of three personages and not merely of one. The Rule speaks of "the coming of the Prophet and of the Messiahs of Aaron and of Israel."[11] It is not hard to find the basis of the expectation of these three personages. There was a passage in Deuteronomy which promised that God would raise up in the midst of the sons of Israel a prophet like Moses.(Dt 18:18) Like so many other divine promises, this one was clearly capable of several levels of interpretation. Its realization might have been seen in the course of successive centuries in the person of such great prophets as Elijah and Elisha. It should be noted, however, that the final editor of Deuteronomy, who lived after Elijah and Elisha, was not of this opinion, for he observes at the end of the book:

There has no more been raised up in Israel a prophet like Moses. (Dt 34:10)

The full realization of the promise expressed in Deuteronomy 18:18 was therefore yet to come. This same position was taken at Qumran, as also at Jerusalem, according to the witness of the Fourth Gospel (Jn 1:21).

In addition to the Prophet, the text of the Rule mentions two other personages, whom it designates by the name of "Messiahs" (in Hebrew *meshihe*, the plural of *mashiah* preceding a complement). It is true that this rendering could be contested by the observation that the Hebrew word *mashiah* had more semantic breadth than its English derivative, *messiah*. Its immediate meaning, "anointed," was perceived. The term could then be applied just as well to a Jewish high priest as to a king of Israel, for in both cases the induction into office included a ceremony of anointing. However, in the text before us the

two "anointed" persons under discussion were also persons expected
in the Last Days, and this justifies translation by the term *Messiah.*
Obviously "the Anointed One of Israel" is here the royal Messiah,
whose advent was expected on the basis of the oracle addressed by
the prophet Nathan to King David, as well as on a whole series of
other texts.[12] "The Anointed One of Aaron" is presented in parallel
fashion as the supreme heir of the priestly institution. The expectation
of his coming was based on the biblical texts already cited above and
on the awareness, very much alive at Qumran, of the importance of
the priesthood.

It may in fact be noted that in the words of the Rule it is the
Anointed of Aaron, the priestly Messiah, who is placed first, not the
royal Messiah. This order corresponds with the order of precedence in
the sect. Some lines earlier in the text of the Rule it is prescribed that

> Only the sons of Aaron shall exercise authority in matters of law
> and property; and it is under their authority that the ballot shall go
> out for every decision concerning the members of the Commu-
> nity.[13]

Another document, of which we possess only a fragment, applies the
same principles to the Messianic times, "when God will have caused
the Messiah to be born among them." It gives pre-eminence to the
Priest. He will be the first to enter in his capacity as "chief of the whole
assembly of Israel" and he is followed by the chiefs of the priests.
Then the Messiah of Israel will enter. At the table,

> no one will extend his hand over the first fruits of the bread and the
> sweet wine before the Priest, for he is the one who will bless the
> first fruits of the bread and the sweet wine and will first extend his
> hand over the bread. Then the Messiah of Israel will extend his
> hands over the bread. (1 QSa II:11-12)

In the Damascus Document, which comes from the same sect but was
discovered in Egypt at the end of the nineteenth century, the perspective changes. The word *messiah* is no longer employed in the plural,
but in the singular, while preserving the double qualification expressed in the Qumran manuscripts. The document refers several
times to the hoped-for coming of the "Messiah of Aaron and of Israel."[14] It declares that the wicked "will be delivered to the sword,
when the Messiah of Aaron and of Israel comes."[15] It seems that either
at some given time or in some communities the messianic expectation

was centered on a unique personage, who would receive both the priestly anointing and the royal coronation at the same time. Other writings, which are not from Qumran, attest similar traditions. This is especially the case with the "Testament of the Twelve Patriarchs," an apocryphal work which utilizes texts of Jewish origin, in particular a *Testament of Levi* written in Aramaic, two fragments of which have been found in Cairo and some fragments at Qumran. The complete version that we have is a Greek adaptation; there is also an Armenian version.[16] The first edition may be dated at the beginning of the first century before Christ, but the text that has come down to us includes additions that appear to be Christian interpolations. Whatever we think about this controverted point, the passages that interest us cannot be the work of Christian editors, for the messianism that they express is far from Christian perspectives. Indeed, they do not give preference to the tribe of Judah, but to that of Levi.

From the first Testament, which is that of Reuben, the oldest of the sons of Jacob, the priority of Levi is affirmed:

> To Levi the Lord has given the principate, and to Judah. (Test. Reuben, VI:7)

Reuben tells his sons to listen to Levi:

> for he will sacrifice for the whole of Israel until the fulfillment of the times of an *anointed high priest* of whom the Lord has spoken. (Test. Reuben, VI:8)

Instead of "anointed high priest," the Greek text may be translated "Messiah high priest" or even "Christ high priest," for it contains the word *christos*. The second Testament, that of Simeon, enjoins obedience on Levi and Judah and continues:

> Do not rise against these two tribes, for from them the salvation of God will be raised up for you. For the Lord will raise from Levi a high priest and from Judah a king, God and man, who will save all the nations and the race of Israel. (Test. Simon VII:1-2)

In the phrase "God and man," that describes the king who comes forth from Judah, we recognize a Christian addition, but the place given to Levi in the text reflects an earlier tradition.

The Testament of Levi is still more explicit. It describes the history of the Israelite priesthood and foretells that in the end, after countless abuses the priesthood will disappear, and then the Lord will raise up a *new priest*, to whom all the words of God will be revealed and he will execute a judgment of truth upon the earth for a multitude of days. And his star will mount up into the sky, like a king. (Test. Levi XVIII:1-3)

Even the Testament of Judah proclaims the pre-eminence of Levi when it says:

My children, love Levi in order to survive; and do not rise against him lest you be destroyed. For the Lord has given me the royalty and to him the priesthood, and he has subjected the royalty to the priesthood. (Test. Judah XXI:1-2)

Whatever the controversies raised by these Testaments, one cannot deny their witness as far as it concerns the existence of a priestly type of eschatological expectation. This expectation was alive at the beginning of the Christian era. We must recognize that it was an entirely normal feature of the religious aspirations of the period. People were waiting for the total and definitive fulfillment of God's plan. It was only reasonable then for the priestly aspect to be included, since the priesthood occupied a foremost place in biblical revelation and in the life of the people of God.

In this historical context, the Christian community had undertaken to affirm that God had answered the expectations of his people and that the fulfillment was now a tangible reality: by his life, his death and his glorious resurrection, Jesus had brought God's plan to a successful conclusion. One question remained to be answered: was there a priestly dimension in the Christian fulfillment? What connection could be established between the expectation of a renewed priesthood and the story of Jesus?

3. The Apparent Absence of the Priestly Dimension in Jesus

The question was formidable, because it could put the Church in a quandary. Indeed, at first sight it seemed as if the answer would have to be negative and that it might reveal a weakness in the Christian fulfillment of revelation. We have already observed, in Chapter I, that the relationships between Jesus and the Jewish priesthood had not been harmonious. This inquiry must now be completed by examining Jesus' own position more closely. Could one discover a priestly dimension in his person and in his work?

a) *The person of Jesus*

The person of Jesus had aroused much astonishment in the course of his public life, and numerous questions had been raised in his regard. Who was this man? In what category could he be placed? The Gospels echo everyone's perplexities and record the most diverse opinions: Jesus, God's elect or tool of Satan, master of wisdom or dangerous seducer, Son of David or ancient prophet returned to earth, and so on. It is significant that among so many hypotheses one never finds any suggestion that he might be a priest. No one, it seems, had ever asked if Jesus might be the priest of the Last Days, come in order to offer the perfect worship to God. It may appear strange that this question was never asked, but it is enough to recall the then current notion of the priesthood to find the reason for this omission. It was clear to everyone that Jesus was not a Jewish priest. It was known that he did not belong to a priestly family, and that in consequence he had no right to any priestly function. The priesthood had been given by God "to Aaron and his sons." God himself had excluded all other claimants.[17] The precept of the Law was extremely severe on this matter: "Establish Aaron and his sons in the exercise of their priesthood: every lay person who approaches shall be put to death."[18] In this way the "holiness" of the priesthood was manifested: an impassable separation was maintained between the priestly families and the rest.

Jesus belonged by birth to the tribe of Judah. Thus, according to the Law, he was not a priest. No one thought of attributing this office to him and he himself never laid the least claim to it.

b) *His activity*

His activity had nothing priestly about it in the then traditional sense of the word, but placed him rather in the line of the prophets. He had undertaken to proclaim the word of God, as the prophets had formerly done, and to announce that the restoration of the kingdom of God was at hand. He expressed this sometimes through symbolical actions (Mt 21:18-22), in this respect imitating Jeremiah, Ezekiel and other prophets.[19] His miracles were reminiscent of the time of Elijah and Elisha: the multiplication of the loaves, the raising of the widow's son, the healing of the leper.[20] In one of Luke's stories, Jesus himself invites the comparison; several times he implicitly ranks himself with the prophets.[21] In fact, many people recognized him as a prophet and even a great prophet, "the" prophet who was expected.[22] After the Resurrection, the apostle Peter proclaims Jesus to be the prophet comparable to Moses, the one promised by God in Deuteronomy.[23]

The prophets of Israel, as we know, often kept their distance with respect to the priesthood. They would strongly criticize the formalism that infected ritual worship and they would insist, in contrast, on a true docility to God in the reality of existence. The preaching of Jesus was similarly oriented. The Gospels witness that Jesus took systematic action, not against the priests personally, but against a ritualistic conception of religion. By firmly refusing to grant any importance to rules of external "purity," by not hesitating to put the healing of the sick before the observance of the Sabbath, Jesus was rejecting the traditional manner of understanding holiness.[24] He was taking sides against the system of ritual separations, which culminated in the priestly offering of sacrificial animals, and was opting for the opposite attitude: instead of a holiness obtained by separating oneself from others, he proposed a holiness obtained by welcoming them. The word *thysia*, which designates the ritual sacrifices and occurs very often (almost 400 times) in the Old Testament, occurs only twice on the lips of Jesus in the Gospels, and on both occasions he is recalling that God does not like this kind of worship.[25] In Mark, *thysia* occurs only once, in a phrase spoken by a scribe and approved by Jesus, and the perspective is the same: the love of God and one's neighbor "is worth more than all holocausts and all sacrifices."[26] Without employing the word *thysia*, another saying of Jesus has the same sense: it prescribes that reconciliation with a brother should precede the offering of a gift at the altar of the Temple.[27]

On the other hand, the Gospels record a forceful intervention by Jesus within the Temple itself.[28] In reproaching the sellers of animals destined for sacrifice, Jesus was effectively criticizing the whole of sacrificial worship. John carefully notes that Jesus "drove out of the Temple the sheep and the cattle," that is to say, the animals that were to be offered in sacrifice. Mark observes that the high priests were greatly chagrined and it is not difficult to understand their position.

A connection can be seen between this initiative on the part of Jesus and the prophecy of Malachi: "Suddenly the Lord whom you are seeking will enter his sanctuary . . . . He is like a refiner's fire . . . . He will purify the sons of Levi . . . ." The negative part of the prophecy is thus accomplished, but there is nothing to show how its positive part will be fulfilled, that which announces the institution of a worship pleasing to God.[29]

c) *Royal Messianism*

The Messianic hopes aroused by the person and activity of Jesus did not then take on a priestly color, but rather suggested the royal Messianism. The questions and the discussions about the identity of Jesus finally came to focus about this point: was he the Messiah, son and successor of David,[30] whose reign had been foretold by a whole series of prophecies? This was the question that was put to Jesus during his interrogation before the Sanhedrin. In his reply, Jesus refers to a text that belongs to the Davidic tradition.[31] After the Resurrection, the same text is cited in an address by Peter in which he proclaims that God has established Jesus as "Lord and Messiah."[32] This is the earliest expression of the Christian faith.

d) *His death*

It must be acknowledged then that the person and activity of Jesus in no way corresponded to what would have been expected of a priest at that time. But did the situation not change with his death? We would be inclined to reply in the affirmative, for we have learned to consider the death of Jesus as a sacrifice, that is to say, as a priestly offering. In reality, the question is less simple than it seems, and one cannot immediately give a positive answer. From the point of view of Old Testament cult, the death of Jesus in no way appeared as a priestly offering; it was in fact the very opposite of a sacrifice. Indeed, sacrifice did not consist in the putting to death of a living person, still less in his sufferings, but in rites of offering performed by the priest in the holy place. The Jewish Law carefully distinguished between slaughter and ritual sacrifice (Dt 12:13-16). Now Jesus' death had taken place outside the Holy City. It had not been accompanied by liturgical rites. It was viewed as a legal penalty, the execution of a man condemned to death.

The Israelites—and therefore also the first Christians—saw the most thorough opposition between the execution of a criminal and the offering of a sacrifice. The rites that accompanied a sacrifice made it a solemn and glorious act, which would bring about a union with God and obtain divine blessings. Because it was offered during the course of religious ceremonies, the victim would be symbolically lifted up to

God. A legal penalty, on the contrary, was a juridical and not a ritual act that had nothing glorious about it, but covered the criminal with dishonor. Far from uniting to God and drawing down his blessings, it was truly a curse.[33] It would seem to follow then that the Calvary event would only increase the distance between Jesus and the priesthood.

e) *Non-priestly formulations*
In these circumstances it is not surprising that primitive Christian preaching did not speak of the priesthood in connection with Jesus. Neither in his person nor in his ministry nor in his death did the first Christians find any close connection between Jesus and the institutional priesthood as they knew it.

To designate the person of Jesus and to define his work, they turned first, therefore, to a Messianic and existential vocabulary. Jesus is the Messiah, Son of David and Son of God. "He died for us" (1 Thess 5:10). To die for someone is not a "sacrifice" in the ritual sense, but an act of supreme devotion. Even if we specify, with the profession of faith of 1 Cor 15:3 that "Christ died for our sins," *we still have not reached a formulation that is properly sacerdotal*. The Old Testament never says that a victim offered in sacrifice "has died for sins." Paul's magnificent phrase regarding "the Son of God who loved me and delivered himself up for me" (Gal 2:20), does not contain the slightest allusion to sacrifice; it expresses the existential gift of one person in favor of another. This also applies to that passage of the Gospel which declares that the Son of Man "did not come to be served but to serve and to give his life as a ransom for many."[34] The same observation also applies to the vocabulary of liberation or salvation, of purchase or of redemption, employed in the New Testament to describe the work of Christ.

Since nobody thought of using the sacrificial and priestly vocabulary for Christ, it was even less likely that they would think of it for his disciples. None of the functions exercised in the Christian communities corresponded to the specific activities of the Jewish priests. Therefore the leaders of the Christians did not take the title of *kohen* or *hiereus*. They were given names which expressed the notion of mission, or of service, or of a position of responsibility and authority, such as *apostolos*, apostle, which means "one who has been sent;" *diakonos*, deacon, "one who serves;" *episkopos*, from which the word "bishop" comes and which means "overseer;" *presbyteros*,[35] which gives us the word "priest" and which means an "elder;" *hegoumenos*, which means "a leader."

4. Some Contacts

These various considerations clearly show the difficulty of the problem that faced the newly-born Church: was it possible to find in the mystery of Christ the fulfillment of the traditional priesthood? At first sight, there seemed rather to be a complete break.

a) The Messiah and the Temple

The situation, however, was not entirely negative. One might note a certain connection between the mystery of Christ and Old Testament worship. This connection was based primarily on the tradition of royal Messianism itself. This tradition offered a very strong link between the Messiah and the Temple. The prophecy of Nathan, the basis of royal Messianism, was directly linked with David's project of constructing a House for God and it proclaimed that the Son of David would construct the house of God (2 Sam 7:1-5, 13). This aspect of the tradition had not been ignored by the evangelists. In a new and surprising form it even occupies a foremost place in their narratives. The life of Jesus is closely connected with a threat to destroy the Temple and with the proclamation of the construction of a new one. The Synoptics relate first of all that Jesus had foretold the complete destruction of the Temple (*hieron*) of Jerusalem, which evidently included the destruction of the actual sanctuary, called in Greek the *naos*.[36]

A text in Luke, which extends the same prediction to the entire Holy City, discloses the fundamental cause of this disaster: Jerusalem has failed to recognize the time of its "visitation," in other words, it did not receive as it should the person and preaching of Jesus.[37] A close link is therefore affirmed between the fate of Jesus and the destruction of the Temple. The same theme reappears insistently in the account of the Passion. When Jesus was arraigned before the Sanhedrin, the only explicit accusation against him was that of having planned the destruction of the sanctuary: "We heard him say, I will destroy this sanctuary (*naos*) made by human hands . . . ."[38] The accusation is presented by the evangelists as "false testimony," and, in fact, there is no record of Jesus having said, "I will destroy . . .", but underlying the false witness it is easy to discern the expression of an accurate datum, one that is mentioned again at two other moments in the account,[39] and which has two sides, one negative and one positive. It is not just a question of destruction, but also and above all of a new reconstruction: "in three days" Jesus will construct "a new sanctuary not made by hands." The allusion to the Resurrection is obvious. The destruction of the old sanctuary clearly puts an end to the Jewish priesthood, because the sanctuary was the building in which the Jewish priests and the high priest performed the ritual worship prescribed by the Law of Moses. The construction of a new sanctuary is normally bound up with the setting up of a new priesthood. But the Synoptics do not express this corollary: they are content with forcefully pointing out the link between the sanctuary and the mystery of Jesus. For his part, John bears witness to the same link when he quotes a saying of Jesus about the sanctuary:

Destroy this sanctuary and in three days I will rebuild it. (Jn 2:19)

and when he specifies that this saying refers to "the sanctuary of his body" (2:21). In the rest of the Fourth Gospel, the theme of the new temple and the new worship returns more than once, under different aspects.[40] All this is in perfect harmony with the tradition of royal Messianism: the principal mission of the Son of David was to construct the house of God.[41]

b) *The account of the Last Supper*
Another Gospel tradition goes even further. It suggests a connection between Jesus' death and a sacrificial rite. It occurs in the account of the Last Supper, which has been transmitted both by St. Paul and by the three Synoptics.[42] In themselves, Jesus' actions—rendering thanks to God for the bread and the wine, breaking the bread and passing the cup—do not constitute a ritual sacrifice, but belong to the normal course of a meal. Neither is the new value that Jesus confers on these traditional actions necessarily sacrificial. To hand over one's body, to shed one's blood to save others is not a ritual sacrifice, but an act of heroic dedication. Among the words spoken by Jesus, however, there is an expression that possesses an undeniably sacrificial connotation, for it unites the word "blood" with the word "covenant." These words have an obvious connection with the words pronounced by Moses at the sacrifice accomplished on Sinai as a way of sealing the

covenant between the People of Israel and Yahweh. "This is," said Moses, "*the blood of the covenant* which the Lord has concluded with you . . ." (Ex 24:5-8). The connection is particularly evident in the wording of Matthew and Mark, where the expression "the blood of the Covenant" is literally reproduced, only with a possessive pronoun to give it specific application: "This is my [blood] *the blood of the Covenant* . . . ." But the connection is also visible in the wording of Luke and Paul, who say: "This cup is the new Covenant in my blood." It may also be noted that the date of this event facilitates the connection with the story of the Exodus: the Passion of Jesus took place at the time of the Feast of Passover.[43] It is possible that the immolation of the lamb was in mind as well as the covenantal sacrifice.[44]

The first Gospel joins the aspect of the sacrifice of expiation to that of the sacrifice of the covenant: the blood of Jesus is the blood "shed for many for the remission of sins" (Mt 26:28). While not belonging to the Old Testament ritual as a precise quote, the expression "for the remission of sins" is close to the phrase which in Leviticus (4:20) concludes the description of the sacrifice offered for the sins of the whole community of Israel: "The priest will make expiation for them and the *sin* will be *remitted.*" The same phrase is used again for individual sacrifices and, in slightly modified form, it recurs like a refrain.[45]

A number of exegetes believe that a supplementary confirmation of the sacrificial character of Jesus' death may be discerned in the words "for many" ("the blood . . . shed *for many*), where they see an allusion to the prophecy of Isaiah about the Servant of Yahweh. It is written of the Servant that "he will justify *many*" and that "he has borne the sins of *many*" (53:11-12). Moreover, according to a current rendering of an earlier verse, the prophet foresees that the Servant will offer his life in sacrifice: "If he offers his life as a sacrifice of atonement, he will see a posterity" (53:10). The sacrificial interpretation of which we are speaking is based on this verse.[46] Actually, we are far from certainty on this point, since the exact meaning of Isaiah's statement is doubtful. Neither the Hebrew text nor the Septuagint rendering says: "If he offers his life . . . ." The wording of the modern versions is that of the Vulgate.[47] We do not find it cited anywhere in the New Testament. The other passages of the same prophecy that the New Testament applies to Christ do not, properly speaking, have a "sacrificial" sense. Verse 7, in particular, which is quoted in Acts 8:32, speaks of slaughter and not of sacrifice: the parallel drawn in this text between the shearing of the sheep and their slaughter shows that the author is not thinking of sacrificial worship.

After careful consideration, one cannot say that the Gospel tradition establishes many connections between the mystery of Jesus and what is properly called priestly worship. There is clearly no tendency here to emphasize this perspective.

c) *Possible points of contact*
Several exegetes have nevertheless made great efforts to multiply the connections by examining the texts for all possible points of contact. Friedrich[48] sees an allusion to the priesthood in the title "the Holy One of God," applied to Jesus in Mark 1:24 and John 6:69; he thinks that the baptism of Jesus and the titles of Son of God and Christ are connected with the priesthood; he perceives examples of priestly power in the expulsion of demons by Jesus, in the healing of the lepers, the blessing of children and in the pardon granted to sinners. For his part, A. Feuillet thinks that "every time the role of Christ is mentioned in the New Testament in connection with the offering which the Servant of the Lord makes of himself, Jesus is being implicitly presented to us as the priest of the new Covenant."[49] Feuillet is particularly anxious to demonstrate "the priestly character of the prayer in John 17" and says in this regard: "The clearest indication of this priestly character is the reference to Isaiah 53." According to him, another important indication is furnished by the division of Jesus' prayer, which corresponds to the priestly ritual of the Atonement: Jesus prays first for himself and for his apostles, then for all other believers, just as the high priest had "first to atone for himself and his house," and then "for the whole assembly of Israel."[50]

Though these suggestions are very interesting, they remain problematical.[51] One must be careful not to confuse uncertain allusions with explicit statements. Moreover, in a study of this kind, it is important to distinguish carefully between the successive points of view. In the first, that of the time of Jesus and of the first years after his death and Resurrection, the prevailing concepts of priesthood and of sacrifice were those of the Old Testament. As we shall see, the light of Christ has triggered a reworking of these ideas which has culminated in their radical transformation. Once this reworking was completed, certain elements of the Gospel tradition which initially had no priestly or sacrificial connotation whatsoever are henceforth closely and directly connected with the priesthood and the sacrifice. This is the case, for example, with "dying for sins" or "delivering himself up for . . . ." At this point in our inquiry, we can only observe that the Gospel traditions concerning Jesus never describe either his person or his activities or his death in explicitly sacerdotal terms and only once do they use a sacrificial formula.

In the final version of the Gospels, the text that most clearly suggests a sacerdotal christology is undoubtedly that of the conclusion of Luke's Gospel. Here Jesus is shown in a typically priestly attitude, "raising his hands" in "blessing."[52] This is the final image Luke leaves us of Jesus, as he takes leave of his disciples at the moment of his Ascension.

Raising his hands, he blessed them; and it happened that while he was blessing them, he was separated from them and was carried up to heaven. (Lk 24:50-51)

There are only two occasions in the Old Testament where we find someone lifting up his hands and blessing, and in both the person is the high priest at the conclusion of a sacrifice. In Leviticus 9:22, at the conclusion of the sacrifice for his priestly consecration, Aaron "raised his hands over the people and blessed them;" in Sirac 50:20, at the end of a solemnly described liturgy, the high priest Simon "raised his hands over the whole assembly of the sons of Israel in order to give the Lord's blessing." In both these texts the blessing is followed by a prostration, a trait that is also found in Luke's account. Sirac then concludes with an invitation to bless God: and this is precisely what the disciples do, according to the last verse of Luke. We are therefore justified in thinking that Luke wished to suggest, at the end of his Gospel, a priestly interpretation of the mystery of Jesus. However, it must always be remembered that this presentation remains implicit. Here again we have an allusion but not an affirmation. The conclusion already reached therefore holds good: the Gospels never speak explicitly of the priesthood in connection with Jesus. They provide several elements which prepare the way for a positive solution of the problem, but they themselves do not provide this solution. To find it, we must explore the other writings of the New Testament.

Notes

[1]Lev 1-7;11-16; 21-22; 23.
[2]Num 1:48-53; 3-4; 8; 16-17.
[3]Gen 1:1-2:4a.
[4]Hag 1:1, 12, 14; 2:1, 4, 21, 23.
[5]Hag 1:1, 12; Zech 3:1, 9; 6:11. The same expression is in Neh 3:1, 20; 13:28; Jdt 4:6, 8, 14; 15:8; and Sir 50:1.
[6]de Vaux, *op. cit.*, pp. 241, 266-267 [English ed., pp. 377, 397-398.]
[7]These discontents led to violent arguments, echoes of which are passed on in the Second Book of Maccabees and the Qumran manuscripts.
[8]Cf. Hos 5:1; 8:13; Amos 5:21-23; Is 1:10-16; Jer 2:8; Mal 2:1-9.
[9]Cf. Ez 40-44; on the Levites and the priests, 44:10-31; Jer 7:12-14; 33:18.
[10]Sir 45:7, 15, 24f.
[11]1QS IX, 10-11.
[12]2 Sam 7:12-16; Is 11:1-9; Jer 33:15f.
[13]1 QS IX, 7.
[14]DamD XII:23; XIX:10; XX:1.
[15]DamD XIX:10.
[16]The detail of the text is often uncertain, for the manuscripts present a great number of variants; cf. the critical edition of R.H. Charles, *The Greek Version of the Testaments of the Twelve Patriarchs*, Oxford, 1908; Darmstadt, 1966; and the recent edition of M. de Jonge, *The Testaments of the Twelve Patriarchs*, A Critical Edition of the Greek Text, Leiden, 1978. The expectation of a "priest savior" has been specially studied by A. Hultgard, *L'Eschatologie des Testaments des Douze Patriarches*, v.I. Interprétations des textes, Uppsala, 1977, pp. 268-381. See also P. Grelot, *L'Espérance juive à l'heure de Jésus*, Desclée, 1978, pp. 77-90.
[17]Cf. Ex 28:1; Lev 8:2; Num 16-17; Sir 45:15, 25.
[18]Num 3:10; cf. 3:38.
[19]Cf. 1 Kg 22:11; Jer 19:10; Ez 4:1-3.
[20]Cf. Mt 14:13-21 and 2 Kg 4:42-44; Lk 7:11-17 and 1 Kg 17:17-24; Mt 8:1-4 and 2 Kg 5.
[21]Cf. Lk 4:24-27; Mt 13:57; Lk 13:33.
[22]Lk 7:16, 39; Mt 21:11, 46; Jn 4:19; 6:14; 7:40; 9:17.
[23]Ac 3:22 quoting Dt 18:18.
[24]Cf. Mt 9:10-13 and par.; 12:1-13 and par.; 15:1-20 and par.; Jn 5:16-18; 9:16.
[25]Mt 9:13; 12:7; both cite Hos 6:6.
[26]Mk 12:33. Beyond these three occurrences (Mt 9:13; 12:7; Mk 12:33), *thysia* is mentioned only twice in the Gospels: Lk 2:24; 13:1; none in Jn.
[27]Mt 5:23f. In Greek the word "altar" (*thysiasterion*), related to "sacrifice" (*thysia*), is also very frequent in the O.T. (more than 400 occurrences), but is rare in the Gospels (8 instances). In addition to Mt 5:23, it is found in Mt 23:18-20—where Jesus criticizes the casuistry of the scribes and Pharisees—and in Mt 23:25; Lk 1:11; 11:51, where it serves to define a location.
[28]Mt 21:12f. and par.; Jn 2:14-16.
[29]Mal 3:1-4.
[30]Mt 12:23; Mk 8:29; Jn 7:26, 41; 12:34.
[31]Mk 14:61 and par.; cf. Ps 110:1.

³²Ac 2:34-36.
³³Cf. Dt 21:22f. However, the Book of Wisdom outlines a connection between the result of punishment suffered by the just and the outcome of a ritual sacrifice, by taking as a middle ground the idea of a purifying trial. The just "in the eyes of the foolish have seemed to die," (3:2) "in the eyes of men, they have been subjected to a penalty," (3:4) in reality "(a) God has put them to the test and (b) has found them worthy of him; (a') like gold in the crucible he has tested them and (b') *like a burned sacrifice*, he has accepted them" (3:5f). The legal penalties undergone by the Jewish martyrs during the persecution of Antiochus (167-164 B.C.) are presented in 2 Mac 7:32-38 as an expiation which prepares the reconciliation of the people with God, but the vocabulary employed is not sacrificial (cf. also 4 Mac 6:28f; 17:17-22). On the other hand, from the Jewish point of view, an enormous difference is evident between these martyrs and Jesus. The former had been condemned to death by pagans because of their fidelity to the Law of Moses; Jesus, on the other hand, had been handed over by the Jewish authorities for having transgressed the Law on the most serious matter. (cf. Jn 19:7; 5:18; Mt 27:65f; Mk 14:64)
³⁴Mt 20:48; Mk 10:45.
³⁵On the evolution of the meaning of *presbyteros*, cf. Ch. X, 6.
³⁶Mt. 24:1f. and par.
³⁷Lk 19:41-44; cf. 1:68, 78; 7:16.
³⁸Mk 14:58; cf. Mt 26:61; Ac 6:14.
³⁹Mk 15:29, 37-39; Mt 27:40, 51-54.
⁴⁰Jn 4:20-24; 7:37-39; 11:48; 14:1-3; 17:24.
⁴¹2 Sam 7:13; 1 Kg 5:19; 8:13, 19; 1 Chr 17:13, etc.; Wis 9:8.
⁴²1 Cor 11:23-25; Mt 26:26-29; Mk 14:22-25; Lk 22:19f.
⁴³Cf. Mt 26:2, 17-19; Mk 14:1, 12-16; Lk 22:1, 7-13, 15; Jn 18:28, 39; 19:14.
⁴⁴Cf. 1 Cor 5:7.
⁴⁵Lev 5:6, 10, 13, 16, 18; 6:6; 19:22.
⁴⁶Cf. A. Feuillet, *Le Sacerdoce du Christ et ses ministres*, Paris ed., 1972, pp. 22-23, 70-74.
⁴⁷In Hebrew, the verb is in the feminine singular 3rd person, or—the form is the same—in the masculine singular 2nd person; in the Septuagint, it is in the 2nd person plural. The Hebrew may be translated either: "If his soul offers a sacrifice of reparation, it will see a posterity," or "If you (sing.) make of his life a sacrifice of reparation, he will see a posterity . . . ," and the Greek translates: "If you give for sin, your soul will see a posterity . . . ."
⁴⁸G. Friedrich, "Beobachtungen zur messianischen Hohepriestererwartung in den Synoptikern," *ZTK* 53 (1956), pp. 265-311.
⁴⁹Feuillet, *op. cit.*, p. 23.
⁵⁰*Ibid.*, pp. 47-48. Cf. Lev 16:11-16.
⁵¹Friedrich's study has been criticized in detail by J. Gnilka, "Die Erwartung des messianischen Hohepriestertums in den Schriften von Qumran und im Neuen Testament," *RQum* 7 (1960), pp. 395-426, as well as by J. Coppens, "Le messianisme sacerdotal dans les écrits du Nouveau Testament," in *La Venue du Messie*, Bruges, 1962, pp. 101-112. Feuillet's study has been criticized by J. Delorme, "Sacerdoce du Christ et ministères," *RSR* 62 (1974), pp. 199-219. Moreover, in his article (Ch. 2, note 27), p. 306, n. 12, O'Fearghail deprives Feuillet of two supports (*Le Sacerdoce*, p. 48) by showing that

the pronouncement of the divine Name was not limited to the liturgy of the Atonement and that the text of Sirac does not refer to this liturgy. [52]This observation has been made by P. Van Stempvoort, "The interpretation of the Ascension in Luke and Acts," *NTS* 5 (1958-59), pp. 34-35; then by J. Coppens, "Le messianisme sacerdotal," p. 109; H. Schlier, *Essais sur le Nouveau Testament*, Cerf, 1968, pp. 265-266; W. Grundmann, *Das Evangelium des Lukas*, Berlin, 1961, pp. 453-454, and by other authors.

PART TWO

JESUS CHRIST, THE NEW PRIEST

Priestly Terminology
in the New Testament

To give some guidance for the second stage of the research, a quick survey of the terminology is needed. In the course of the preceding chapters we have already noted the use of the words "priest" and "high priest" in the narrative writings of the New Testament. The analysis of these uses has made it possible to grasp the problems before us. It is now appropriate to complete the survey in two ways at the same time: on the one hand, to extend it to the whole of the New Testament and, on the other, to include all the words that have a direct relationship with the theme of the priesthood. Thus we get the following table (the label *Pl* stands for all the Pauline Epistles, including the Pastorals):

	Mt	Mk	Lk	Jn	Ac	Pl	Heb	1P	Rev	Total	LXX
1. priest, *hiereus*	3	2	5	1	3		14		3	31	800
2. high priest, *archiereus*	25	22	15	21	22		17			122	40
3. high-priestly *archieratikos*					1					1	0
4. priesthood, *hierosyne*							3			3	9
5. priesthood, *hierateia*			1				1			2	16
6. priesthood, *hierateuma*								2		2	3
7. to exercise priesthood, *hierateuein*			1							1	26
8. to perform a sacred action, *hierourgein*						1				1	[1]

In this list we find three different words used to denote the priesthood, but each has a particular nuance. *Hierosyne* (4) expresses the quality of one who is a priest; the suffix *-syne* in Greek indicates quality (for example, *dikaiosyne*, justice). *Hierateia* (5) expresses the sacerdotal office, as *strateia* expresses the military office. *Hierateuma* (6) is a rare word, the meaning of which is disputed;[1] it can mean either "the priestly organism" or "priestly functioning." Another word open to discussion is the verb *hierourgein*, which does not belong to the contemporary priestly vocabulary; there is some question whether or not it does apply to a priestly activity.[2]

A comparison of the numbers gives rise to intriguing observations: outside of the narrative writings, where the title "high priest" appears often, the frequency with which the priestly vocabulary is used varies greatly. There is practically none in Paul, but a great deal in the Epistle to the Hebrews which, unlike the narrative writings, uses "priest" as often as "high priest"; it is infrequent in the Catholic Epistles, where it is used only in 1 Peter, and a little more frequent in Revelation. Statistics, of course, do not tell everything; even when the usages are rare, they may be highly significant.

It is informative to further pursue the analysis of the usages and to list separately the cases where the priestly vocabulary is applied to the Jewish (or even the pagan) priesthood, and those where the terms are applied either *to Christ* or *to Christians*. If we retain only the latter category, we get a quite different table:

	Mt	Mk	Lk	Jn	Ac	Pl	Heb	1P	Rev	Total
1. priest, *hiereus*	0	0	0	0	0		7		3	10
2. high priest, *archiereus*	0	0	0	0	0		10			10
4. priesthood, *hierosyne*							1			1
6. priesthood, *hierateuma*								2		2
8. to perform a sacred action, *hierourgein*						1				1

This table brings to light the observation already made in the course of the preceding chapters: the Gospels and the Acts never apply priestly vocabulary either to Jesus or to his disciples. But another fact also attracts our attention: some New Testament writings have brought together the Christian faith and the theme of the priesthood. This appears very clearly in three writings: the Letter to the Hebrews, the First Letter of Peter, and Revelation. In a fourth instance, that of one text of Paul (Rom 15:16), the connection needs to be proved.

To be more precise, it is necessary to specify that only the Epistle to the Hebrews applies to Christ himself the titles of "priest" and "high priest," and attributes to him the quality of priesthood (*hierosyne*). In

Paul's text it is the Apostle's ministry that is presented as the fulfillment of a sacred action. In the First Letter of Peter and in Revelation, the terms "priestly organism" and "priest" are employed in reference to Christians.

These writings give a positive answer to the question which was confronting Christians: "Does the mystery of Christ have a priestly dimension?" The fact is surprising since, as we have seen, the Gospel data suggested a solution in the opposite direction. Relying on what was known about the person and about the life and death of Jesus, a preacher of the Good News could very well have given a negative answer and declared that in the New Covenant the priesthood had been abolished. The Old Covenant involved a priestly ritual which offered sacrifices and celebrated various ceremonies; the New no longer involves these things. The New Testament establishes a desacralized religion or, to put it better, an existential faith, a faith without religion in the ritual sense of the term. It is legitimate to believe that St. Paul, with his decided taste for contrasts, would have spoken freely in this way. We need only recall his sharp negative statements concerning submission to the Law: "You are no longer under the Law," he writes to the Romans, "but under grace,"[3] which does not prevent him from proclaiming elsewhere: Do we then overthrow the law by this faith? By no means! On the contrary we uphold the law!"[4] Regarding priesthood then, a negative answer appeared possible, but such a response is not expressed anywhere in the New Testament. None of its writings declares that there is no longer a priesthood. The few writings that pronounce on this subject give a positive response. In a sense they represent a kind of case apart with respect to the others, as the statistics reveal. But in another sense, they are in agreement with all, for none of these writings takes a contrary stance. This preliminary observation is not lacking in importance. It does not dispense us however from examining the relationships more closely, so as to arrive at an exact idea of the New Testament position regarding priesthood.

The text that must hold our attention first of all is, of course, that of the Epistle to the Hebrews, for it is this Epistle that treats the fundamental point, that of the relationship between Christ and the priesthood and its treatment is extensive and profound. It furnishes the material for six chapters of our second part. Since they treat other aspects of the subject, the texts of Peter, of Paul and of Revelation will only afterwards be analyzed, in a third and final part.

The Epistle to the Hebrews, as is well known, does not at all have the character of a letter, but, with the exception of a few sentences appended at the end, it has all the appearance of being an admirably composed homily or sermon.[5] This makes it possible to proceed with order in the study of the subject by simply following the Epistle's course as it unfolds section by section.

After an initial presentation of Christ High Priest (chapter IV), we are invited to consider in him the twofold relationship on which all priesthood is based: the priest must be accredited before God (chapter V) and bound to human beings by a real solidarity (chapter VI). Having established this basis, we are led to a discernment of what is unexpected and unsurpassable in the priesthood of Christ: priest of a new kind (chapter VII), Christ has accomplished a decisive sacerdotal action (chapter IX), whose efficacy has completely transformed the situation of human beings (chapter X). This rapid outline allows us to glimpse the strength of the construction and the importance of the themes treated. A doctrine elaborated with such care surely merits an attentive study.

Notes

[1]Cf. below. "The meaning of *hierateuma*," Ch. X, 2.
[2]Cf. below, Ch. X, 7.
[3]Rom 6:4; cf. Gal 5:18.
[4]Rom 3:31; cf. 8:4; 13:8, 10.
[5]The ancient tradition ranked the Epistle to the Hebrews among the Pauline letters, while recognizing that its Greek text was not of the Apostle Paul. Modern criticism does not have the means to determine with certitude the circumstances of its composition, and hesitates for its dating between the end of the reign of Claudius (d. 54), the last years of Nero (d. 68), and the reign of Domitian (81-96). The first position has few partisans. The sum total of the data in my view rather favors the second position: the Epistle appears to have been composed by a companion of Paul some time before the outbreak of the Jewish War of the years 66-70, which led to the destruction of the Temple of Jerusalem.

CHAPTER IV

Christ Has Become High Priest

The Epistle to the Hebrews affirms insistently that we, Christians, *have a Priest*, "an eminent priest;"[1] even more, that "we have a *high priest*," "an eminent high priest."[2] And it identifies him plainly: he is "Jesus, the Son of God," (4:14) "Jesus, the apostle and the high priest of our profession of faith," (3:1), "Christ, who has appeared as high priest of the good things to come" (9:11). The clarity and the force of the affirmation leave not the slightest room for doubt.

And yet the author was fully conscious of the difficulties of the question. He knew very well that Jesus did not belong to a priestly family, and he does not hesitate to recall this:

> It is common knowledge that our Lord is sprung from Juda, a tribe of which Moses said nothing in his statements about the priests. (Heb 7:14)

He knew that there was no place for Jesus in the organization of the priesthood according to the Law of Moses:

> If he was on earth he would not even be a priest (Heb 8:4)

and therefore still less a high priest,

> because there are those who present the offerings in conformity with the Law. (Heb 8:4)

On the other hand, the author of the Epistle knew the traditional Christian catechesis, which did not employ priestly categories. None of this prevented him from boldly giving an affirmative response to the question that had been raised.

1. Preparations

Before him, no one had confronted the problem directly. A few efforts had nevertheless been made which prepared the way for a solution, but they remained far from complete. Christian thinking had only just begun to employ cultic terms in describing the mystery of Jesus. The oldest text is undoubtedly the one in which St. Paul boldly assimilates Christ to a paschal sacrifice:

Christ, our Passover, has been sacrificed. (1 Cor 5:7)

In the same Epistle, Paul establishes a connection between eucharistic communion and participation in pagan sacrifices, and shows that they are mutually exclusive (1 Cor 10:14-22). His argument implies a sacrificial interpretation of the death and resurrection of Christ. In Romans 3:25 we find the Apostle penning another phrase that evokes the Old Testament cult: Christ is likened this time to "the Propitiatory" (*hilasterion*), a sacred object whose symbolic importance was of prime importance in the sacrifices of Atonement (Lev 16:13-15). St. John likewise employs an analogous term when he says that Jesus Christ "is a propitiation (*hilasmos*) for sins" (1 Jn 2:2), and that God "has shown us his love by sending his own son as a propitiation for our sins" (4:10). In these various expressions the mystery of Christ was gradually beginning to be viewed in the light of the priestly world, but the "priesthood of Christ" was not yet spoken of. To present Christ as an immolated victim or as an "instrument of propitiation" was by no means equivalent to affirming that he was a priest.

The same comment is also valid for the text where St. Peter speaks of our redemption by Christ (1 Pet 1:18-19). The passage as a whole does not call to mind a sacrifice, because the metaphor used is the very different one of liberation by means of a ransom: Christians have not been ransomed with gold or silver, but by precious blood. A sacrificial connotation can, however, be discerned when the apostle goes on to add, "a precious blood, *like that of a lamb without defect or blemish, Christ.*" The expression "lamb without defect (*amnos amomos*) does indeed belong to the vocabulary of ritual.[3] The Law prescribed that only animals without any defect could be chosen for sacrifices offered to God. Christ, "a lamb without defect," was worthy to be offered. His integrity qualified him to be a sacrificial victim. But can a lamb be a priest?

A passage of the Epistle to the Ephesians opens up a new vista when it completes in sacrificial terms a Pauline expression that speaks of the love of Christ. In his letter to the Galatians, Paul says of the Son of God:

He loved me and gave himself up for me. (Gal 2:20)

We have already had occasion to note that this phrase does not establish any connection between the death of Christ and ancient cultic ritual, but concerns existential relationships between persons and describes an act of extreme generosity. The Epistle to the Ephesians takes up the same expression, but extends it and gives it a sacrificial sense:

Christ loved us and gave himself up for us, *an offering and sacrifice to God* in an odor of sweetness. (Eph 5:2)

Christ's existential gift is thus described as an "offering and sacrifice to God." In themselves, these words do not go beyond the idea of "victim" that we have already encountered. They do not state explicitly that Christ was "priest." But they do occur within a passage which, instead of presenting Christ in the passive attitude of a victim, insists strongly on his voluntary personal dedication: Christ, through love, *gave himself up.* It seems that the distance from this statement to saying that Christ *offered himself* in sacrifice is not great. And if Christ offered himself in sacrifice, should one not conclude that he is priest? This second point is more problematical than the first, because the Bible mentions more than one sacrifice offered without the intervention of a priest. It follows that the Epistle to the Ephesians also leaves us somewhat in the dark regarding the priesthood of Christ. It goes further than the preceding texts, but still does not pronounce explicitly on this question.

To state and solve the problem clearly required a discerning and fearless mind, for there were great difficulties to be overcome. To affirm that Christ was a priest was to run the risk of weakening the Christian faith, by favoring a return to the ritual mentality of the Old Testament. To give a negative answer would be to destroy the proclamation of Christian fulfillment of the Scriptures and to cause a break between the New Testament and the Old. The author of the Epistle to the Hebrews, aware of the gravity of what was at stake, avoided every simplistic solution and undertook the strenuous work of deepening the understanding of the faith. It was thus that he came to work out a stimulating and substantial doctrine.

2. Innovation

The first observation to be made on reading the Epistle to the Hebrews is that the theme of the priesthood does not appear at the beginning but only at the end of Chapter 2, where we find the first mention of the title "high priest" applied to Jesus. This mention deserves to be studied from two points of view, because it represents a twofold innovation: first with respect to the traditional idea of priesthood, and secondly with respect to the primitive Christian catechesis.

For it is not with angels that he is concerned, but with the descendants of Abraham. Therefore he had to be made like his brethren in every respect, so that he might become a merciful and credible high priest in the service of God, in order to wipe out the sins of the people. For because he himself has suffered and been tested, he is able to help those who are being tested. (Heb 2:16-18)

This text gives primary importance to priesthood, because it presents it as the goal of Jesus' whole existence. "The pioneer of salvation," (2:10) Jesus "had to make himself like his brothers in all respects *in order to become high priest* . . . ." The context makes it clear that this purpose has been attained. The beginning of the following paragraph confirms this, for there the author invites us "to consider the apostle and high priest of our profession of faith, Jesus" (3:1).

a) *Complete identification with his brethren*   What is stated directly in 2:17 is the indispensable condition of Christ's accession to priesthood. And this condition appears as an innovation. What is actually new is the idea of "being comparable in all ways to his brethren." The Greek verb, which is passive in form, can be taken here as a reflexive verb as in Matthew 6:8: "to assimilate oneself," "to make oneself like." Even if the passive sense is retained, the phrase implies at least that Jesus had to agree to be made like men. This is confirmed by another passage in the Epistle which speaks of "obedience" (5:7-8). Here the author specifies that the assimilation must be total, "in all respects."

The previous context and the following verse show that the most dramatic and painful aspects of human existence are the ones especially referred to: trials and temptations, suffering and death.[4]

This complete assimilation was therefore the necessary condition for gaining the priesthood. A surprising condition, for it corresponded neither with the ideas of the time nor with the tradition of the Old Testament.

At the time of Jesus, as we know, the position of high priest represented, in the eyes of the Jews, the highest dignity that a man could attain, the highest rank in both the civil and religious hierarchy. Our author does not entirely reject this point of view; he speaks later of "the glory" of the priesthood (5:5). The originality of his teaching concerns not so much the glory itself as the path that must be followed to reach it. At the same time, however, the internal quality of the glory to be obtained also changes.

The Books of the Maccabees and the writings of the historian Josephus reveal the extent to which the dignity of the high priest, which included political power, had become the object of frantic ambition and of implacable rivalries. Some claimants would stop at nothing to raise themselves to this office, just to satisfy their lust for power. We read in the Books of Maccabees how, in the reign of Antiochus Epiphanes (175-164 B.C.), the brother of the high priest Onias "usurped the high priesthood by unlawful means: he promised the king, in the course of an interview, 360 talents of silver and 80 talents more from another source of revenue" (2 Mac 4:7-8). Once promoted to high priest, Jason—as this ambitious man was called—set out to hellenize his country. But soon he was supplanted by another claimant called Menelaus, who "got the high priesthood for himself, by offering 300 silver talents more than Jason" (2 Mac 4:24). The rivalries accelerated to the point of violence and murder: the high priest Onias was assassinated at the instigation of Menelaus (4:32-34). The documents of Qumran echo other conflicts of a similar kind, at a time quite close to that of Jesus. They bitterly criticize a high priest whom they call "the wicked priest;"[5] they reproach him for his pride, his insatiable avarice and his "abominable actions." The historian Josephus likewise confirms these harsh judgments with his detailed accounts of scandalous deeds.[6] Later on we shall have occasion to mention some of these.

According to the customs of the time, therefore, access to the priesthood was through the path of ambition. The Epistle to the Hebrews rejects this way, and resolutely points to the opposite course. It declares that, far from seeking to raise himself above other men, Christ on the contrary had to renounce all the privileges and to descend to the very lowest level by accepting complete likeness to his brothers, even to sharing their sufferings and death.

b) *Change of perspective*
This way of looking at the priesthood contrasts not only with the deplorable practices that dishonored it at this time, but—more sur-

prisingly—it is also at odds with the traditional Jewish attitude that was based on Holy Scripture. Instead of speaking of assimilation, the texts of the Old Testament in fact insist on the necessity of a separation. To become high priest it was necessary to undergo rites of consecration, which clearly distinguished the man whom God had set apart for his service from all others:[7] the ritual bath, which preceded the priestly consecration was a rite of purification and separation; the changing of garments and the putting on of priestly vestments expressed a transformation and an elevation; the anointing with perfumed oil signified an impregnation with sanctity. All these ceremonies set an impassable distance between the elect of God and the commoner, and this distance was to be scrupulously maintained from then on by the observance of very strict regulations.

Among the conditions required for the exercise of the priesthood, the Law of Moses prescribed in particular freedom from all physical defect or deformity: "None of the descendants of Aaron the priest, if he has a physical defect, will be able to draw near to offer the food of the Lord" (Lev 21:21). Leviticus is particularly insistent on this point, giving a list of these defects and repeating the prohibition no fewer than five times in the space of seven verses (21:17-23). The historian Josephus relates an incident which gives a good illustration of the importance attached to this regulation. In 40 B.C. Antigonus, the rival of the high priest Hyrcanus, incited the Parthians to capture Jerusalem and to depose Hyrcanus. After they had succeeded in doing so, the Parthians handed Hyrcanus over in chains for his rival to abuse. Josephus records that "when Hyrcanus cast himself at his rival's feet, Antigonus himself tore off his ears with his teeth, to prevent him ever recovering the high priesthood, even if a revolution should restore his freedom; for no one can be high priest if he is not free from bodily defect."[8] The final words clearly refer to the prescription of Leviticus, which excludes from priestly functions anyone "deformed or disfigured" (21:18). In the same connection, Leviticus warns against all contact with a dead person: the high priest must totally avoid approaching a corpse, and he is not permitted to go into mourning, even for his father or mother. Physical infirmity and death appeared irreconcilable with the holiness of the living God. In their preoccupation with preserving the sanctity of the priesthood, pious Jews attached the greatest importance to the rigorous maintenance of all these legal separations. To require of the high priest a complete assimilation to the other members of the Jewish people would have been for them an unthinkable absurdity.

However, we find that our author lays down precisely this requirement and no other. He does not invoke any rite of consecration, or any ceremony of investiture, but only the "duty" of "rendering himself like his brethren in all things." It nevers enters his head to exclude physical wounds or contact with death; on the contrary, he sees them as included in the road that leads to priesthood: it was necessary for Jesus to suffer, it was necessary for him to suffer death. What a reversal of attitudes! It would be difficult to imagine a more radical one.

3. Connection with the Primitive Christian Catechesis

How could the idea of such a reversal of values enter the author's mind? A comparison of texts may help us to answer this question. Indeed the verse of the Epistle is clarified when it is compared with the Gospel passage where the risen Jesus explains the events of Good Friday to the disciples at Emmaus.

Lk. 24:6	Heb 2:17
a) Was it not necessary	a') He had to
b) for the Christ to suffer these things	b') be made like to his brethren in all things
c) and to enter into his glory?	c') in order to become high priest...

The question: "Was it not necessary . . ." which suggests a positive answer, is echoed in the Epistle by the affirmation: "He had to be . . ." The phrase "made like to his brethren in all things" corresponds to the expression "to suffer these things"; and "to become high priest" corresponds to "and to enter into his glory." The Epistle's formulation is seen, therefore, to be a transposition in sacerdotal terms of the Gospel proclamation of the mystery of Jesus. This priestly transposition has a twofold significance. On the one hand, it throws new light on the mystery thus expressed: the Passion of Jesus becomes a priestly consecration, and the glory of Christ becomes the glory of being high priest (cf. 5:5). On the other hand, it brings about a profound transformation in the ideas previously held about the priesthood. Consecration to the priesthood is no longer accomplished by rites of separation, but by the acceptance of a total identification with mankind, and the glory of the high priest is defined by the present and permanent position of Christ in relation to God and to mankind.

We now begin to perceive that the transition from the Old Testament attitudes is not the result of abstract speculation. The facts themselves have been the determining factor. The author of the Epistle has given all his attention to the events of the Passion and glorification of Jesus, and he has concluded that these events have in fact achieved what the Old Testament rites for the consecration of a priest sought in vain to accomplish: the establishment of an effective mediation between mankind and God. It is this observation that led him to reverse the perspectives, that is, to abandon the requirement for ritual separation and to insist instead on the necessity for fraternal solidarity.

a) *Humiliation and glorification*

Before taking up these important themes in greater depth, it would be useful to establish more solidly the connection that has just been affirmed between Hebrews 2:17 and the primitive expression of the Christian faith. If the only argument in its favor is the possible agreement with one passage of Luke, the conclusion would remain uncertain. But there is much more: we can find the elements necessary for proof in the very text of the Epistle.

The author, in fact, clearly presents the formula of 2:17 as the conclusion of the preceding argument, which defined the mission of Christ. The logical connection is expressed by the Greek adverb, *othen*, which literally means "whence" and which indicates a deduction: "from whence it follows that . . ." The necessity of being made like men to attain the priesthood is the *result* of the mission undertaken by Christ, as it was defined in 2:16 and described in the whole previous context. Christ "has taken responsibility for the descendants of Abraham," in order to open "for all mankind" the way to salvation and glory.[9]

As the conclusion of the section beginning at Hebrews 2:5, the affirmation of 2:17 applies at the same time to the two contrasting phases of the mystery of Christ—"to suffer these things" and "to enter into his glory," (Lk 24:26)—for the entire section (Heb 2:5-17) has as its only theme the realization of these two stages. The author has them in view from the beginning, when he quotes the passage from Psalm 8 in which the condition of man is described by a similar contrast between a humiliation and a glorification:

You make him a little lower than the angels,
with glory and honor you crown him. (Heb 2:7; Ps 8:6)

Commenting on this text, the author in fact immediately observes that we see its realization in Jesus and that his humiliation consisted for him in "suffering" his Passion:

Made a little lower than the angels, *because he suffered death*, Jesus has been crowned with *glory* and honor. (Heb 2:9)

Suffering and glory are the very two themes that occur in Luke 24:26 and they are expressed in Greek by identical or related words.[10] Developing his thought further, the author of the Epistle goes on to employ other terms as well. He speaks not only of suffering but also of humiliation, as does Paul who emphasizes the humiliation of Christ (Phil 2:8), and he specifies that "suffering *these things*" (Lk 24:26) means in fact "suffering *death*" (Heb 2:9). On the other hand, he adds to "glory" the words "honor" and "crowned" supplied him by the Psalm.[11]

The following verse (2:10) takes up the word "sufferings," but this time in the plural, to express the first phase of the mystery of Christ. For the glorious phase, the author employs a new term, the Greek verb *teleioun* which means "to make perfect." Instead of "to suffer these things and enter into his glory" we have "made perfect through sufferings" (with God as the subject and Christ as the recipient of the divine action). This is another way of referring to the glorification.

A little further on we find a new variation (2:14-15): instead of speaking of glory, the author speaks of victory or, more precisely, of the annihilation of the adversary and of the deliverance of the oppressed: Christ had "by his death to reduce to impotence the one who held the power of death, that is to say, the devil," and by the same action "to free those whom fear of death kept in a state of slavery throughout their lives."

Beyond the diversity of these expressions, we have no difficulty in perceiving in each the same antithetical couplet of fundamental themes, and so we are led to recognize them when they appear again at the end in a formulation that employs priestly concepts. In saying that Christ had "to become like his brethren in everything," the author intends to reaffirm the necessity for the Passion—"it was necessary for the Christ to suffer these things"[12]—and in making the gaining of the priesthood the objective of this total identification with mankind, he wishes to define the glory of the risen Christ and to make it understood that for Christ "to be crowned with glory and honor" (Heb 2:9) simply means "to become high priest" (2:17).

The verse of the Epistle presents an antithetical and even paradoxical aspect which constitutes a further resemblance to the earlier statements. "To be made like to his brethren in order to become high priest" is at first sight no less contradictory than to humble oneself in order to enter into glory or to die in order to triumph over death. The connections between the priestly formulation of Hebrews 2:17 and the traditional expression of the Christian faith are therefore very close. The analysis of the entire section, Hebrews 2:5-18, has provided the proof.

b) *Traditional catechesis*

It would be wrong, however, to limit our investigation to this section alone, because it does not constitute a self-contained whole. It is integrated into a more extensive doctrinal exposition that begins immediately after the introduction to the Epistle and goes from 1:5 to 2:18. It is this large section as a whole that finds its conclusion in 2:17-18. It would be useful, then, to take an overall view of it if we wish to appreciate the train of thought which ends in the affirmation of the priesthood.

The theme announced at the end of the introduction (1:4) is the "Name" won by the Son as the result of his redemptive intervention. In other words, the author intends to give us a synthetic exposition of Christology. It is interesting to watch how he proceeds: he faithfully presents the principal points of the Christian *kerygma* returning to the Old Testament texts which had, from the start, been its foundation. His doctrinal exposition is divided into two sections (1:5-14 and 2:5-18), which are separated by a brief exhortation (2:1-4). The theme of the first is the present glory of Christ, enthroned beside God and by this very fact established in a position superior to that of the angels themselves. The theme of the second doctrinal section, as we have just seen, concerns the way in which Christ gained this glorification: through suffering and dying for his brethren. Thus, the order adopted is retrospective, starting from the present condition of Christ and explaining it by reflecting on earlier events. The same arrangement was already found in the Book of the Acts, in the first proclamations of the Paschal message.[13]

Primitive Christian preaching normally presented the risen Jesus as the Messiah, the Son of David,[14] and therefore went back to those Old

Testament texts which formed the basis of royal Messianism. Our author proceeds in the same way. To describe the glory of Christ with God, he uses the Davidic oracles. The first text that he cites:

You are my Son; today, I have begotten you. (Heb 1:5a; Ps 2:7)

is taken from a royal psalm that is used several times in the New Testament in reference to Jesus.[15] The second text:

I myself will be a father to him, and he will be my son. (Heb 1:5b; 1 Chr 17:13)

is an excerpt from Nathan's prophecy concerning the Son of David, which is the pre-eminent messianic text.[16] Next, the author uses another royal psalm, one which the targums apply to the Messiah;[17] and to conclude his first section he quotes Psalm 110, a psalm of royal enthronement, which was employed more than any other by the apostolic catechesis.[18] The application of this text to Christ Jesus was so familiar to Christians that the author does not need to explain it and can even omit the first words of Psalm 110: "The Lord said to my Lord," and quote at once the decisive phrase:

Sit at my right hand . . . (Heb 1:13; Ps 110:1b)

Everyone would immediately understand that it referred to the heavenly glorification of Jesus, the Messiah-king.

In the second half of his exposition (2:5-16) the author shows the same fidelity to the tradition and continues to use the familiar texts. He begins by citing Psalm 8:

What is man that you are mindful of him?
. . . You have put everything under his feet. (Heb 2:6-8; Ps 8:5, 6, 7b)

Paul applies the same psalm to Christ and connects it with Psalm 110.[19] Next, the author cites a verse of Psalm 22:

I will announce your name to my brethren . . . (Heb 2:12; Ps 22:23)

Psalm 22 is the psalm of the Passion; before foretelling Jesus' triumphal act of thanksgiving, it describes his abandonment on the cross and his sufferings.[20] Finally, the author uses two other texts connected with royal Messianism. One is taken from David's song of victory, a song referred to by Luke and quoted by Paul:[21]

I myself will have full confidence in him. (Heb 2:13a; 2 Sam 22:3)

The other belongs to the "Book of Emmanuel" (Is 6—12), which is rich in Messianic oracles and therefore abundantly exploited in the New Testament:[22]

Here am I, and the little children whom God has given me. (Heb 2:13b; Is 8:18)

It must be observed then that in the first part of his letter (1:5—2:16) the author faithfully reproduces the traditional teaching. The originality of his doctrine does not appear until the conclusion of his exposition (2:17-18), and it consists in suddenly showing that *it is possible to pass without the least difficulty from the traditional description of the mystery of Christ to a priestly description that is no less valid.* In fact, by proclaiming that Jesus is the glorious Messiah, enthroned as Son of God at the Father's right hand, and that he has also won this heavenly glory by dying for us on the cross, the Christian teaching has brought to light this double relationship—with God on one side and with mankind on the other—which makes the glorified Jesus the perfect mediator for men with God or, in other words, the perfect high priest.

c) *Relationship with the priesthood*
While reproducing the traditional teaching, the author has been skillfully and gradually preparing for the change in formulation. Already at the end of his introduction, before referring to Christ's heavenly enthronement in an expression that is tied up with royal Messianism (Ps 110:1), he has used a formula of a notably different sort to recall the redemptive intervention of Christ: the Son, he says, "has brought about the *purification* of sins" (Heb 1:3). He is here employing cultic terms for an affirmation of the faith which was normally presented in existential terms: "Christ *died* for our sins" (1 Cor 15:3). The language of purification is, as we know, characteristic of ritual laws.

As a result of this preparation, one of the subsequent quotations reveals some priestly harmonics which are added on to its royal tone. The psalmist addresses the following words of praise to the king in Psalm 45: "You have loved justice and hated iniquity" (Ps 45:8; Heb 1:9). In the context of royal Messianism these words automatically suggest an armed struggle that the king has been conducting against oppressors. The king "girds on his sword" and sets out to fight "for the cause of justice" (Ps 45:4). But when applied to the Son who "has brought about the purification of sins," these words tend to take on, in the context of the Epistle, a sacrificial meaning, for it is clear that Christ's love of justice and his hatred of iniquity are shown by the "purification of sins," and this purification is normally obtained by the offering of sacrifices (cf. Lev 16:30).

The conclusion of the exposition in 2:17 can therefore express this perspective in full clarity and can further specify that Christ's task consists in "washing away the sins of the people," which is a priestly task. The Greek verb used belongs very clearly to the language of expiation by a priest.[23] The author will later emphasize that the particular role of the priest is to eliminate effectively the obstacle of sin (Heb 5:1-3) so as to re-establish communication between mankind and God.

If the love of justice that the psalm speaks of is revealed by "the purification of sins," then it follows that the anointing mentioned next[24] could be understood as a priestly consecration no less than as a royal coronation. This would be the anointing of a priest-king. It should be noted in this connection that there is no royal anointing in the Law of Moses, but only the priestly anointing, as well as that of the altar and of the divine dwelling.

The orientation toward the priesthood, already apparent in the first section (Heb 1:5-14), becomes gradually more explicit in the second half of the christological exposition (2:5-16). It is muted at first, but can be detected in the expression "glory and honor," which can have a priestly meaning. In fact, several biblical texts celebrate the "honor and glory" of the priesthood.[25] It is true that the context of the psalm tends rather to describe a royal glory, the glory attached to power: "You have put all things under his feet" (Ps 8:7; Heb 2:8). But some unexpected elements are added in the way it is then applied to Christ: it is "because he has suffered death" that Jesus has "been crowned with glory and honor" (Heb 2:9). Is a glory won by "having suffered death" a merely royal glory? We may think not and we ought, in any case, to note the profound doctrinal advance that this clarification represents. It controls all the remainder of the paragraph (2:10-18) and the whole development of the priestly theme.

4. A New Doctrinal Dimension

The first formulations of the Calvary event were limited to describing the contrast between its two successive phases: death and resurrection, humiliation and glorification.[26] This is also the case with Luke 24:26, which was our point of departure: it affirms the necessity of the two opposite aspects, suffering and entering into glory. Their juxtaposition suggests that there may be a relationship between them, but there is nothing in the phrase that describes what this is. It is not unusual for translations to add to the text, beginning with the Vulgate, which inserts an *ita* after the conjunction *et*, and so presents the Passion as the means that Christ had to take to enter into his glory. Luke's Greek phrase does not say as much. Hebrews 2:9, however, clearly defines the connection: it is *"because of* his passion" (*dia to pathema*) that Jesus "has been crowned." A causal relationship has been added to the contrast between his suffering and his glory. This presentation is in accord with that of the christological hymn of Philippians, which links the glorification of Christ to his voluntary humiliation in the same way:

> He humbled himself, becoming obedient unto death, even the death of the cross; *wherefore (dia)* God has exalted him . . . (Phil 2:8-9)

The Resurrection of Christ is not only the annulment of his death, it is at the same time its consequence. The death of Christ produced the glorious outburst of a new life. The hymn of Philippians explains this paradox very succinctly by pointing out that the death of Christ was an act of obedience; that is why it won him glorification by God. The general context (Phil 2:1-5) suggests a complementary explanation by situating the event in a context of fraternal love. The same doctrine is found in the Epistle to the Hebrews, expressed in different terms, and there it forms the basis of the sacerdotal christology; if Christ's death resulted in his glorification as high priest, it was because it was an act of filial obedience toward God and of fraternal solidarity with mankind. These two aspects are inseparable, the first governing the second. The Epistle offers more than one opportunity for deepening our understanding of both.

In the text with which we are now concerned (Heb 2:5-18), the order of these two aspects is opposite to that which we have just observed in the letter to the Philippians: the aspect under immediate consideration is that of fraternal solidarity and the aspect of filial submission remains in the background. We shall have to await further developments[27] for this second aspect to come to the fore. Here, the submission of Christ is only suggested in the general tenor of the text, which clearly shows that the initiative belongs to God. It is God who is concerned with the fate of mankind and who actively intervenes in Christ's humiliation and in his coronation (2:6-7). It is God who, in order to accomplish his design, submits Jesus to a painful transformation that leads to glory; it is God who entrusts Christ with "the little children" that he is going to rescue (2:10, 13). The author shows that Jesus has fully corresponded to this divine initiative: "Here I am, and the little children whom God has given me." Jesus has taken upon himself all the consequences of the mission willed by God, including death (2:14-15), and so he has done what he "had to do" (2:17), directing his course from the start toward the honor of the Father:

I will announce your name to my brethren,
in the midst of the assembly I will praise you. (Heb 2:12)

It is in this way that he became "worthy of trust for the relationships with God" (2:17). We see that even if the author does not employ here the term "obedience," he nevertheless attributes an attitude of filial submission to Christ throughout this section.

But the theme that he develops explicitly is that of the solidarity of Jesus with men, a solidarity that constitutes the fundamental characteristic of the plan of salvation. He provides a very clear affirmation of it:

Since the little children[28] are united among themselves through a sharing of flesh and blood, he too, in like manner, shares this condition. (Heb 2:14)

Sketched out early in the section (2:5-9), this perspective stands out in the very order of the development. Before introducing the name of Jesus, the author has in fact taken care to recall the essential lines of man's destiny—the destiny of all men—as they are drawn in Psalm 8. Christ's human existence is outlined against this background and is found to be an exact case in point (2:9). Christ is seen to be fully human, the only man in whom the human vocation has been perfectly fulfilled. And the author demonstrates that this exemplary success is doubly characterized by the principle of solidarity: on the one hand,

Christ has rejected nothing of the human condition; he has accepted its humiliation before receiving its crowning; his solidarity has been total. On the other hand, it is universal, for it was for the benefit of all men that Christ carried God's project for mankind to its conclusion:

> Because of the death that he suffered, he has been crowned with glory and honor, so that by God's grace it would be *for the profit of every man* that he tasted death. (Heb 2:9)

Returning immediately to this point, the author discovers a profound coherence in this manner of saving mankind:

> It was fitting that God, undertaking to lead a multitude of sons to glory, should lead the pioneer of their salvation through sufferings to the fulfillment. (Heb 2:10)

This extremely concentrated sentence is not easily translated. The suggested rendering respects, as far as possible, the order of the words in the Greek text, so as to maintain its dynamism. Here also, what is first called to mind is God's design for the human race: God has undertaken to lead it to the glorious realization of its calling.[29] Christ's role in this design is defined in the following way: he has to place himself at the head of the company, as both leader and pioneer (*archegos*). Without him, mankind would not know what direction to take and would be condemned to perdition. His role is to open up for them a road to salvation. This can only be done by his first joining them in their present situation, that is to say, in their lives of temptation and suffering. It is this very existence which he is to transform into a way of liberation. This is then what God wished to bring about: to use the suffering inherent in the human condition to lead Christ to the glorious destiny assigned to mankind and so to open a way of salvation to all. The principle of solidarity comes into play first in one sense so that it may later be able to come into play in the other sense. Christ makes himself one with mankind in his suffering in order to be able to communicate to them the glory that he will acquire at the price of this solidarity itself. His glory, won in this fashion, is truly the glory of man of which Psalm 8 speaks, and therefore it may be communicated to all.

We see that Christ's glory is founded at the same time on his solidarity with mankind and on filial obedience. This is not only the glory of the Son who is completely pleasing to God, but also the glory of one who has been made like his brothers, in conformity with the

Father's loving design. It is clear that by insisting on this point, the author of the Epistle is in no way departing from the primitive catechesis. He is simply underlining one obvious aspect of it. One cannot, in fact, think of the Passion of Jesus without acknowledging that he suffered and died as a man, and at the same time, the preaching of the faith consists in the proclamation that he has died "for us," "for the multitude," "for all,"[30] and that he has thus triumphed over death.

The innovation introduced by the author consists in showing that the position won in this way by Christ corresponds to what one would expect of a high priest: it is a position of mediation. To put it even better: the author does not only speak of a position to be won or a path to be traveled. He speaks of a profound transformation to be undergone. Through his Passion, Christ has been transformed and has *become* high priest in the fullest sense. This bold statement already appears in 2:10, where a Greek verb rich in implication is used in connection with the result of the Passion: *teleioun*, the first meaning of which, "to render perfect," describes a transformation. This verb, in the Greek translation of the Pentateuch, has a well-defined meaning: there *teleioun* always signifies the priestly consecration. Therefore, when the author says that it was fitting for God "to render perfect" by sufferings the head and leader of men's salvation, he was suggesting that the Passion of Christ was a priestly consecration of a new kind. Certainly the allusion is fleeting, but it will recur and be reinforced later on[31] and we shall have occasion to return to it. The following sentence turns our thoughts in the same direction, for it describes Christ as "he who sanctifies":

He who sanctifies and those who are sanctified are all of one origin. (Heb 2:11)

The principle of solidarity, expressed in terms of sanctification, is implicitly applied to priestly mediation. And this principle governs the whole conclusion of the exposition. Because, in accordance with God's designs, he has fully accepted identification with his brethren and so arrived at his enthronement with God, the glorified Christ must be recognized as the perfect mediator. He is intimately united to God in heavenly glory and yet remains closely united to us. In him, therefore, life-giving communication between God and mankind is assured: he is effectively high priest. Pursuing his thought further, the author recognizes that the result obtained required the means employed. In order that the Son of God might become our high priest, complete identification with us was the necessary way:

> He had to make himself like his brethren in everything in order to become a merciful high priest, and one worthy of credence as regards relationships with God, in order to wash away the sins of the people. (Heb 2:17)

Far from appearing suddenly at the end of an explication that did not say anything about the priesthood, the title of high priest is presented as the cleverly prepared conclusion of all that has gone before. And it is precisely the close link with the traditional christology which explains the distance maintained with respect to the Old Testament. The author's attention has been fixed on the essential goal of the priesthood, so that he no longer attaches importance to the ritual organization which appeared to be inseparable from it.

The insistence on the aspect of solidarity with men comes from careful reflection on Christ's peculiar situation. In the Old Testament this essential aspect did not receive much attention, because the great problem then was to make sure of the other relationship required for the exercise of priestly mediation: the communication between the priest and God. There was no need to worry about the connection between the priest and other men, for he was already only too closely joined with them. They were more afraid of the danger of a complete union, of the all too obvious resemblance on those points that compromised the priest's relationship with God. It was necessary somehow to forget that the priest was only a man like the others, wretched and sinful in the same way as his brothers, because this made him unworthy to present himself before God. That was the reason for the insistence on the rites of separation.

But in the case of Christ, the problem was precisely the opposite. Relationship with God presented no difficulty, since Christ was "the Son of God," (Heb 4:14) "the splendor of his glory and the expression of his being" (1:3). What had to be established was his relationship with mankind. On this side, solidarity could not be presumed in advance. What could there be in common between the Son of God and carnal human beings, sold into sin?[32] One would rather have to speak of distance and of radical opposition. "Oh faithless generation, how long am I to be with you?" exclaims Jesus in the Gospel.[33] Identification was not an initial given but a relationship to be created, for the sake of a mission that could not be accomplished without it. The "pioneer of salvation" could not in fact bring his task to a proper conclusion without being first tied to mankind by a secure lifeline. He had first to share their nature of flesh and blood (Heb 2:14) and to walk at their head on their road of suffering and death in order to come, by this very road, to his place with God and thus become their living link with God.

5. The Name of Christ

One last observation, not without importance, must be made about the relationship between the title of high priest and the doctrinal exposition that precedes it. It follows from two complementary observations. On the one hand, the last words of the introduction (1:4) show that the first part of the Epistle has for its theme the "Name" received by the Son at the conclusion of his redemptive intervention: "After having brought about the purification of sins," the Son "has inherited a name quite different from that of the angels." On the other hand, the conclusion of this same section (2:17), which we have just re-read, applies the title of "high priest" to Christ. Must we not deduce from this that, for the author of the Epistle, the name received by Christ at his glorification is best expressed by the title "high priest"? If we are to judge by the unequaled mastery with which the author has put together his text, an affirmative answer is unavoidable. It is confirmed by a structural analysis of the Epistle.

When commenting on the words of Hebrews 1:4, exegetes often stop at somewhat unsatisfactory interpretations. Because they have failed to observe that the final mention of the "Name" introduces the whole of the following part, they try to define it according to the immediate context and they think it is possible to affirm that the name is that of "Son."[34] But the subject of the sentence is already the "Son" (1:2). What sense is there then in saying that the Son has inherited the name of Son? More insightfully, Westcott offered a different interpretation as probable: that the author means to speak of "the Name which gathered up all that Christ was found to be by believers,"[35] but in order to define this Name, Westcott limited his search "to the remainder of the chapter" and thus was able to assemble only the titles of "Son, Sovereign, Creator and Lord." In reality, that part of the Epistle which treats of the Name of Christ terminates not at the end of

Chapter 1 but at the end of Chapter 2, as a methodical study of the structure of this text demonstrates.[36] The name of Christ is defined by two kinds of relationships and not by one only. To his privileged union with God, which has set him beside God in heavenly glory (1:5-14), Christ adds his very close relationship with mankind, with whom he has forever identified himself (2:5-16). To take one aspect without the other is to truncate in a lamentable fashion the christological doctrine of the author of the Epistle and to distort his teaching on the "Name" of Christ, a teaching which, as we have seen, faithfully conforms to the apostolic tradition.

As the conclusion of the entire argument that goes from 1:5 to 2:18, the title of "high priest" corresponds simultaneously with the two fundamental aspects of the "Name." It describes both the glorification with God and the identification with mankind. None of the other titles applied to Christ in the first (1:5-14) or the second section (2:5-18) of the exposition can provide this synthesis. One group speaks of the glorious relationship of Christ with God: he is the "Son," "the first-born," "God" and "Lord." The other group speaks of his participation in the destiny of mankind: he is "man," "son of man," "Jesus," "the pioneer of their salvation," their "brother." "High priest," in contrast, does suggest the idea of the double relationship, with God and with mankind, and calls to mind both the Passion and the Glory. One may say that this title sums up and completes all the others.

But it must be added that, in choosing this title to conclude his exposition, the author led traditional christology into an important new stage. He moved it from categories of royal Messianism to those of priestly Messianism. Royal Messianism had provided the first formulations of the glory of Christ. Jesus, Son of David, was proclaimed King-Messiah. God had glorified him and given him the throne of his father, David (Ac 2:30-36). But was this royal presentation adequate? Did it correspond fully to the mystery of Jesus? Was there not room to criticize and go beyond it? In fact, the event of Calvary obliged Christian thought to distance itself perceptibly from royal ideology and to abandon entire portions of this kind of messianic expectation. A king has recourse to the force of arms to defend or to liberate his people. He puts himself at the head of his troops and sets out for war. Psalm 45, for example, invites the king to take his sword and smite his enemies. How can one square these warlike images with the contemplation of

Jesus "meek and humble of heart" (Mt 11:29), who expressly refuses to take up the sword[37] and allows himself to be overwhelmed with sufferings and humiliations? It is not impossible, of course, to present the Passion as a combat, but such a presentation is paradoxical and fails to explain the deepest aspects of the event. It does not allow us to grasp its internal coherence. Was it truly necessary for Jesus to undergo such sufferings in order to be proclaimed King-Messiah? This is not obvious. On the other hand, did the royal dignity really require that he should be introduced into intimate union with God? There is no reason to think so. It must at least be recognized that Christ is king in a manner far removed from the ordinary image of royalty, and that this manner corresponds rather to the reality of the priesthood. The priestly function is one of mediation and therefore requires a twofold relationship, as perfect as possible, with mankind and with God. This requirement is realized in the mystery of Christ and allows us to appreciate this mystery much better than the idea of the King-Messiah. The sufferings of Christ appear necessary to complete his identification with mankind. His glorification as Son, which introduced him into the intimacy of the Father, appears necessary to give his relationship with God the greatest possible perfection.

The presentation of the mystery of Christ in the terminology of priesthood therefore offered great advantages for a better formulation of the Christian faith. The title high priest (*archiereus*) was particularly suitable because it permitted the retention of the valid elements of royal Messianism. This title, in fact, expressed at the same time the idea of authority (*arche*) and that of priesthood (*hiereus*), but with the emphasis on priesthood. It is all the more easy to see why the author preferred it to all the other titles in defining the "Name" won by Christ. A later passage in the Epistle confirms this point of view. The end of the second part (3:1 - 5:10) takes up in solemn language the conclusion suggested by the end of the first part (2:17); it declares that the glorification of Christ after his Passion consisted in his being "proclaimed high priest by God" (5:10).

Notes

[1]Literally: "a great priest," (Heb 10:21).

[2]*Archiereus megas* (4:14); *archiereus* (4:15; 8:1).

[3]Cf. Lev 14:10; 23:18; Num 28:3, 9, 11f.

[4]Cf. Heb 2:9, 10, 14, 18. In 4:15 a parallel phrase will say: "tested at all points in a similar way, with the exception of sin."

[5]Commentary on Habbakuk: *1 QpHab* VIII:8; IX:9; XI:4; XII:2.

[6]Book XIV of Josephus' *Jewish Antiquities*, for example, is filled with the story of the struggles in which Hyrcanus and Aristobulus, two high priests who were also brothers, were locked to wrest power from each other. See also Book XX, 179-181, 205-207, 213.

[7]Cf. Ex 28—29; 39; 40:13-15; Lev 8—9.

[8]Josephus, Jewish War I, 270, (trans. R. Harmand, Leroux, Loeb II, 1927), p. 55.

[9]Cf. Heb 2:9-10, 14-15, 16.

[10]*Doxa* (glory) Heb 2:9 and Lk 24:26; *pathema* (suffering) Heb 2:9 and *pathein* (to have suffered) Lk 24:26.

[11]These comparisons are not intended to affirm a relationship of literary dependence between Heb 2:9 (or Heb 2:17) and Lk 24:26. Luke's statement is simply taken as a convenient example. We also find a similar structure in other places, for example in Phil 2:8f.

[12]Lk 24:26; cf. Mk 8:31; Mt 16:21; Jn 12:34.

[13]Ac 2:36; 3:13; 5:30.

[14]Ac 2:30-32; 13:22f; Rom 1:3.

[15]Ac 4:25f; 13:33; Lk 3:22.

[16]2 Sam 7:14 or 1 Chr 17:13; cf. Lk 1:32f; Ac 2:30; Rom 1:3.

[17]Ps 45; Heb 1:8f.

[18]Mt 22:44 and par.; 26:64 and par.; Ac 2:34; 1 Cor 15:25; Col 3:1.

[19]1 Cor 15:25-27; Eph 1:20-22.

[20]Ps 22:2; Mt 27:46 and par.; Ps 22:8; Mt 27:39 and par.; Ps 22:9; Mt 27:43; Ps 22:19; Mt 27:35 and par.

[21]Cf. Lk 1:69; Rom 15:9.

[22]Cf. Mt 1:23; 4:15f; Lk 1:79; Rom 9:33; 1 Pet 2:8; 3:14f.

[23]The only difference is that the author of the Epistle uses the verb *hilaskesthai* without any prefix, instead of the composite *exilaskesthai*, employed very frequently in the ritual laws of Leviticus with "the priest" for its subject, Lev 4:20, 26, 31, 35; 5:10, 13, 16, 18, etc.

[24]Ps 45:8; Heb 1:9.

[25]Ex 28:2, 40; cf. Sir 45:7-13; 50:5-11.

[26]Death and resurrection: 1 Thess 4:14; 1 Cor 15:3; Ac 2:23f; 2:36; 3:15. Humiliation and glorification: Ac 3:13; 4:11.

[27]Heb 5:7f and 10:5-10.

[28]The expression "the little children" (*ta paidia*) is borrowed from Is 8:18, quoted just before and it designates, in the context of Heb, the people entrusted to Christ by God.

[29]In Greek the nuance "has undertaken" is expressed by an ingressive aorist (*agagonta*).

[30]"For us": 1 Thess 5:10; Rom 5:8; "for the multitude": Mk 10:45; 14:24; Mt 20:28; 26:28; cf Rom 5:19; "for all": 2 Cor 5:15; cf. Rom 5:18.

[31]Cf. Heb 5:9; 7:11, 19, 28; see also below Ch. VI, 3-4; Ch. VII, 2c.

[32]Cf. Rom 7:14.

[33]Mk. 9:19 and par.

[34]So, for example, O. Michel: "Es geht hier im Hebr. um den Sohnesbegriff . . ." *Der Brief an die Hebräer*, Göttingen [2] 1966, p. 105; O. Kuss: "Den Namen: Sohn," with the same title, Regensburg, [2] 1966, p. 31; J. Dupont, "Filius meus es tu," *RSR* 36 (1948), pp. 530-535.

[35]B.F. Westcott, *The Epistle to the Hebrews*, London, [3] 1903, p. 17.

[36]Cf. A. Vanhoye, *La Structure littéraire de l'épître aux Hébreux*, DDB, [2] 1976, pp. 38 and 69-85.

[37]Mt 26:52 and par.; Jn 18:36.

CHAPTER V
Priesthood and Divine Authority

The affirmation of the priesthood of Christ, as stated in the verse that we have just analyzed (Heb 2:17), is obviously only the introduction to the subject. The Christians of the first century who heard this text for the first time would certainly have experienced a wonderful joy, but they would also have continued to ask themselves a number of questions. Was it really true that Christ had a right to the title of high priest? How could this new title be justified? In what sense exactly was it to be understood? Was not this way of speaking extremely equivocal? What connection could there be, in fact, between the "priesthood" of Christ and the priestly institution that they knew? So many questions that the author of the Epistle could not avoid. However, he was perfectly aware of them, and if he raised them himself, it was because he knew he was able to answer them. The principal theme of his preaching, as all the commentators recognize, is precisely a thorough explanation of the priesthood of Christ.

1. The Theme of the Priesthood in the Structure of the Epistle

But where does this explanation begin? It is important to see this clearly if one wishes to form a correct understanding of the author's doctrine. However, on this point the commentators are not unanimous. There are some who believe that the doctrinal exposition of the priesthood of Christ begins only at the end of Chapter 4 or the first verse of Chapter 5. What has led them to this position is the presence, at the beginning of Chapter 5, of a description of "every high priest" (5:1-4), which the author then applies to Christ (5:5-10). The impression made by this passage on these exegetes is so strong that they establish a division at this point between two major sections of the Epistle, of which only the second would deal with the priesthood. The first part would be centered on the theme of the Word of God or of Revelation.[1] This point of view reveals itself in the headings and sub-headings chosen to state the content of the first four chapters where one looks in vain for the slightest allusion to the priesthood.[2] One gets a schema like this:[3]

I. The Word of God	1:1–4:16
II. The Priesthood of Christ	5:1–10:18
1. *Description of the high priest applied* *to Christ*	5:1–10
2. A digression	5:11–6:20
3. *Continuation of the exposition on* *Christ the high priest*	7:1–10:18

Such an arrangement, one would guess, is not without consequences for the interpretation of the Epistle.[4] The text of 5:1-10, which gives a description of the high priest, is then separated from the preceding developments, which are supposed to have nothing to say about the priesthood. But it is likewise separated from the rest of the exposition on the priesthood (7:1—10:18) by a long exhortation which is not concerned with this theme. It therefore remains in isolation at the head of the "second major section," as these authors see it, and acts as the "text-program." One is led to believe that it describes the basic idea of the author of the Epistle and that for him it gives an adequate definition of the priesthood.

If it does, anomalies appear. Though the definition is assumed to be complete, it involves some strange omissions. M. Dibelius observes with astonishment that it says nothing about the high priest's entry into the sanctuary;[5] indeed, it does not even mention the existence of the sanctuary; the theme of the house of God is entirely absent. Another and no less surprising silence: "no ministry of preaching" is mentioned;[6] the priesthood seems to have no connection with the Word of God. To judge by the titles chosen, Word of God and priesthood would appear in the Epistle to be two completely distinct themes. When the author treats of the Word of God, he does not speak of priesthood, and when he defines priesthood he makes no further mention of the Word of God. Is this impression justified? If it were, we would be admitting serious lacunae, which would be difficult to explain in the case of the author of Hebrews, who knows his Bible so well. In the Old Testament, as we have seen, the priestly functions can in no way be reduced to the offering of sacrifices. The priest was both the man of the sanctuary and the man of religious instruction. He had the privilege of being able to enter into the House of God[7] and it was to him that the people would come to ascertain the will of the Lord.[8] Would the author of the Epistle have been ignorant of these important aspects of the priestly mediation? Would he have had such a narrow idea of the priesthood? Is he likely to have applied such an inadequate concept to Christ? These questions,[9] whose gravity is immediately evident, have no satisfactory answer when we make the exposition on the priesthood begin at Hebrews 5:1 or 4:14, and exclude the previous chapters therefrom.

But such a presentation does not at all correspond to the text of the Epistle. It falsifies the perspective defined by the author and is reached only as the result of a kind of censorship over his work, a censorship which arbitrarily suppresses the first mentions of priesthood. In fact, as we have already observed, the author introduces the theme of the priesthood not at the end of Chapter 4 but at the end of Chapter 2, when he concludes his exposition on the Name of Christ (1:5—2:18). The title of high priest does not appear here by chance; it announces an exposition which begins immediately and which constitutes a new part of the Epistle (3:1—5:10). The initial sentence of this part immediately takes up the new christological title and solemnly invites the listeners to "consider" this subject:

> So then, holy brothers, who have a share in the heavenly vocation, *consider* the apostle and *high priest* of our profession of faith, Jesus, . . . (Heb 3:1)

The consideration of the priesthood therefore begins at the beginning of Chapter 3 and not at the beginning of Chapter 5. This was recognized as early as 1902 by a Dutch exegete, Thien; and the same observation was made by Vaganay in 1940. One of the great merits of Spicq was that he fully appreciated this point and arranged the structure of his commentary accordingly.[10] For my own part, I have added a whole set of literary clues which confirm this position.[11]

It follows from the convergence of numerous data that the exposition on the priesthood of Christ in the Epistle takes place in two successive stages, which make up the second and third parts of the whole. The second part begins at 3:1 and ends at 5:10; the third part begins at 5:11 and ends at 10:39. These two parts are preceded by a general statement on christology. One obtains the following structure:

In this structure, the text of 5:1-10 finds its place at the end and not at the beginning of a first presentation of the priesthood. This position limits the role it is allowed to fill. One cannot isolate this text, as is done so often, and hold it up as an exhaustive definition of the priesthood. On the contrary, it must be considered as a partial description intended to complement an exposition begun earlier. At the same time, one will not need to be surprised to find gaps here, since the text's limitation corresponds to its position. Before suspecting the author of being tied to an inadequate notion of priesthood, it would be good to first point out carefully the elements he presented earlier in his treatment.

The first observation that strikes us is that the author immediately, in the very process of introducing the title of high priest, brought out two different aspects of the priesthood, which he expressed by means of two adjectives. He did not simply state that it was necessary for Christ to become high priest, but specified *eleemon kai pistos archiereus*, which means literally "merciful and trustworthy high priest" (2:17). These two qualifications merit attention because the author then takes them up, one after the other, to explain their full significance. The adjective *pistos*, which we render as "trustworthy," appears again at the beginning of the following section (3:2,5) and it dominates the whole development which goes as far as 4:14, as is evident from observation of the frequent use of words from the same root or of related meaning.[12] As to the adjective *eleemon*, "merciful," it is recalled by means of the corresponding noun, *eleos*, "mercy," at the beginning of the second development, which extends from 4:15 to 5:10. It is then expounded by a whole series of expressions.[13] We see from this that, in the author's thinking, the two adjectives of 2:17 correspond to two fundamental aspects of the priesthood and that it is necessary then to grasp, on the one hand, the meaning of each, and on the other, why it is so important that they go together.

2. A High Priest Worthy of Trust (Heb 3:1-6)

There is a difficulty here that complicates the task of the exegetes and is liable to confuse the perspectives. The Greek adjective *pistos*, which here expresses one of the two fundamental qualities of Christ the high priest, has several possible meanings: worthy of trust, faithful, believing. In what sense is it to be taken in the text of the Epistle? The single verse 2:17 cannot supply a definite answer to this question, since it uses the term without explanation. But in the following paragraph (3:1-6), the author takes it up again and develops his thought by drawing a comparison in this respect between Jesus and Moses. Exegetes ought, in good method, to take this section as a starting point in establishing the meaning of the adjective. But this is not what they normally do. Usually they choose a meaning for *pistos* when this word appears for the first time in 2:17, although the sentence does not furnish them with enough data to do so, and then they retain the same meaning in 3:1-6, without perceiving that it does not accord with the orientation of these verses.

The meaning usually chosen is "faithful," which is one possible meaning of *pistos*. Christ, they say, has become "a merciful and *faithful* high priest" (2:17). Christians are invited to "consider the apostle and high priest of their profession of faith, Jesus, who is *faithful* to the one who appointed him, as Moses also was in all his house" (3:1-2). Michel explains that the meaning is that of faithfulness through trials and tribulations; Spicq speaks of faithfulness in fulfilling his mission. "Jesus has accomplished his mission exactly according to the divine ordinances." Since this faithfulness was exercised in the past, such a translator does not hesitate to introduce into the text a verb in the past tense: ". . . Jesus, who *was* faithful . . .,"[14] although the Greek has a present participle. And as the text states a relationship between Jesus and "the One who has appointed him," one is led to think of faithfulness toward God.

Is this really what the author meant to say? A more rigorous analysis shows that it is not, and supports the translation of the TOB which, instead of putting "faithful towards God," puts "accredited with God" (2:17). In fact, the author is not referring here to a virtue practiced by Jesus in the past, but of a status he possesses at the present time. He does not understand *pistos* in the sense of "faithful," but in the sense of "worthy of trust." He is inviting Christians to contemplate the glorious Christ, enthroned with God and therefore fully "worthy of trust." Only this rendering completely fits all the requirements of the text and only the same serves to accurately define one of the fundamental aspects of the priesthood, which would disappear completely without it.

It must be said at once that the first meaning of *pistos* is not "faithful" but precisely "worthy of trust," "which can be believed," as the dictionaries testify.[15] When the author comments on *pistos* in 3:1-6, it is clearly this first meaning that he has in mind. In fact, to compare Jesus and Moses, he uses a passage from the Greek Bible (Num 12:7) where the word *pistos* very clearly means "worthy of trust" and not "faithful." In opposition to the claims of Aaron and Miriam, God there declares that Moses stands in a privileged relationship to him, and that he is, for this reason, *"worthy of trust in all his house."* Our author affirms that Christ deserves the same characterization (3:2) by an even better title, because his position in the house of God is higher than that of Moses.[16]

The connections between Hebrews 3:1-6 and Numbers 12:1-8 deserve to hold our attention. Indeed, they are not restricted to a brief quotation, but the author of the Epistle recaptures exactly the point of view adopted by the episode in the Book of Numbers. This is characterized by the close union of two themes: that of the authority of the

Word, and that of position in the house of God. These two themes enter into the scheme of priestly mediation that we established above,[17] and in fact they constitute two essential elements of this mediation. The priest is admitted into the house of God and, thanks to his privileged contact with God, he is in a position to speak with full authority in the name of God.

This is precisely the problematic that appears in Numbers 12:1-8. The point contested by Aaron and Miriam is the authority of Moses, his role as mediator of the word of God. "They said: 'Would God speak only to Moses? Has he not also spoken to us?' " (12:2). The decisive fact which immediately afterwards reduced the disputants to silence is the affirmation by God himself of a privileged relationship between Moses and himself, a relationship that finds expression in the position given to Moses in the house of God:

> The Lord says: "Listen to my words: if there is a prophet among you, it is by means of a vision that I make myself known to him, it is in a dream that I speak to him. But it is not thus with my servant Moses: *in all my house he is the man worthy of trust (pistos)*. I speak to him face to face, openly, not in enigmas, and he sees the form of the Lord." (Num 12:6-8)

The authority of Moses is superior to that of the prophets, because God honors him with a greater confidence by opening his whole house to him.

If the author of the Epistle refers to this tradition, it is because he intends to make a similar point concerning Jesus. His concern is to affirm the priestly authority of the glorified Christ. He therefore presents him to believers as the high priest who transmits the definitive word of God and who has the right to their unreserved allegiance. That this is in fact the orientation of the text can be ascertained from the introduction of this development (3:1) and confirmation for this interpretation is found in the exhortation which follows (3:7 - 4:13) and in the conclusion of the section (4:14).

To introduce the theme in 3:1, the author invites us, in fact, "to consider the apostle and *high priest of our profession of faith*, Jesus." This expression links "high priest" and "profession of faith." What exactly does it signify? We cannot simply translate: "the high priest in whom we believe," for the author is not only speaking of faith, rather, he says, "profession of faith," which goes further (cf. Rom 10:10). Some exegetes propose that it be understood as follows: "Jesus whom we declare our high priest in our profession of faith formula." This interpretation seems improbable, for we know of no early credal formula that applies the title of high priest to Jesus. We must rather see in the statement of 3:1 the affirmation of an active role of the high priest in relation to the profession of faith. As high priest, Christ speaks to us in the name of God; his word demands the allegiance of faith and makes it possible. As high priest, on the other hand, Christ brings our profession of faith to God; "through him," it is to God that we are truly united in faith (cf. 13:15).

To better bring out this sense, the author has prefaced the title of "high priest" with another word, which at first sight seems surprising when applied to Jesus, but which becomes clear if we recognize in it an allusion to the words of Malachi (2:7). In Hebrews 3:1 Jesus is called "the *apostle* and high priest of our profession of faith." No other New Testament text applies to Jesus the title of apostle. As it is used here, it is closely linked with "high priest," the two words being introduced by a single article. For this reason, it is well to explain it with the help of the text of Malachi which concerns the priest and calls him "messenger of Yahweh" in order to underline his teaching function and the authority of his word:

> The lips of a priest should guard knowledge, and men should seek instruction from his mouth for he is the *messenger* of the Lord of Hosts. (Mal 2:7)

To translate the Hebrew word rendered here as "messenger," the Greek bible used *angelos*, a term whose first meaning is in fact "messenger," but which often has the meaning of "angel" in the biblical texts. Because of this ambiguity, the translation *angelos* was not considered appropriate by our author, who had just demonstrated (in 1:5 - 2:18) that Christ "has inherited a name very different from that of the *angels*" (1:4). He therefore chose another word with an equivalent meaning, *apostolos*, which does not risk this confusion.[18]

The author gives greater prominence, by means of this title, to the aspect of transmission of the Word of God and to the aspect of authority in the priesthood of the glorified Christ. Christ, as the author will tell us later, is "the one who speaks from the heavens" (12:25). Because by his glorification he has become "the spokesman and high priest of our profession of faith," he reveals to us our "heavenly vocation" (cf. 3:1) and invites us to enter into God's rest (cf. 3:7 - 4:11);

he asks for our allegiance of faith and our profession of faith. He has the right to this because he is "worthy of trust," declared so by God himself.

The orientation set by the initial statement (3:1) is confirmed by the exhortation of 3:7 - 4:13. There the author takes the words of Psalm 95 and addresses them to the Christian community:

> Today, if you hear his voice, do not harden your hearts. (Heb 3:7-8, 15; 4:7 = Ps 95:7-8)

In the context of the psalm, the voice in question is that of Yahweh, of "our God."[19] By the way in which he introduces his quotation, the author gives it a significant change of interpretation. He makes it understood that the voice which we must now receive with total faith is the voice of the glorified Christ, established "as Son, over the house" of God (3:6) and thus speaking with the authority of God himself.

Making a kind of synthesis of the exposition (3:1-6) and of the exhortation (3:7 - 4:13), the conclusion of the whole section (4:14) again forcefully expresses the connection that exists between the authority of the word and the priesthood. The author recalls that "we have a high priest" and he defines his elevated position in strong terms: he is "eminent," "he has traversed the heavens," and he is "Son of God." He has thus laid the foundation for the authority of his priestly word to which we must respond with an unreserved allegiance, "holding firm the profession of faith." The perspective is extremely clear: Christ is being presented as "high priest worthy of trust."

3. High Priest and House of God

In the brief doctrinal exposition of Hebrews 3:1-6, what especially engages the author's attention is the connection of Christ the high priest with the house of God. This connection defines the level of his relationship with God and therefore constitutes the basis of his priestly.authority. The word *oikos*, "house," occurs six times in this passage within the space of five verses and provides the opportunity for expressing very varied points of view. The author indeed passes so rapidly from one to the other that it is difficult to follow his thought.

The very first formulation leaves the door open to several possibilities. The text says: "Jesus who is worthy of trust for the one who appointed him, like Moses in all *his* house." To whom does the possessive refer? Are we to understand "the house of Moses" or "the house of Jesus" or "the house of the one who appointed Jesus"? A decision is impossible on the basis of grammar alone. To elucidate the text, we must refer to Numbers 12:1-8, to which our author alludes. We then see that the first meaning must be rejected: in Numbers 12:7 it is not the house of Moses that is at issue but the house of the one who is speaking, that is to say, of the Lord. The choice is then between the "house of God" and the "house of Jesus." In Numbers 12:1-8 the word *Kyrios*, "Lord," which recurs six times, evidently refers to God. It is then the "house of God" that is meant. A later phrase in the Epistle gives explicit support to this interpretation when it refers to Christ as "eminent priest set over *the house of God*" (10:21). We should not be too quick, however, to reject the other possibility, making this the exclusive sense in explaining the text. What follows shows that our author wishes rather to keep both meanings simultaneously. For him, the house of the Lord is undoubtedly "the house of God," but it is also, on several counts, "the house of Christ."

a) *Priestly aspect*
In the Old Testament the word "house" (Hebrew *beth*; Greek *oikos*) is a customary designation for the Temple of God. Its usage in Numbers 12:7 sets up a relationship between the position of Moses and that of a priest. This is what H. Cazelles observes with reference to this passage: "Perhaps this statement originally concerned the stability of the priest attached to the sanctuary in order to communicate the laws of the Lord."[20] But by adding the qualification "all" ("worthy of trust in *all* my house"), the text of the Book of Numbers suggests an extension of the meaning: not only the sanctuary itself, but all the objects and all the people who are in any way connected with the sanctuary. This was the interpretation of the Targum Onkelos, which, in its paraphrase of this verse, does not hesitate to see in "my house" the equivalent of "my people." But the people, it should be noted, can be called house of God only to the extent of its relationship to the sanctuary where God dwells. Our author, as we shall soon see, is sensitive to these overtones.

Before dealing with them, he takes care to note that the relationship between Jesus and Moses is not only one of similarity—"Jesus worthy of trust *like Moses*"; it is also one of superiority. And the superiority of Jesus is based on his different relationship with "the house."

In fact, to him belongs a glory superior to that of Moses, in the degree to which the builder of a house is more highly esteemed than the house itself. (Heb 3:3)

This sentence obviously suggests that, despite the authority conferred on him in the house of God, Moses continued to be part of this house; he was not in essence distinct from it. The case of Christ is different. His authority is the authority of the builder; there is a complete change of level.

b) *Messianic foundation*
On what basis does the author put forward this claim? This is not hard to guess, if we recall the preceding developments and in particular a citation made at the beginning of the first part (1:5), which is taken from the oracle of the prophet Nathan.[21] This oracle is wholly devoted to the question of "the house." Nathan comes to David, who was planning to build a house for God, to tell him that God himself will build a house for him, by giving him a son who will rule after him. This son whom God will give to David will, at the same time, be Son of David and Son of God.[22] The oracle ends with a final divine promise, which appears in the First Book of Chronicles in a particularly interesting form. We recall in passing that Chronicles, which is of a later date than the Books of Samuel, heightens the messianic traits of the oracle and, for this reason, constitutes a preferable source for the authors of the New Testament. The likelihood therefore is that our author did not turn to 2 Samuel 7:14 in Hebrews 1:5 in order to express the divine sonship of Christ, but to 1 Chronicles 17:13, which gives a more idealized image of the Messiah. The text of 2 Samuel 7:14 foresees, in fact, some grave lapses on the part of the son of David; but the editor of Chronicles has taken care to suppress this aspect, which would not be fitting for the Messiah Son of God. This is likewise the firm conviction of the author of Hebrews.[23] In the final promise, to which we have just alluded, the difference in formulation is not very important in itself, but it has a more direct relationship with our text. Whereas in 2 Samuel 7:16 God says to David: "*Your* house and your royalty will endure before me," in 1 Chronicles 17:14 God's focus is on the promised Son and he declares in his regard: "I will maintain *him* forever in *my* house." In Greek this promise becomes: *Pistoso auton en to oiko mou*, a phrase in which one recognizes the expressions used in Hebrews 3:2 and which literally means: "I will render him *worthy of*

trust in my house." There is good reason to think that the Greek text of
1 Chronicles 17:12-16 is the scriptural basis on which our author relies
in presenting Jesus as "worthy of trust for him who appointed
him . . . in his house,"[24] and when he immediately links to this affirmation the theme of building, and, a little later, that of sonship,[25]
already explicitly referred to in Hebrews 1:5. At the same time, he has
established the link between Davidic messianism and priestly christology; the latter now appears capable of accommodating the whole
substance of the traditional doctrine within a more illuminating overall perspective.

To bring the glorious authority of the priest builder into greater
relief, the author adds an observation which links this authority with
the glory of the creator himself:

Every house has its builder and the builder of everything is God.
(Heb 3:4)

Thrown out in passing, this allusion to the creation is here very
suggestive, but it is not easy to define its precise significance. What
connection does our author intend to suggest between the house of
God and the entire universe? And what role, above all, does he wish
to attribute to Christ? It would take too long to discuss in detail the
various possible interpretations. A few comments must suffice. The
text is not saying that it is God who created everything, but that he
who created everything must be acknowledged as God. His glory is
the divine glory in the proper sense of the term. The conclusion that
the builder of a house enjoys a glory comparable to this divine glory
comes from the analogy that exists between the action of building a
house and the action of creating the universe. His position is then
much superior to that of the house. Thus the assertion in verse 3
regarding the honor due to a builder is established, and this is the
immediate function of verse 4, which thus helps to demonstrate that
the credibility and authority of Jesus surpass, beyond all question,
those of Moses.

But now other aspects stand revealed, which strengthen the argument and even render it quite dazzling. When we recall the preceding
developments, the author's allusion opens up deeper perspectives.
The glory of Christ is not only a glory comparable to that of the
creator, but is that very glory, for Christ himself is "the builder of
everything." At the beginning of the Epistle he was acclaimed such:

"You, oh Lord, at the beginning established the earth, and the heavens are the work of your hands" (1:10).

One more point should be made: the house of God which he has built should not be thought of as simply a component of the created universe—a component which would obviously be inferior to the whole of which it would be only a part[26] —rather, it constitutes a new creation of greater value than the first. The first creation will, in fact, perish[27] while the house of God constructed by Christ will remain for all eternity; it is "the eternal heritage" (9:15), the "indestructible kingdom" (12:28), into which the believers are admitted.

The author does not pause to develop this doctrine at this point: he is content to orient our minds in this direction and he immediately returns to the text of Numbers to draw another argument from it. In the Book of Numbers, Moses is introduced by God as "his servant":

My servant Moses is the man of trust in all my house. (Num 12:7)

In this context, as in many similar ones, the title of "servant" has nothing demeaning about it. On the contrary, it is an honorable title, for it expresses a personal relationship with God. The Greek Bible was careful to bring out this nuance. Instead of using the word *doulos*, "slave," it chose a nobler term, *therapon*, which would refer to a free man admitted to the service of an important personage. Moses therefore occupied an enviable position in the house of God. Our author observes this and he goes on to specify the reasons for this honor being granted him: it was a question of "guaranteeing what was going to be said." The perspective is clearly that of the authority of the word. Passing then to the case of Christ, the author has not the least difficulty in showing that his position is still more glorious: in fact, it is by virtue of being "Son" and not "servant" that Christ has taken his place with God and his relationship with the house is therefore different:

Though Moses was worthy of trust *in* all his house as a servant, in order to guarantee what was going to be said, Christ himself is so as Son *over* his house. (Heb 3:5-6a)

His authority is therefore incomparably superior and his word merits that much more assiduous attention and acceptance.

c) *We are "his house"*

Having arrived at this point, the theme of the "house" is suddenly enriched with a new overtone. The author defines the house in unexpected terms. He proclaims:

We are that house. (Heb 3:6b)

In saying this, he is clearly moving on to the Christian conception of sanctuary. The house of God constructed by Christ is not a material building like Solomon's Temple. It is a construction of "living stones" (1 Pet 2:5). By adhering to Christ, the believers themselves become "the sanctuary of God." This doctrine is Pauline,[28] but our author presents it here in a more vivid light by connecting it to the priesthood of Christ. As high priest, Christ is "the man of the sanctuary," and he is so with a fullness of meaning that could not previously have been imagined. The significance of his death and glorification is not only that he himself has entered into heavenly intimacy with God, but also that the religious situation of all men has been thereby radically transformed. For all people now have the possibility of becoming the house of God by becoming the house of Christ. All they have to do is to be obedient to the voice of Christ summoning them to hope and to persevere in their faithfulness to him:

> We ourselves are his house, if we hold fast our confidence and pride in our hope. (Heb 3:6b)

Having become "sharers in Christ," as the author says a little later (3:14), Christians form a community which has a much better claim than any material building to be called God's dwelling. This transformation of the theme of the "house" was not without some preparation in the Old Testament and in the Jewish tradition. Reflecting on the Exodus, a psalm invites us to praise Yahweh because at that time "Judah became *his sanctuary*" (Ps 114:2); towards the beginning of our era the community of Qumran had ambitions to become "the house of holiness for Israel, the society of highest holiness for Aaron."[29] But the affirmation of the New Testament is clearer and stronger, for it is founded on the glorification of Christ. We find this idea again in the priestly text of 1 Peter, which will be analyzed later. It has far-reaching consequences for the understanding of cult and of the Christian life.

We may note immediately that the insistence on the theme of the "house" in this section which presents Christ as "high priest worthy of trust," bars the way to individualist conceptions of faith. It shows that the allegiance of faith has, of necessity, two dimensions: it puts the believer in a personal relationship with God through the mediation of Christ glorified, but, at the same time, it brings him into a "house," that is to say, into a community animated by faith. The two dimensions cannot be separated from one another, since their union defines the mediation of Christ, who is "high priest worthy of trust for the relationship with God" (2:17), "worthy of trust . . . in all the house" (3:2). To wish to shut oneself up in religious individualism is to cut oneself off from the mediation of Christ. From this it can be seen that the first characteristic of the priesthood of Christ, as stated in 3:1-6, is not unconnected with the second, which concerns brotherly identification (4:15 - 5:10).

d) *Eschatological dynamism*

Before passing to this second characteristic, the author once again finds a way to fill in the theme of the house in an important respect: he expresses its eschatological dynamism in the long exhortation (3:7 - 4:14) which separates the two expositions of 3:1-6 and 5:1-10. For this purpose he uses a formula borrowed from Psalm 95, that of "entry into the rest of the Lord." There is a natural link between "rest" and "house" which the Bible applies several times to the "rest" and the "house of God." In Psalm 132, God declares with regard to Zion, where his "house" will be located: "Here is my rest for ever; here I will establish myself, for I have desired it" (v. 14). Adopting another point of view, an oracle of Isaiah casts doubt on whether men can really build on earth a "house" for God and provide a place of rest for him here below. The true rest of God is not earthly but heavenly (Is 66:1). The Epistle to the Hebrews adopts this view and uses Psalm 95 to remind Christians of their "heavenly vocation" (Heb 3:1). The relationship of believers with the house of God includes, therefore, several aspects; in one sense, the believers are even now the "house of God," by virtue of their belonging to Christ (3:6, 14). In another sense, they are not as yet fully introduced into the house of God, for they do not yet enjoy the "rest of God." Christ himself enjoys it (Heb 4:10); he has opened up for us the road that leads to it (4:14) and that is why he is "high priest" and "high priest worthy of trust." We have to "listen to his voice," when he shows us the route to be followed in order to enter permanently into the intimacy of God.

We see in all this how wrong it would be to think that the author has separated the Word of God from the priesthood and that he has forgotten, in describing Christ's priesthood, the priestly function of teaching. On the contrary, this is the first point he insists on. Christ is "apostle and high priest of our profession of faith" (3:1). The authoritative aspect of the word is given priority (3:1 - 4:14). The aspect of priestly compassion and sacrificial offering comes only subsequently (4:15 - 5:10) and its effectiveness is also subordinated to that of the word, because the author will conclude his second point by underlining the necessity of *listening obediently* to Christ in order to obtain salvation (5:9); the verb employed will be *hyp-akouein*, derived from *akouein*, "to listen." More immediately necessary, the mediation of the word signifies a more direct relationship with the present situation of Christ as Christians view it in faith. Whereas the Passion of Jesus is an event in the past, which has taken place once and for all (cf. 9:25-28), the authority of Christ is a present reality. The glorified Christ possesses it and is exercising it at the present time. It is now that he is speaking to the believers in his capacity as heavenly high priest. We now understand much better why the author began his exposition in this way.

e) *Authority of the priesthood*

Having said this, we must recognize that there is less insistence on the title of high priest in this section (3:1 - 4:14) than in the second (4:15 - 5:10). This difference is not hard to explain. It stems from the fact that the first element of the priesthood is developed on the basis of the figure of Moses, and the second on that of the figure of Aaron. Now the Bible applies the title of "priest" to Aaron but not to Moses. Therefore one could not insist on this title in the first section.

To be sure, Moses did not lack some connection with the priesthood. He belonged to the tribe of Levi and we see him exercising the highest functions of the priesthood. It is he who at the foot of Sinai performs the rites of sacrifice which serve as the basis for the first covenant.[30] Furthermore, it is he who performs the priestly consecration of his brother Aaron (Lev 8). One could therefore say that Moses possessed the priesthood before Aaron and more fully than he. Philo does not hesitate to call him high priest and to demonstrate at length the correctness of this appellation. Our author, with greater fidelity to the text of the Bible, refrains from attributing the dignity of the priesthood to Moses, and bases his comparison of Moses with Jesus solely on the qualification "worthy of trust in the house of God," as found in Numbers 12:7. He does not say: "Consider Jesus, who is, like Moses, a high priest worthy of trust...," but: "Consider our high priest Jesus, who is worthy of trust as Moses was ...." At the same time, the direction he has taken prevents him from mentioning again the title of "high priest."

But his method of proceeding shows all the more clearly his desire to treat the aspect of authority and to link it with the priesthood. If the matter of the authority of the word had seemed to him to be secondary, he would have been content to refer to the priestly figure of Aaron which, strangely enough, does not include this aspect. On the other hand, if he wanted to underline the authority of Christ without concern as to how that authority relates to priesthood, he would immediately have made the comparison with Moses without giving Christ the title of high priest. In fact, he has deliberately placed the two elements together, "high priest" and "worthy of trust," already in 2:17 and again in 3:1-2, in spite of the difficulty caused by the comparison with Moses. In this way he shows the importance he attaches to their conjunction.

To develop the theme of the word, he certainly could not have found anything better than a comparison with Moses. In the Old Testament Moses is the most important mediator of the Word of God, the one whose authority is recognized as supreme. If one of the most important functions of the priests was to consult God on behalf of the faithful and to convey back to them the divine answers for the conduct of their lives, Moses appeared, from this point of view, superior to all others. What he had received from God was not just a few occasional oracles, or opportune instructions (*tora*, in the plural) but the complete revelation of the "ways of the Lord," the incomparable Instruction (*Torah*, in the singular), which was to govern the whole divine worship and life of the people. In the last resort, all the priests depended on him, for according to Deuteronomy 31:9-13 it was he who had entrusted the divine Law to the priests and elders, ordering them to make it known. It was therefore not only useful and enlightening to define in this respect the position of Christ as high priest, but truly indispensable to compare his priestly authority with that of the first guide of the People of God. And it is this which our author has not failed to do in this first section, often badly interpreted, where he presents Christ as "high priest worthy of trust."

Notes

[1] The commentators are not agreed on the precise limits to be given to these two parts. Some put the beginning of the second part at 4:14, others at 5:1, and the end is situated either at 10:18 or 10:31 or 10:39.

[2] See for example the titles and sub-titles proposed by R. Gyllenberg, "Die Komposition des Hebräerbriefes," *SvExAb* 22-23 (1957-58), p. 145, or those of O. Michel, *Der Brief an die Hebräer*, Göttingen, 1966, p.8.

[3] Gyllenberg, *op. cit.*, pp. 141, 145-6.

[4] I have shown this in "Situation et signification de Hébreux, v. 5:1-10 " *NTS* 23 (1976-77), pp. 445-456.

[5] M. Dibelius, "Der himmlische Kultus nach dem Hebräerbrief," *Theol. Blätter*, 21 (1942), p. 8 (= *Botschaft und Geschichte*, Tübingen, 1956, v.II, p. 171.)

[6] Spicq, *op. cit.*, II, p. 129.

[7] Cf. Num 3:38; Lev 16.

[8] Cf. Dt 33:8a, 9b-10a; Jer 18:18; Mal 2:7.

[9] Among other consequences, they have direct repercussions on one's own concept of the ministerial priesthood. One should ponder the Vatican II debates on the relationship between preaching and sacramental worship.

[10] F. Thien, "Analyse de l'épître aux Hébreux," *RB* (1902), pp. 74-86; then L. Vaganay, "Le plan de l'épître aux Hébreux," in *Mémorial Lagrânge*, Gabalda, 1940, pp. 269-277. Cf. C. Spicq, *L'Épître aux Hébreux*, 2 vol., Gabalda, 1952-53; M.M. Bourke, "The Epistle to the Hebrews," in *The Jerome Biblical Commentary*, Englewood Cliffs, 1968, v. II, pp. 381-403; A. Cody, "Hebrews" in *A New Catholic Commentary on Holy Scripture*, London, 1969, pp. 1220-1239; P. Andriessen - A. Lenglet, *De Brief aan de Hebreeën*, Roermond, 1971.

[11] Cf. Vanhoye, *op. cit.*, Ch. IV, 5, note 36. "Le message de l'épître aux Hébreux," *Cahiers Évangile*, 19, Paris, 1977.

[12] *Pistis*, "belief": 4:2; *pisteuein*, "to believe": 4:3; *apistia*, "unbelief": 3:12, 19; *apeitheia*, "disobedience": 4:6; *homologia*, "profession of faith": 3:1; 4:14.

[13] *Charis*, "grace": 4:16; *boetheia* "help": 4:16; *sympathein*, "to suffer with": 4:15; *metriopathein*, "to be comprehensive": 5:2; *sozein*, "to save": 5:7; *soteria*, "salvation": 5:10.

[14] S. Zedda, *Lettera agli Ebrei*, Rome, 1967. "Jesus, the one who was faithful to him who made him."

[15] Cf. M. A. Bailly, *Dictionnaire grec-francais*: "qu'on peut croire, digne de foi"; Liddell-Scott-Jones, *Greek-English Lexicon*: "to be trusted or believed;" W. Bauer, *Wörterbuch zum N.T.*: "Glauben oder Vertrauen weckend, glaubwürdig." The suffix -*tos* in Greek corresponds to the suffix -*ible* or -*able* in French and English: *pistos* means "credible," as *horatos* means "visible." That is why *pistos* is often used to qualify a word: "*Worthy of belief* is this word . . ." (1 Tim 1:15; 3:1; 4:9; Rev 21:5; 22:6), or even a witness (Rev 1:5; 2:13).

[16] The dative which follows *pistos* in Heb 3:2 in no way calls for the meaning of "faithful." It is a dative of interest. The rare examples of *pistos* with the dative in the Greek Bible all have this meaning: cf. Sir 33:3: *ho nomos auto pistos*, which the *Jerusalem Bible* correctly translates as: The Law is *for him* dependable; 1 Sam 3:20; *pistos Samouel* . . . *to Kurio*, "Samuel was accredited *before the Lord*"; in 1 Mac 7:8: *piston tô basilei* takes up 1 Mac 7:7: *andra ho pisteueis*, "a man who has your confidence," and must be translated "a man having the King's confidence."

[17]Cf. Chapter II, 3c.

[18]*Apostolos* means "someone sent" and is therefore very close to *angelos*, "messenger". In the N.T. the "apostles" are charged with spreading "the Gospel" or "Good News" (*euangelion*).

[19]Ps 95:6f.

[20]In the fascicle edition of the *Jerusalem Bible, Book of Numbers*, note on Num 12:7.

[21] 2 Sam 7; 1 Chr 17.

[22] 2 Sam 7:13; 1 Chr. 17:12.

[23] Cf. Heb 4:15; 7:25; 9:14.

[24] In Heb 3:2, the textual tradition hesitates between two variants: "in his house," or "in all his house." The witnesses are more numerous for the latter, which corresponds to Num 12:7 and Heb 3:5. But there are grounds for preferring the former as a *lectio difficilior*. It corresponds to 1 Chr 17:14. This allusion being less readily noticeable, there was a tendency to correct the text to bring it into line with Num 12:7.

[25] The theme of building in Heb 3:3b-4 is in line with 1 Chr 17:12; that of sonship in Heb 3:6 is in line with 1 Chr 17:13.

[26] Cf. Is 66:1-2.

[27] Heb 1:11f; 12:26f.

[28] Cf. 1 Cor 3:16f; 6:19; 2 Cor 6:16; Eph 2:21.

[29] 1 *Qs* VIII, 5-9.

[30] Ex 24:4-8; Heb 9:19-21.

CHAPTER VI
Priesthood and Human Misery

To exercise the priesthood, it is not enough to hold a privileged position in relation to God and to be able to speak in God's name. It is also necessary to be closely linked with mankind. The role of the priest, in fact, is to bring about a mediation between humanity and God. That is why our author is not content to draw attention to the glorious authority of Christ. He turns at once to the consideration of his mercy:

> In fact, we have not got a high priest who is not capable of sympathizing with our weaknesses, but a high priest who has been tested in a similar way in everything, with the exception of sin.
> Let us then approach the throne of grace with assurance in order to receive mercy and to find grace to help us in time of need. (Heb 4:15-16)

The rather solemn manner in which our author moves to this second aspect of the priesthood corresponds to a precise intention, that of forestalling a possible error. The description of the compassionate high priest is introduced by a double negative: "We *have not* a high priest *who is not* capable of sympathizing . . . ." It is presented as a denial, opposing a false idea that one could form about the glory of Christ and, at the same time, it answers the objections that could arise from this. Just before this, the author has argued from the glorious position of Christ the priest as a basis for an appeal to faith:

> Having therefore an eminent high priest, who has passed through the heavens, Jesus the Son of God, let us hold firm the profession of faith. (Heb 4:14)

In itself the argument is perfectly valid; his heavenly glorification confers on Christ the highest possible priestly authority. But for such poor creatures as we are, such an exalted position can have the effect of dissuading us from approaching him. Is the glorified Christ really the kind of high priest for us? Is he not too far above us for us to dare to approach him? How can we believe that the "Son of God" could welcome such wretches as ourselves? It is to objections of this kind that the author is responding when he asserts that the priestly character of Christ includes a second aspect, specifically, an extraordinary capacity for compassionate acceptance.

What makes the priest is not the first aspect or the second, but the combination of both. A priest acceptable to God but lacking the tie of solidarity with humanity would not be able to help them in their wretchedness. His elevated position would cut him off from them: it would effectively be useless to them. Conversely, a priest filled with compassion for his peers but not acceptable to God could not intervene effectively. His compassion would be futile. The whole value of the priesthood of Christ comes from the perfect union of the two priestly qualities in him: Christ is "the merciful high priest who at the same time is pleasing to God" (2:17). And what assures this perfect union is the very manner in which Christ acquired his glorious position: not by separating himself from other men, but in carrying his identification with them to its furthest limit. Christ attained his present glory by way of his Passion, that is to say, by the way of human suffering and death. His glory is in no way the glory of satisfied ambition, but the glory of generous love. It therefore establishes him in mercy and gives him the means of coming to the aid of mankind. This is the point that the author undertakes to demonstrate in this second section of his expositions (4:15 - 5:10). Its text is not lengthy, but it is of a rare richness.

1. Priestly Compassion (Heb 4:15-16)

Of the two introductory phrases already cited, the first, in the indicative, affirms Christ the high priest's capacity for compassion; the second, in the imperative, invites the faithful to deduce the consequences of this situation. The more encouraging the priestly authority of Christ, the more attractive is his priestly compassion. The authority of his word assures the steadfastness of the faith; the certainty of his compassion triggers the dynamic of confidence.

One recognizes in these two phrases many terms already used in 2:17-18 to describe for the first time the priesthood of Christ. But one also notes some precise details that are significant. The invitation to approach had not been formulated before. It marks an important advance in the understanding of the Christian situation, and it will be taken up again as the conclusion of the great central exposition (10:22). The priesthood exists to serve. Our author is convinced of this; that is why he is not satisfied with theoretical exposition but continuously ties exposition and exhortation together. The designation "compassionate" (2:17) is taken up again in another form: our high priest is "capable also of sympathizing with our weaknesses" (4:15). By mentioning "our weaknesses," the author shows how much need we have of "compassion" and "assistance." He completes the picture by adding the word "grace": the mercy and assistance that we receive are gratuitous favors, which come to us through the divine generosity. But at the same time, they have a very human expression and basis. They come to us, in fact, through the compassion of Jesus, which is founded on the direct experience of all our trials. "He has been tested in all respects like us." The verb "to test" (*peirazein*), which in 2:18 was used in the aorist and signified therefore trials undergone by Jesus as events in the past, now appears in 4:15 as a perfect participle which describes the enduring effect of past events. Henceforth Christ possesses the experience of our difficulties; he is a tried man; he knows our human condition from the inside. It was in this way that he acquired a profound capacity for compassion. For one must have suffered in order to truly feel for others.

On the subject of Christ's resemblance to his brethren (2:17), the author here introduces a significant clarification. The resemblance extends to every area, he says, "with the exception of sin" (4:15). Thus we see the clear distinction between testing and failure, between temptation and sin. The man who passes through the test is tempted to revolt and to become discouraged, but as long as he does not yield, he is without fault, and the test only increases his stature. Jesus has been tested and tempted, but he has not sinned. This point is of primary importance and it was essential that it should be clarified, otherwise some may have imagined the contrary. One might easily deduce from the total assimilation of Christ with his brethren that he too must have succumbed to temptation and committed sins. But this would be a serious misunderstanding. Our author does not think this at all, and he says so with great clarity. He repeats it again later: Christ is a high priest, "holy, innocent, without stain" (7:26), who "has offered himself to God as a spotless victim" (9:14). The other witnesses to Christ proclaim the same thing.[1]

Does not this absence of sin diminish Christ's solidarity with mankind? One might think so at first sight, but a little reflection shows that this is an illusion. Sin, in fact, makes no contribution at all to the establishment of true solidarity. On the contrary, it is always a factor of division, for it plunges each person into his own egoism. Authentic solidarity with sinners does not consist in becoming an accomplice of their faults, but in bearing with them the whole weight of the penalty that results from these faults. Jesus has had this unheard of generosity. He, the innocent one, has "borne the sins of the multitude."[2] He has taken on himself the fate of wretched mortals, and more: the disgraceful punishment of the worst of criminals (Heb 12:2). The consequence is that from now on no one can be bowed down under a painful situation without finding that Christ is, by that very fact, at his side. Far from creating an abyss between Christ and ourselves, our trials and weaknesses have become the privileged place of our encounter with him, and not only with him, but with God himself, thanks to him.

It is, in fact, the trials of human existence which have given Christ his present position close to God: "for having suffered death, he has been crowned with glory and honor" (2:9). It is because of his identification with us that he has been enthroned at the right hand of the Father. By this same fact, the throne of God, whose dominant aspect until then was one of formidable holiness, has become for us "the throne of grace" (4:16) and we are invited to approach it with "full confidence" (*parresia*). The Greek word, we should note, expresses not only a feeling of confidence, but also an acknowledged right, a solidly based situation. The presence of "our" high priest at God's right hand has effectively and entirely transformed our religious situation.

The author does not underline here the change that has occurred. He does not make an explicit comparison between the new priesthood and the old. His purpose is not, for the moment, to bring out the differences. His way of expressing himself does, however, allow us to perceive several of these differences, two of which are not without importance. The first concerns the relationship with sin; the second, the capacity for compassion.

The Old Testament, as we have seen, never dreamt of requiring the high priest to make himself like his brethren, but was preoccupied on the contrary with separating him from them. It is all the more striking, therefore, that on one essential point no distinction was made: no text ever required that the high priest should be free from all sin. The Law required him to possess perfect physical integrity and the most rigorous ritual purity; it even specified that he could marry only a virgin (Lev 21:13-15); but it did not stipulate absence of sin. On the contrary, it explicitly foresaw the opposite situation, that of a high priest "who sins and thus makes the people guilty" (Lev 4:3). Instead of then ordering his removal, it simply called for the offering of sacrificial animals, as a remedy for this paradoxical situation of a mediator who had become an obstacle between the people and God.[3] The history of the priesthood effectively witnessed, from the beginning, the sinful condition of the high priest: Aaron had allowed himself to be drawn into idolatry and "burdened the people with a great sin."[4]

One might have thought that, because this weakness is common to all, the capacity for compassion must have been spontaneously included in the priestly ideal of the Old Testament. But it is not so. Though himself an accomplice in the people's crime, Aaron does not excuse the people, but throws the whole blame back on them (Ex 32:22-23), imitating in this Adam's attitude after the first sin (Gen 3:12). It is clear from this that sin does not establish a current of solidarity! The continuation of the story shows, moreover, that in the Old Testament an attitude of compassion toward sinners appeared to be incompatible with the priesthood. It was, in fact, due to a harsh intervention that the tribe of Levi was granted the priesthood.[5] The Levites, answering the appeal of Moses, had raged against the idolators, massacring them without pity, and Moses had then announced to them: "Today you have ordained yourselves as priests of the Lord, one at the cost of his son, another at the cost of his brother . . . ." (Ex 32:29). A similar episode is narrated about Phinehas who, for having transfixed an unfaithful Israelite and his accomplice with his lance, had obtained the promise of a perpetual priesthood.[6] In the blessing given to Levi, the priesthood is based on the breaking of all family ties: "He says of his father and mother, I have not seen them; his brothers, he does not know them; his sons, he ignores them" (Dt 33:9). These traditions clearly show that, in the traditional concept of the priesthood, all the attention was directed toward the relationship between the priest and God.[7] And one has the impression that the establishment of this relationship required the breaking of all human attachments and the denial of compassion. At the time of Christ, this traditional priestly ideal was still very much alive. It had even been affirmed with renewed vigor at the time of the revolt of the Maccabees, which had begun with an episode similar to that of Phinehas; seized by a holy anger, the priest Mattathias had slaughtered a Jewish idolator: "his zeal for the Law was like that of Phinehas" (1 Mac 2:26).

The contrast between this traditional attitude and the image that the author of Hebrews puts forward for Christ, the compassionate high priest, is extremely great. It is true that one can find certain elements in the Old Testament which prepare for this innovation. The Book of Numbers records an intervention by Aaron—instigated by Moses— which succeeds in preserving the people who had rebelled from being exterminated.[8] But even this text does not speak of compassion. Our author therefore has not found his inspiration in this source. Where did it come from? We can easily find it if we re-read in their context the verses that precede this section (2:17-18), and if we then consider the way in which the theme is developed in 5:7-8. The author has formed a new image of the priesthood by contemplating Jesus in his passion and has been led to bring to the fore an aspect which until then had hardly been noticed.

2. Description of a High Priest (Heb 5:1-4)

The two sentences of 4:15-16 serve as introduction to a doctrinal exposition which occupies the entire remainder of the section and which divides clearly into two parts: first, a general description concerning "every high priest" (5:1-4); then, an application to the particular case of Christ (5:5-10), which we read in the following section:

> Every high priest taken from among men is, in fact, established on behalf of mankind for their relationship with God, in order to offer gifts and sacrifices for sins, being capable of understanding for those who are ignorant and wayward, for he himself also is beset with weakness on all sides and, because of this, he must offer sacrifices for sins for himself as well as for the people. And no one takes this honor upon himself, but is appointed by God, as Aaron was. (Heb 5:1-4)

This general description includes three consecutive elements. The first describes (a) the double relationship of the high priest, with mankind and with God, and at once adds (b) the sacrificial function of atonement: "In fact, every high priest (a) taken from among men is established on behalf of mankind for their relations with God, (b) in order to offer gifts and sacrifices for sins."

The second element brings further precision (a') on the relation with mankind as evidenced in (b') the function of atonement. The high priest is "(a') capable of understanding those who are ignorant and wayward, for he himself is also beset with weakness on all sides and (b'), because of this, he must offer sacrifices for sins for himself as well as for the people."

The third element returns to the relationship with God and notes in this regard: "No one takes this honor upon himself, but is appointed by God, as Aaron was."

Many commentators let themselves be guided by their first impression and offer this description as a complete definition of the priesthood, one which expresses "all the conditions necessary to be a perfect pontiff."[9] But we have seen earlier that this is not the case. Undoubtedly this text applies to "every high priest," but it does not follow that it contains all the fundamental characteristics of priesthood. It is easy to see that the author is, on the contrary, dealing with only a single specific point of view and is ignoring other matters not related to this. This point of view is the one that was defined in the introductory sentences, which, as we have remarked, emphasize the theme of the compassionate high priest, and speak of the capacity for compassion which springs from a personal participation in the trials of human existence. The description of the priesthood in 5:1-4 takes up this particular viewpoint very faithfully. The conjunction (*gar*, "in fact") placed at the beginning of the clause makes the connection and shows that the author intends here to justify his summons to confidence.

a) *Primary characteristics*
In fact, the author at once underlines in the *first element* the double bond of solidarity that exists between the high priest and mankind. Both by his origin and by his destination, the high priest is closely united to the other members of the human family: for "he is taken from among men" and he "is established for the sake of mankind." He is a man in service to mankind. The other side of his mediation is not

described until later and without any emphasis, in order to specify the area in which his priestly service is to be exercised: "for the relationship with God." In the Old Testament, on the contrary, the interest is totally centered on this other side: it is a matter of being a priest *for God*.[10] One did not think of specifying that the priest is established *for mankind*. This remained implicit. Our author, for his part, affirms it clearly.

The way he subsequently describes the functions of the priest reflects the same orientation. In his text he chooses to emphasize solely the function corresponding to the most important human need. As we have already noted, he does not speak of the entry of the priest into the house of God, nor of the transmission of the oracles of God, nor even of the offerings made to give thanks to God, but restricts himself to describing only one kind of sacrifice, that of atonement, without even specifying to whom it is offered: the priest is established "in order to offer gifts and sacrifices for sins." Mankind's concrete situation is marked by its weakness and its malice. The first thing to be done is to apply a remedy to this, all the more because this weakness and malice constitute the most formidable obstacle "to relationship with God." The priest's most important task "on behalf of mankind" is therefore the offering of sacrifices of atonement. The author expresses this by using, for the first time in the Epistle, technical, ritual vocabulary.

b) *Priestly solidarity*

This specific emphasis in the first element of the description allows the author to insist still more in the *second element* (5:2-3) on the aspect of solidarity. He is clever enough to find in the very ritual of the Old Testament a confirmation of the community of destiny which unites the priest with the people. His attention is concentrated for this purpose upon the legislation of Leviticus regarding atonement. When Leviticus speaks of sacrifices offered for sins, it envisages not only the case of faults committed by one or other "man of the people" (Lev 4:27), but also—and foremost—the case in which "it is the consecrated priest who has sinned" (Lev 4:3). It instructs him to offer a sacrifice for his personal sin. Far from being reserved for exceptional situations, this kind of sacrifice regularly occupies the first place in the ceremony of commencing his function as high priest: before any other offering, Aaron must offer a sacrifice for sin for himself.[11] The same rule held for the great annual liturgy of the Atonement.[12] Our author lays stress on this incontestable biblical fact: the high priest "is under an obligation to offer sacrifice for sins for himself as well as for the people." He correctly recognizes here the proof of the human weakness of the high priest. This aspect of the priesthood had never been emphasized in the Old Testament. When the high priest was spoken of, it was rather in order to exalt his extraordinary dignity.[13] The description given in the Epistle deviates here from the usual perspectives in order to direct the attention to the second fundamental characteristic of the priesthood, that of solidarity with sinful mankind.

The author declares that "every high priest" is "capable of understanding those who are ignorant and wayward, for he himself is also beset with weakness." In themselves, the terms chosen present a certain ambiguity; the context encourages us to interpret them in the broadest sense. *Metriopathein*, for example, in Philo means self-mastery, resistance to the passions; employed here with a personal complement—which it does not have in Philo—it designates an attitude of "understanding," of indulgent moderation toward the guilty, based on personal experience of the same frailty. Sinners are called "those who are ignorant and wayward"; to "be ignorant" and "to err" are two expressions that tend to diminish the guilt.[14] It is true that the expression can also be understood in a restrictive sense. The Old Testament distinguishes between two categories of sins, those that one falls into through ignorance, and those committed "with raised hand," that is to say, with full knowledge. Atonement sacrifices were permissible only for the first category.[15] The phrasing adopted here by the author corresponds to this limitation and therefore faithfully reflects the teaching of the Old Testament. None the less, the text is positively oriented: there is no mention of the exclusion of any particular category of sins; what is underlined is only the relationship of solidarity between the high priest and sinners.

c) *A path closed to the ambitious*
But should one not recognize that the point of view changes in the *third and last element* of the description (5:4)? Does the author not abandon the theme of identification with mankind in order to take up that of the relationship with God? And does he not therefore pass from a perspective of humility to one of glorification? He speaks in fact of the "honor" of the priesthood, which leads some commentators to

see a "contrast." According to Spicq, the author of the Epistle "after accentuating the humanity and the weaknesses of the high priest, . . . asserts his divine calling and underlines its necessity and authority."[16] In reality, a closer inspection of the text reveals no such contrast. Rather, one notes that the author remains faithful to his point of view. What his expression states directly is, in fact, neither the glory of the priesthood, as in the preceding section,[17] nor the grandeur of the divine calling but, on the contrary, the humility that the priest needs to have. The word "honor" is set in a negative statement and serves to describe an attitude of humility: "One does not take this honor upon oneself" (5:4). Far from contrasting with the preceding characteristics, this sentence—as Westcott had already noticed—completes them admirably. The identification with wretched mankind leads to humility before God.

To confirm this viewpoint, the author returns to the example of the first Israelite high priest, Aaron. The Bible, in fact, shows that Aaron did not claim the priesthood for himself, but that the initiative was taken by God. It was God who commanded Moses to bring Aaron forward, with his sons, "so that he may exercise my priesthood" (Ex 28:1). Since it was a matter of relationships with God, it followed that no man could claim this privilege for himself. The priest does not take; "he is taken," "he is established," "he is named."[18] An episode in the Book of Numbers strongly inculcates this basic condition. When Korah the Levite and his partisans undertook to challenge Aaron and claimed for themselves the right to exercise the priesthood (Num 16:3), God's answer was not slow in coming. By two miraculous signs, that of the thuribles and that of the rods, God made known "who is the consecrated person whom he permits to approach him," and he destroyed the claimants.[19] The priesthood is not a position to which a man can raise himself in order to be above his peers. It is a gift of God which puts the priest at the service of his brethren. "Every high priest is *established on behalf of mankind* to represent them before God." From beginning to end of his general description of the priesthood, the author has remained faithful to the point of view set out in the introduction; he has described the solidarity of the priest with mankind.

3. How Christ Became High Priest (Heb 5:5-10)

Having said all he wished to say here about "all high priests," the author proceeds to a consideration of the case of Christ. The transition is made without difficulty, thanks to the mention of Aaron which concludes the first part of the text (5:4). From the situation of Aaron, he turns to the situation of Christ.

So also Christ did not glorify himself to become high priest, but he who said to him: "Thou art my son; I, today, have begotten thee" [named him a priest], as in another place, "Thou art a priest forever after the order of Melchizedek," who, in the days of his earthly life [having offered] prayers and supplications to him who was able to save him from death, with a loud cry and tears, having offered and having been heard for his deep respect, although he was Son, he learned obedience from what he suffered, and having been made perfect, he became for all those who obey him the source of eternal salvation, having been proclaimed by God high priest after the order of Melchizedek (Heb 5:5-10).

Again, we can distinguish three consecutive elements in the text: the first (5:5-6) concerns the manner of becoming high priest; the second (5:7-8) describes a dramatic offering; the third (5:9-10) describes the final result of this offering. To what extent do these three elements correspond to the three elements of the general description (5:1-4)? That is a question of prime importance, but one that can receive a complete answer only when the text has been analyzed.

a) *The humility of Christ*

A first connection can, however, be noted at once. The author takes up the last trait of the preceding description (5:4) in his first element (5:5-6) in order to apply it to Christ. The two phrases present the same antithetic structure ("not himself . . . . but") and use parallel terms ("just as" and "so," "honor" and "glorify"). The viewpoint is identical. What is directly expressed in 5:5-6 is not the nomination by God but the attitude of humility adopted by Christ. "He has not glorified himself": this is the literal rendering of the principal words of the Greek text. The movement of the thought, both here and in the following verses, is similar to that of the christological hymn in the Epistle to the Philippians (2:6-8): "Christ Jesus . . . did not consider the position of equality with God something to be grasped, but he emptied himself . . . he humbled himself." The difference is that our author speaks here about priesthood. There is significance in the way he words the entire phrase:

So also Christ did not glorify himself to become high priest, but he who declared to him, "Thou art my Son; I, today, have begotten thee [have named him priest] according as he says in another [oracle]: "Thou art a priest forever, after the order of Melchizedek" (Heb 5:5-6).

The statement, as one can see, is elliptical. In the positive part which begins with "but," the subject is in the nominative ("he who") without a corresponding verb. This subject consists of a long periphrasis which includes a citation from Psalm 2. There follows another proposition, introduced by "according as" (*kathos*), which leads to a second citation, drawn from Psalm 110. It is clear that the long periphrasis describes God. It is he, in fact, who in Psalm 2 addresses himself to the enthroned king and declares to him: "Thou art my Son." It is he too who pronounces the oracle of Psalm 110:4. The movement of the sentence and its parallelism with the preceding verse allow us to supply the missing verb—as we have done within square brackets— and to understand that God has given to Christ the glory of the priesthood. The author has however avoided speaking explicitly here of glory received. What he wished to emphasize was that Christ had renounced glorifying himself personally. This trait fully corresponds to the orientation of the first half of the text (5:1-4) and it prepares directly for the mention of the Passion which follows immediately. There Christ will be portrayed in the attitude of a man who begs, who suffers, who learns obedience, an attitude of extreme humility.[20]

The function of the two quotations has aroused much discussion among exegetes. Some, allowing themselves to be guided by their order in the text, attribute to the first of the two the most decisive function in the demonstration of Christ's priesthood: "There are two formulas of investiture in the priesthood," writes Bonsirven, "the first of which is the most fundamental, with the second appearing as its external promulgation."[21] The point is not without importance, for it concerns the relationship between divine sonship and priesthood. Is the divine sonship of Christ presented by our author as *the* foundation of his priesthood, so that we would have to say with Médebielle: "When on the day of his incarnation as man Christ received the quality of sonship which the Father transmits to him as the Word from all eternity, he is then by that very fact made the sovereign priest."[22]

Is this the doctrine of the Epistle? Or should we understand the priestly consecration of Jesus in a different way? We shall return to this question later (Ch. VII, 1 c). For the moment, let us observe only that our text says nothing of the sort. The first quotation acts here as a paraphrase to designate God. It does not directly serve to describe a quality on which priesthood is based. It is the second quotation that fulfills this task, introduced as it is by a conjunction appropriate for introducing a scriptural proof.[23] The meaning, therefore, is that God named Christ a priest according to the word of Scripture that says: "Thou art a priest . . . ." This interpretation is more coherent in itself. In order to name someone a priest, one does not take a word which declares him to be Son (Ps 2:7), but rather an oracle that proclaims him priest (Ps 110:4).

The continuation of the exposition will confirm that this is indeed the thought of the author. Already in 5:10 he returns to the affirmation of Psalm 110 and not that of Psalm 2; he will do the same at 6:20 and the whole argument of chapter 7 will have the solemn oracle of Psalm 110 as its basis.

The most significant passages in this regard are those which, in contrasting the traditional priesthood with the priesthood of Christ, affirm clearly that Christ has been made priest by the solemn oath of God reported in Psalm 110:

> The former ones became priests without the utterance of an oath; but in his case, it was by the utterance of an oath by the one who says to him: "The Lord has sworn and will not forswear: Thou art a priest forever" (Heb 7:20-21).
> Indeed the Law appoints men in their weakness as high priests; while the utterance of an oath, which came later than the Law, appoints a Son who has been made perfect for ever (Heb 7:28).

Our author certainly suggests that a relationship exists between the priesthood and the divine sonship—the precise nature of which will have to be defined —but he does not offer the text of Psalm 2 on the sonship as the foundation of Christ's priesthood.

b)   *The way followed by Christ*
The one who was appointed priest by God is a man who "did not exalt himself." The second element of the text (5: 7-8) gives dramatic attestation to this.[24] It shows Christ

who, in the days of his flesh, having offered prayers and supplications to him who was able to save him from death,
with a loud cry and tears,
having offered and having been heard because of his godly fear,
although he was son, he learned obedience through what he suffered . . . (Heb 5:7-8)

The sentence does not end here. Its intense movement leads immediately to a triumphant conclusion, which constitutes the third element of the whole and will be analyzed in Chapter VI, 3 c.

The principal affirmation comes at the end of v. 8, where we find
the only main verb which depends directly on the initial relative
(who). Christ "learned obedience." Before this stunning affirmation,
two participles, preceded by a long series of complements, present
another aspect of the same events: "having offered and having been
heard." We have then, in the same sentence, two different perspectives on the passion of Christ. It is first described as a prayer that was
heard, then as a painful learning process. These two perspectives
seem to harmonize poorly with one another. According to the first,
God does the will of Christ, because he hears him. According to the
second, on the contrary, it is Christ who submits through extreme
suffering to the will of God. A more attentive analysis, however, leads
to the recognition that there is no contradiction here, but a profound
insight into a complex reality.

The two perspectives are both characteristic of the human condition, so that this poignant text demonstrates to what extent Christ
became one with us. The beginning of the phrase is already significant
in this respect. It situates the event "in the days that he was in the
flesh," that is to say, in the time of the mortal life of Christ. When it
speaks of a man's life, the Bible says "his days," suggesting at the
same time that this life covers only a limited period. On the other
hand, it also uses the word "flesh" to express the weakness and
mortality of mankind.[25] Our author therefore evokes the human existence of Jesus and makes us realize that this put him on the same level
as other men, fragile and mortal.

1) A SUPPLIANT OFFERING

What is immediately described is precisely an agonizing situation
provoked by the threat of death. Jesus prays and beseeches the One
who can save him from death; he cries and weeps. The "prayers and

supplications" addressed "to him who can save him from death" make us think of the Gospel accounts of the agony of Jesus: "In the grip of fear and anguish . . . he fell to the ground," writes Mark, "and he prayed: Father, everything is possible to thee, take away this cup from me" (Mk 14:33-36). The "loud cry" that the Epistle then recalls is not uttered in these painful circumstances, but at an even more dramatic moment, on Calvary, when "Jesus cries with a loud voice: My God, my God, why hast thou forsaken me?" (Mk 15:34). It does not seem to be our author's intention to recall a particular episode in the Passion of Christ, but rather to evoke its whole atmosphere. With this in view, and inspired by statements that he finds in the psalms of supplication—but without limiting himself to any specific text[26]—he puts before us the image of a prayer that springs from the agony itself. It is not a matter of a conventional liturgy, with its rites fixed in advance, but of the violent reaction of a man whose whole existence is in danger.

The chief contribution of this text does not consist in the details of the description, but in the fact that Christ's Passion is presented as being at the same time a *prayer* and an *offering*. Out of the long series of painful episodes which subjected Jesus to the worst trials that a man can know (treachery, abandonment and denial, an iniquitous trial, an unjust condemnation, blows and insults, scourging, crucifixion), our author retains only the manner in which they had been confronted in prayer. The tragic events which threatened the whole work of Jesus, his mission and even his very individuality, these events which threatened to engulf him entirely in death, brought about in him an intense prayer which constituted a priestly offering. It is clearly not by chance that the author uses here the verb "to offer." After having declared that "every high priest . . . is established . . . to offer" (5:1), he now states that Christ "has offered." Taken into the prayer, transformed by the prayer, the dramatic situation has become an offering.

This offering, he adds, has been accepted. The prayer has been heard. How is this declaration to be understood? To determine its precise meaning, we must first find out what Jesus asked for in his prayer. A literal reading of the text immediately suggests that the object of the prayer was to be preserved from death. This is how it is interpreted by Harnack, who then observes that this prayer was not answered. Jesus suffered death, as the whole New Testament bears witness. Harnack therefore concludes that our present text is not authentic. The author must have written the opposite, that is, that Christ *"was not* answered, although he was the Son," but that very early a copier, scandalized by this negation, must have suppressed it in order to obtain a text more in tune with his piety.

Harnack's conjecture cannot be accepted. It has no support whatever from textual criticism and it starts from an incorrect interpretation of the phrase. The author does not in fact say that Jesus asked not to die. He does not give any precise indication of the content of Jesus' prayer. He indicates only to whom Jesus addressed himself: Jesus prayed to "the One who had the power to save him from death."

It is true, however, that without specifically stating it, this expression suggests that the prayer was a request for deliverance. But in this connection Joachim Jeremias observed that there are two possible ways of being "saved from death," one consisting in being preserved from it for the moment, the other consisting in triumphing over it definitively after having endured it. According to this exegete, it is in this second sense that we must understand the prayer of Jesus, a prayer which indeed was answered in the event of the Resurrection. The solution proposed by Jeremias resolves the difficulty but has the unfortunate effect of flattening the text. Does the author really want to suggest that at this moment Jesus was praying for his Resurrection? One hesitates to believe this, for the phrase does not say so and its troubled character conveys the torment of an agonized supplication rather than the serenity of a prayer that knows where it is going. It is undoubtedly far better to respect its lack of precision, which leaves it open to several possibilities, and at the same time allows a transformation of the demand in the course of the prayer. In this way a living dynamism is revealed.

An expression that follows the verb "to hear" helps to clarify this dynamism. Christ has been heard *apo tes eulabeias*. The meaning of these words is disputed. Some think that *eulabeia* here describes the fear of death, and take it in the sense that Christ has been answered by being "freed from the fear."[27] The result of his prayer would then be that he has obtained the strength to overcome his agony and face death without flinching. This interpretation certainly finds a measure of support in the Gospel accounts: after the entreaties of his agony, Jesus no longer shows fear and announces the arrival of the traitor without a tremor (Mk 14:42). But it is difficult to justify the proposed translation of the text of the Epistle, for it forces the meaning of the Greek words. No other text can be cited where *eisakouein apo* would have the sense of "answer by freeing from . . . ." An exegete has recently suggested the temporal sense of "after" for the preposition *apo*, which is possible in certain contexts. Christ has been answered "after his agony."[28] This interpretation is the opposite of the preceding one, since it affirms that, far from being freed from fear, Christ was obliged to submit to its full weight and was not answered until afterwards. However, the two interpretations have one point in common: the meaning of "agony" attributed to *eulabeia*. This meaning is contestable. *Eulabeia* does not normally describe an attitude of agony, but one of religious fear, which is very different. The etymological sense of this word is "good understanding" (*eulabein*), "careful attention." The corresponding adjective, *eulabes*, is employed by Luke in the sense of "religious," "observant,"[29] and is almost synonymous with *eusebes*, "pious." As for the preposition *apo*, which indicates a point of departure, its most normal sense after "to answer" is "because of," here as in Exodus 6:9: "They did not agree *because of* their faint-heartedness."

The best way to understand the text is therefore the one adopted by the majority of the translators: "answered because of his profound respect." What permits the answering of a prayer is really the attitude of profound respect toward God, for this attitude makes a prayer authentic and opens the soul to the action of God. A psalm states this very clearly: God "will do the will of those who fear him, he will listen to their petition and will save them" (Ps 144:19, LXX).

In light of the above, the internal dialectic of our text can be discerned. Assailed by the anguish of impending death, Jesus experiences the instinctive urge to escape. He does not thrust this impulse aside but presents it to God in a suppliant prayer that springs forcefully from his human will to live. This prayer, however, was totally imbued with profound respect toward God (*eulabeia*) and in consequence avoided imposing any predetermined solution on God. One who prays refrains from deciding for himself and from freeing himself. He opens himself to God's action and consents to the interpersonal relationship. He submits himself at the same time to a magnetic force, which works a transformation in him, though not without a painful struggle. The object of the prayer becomes secondary. What matters above all is the relationship with God. In the Gospels, Jesus adds, after having begged for deliverance: "Yet not as I myself will, but as thou willest" (Mt 26:39). And so what at first appeared to be a redundant clause becomes, little by little, the principal request: "My Father, . . . *may Thy will be done*" (Mt 26:42). In this way the prayer transforms the desire, which models itself on the will of the Father, whatever that may be, because the one who is praying desires above all the union of their wills in love. We now begin to understand why the author of the Epistle refrained from defining the object of Christ's prayer, which would have amounted to freezing its movement. We also understand why he calls the prayer an offering. The initial aspiration is not, for all this, rejected; rather it is supported in its deepest sense. Jesus does not give up asking for victory over death; but he leaves the choice of the path to be followed entirely to God.

A prayer of this kind cannot but be heard, precisely because it is open, with a total respect, to God's action and puts no obstacle in the way of the divine generosity. In the case of Christ, the answering consisted in the complete victory over death, a victory won by means of death itself.[30]

2) A PAINFUL EDUCATION

The second part of the phrase joins the aspect of education through suffering to that of answered prayer. After what has just been said, it is easy to see how these two aspects are in harmony with each other. The answer to his prayer did not mean that Jesus escaped the testing, but represented a transformation of the suffering into a path of salvation. Here again we find the preposition *apo*, which indicates once more the source of a result that has been achieved: "From (*apo*) what he suffered, he learned obedience," that is to say, "he learned obedience through his sufferings." That suffering can have an educative value is a matter of universal experience. We find this expressed particularly in Greek literature, which for this purpose deliberately uses the assonance *pathein/mathein*, adopted here by our author: in suffering, one learns. But it must be noted that the Bible gives a new depth to this fundamental fact of human experience, for it draws attention to the role played in suffering by the personal relationship with God.[31] By means of this testing, God reveals himself to the person, either as a judge from whom no one can escape,[32] or as a father who wishes to help his children to improve.[33] Suffering serves to establish a closer and more authentic relationship between mankind and God. Through suffering, God purifies a person and transforms him, imbues him with his sanctity (Heb 12:10) in order to be able to bring him close to himself. He gives him docility and true availability, the condition of perfect union in love. Such is the path of humanity: by suffering we learn the obedience that unites us to God. But is it not amazing that this was also the path of Christ? Did he need to learn obedience, he who—as our author has announced from the start—was the "Son," "the splendor of the glory" of the Father and the "expression of his being" (1:2-3)? No, this education was not necessary for him personally. He submitted himself to it "although he was the Son" (5:8). This precise qualification, given so clearly here, shows very well the difference of level which exists between his Sonship, defined in a unique manner (1:3; 4:14), and our own filial relationship which, according to a later text (12:8), necessarily implies a "disciplining."

In spite of this, Christ suffered and not only did he suffer, but he was transformed by his suffering; he learned obedience through it. A daring assertion, one that theologians are sometimes tempted to ignore or to attenuate, but one which reveals the whole seriousness of the incarnation and of the redemption. Of course, we are not expected to think that Jesus at some time or other refused to obey and that God punished him in order to reduce him to submission. Such a supposition has been excluded in advance by the words of 4:15 which declared that Jesus remained "without sin." At no time was Jesus personally disobedient to God. From his entry into the world, he made it his aim to "do the will" of God.[34] But our nature "of flesh and blood" which he had agreed to share (2:14) had been deformed by disobedience and needed to be set right. It was necessary for it to be melted down again in the crucible of suffering and transformed by the action of God. No man, however, was in a position to welcome this terribly trying divine action in the way required. Only Christ, who had no need of it for himself, was capable of it and did indeed actually submit himself to it in the drama of his Passion. In him, therefore, a new man has been created who corresponds perfectly to the divine intention, because he has come to be by accepting the most complete obedience.

The apprenticeship in obedience and the answering of his prayer thus come together at the deepest level. On one side as on the other, the action of God and the action of Christ come together in an admirable unity. The action of Christ consists in calling for the action of

God in his prayer and in welcoming it in obedience. The answering of the prayer is precisely the transformation of Christ wrought by God through an educative suffering. The author will show us later that this offering which has been answered constitutes the most perfect of sacrifices. The vistas that it has opened up throw an inexhaustible light not only on the mystery of Christ but also on the depths of all spiritual life.

c) *The priestly outcome*
The end of the phrase (5:9-10) is immediately linked with the mention of the Passion of Christ. It simply describes its consequences in three closely connected affirmations, all of which concern Christ:

> and, 1) having been made perfect,
> 2) he became for all those who obey him the cause of eternal salvation,
> 3) having been proclaimed by God high priest after the order of Melchizedek.

The first and the third of these affirmations are expressed by participles; the central one alone takes the form of a main proposition with a personal verb: "he became . . . the cause of salvation." It therefore acquires more emphasis. This is significant, for this affirmation is the one that corresponds most closely to the theme developed in this section, that of the solidarity between the priest and mankind. This theme was not directly revealed in the description of the Passion (5:7-8), which refers only to Christ and does not say a word about other men. It now reappears in a revealing manner, linked as it is to the transformation of Christ on the one hand and to the proclamation of his priesthood on the other. We understand that transformation of humanity and proclamation of priesthood have no other purpose than to enable Christ to offer salvation to all.

The first point is the decisive one: the transformation of Christ "made perfect." Here is discovered the foundation of all the rest. It is because he has been made perfect that it has been possible for Christ to be proclaimed high priest.
In what sense should we understand this astonishing declaration? In the Greek text, it is expressed by the verb *teleioun*, formed from the adjective *teleios* which means finished, accomplished, perfect. Here the verb is in the passive and its form is that of an aorist participle

(*teleiotheis*), which indicates an action considered as ended and therefore belonging to the past. The most literal translation is the one we have given: Christ "was made perfect." The placing of the phrase puts this affirmation in direct relation with education through suffering. Christ "learned obedience from what he suffered" and so was "made perfect." It is therefore a matter of the transformation effected by means of the painful Passion. A phrase from the first part of the Epistle (2:10) confirms this interpretation, explicitly speaking of "*making perfect by suffering.*" It specifies that God was the author of this transformation. Like the Greek text that we are analyzing (5:9), it establishes a relationship between the "perfection" to be received and the "salvation" to be procured. This sentence says, indeed, that it was fitting for God "to *make perfect* through suffering the initiator of their *salvation.*"[35] Our context completes the thought by showing that the transforming action of God has been asked for by Christ in his prayer and accepted by him with docility. We have just seen that the transformation in question consists in a radical renewal of human nature, which makes it fit for perfect communion with God. The renewal takes place thanks to the relationship with God—it is indeed God who acts—and he has in view the establishment of a more perfect relationship. God renews mankind in Christ in order to introduce him for ever into his presence (9:24). It is in this way that Christ has been saved from death by passing through the throes of death.

The author now reveals the profound connection which exists between this transformation accepted by Christ and the capacity that he has acquired to save all men. In the words of 5:7 the supplication of Christ is not presented as a prayer made on behalf of the people, but as the agonized request of a man seeking something for himself. Neither does the corresponding answer seem to concern the people. It is Christ himself who has been transformed by the divine glorifying action. But the conclusion that immediately follows shows that in this dramatic event the people, far from being left out, are included: the transformation that has taken place ends by making Christ the source of salvation for all those who adhere to him. We see from this on the one hand that Christ has taken on the human condition in so real a manner that he has been obliged to offer for himself "prayers and supplications . . . with a very loud cry and with tears," but, on the other hand, that he has carried his identification with us to such a point that in praying for himself he was at the same time praying for us, and that being answered himself, he was obtaining our own salvation at the same time. The transformation wrought in him is not the individual transformation *of an* isolated man, but it is the transformation *of* man, which is communicable to every man.

What is the connection between the third and last affirmation, "proclaimed high priest by God," and the two preceding ones? Its connection with the second is easily grasped. The proclamation of the priesthood reveals the capacity to intervene to save mankind and defines the manner of this intervention. From now on Christ occupies the position of accredited intercessor in favor of his brethren. "He is in a position to save in a definitive manner those who approach God through him" (7:25). His manner of intervening will not consist in taking up the sword and fighting, like the king in Psalm 45, but will be done in a priestly fashion, the diverse forms of which are explained in the remainder of the Epistle.

The connection with the first affirmation is just as close, but different. The proclamation of the priesthood (third affirmation) finds the foundation that it needs in the transformation of the humanity of Christ (first affirmation). It is by virtue of this transformation, which has "made him perfect," that Christ has become high priest and so can be proclaimed as such. The words of 5:9-10 are, basically, parallel to those of 2:17, which were commented on earlier: Christ "had to become like to his brethren in everything in order to become high priest" (2:17). Christ had to suffer and learn obedience in order to be proclaimed high priest.

However, the thought has progressed between 2:17 and 5:9-10 and this progress is expressed precisely by the participle *teleiotheis*, "made perfect." By accepting this likeness to his brethren in suffering, Christ has been made perfect, which his brethren are not. We therefore note a twofold movement of transformation: on the one hand, an assimilation of Christ to mankind, and on the other, the elevation of mankind, in Christ, to perfection. What is unusual is that the ascending movement of raising up takes place at the same time as the descending movement of assimilation, and by means of it. It is by making himself like sinful men that, paraxodically, Christ has been made perfect. The key to the paradox is not found on the external surface of events, but in the interior dispositions that animated Christ: his total docility toward God and his fraternal love for mankind. These two dispositions led Christ to take upon himself, to the very end, our wretched human condition, but they introduced into this condition an internal dynamic of radical change. Thus the situation of mankind has been transformed not by some exterior intervention, which would inevitably have been superficial, but from within. Motivated by love, the descending movement of humiliating assimilation (Phil 2:8) has become the ascending movement of glorious transformation. And for Christ this transformation is revealed to be a priestly consecration. The close connection that the words of 5:9-10 establish between the acquisition by Christ of "perfection" and the proclamation of his priesthood takes on its full meaning only in light of the use of the verb *teleioun*, "make perfect," in the Greek version of the Pentateuch. This verb is always connected with the priestly consecration envisaged by the Law of Moses. In Hebrew the expression used (*millé' yad*) means literally "to fill the hand." Thus, Moses saw himself as charged by God with "filling the hand of Aaron and his sons," that is to say, with consecrating them priests. The Greek translators preferred to change this and instead of "to fill" they usually translated it "to perfect," to make the hands perfect.[36] The word that describes the corresponding action, *millu'im* in Hebrew, is translated as *teleiosis* in Greek, "the act of making perfect," a phrase often found in the texts regulating the ceremonies of priestly consecration.[37] With his admirable knowledge of the Greek Bible, our author could not have been unaware of this technical use of the verb *teleioun*, an exclusive use, we repeat, in the Pentateuch. His intention to allude to this usage here becomes fully evident a little later.[38] Here already one can and must recognize that he is suggesting a link between the transformation won by Christ and the consecration of Jewish priests. We shall have occasion to return to this point later (Ch. VII, 2 c).

4. Relationship Between "Every High Priest" and "Christ"

Having completed the analysis of the different elements of the text, we can now turn our attention to the composition as a whole and examine in particular the connections which appear between the description of "every high priest" (5:1-4) and what is subsequently said of "Christ" (5:5-10).

a) *Parallels*
It is evident that the author intends above all to underscore a relationship of similarity. His intention is revealed clearly in the middle of

the section, when he passes from a general description to the particular case of Christ. The purpose of his first words is then to affirm that the description given applies to Christ: "So also Christ . . ." (5:6). He shows here the continuity between the traditional priesthood and the position of Christ. What the Bible says about Aaron is also verified in Christ. It follows that Christ must be recognized as high priest and that the Christians have a high priest (4:14,15). They do not find themselves in a position that conflicts with that of Israel.

This affirmation of a relationship of similarity between the mystery of Christ and the institutions of the Old Testament is characteristic of the second part of the Epistle (3:1 - 5:10). Already in the first section, this connection was expressed in the first place between Jesus and Moses. The high priest Jesus is declared "worthy of trust . . . as Moses was" (3:2), and Christian evangelization is likened to the Good News announced to the Israelites of the Exodus (4:2). Commentators often fail to discern this orientation. In 3:1-6, they insist unilaterally on the relationship of superiority: "Jesus superior to Moses," a relationship that comes there only in second place, and in 5:4-6 they at once emphasize the difference that exists between Christ and Aaron, noting that the oracle attributes to Christ priesthood "according to the order of Melchizedek."[39] This kind of commentary is a flagrant contradiction of the orientation of the text. In this passage, indeed, the author is in no sense seeking to show any opposition between Christ and Aaron. He uses Psalm 110 only to demonstrate a relationship of resemblance. The quotation of this psalm in 5:6 proves that, for Christ as well as for Aaron, the priesthood is not founded on a personal claim, but on a call from God.

In the following section (5:11 - 10:39), the point of view will change. Instead of underlining the points in common, the author will insist on the differences, so as to reveal the originality of the Christian fulfillment. But that is another aspect of the demonstration which can only come in a second moment. For there to have been fulfillment, indeed, the first condition is that a correspondence be revealed between the proposed realization and its preparation in the Old Testament. Otherwise it would not be possible to speak of a fulfillment, but we would instead have to speak of an innovation pure and simple, something having no connection with God's plan, and therefore not capable of verification. Conscious of the necessity of ordering the content in this way, our author, in his first expositions on the priesthood (3:1—5:10), begins by establishing the relationship of continuity.

In our text (5:1-10), he uses a parallelism of structure for this purpose. We have already noted that the construction of the paragraph presents a certain symmetry—there is a ternary arrangement in 5:1-4 as in 5:5-10—which invites us to make comparisons. The closest parallel is that between the last element of the description (5:4) and the first element of its application to Christ (5:5-6), which follows immediately. We can demonstrate this by means of the following schema, in which the letters A, A′ and B, B′ indicate the correspondences:

> (A) 1. One does *not* take this HONOR for *oneself*
>   2. *but* one is nominated BY GOD
> (B)   *just as* Aaron was.
> (B′)   *So also* Christ
> (A′) 1. did *not* GLORIFY *himself* . . .
>   2. *but* HE WHO SAID TO HIM . . .

This is a good example of concentric symmetry.

The connections between the central elements of each half of the text are much less apparent. Verbal contacts are not conspicuous and the style of the sentences is entirely different: on the one side, the tone has the calm of juridical texts (5:2-4), on the other, it is moving and uneasy (5:7-8). But on looking more closely, one can perceive beneath the superficial differences a strong and deep correspondence: the description of the prayer and the agony of Christ (5:7) constitutes, indeed, an impressive illustration of the formula which in 5:2 defines the situation of every high priest: "he is himself beset with weakness." Moreover, the verbal connections, though infrequent, are not lacking in significance. One of them in particular deserves to be emphasized, for it is certainly intentional. We have already mentioned it: after having said that every high priest must "offer" on account of his own weakness, our author has managed to use the same verb for Christ. To do so, he has created a new expression, "to offer . . . prayers and supplications," and he has thus been able to affirm that Christ has "offered," which is an essential point for his demonstration.

The correspondences are quite numerous between the first element of the description (5:1) and the last one of its application (5:9-10), even though they are supplied with variant terminology. The principal correspondence is the actual title of "high priest" (v. 1 and 10) which frames the entire text and the name "God" which goes more or less closely with it. On the other hand, the first sentence says that the high priest "is established" (5:1), and the concluding one specifies how Christ has been established: "having been made perfect," he has been "proclaimed high priest by God." These two phrases have been prepared for by intermediate developments, the first one by v. 8, the second by vv. 4 and 5-6. The concluding phrase therefore has a richer content than the introductory one, which is indeed perfectly normal. This same observation applies to the terms which indicate, in both cases, the final purpose of the priesthood: at the beginning its purpose, "on behalf of mankind," is still vague; at the end, the author can affirm much more with regard to Christ: "he became for all those who obey him the cause of eternal salvation."

The analysis could be taken still further, but the parallels which we have indicated are sufficient to bring out a first aspect of the author's argument: the insistence on the correspondence that exists between "every high priest" and "Christ."

b) *Scripture and event*

Within this general framework, one can easily observe that the author uses two quite distinct kinds of argument, which give a composite character to the second part of his text (5:5-10). The first verses (5:5-6) quote Scripture. The following verses (5:7-8) recall certain events. What connection can we discern between the text quoted and the events recalled? The answer to this question is given in the concluding sentence (5:9-10), which shows the intimate connection between the two arguments.

To prove that Christ is the high priest, the author first uses Psalm 110, a messianic psalm, recognized as such by the primitive tradition,[40] which frequently applies its first verse to Christ: "The Lord said to my Lord, Sit at my right . . ." (Ps 110:1). Our author has not failed to quote this text in the first part of his Epistle—in 1:13—the part which constitutes, as we have seen an exposition of traditional christology.[41] Now all he has to do is to go from the first to the fourth verse of the same psalm to find the biblical witness to the priesthood of Christ: "The Lord has sworn and he will not retract: Thou art a priest forever . . ." (Ps 110:4). God himself there proclaims that his Messiah is a priest.

The existence of this scriptural argument evidently is of paramount importance for the doctrine developed in the Epistle. If the author had not had any word of God on which to base his argument, the presentation of the mystery of Christ as priest would have remained on the level of theological speculation, interesting no doubt, but also problematical. It would not have had the weight of a divine revelation which appeals to and arouses faith. But since the author is able to show here that God has spoken and has truly named Christ a priest, doubt is no longer permissible, the light has dawned. We must recognize as a matter of faith that Christ has received the priesthood.

There is, however, reason for going more deeply into the scriptural argument to show how the word of God provides the key to the disconcerting events that took place. In the light of the biblical proclamation of the priesthood of the Messiah, the author turns his attention to the human existence of Jesus and especially to his Passion, which ended in his glorification by God. There he then perceives, in an unexpected way but without any doubt, the foundation of the divine proclamation of the priesthood. The Passion constitutes the path to the priesthood for Christ, it is his way of becoming a priest, his consecration as a priest. Why? Because it carries to its perfection, in his humanity, the double relationship which is the basis of priestly mediation. In one and the same action, Christ has pushed to its limit his identification with mankind, he has descended to the depths of their distress, and on the other hand he has opened this same distress, by his suppliant prayer and his agonized constancy, to the transforming action of God, who has therefore been able to create in him the New Man, perfectly united to the Father and at the service of his brethren. In Christ, transformed in this way, mediation is effected between the lowest level of human misery and the hitherto inaccessible summits of divine holiness. Christ, who "has offered and been answered," who "has learned obedience by his sufferings," has become in his own person the accomplished mediator. The divine proclamation is applicable to him in its fullness: he is priest forever.

Though at first sight it appears composite, the text of 5:5-10 in reality possesses a very strong unity. From first to last, it shows how Christ has become the high priest: "Christ did not glorify himself in order to become high priest" (5:5) but, on the contrary, he humbled himself by sharing the lot of the most wretched of men and by submitting himself totally to God (5:7-8), and it is precisely in this way that he has won for himself the transformation which makes a man a priest (5:9-10).

c) *New perspectives*

To complete the analysis, there is reason here to add some observations on the originality of the doctrine unfolded by the author. Although his purpose has been to show the continuity between the Old Testament priesthood and the mystery of Christ, he has not in fact been able to avoid allowing some new perspectives to appear.

Let us begin by re-reading his description of "every high priest" (5:1-4). Certainly, this can be presented as universally valid and in conformity with the ancient traditions. It faithfully reflects the condition of the priesthood in the Old Testament. However, it includes certain omissions and certain emphases which give it a new direction.

It is unnecessary in this context to mention the omissions due to the limitation of the subject matter. If the author does not say anything about the connection between the priesthood and the House of God nor about the teaching function of the priesthood, it is because he treats these topics elsewhere. There is no need, therefore, to be surprised. But on some other points his silence is more surprising. When he speaks about the institution of the priesthood, he does not say a word about the rites of consecration of a priest, which are however the object of minute descriptions in the Law of Moses and which are recalled with satisfaction by the author of the Book of Sirac.[42] He does not make use of the vocabulary of ritual sanctification, but uses a catch-all verb (*kathistatai*, "is established"), which can serve to designate a nomination to any kind of occupation. In this way, he lets us see that he does not consider the sanctification effected by means of ritual segregation to be an essential aspect of the priesthood.

Another detail supports the same interpretation: the manner of choosing the high priest is left as vague as possible. The author notes only that the high priest is "taken from among men." In the Law of Moses one never finds so imprecise a formula. On the contrary, the Law is careful to determine the tribe from which the priest must come and the family to which was entrusted the office of high priest. All the other tribes were excluded, and all the other families.[43] Our author takes the most general term, *anthropos*, which applies to every human being, without distinction of race, culture, social condition or sex, and employs it in its most indeterminate form, in the plural without the article. The same universal openness is to be noted in the formula which indicates the purpose of the priesthood: the high priest is established "for mankind." Here, too, there is an innovation. On one hand, the Old Testament prefers to say, as we have already noted, that the priest is at the service of God.[44] And, on the other hand, when it speaks of those who are to have recourse to the mediation of the priest, it never uses so general an expression but specifies either the children of Israel or such and such an individual member of the people.[45] Because they are more vague, the formulas of the Epistle also include these cases, but they are not limited to them. They tend to expand to infinity the priestly solidarity of the high priest, who is "taken from among men" and "established for mankind."

The most striking characteristic of this description, the insistence on the identification which unites the high priest with the rest of humanity, is also the point at which the author diverges most from the customary Jewish point of view. It is true that he endeavors to discover this characteristic in the ritual law of the Old Testament, and succeeds in doing so. The argument that he draws from the sacrifices prescribed for the sins of the high priest is proof against any test. But it must be recognized that the Jews had never considered things in this way. It never occurred to them to emphasize the idea that the high priest "was enveloped in weakness." Rather, they saw him as clothed with glory. This is the point of view of the author of the Book of Sirac, when he speaks of Aaron: he writes that God "covered him with a glorious garment; he clothed him with perfect glory and put rich vestments on him" (Sir 45:7-8). Some chapters later, he describes the high priest of his time with the same enthusiasm: "How magnificent he was . . . when he put on his robe of office and his superb vestments" (Sir 50:5, 11). In the eyes of the author of Sirac, the high priest seems like a heavenly apparition. For our author, he is a man closely tied to other men.

The difference of outlook comes, one suspects, from the fact that our author has let himself be guided by the light of Christ when defining the fundamental traits of the traditional priesthood. This light, which emanates from the Passion, has led him to pass over as less important certain aspects of the priesthood which until then had been in the foreground and to bring forward instead other existing aspects that had tended to be ignored. As it turns out, the picture that he draws in these verses is that of a high priest "meek and humble of heart,"[46] gentle toward his unfortunate brethren (Heb 5:2-3), humble with them before God (5:4).

The same understanding facilitated the application of this image to the priesthood of Christ. There is no reason, however, to think that he has confused the levels. Far from it! The description of "every high priest" is not an anticipated presentation of the figure of Jesus. To be sure of this, it is sufficient to observe the differences that exist between the two parts of the text. The application made to Christ (5:5-10) no longer speaks of sins, although the description insisted upon this point. Human weakness and sin went together, the weakness of the priest and the sins of the priest. In the case of Christ, the weakness is revealed in a touching way, but it no longer involves falling into sin. Whatever his anguish, Christ remained united to God in absolute devotion (*eulabeia*) to the will of God and, far from yielding to evil, he "learned obedience."

Another difference is seen in the relationship between the weakness and the offering. The description expresses a relationship of causality: the priest must offer because of his weakness (5:3); and it allows us to perceive a distinction: what the priest offers is not his weakness but "gifts and sacrifices" (5:1). In the application to Christ, the distinction disappears. Christ does not offer gifts and sacrifices that are outside his own person, rather, he presents his condition of weakness and anguish to God in a suppliant prayer. One could say that Christ's offering is his very weakness. In this way we pass from ritual sacrifices that are external to a personal and existential sacrifice.

This fusion between the weakness and the offering has been made possible precisely by the disjunction that we have just observed between weakness and sinfulness. The human weakness of the Old Testament priests could not constitute an offering worthy of God, because it included sin which offends God. On the contrary, the weakness of Christ,[47] being completely free from all involvement in sin, contains nothing opposed to the upward movement of the offering.

The description speaks only of the offering and says nothing about the result obtained by the offering. The high priest is "established to offer," indeed, "he must offer." What is the outcome of this activity? The account does not specify. But in the case of Christ, the mention of the offering is immediately followed by a complementary affirmation:

Christ "has offered, and has been answered." An essential difference. The author will return to it later, in order to demonstrate its full significance.[48] He knows that the making of a human offering does not suffice to constitute a true "sacrifice." The decisive element is its acceptance by God, for if the offering is not accepted, neither is it sanctified—it is God who sanctifies—and the sacrifice is not accomplished. It follows from this that the ancient ritual offerings were not truly sacrifices, but only ineffectual attempts. Only the offering of Christ, who "offered and was answered," constitutes a sacrifice in the full sense of the word. This outcome is due to Christ's prayer, which has opened human suffering to the sanctifying action of God.

The words of 5:8 make it clear that the resulting transformation did not affect merely the external situation, as happens when a person who has been threatened suddenly finds himself free from danger. There has also and above all been a personal transformation of the offerer himself through his education by suffering. Here we find the most radical innovation with respect to the Old Testament priesthood. The description of 5:1-4, true to the Old Testament statements, does not contain the slightest indication of a change in the person of the high priest. The application to Christ proclaims that he has been "made perfect" and grounds this assertion by showing in realistic terms how the transformation was effected.

Indeed, we pass from the vague *kathistatai* ("is established"), which is applicable to "every high priest" (5:1), to a vigorous *teleiotheis* (5:9), which when understood, as it must be, in the light of the preceding verse, defines the existential transformation of Christ. According to the Law of Moses, the consecration of the high priest was accomplished by means of a ritual sacrifice, described in Greek as *teleiosis*, which then enabled him to offer other ritual sacrifices. It was in this way that every high priest was "established to offer gifts and sacrifices . . . ." In the case of Christ there was no ritual sacrifice of consecration, but an existential transformation realized by means of painful events confronted in prayer. Such was the *teleiosis* of Christ, his priestly consecration (5:8-9). To this is added another difference: this sacrifice of consecration has not been followed by a sacrificial ministry comparable to that of the ancient high priests. Our author does not say that Christ has been consecrated "in order to offer sacrifices." On this point, the parallelism is not confirmed, because Christ's sacrifice of consecration suffices for everything. Having "been made perfect" by his personal offering which God has accepted, Christ, "proclaimed high priest," no longer needs to present further sacrifices,[49] since "he has become for all who obey him the cause of eternal salvation." His unique offering is totally sufficient: it is at the same time a sacrifice of priestly consecration for himself and a sacrifice of expiation for the sins of all mankind, a sacrifice which is the basis of the Covenant and a sacrifice of thanksgiving. In short, it replaces, and surpasses, all the ancient sacrifices, precisely because it is a fundamental transformation of mankind, a sanctification that is not ritual but real.

We repeat, however, that the author does not emphasize these differences here. That is not part of his purpose. But his text allows us to glimpse them and so prepares us for the next stage of his exposition, which will fully illuminate them in such a way as to demonstrate the powerful originality of the priesthood of Christ.

We should notice in closing this chapter that the final phrase of 5:9-10 not only ends the brief exposition that precedes it, but is also the conclusion of the whole section (3:1 - 5:10), and that the author has taken pains to recall here the two fundamental traits of the priesthood. When he declares that Christ, "made perfect" by his Passion, "has become . . . the cause of eternal salvation," he completes the delineation of the merciful high priest who has acquired through suffering the capacity to suffer with, and to bring help to, his brethren. This is the subject of the second section (4:15 - 5:10). When he specifies that it is "to those who obey him" that Christ brings salvation, he recalls the other aspect of the priesthood: the authority of the word. Christ is a "high priest worthy of trust" (3:1-6). The glorious affirmation of 5:10 is to be taken also in this sense. It proclaims that Christ is the high priest recognized by God. This is the subject of the first section (3:1 - 4:14).

Thus the strong internal coherence of this section is confirmed. Its twofold structure corresponds to the necessity of a double relationship for the exercise of priestly mediation. As a first approximation, one can say that the first section, in speaking of the high priest worthy of trust, is concentrating on the relationship with God, while the second, which directs attention to the quality of mercy, concerns the relationship with mankind. But when we look more closely we find that the relationship with mankind is not absent from the first section, for this calls men to faith, and the relationship with God has an important place in the second section, which speaks of prayer and offering. The author therefore always shows himself attentive to the combination of these two relationships in the person of the mediator. What distinguishes these two sections is rather the direction of the movement of mediation. In the first section, Christ is presented to the faithful as the high priest invested with the divine authority, who speaks in the name of God. The movement is a descending one, from God to mankind. In the second section, Christ is presented as the high priest who has truly taken on our human condition and raised it up to God. The movement is ascending, from mankind to God. Because they are grounded in a unique dynamism, the two movements assure a perfect mediation.

Notes

[1]Cf. Jn 8:46; 1 Jn 3:5; 2 Cor 5:21; 1 Pet 1:19; 2:22; 3:18.
[2]Heb 9:28; cf. 1 Pet 2:22-24; Rom 5:6-8.
[3]Lev 4:3; 9:7; 16:6.
[4]Ex 32:1-5, 21-24.
[5]Ex 32:26-29.
[6]Num 25:6-14.
[7]Cf. Ex 32:26; Num 25:11.
[8]Num 17:1-5; cf. Wis 18:21-25.
[9]Cf. C. Spicq, *L'Épître aux Hébreux*, v. II, p. 105; R. Gyllenberg, "Die Komposition des Hebräerbriefes," *SvExAb* 22-23 (1957-68), p. 141; D. Bertetto, "La natura del sacerdozio secondo Hebr 5:1-4 e le sue realizzazioni nel Nuovo Testamento," *Sal* 26 (1964), pp. 395-440.
[10]Ex 28:1-3; 29:1.
[11]Lev 9:2, 7, 8-11.
[12]Lev 16:6-11.
[13]Cf. Sir 45:6-13; 50:5-14.
[14]Cf. Lk 23:34; Ac 3:17.
[15]Cf. Num 15:22-31.
[16]Spicq, *op. cit.*, p. 110.
[17]Heb 3:3-6; 4:14.
[18]Heb 5:1-4; cf. Lev 8:2.
[19]Cf. Num 16:5, 16-35; 17:1-5, 16-26.

[20]Cf. Phil 2:8: "He humbled himself, becoming obedient unto death, and the death of the cross."

[21]J. Bonsirven, *Épître aux Hébreux*, Beauchesne, 1943, p. 41. This point has been discussed in greater detail in my work, *La Structure littéraire . . .*, pp. 111-113, where other references are to be found.

[22]A. Médebielle, *Épître aux Hébreux*, Letouzey, 1935, in loc.

[23]*Kathos*, "according to"; cf. Mt 26:64; Jn 6:31; 7:38, etc.

[24]This text has been the object of countless studies and discussions, above all since the article by A. Harnack, "Zwei alte dogmatische Korrekturen in Hebr" in *Sitzungsber. der Preuss. Akad. Wiss. Berlin*, Philol-hist, Kl, (1929), pp. 62-73. Cf. especially J. Jeremias, "Hbr 5:7-10," *ZNW* 44 (1952-53), pp. 107-111; G. Friedrich, "Das Lied vom Hohenpriester im Zusammenhang von Hbr 4:14 - 5:10," *TZ* 18 (1962), pp. 95-115; E. Rasco, "La oración sacerdotal de Cristo en la tierra segun Hebr. 5:7," *Greg* 43 (1962), pp. 723-755; E. Brandenburger, "Text und Vorlagen von Hbr. 5:7-10," *NT* 11 (1969), pp. 190-224; P. Andriessen, "Angoisse de la mort," *NRT* 96 (1974), pp. 283-292; A. Feuillet, "L'évocation de l'agonie de Jésus dans l'épître aux Hébreux," *Esprit et Vie* 86 (1976), pp. 49-57.

[25]"His days": cf. Gen 6:3-5; 9:29, etc. - "Flesh", cf. Gen 6:3; Is 40:6, etc.

[26]The authors who try to identify the source of our passage in the O.T. are not in agreement. M. Dibelius suggests Ps 31:23 and 39:13. A. Strobel proposes Ps 116. In reality, our author does not restrict himself to reproducing the formula of any one psalm nor even to drawing all his terms from the psalter. The terms *iketeria* and *eulabeia* are not found there, nor the expressions *krauge ischyra* or *deeseis . . . prospherein*.

[27]Thus, for example, J. Héring, *L'Épître aux Hébreux*, Neuchatel-Paris, 1954, pp. 53-54. But, contrary to what this author states, O. Michel does not adopt this interpretation.

[28]P. Andriessen - A. Lenglet, "Quelques passages difficiles de l'épître aux Hébreux" (5:7, 11; 10:20; 12:2), *Bib.* 51, (1970), pp. 208-212; P. Andriessen, "Angoisse de la mort," *NRT* 96 (1974), p. 189; "Exaucé après avoir enduré l'angoisse."

[29]Lk 2:25; Ac 2:5; 8:2; 22:12.

[30]Cf. Heb 2:14f.: "by death to reduce to powerlessness the devil, the prince of death."

[31]Cf. J. Coste, "Notion grecque et notion biblique de la souffrance éducatrice," *RSR* 43 (1955), pp. 481-523.

[32]Cf. Ez 6:7, 10, 14; 7:4, 9, 27; Job 19:29.

[33]Cf. Prov 3:11f. cited in Heb 12:5f; Ps 119:64, 67, 71.

[34]Cf. Heb 10:5-9; Jn 4:34; 6:38; 8:29.

[35]Allow me to refer the reader to the detailed commentary I made on this phrase in *Situation du Christ*, Cerf, 1969, pp. 315-328.

[36]Ex 29:9, 29, 33, 35; Lev 4:5; 8:33; 16:32; Num 3:3.

[37]Ex 29:22, 26, 27, 31, 34; Lev 7:37; 8:22, 26, 28, 29, 31, 33.

[38]In Heb 7:11, 19, 28.

[39]References will be found in *NTS* 23 (1976-77), p. 454.

[40]Cf. Mt 22:44; 26:64; Mk 12:36; 14:62; 16:19; Lk 20:42, 43; 22:69; Ac 2:34; 1 Cor 15:25; Col 3:1.

[41]Cf. above, Ch. IV 3 b.

[42]Ex 29:39; Lev 8 - 9; Sir 45:7-15.

[43]Ex 29:9, 44; Num 1:50; 17:27 - 18:7.

[44]*Hierateuein moi*, "to exercise the priesthood for me" (the Lord): Ex 28:1, 3, 4; 29:6, etc. Cf. above, Ch. II 3 c.

[45]Lev 4; 16:34; Dt 33:10.

[46]Cf. Mt 11:29.

[47]Cf. 2 Cor 13:4.

[48]Heb 10:11f.

[49]Cf. Heb 7:27; 9:25; 10:11-14.

CHAPTER VII

A High Priest of a New Kind

The second doctrinal exposition on the priesthood of Christ presented in the Epistle to the Hebrews differs considerably from the first. It is more extensive, comprising three sections instead of two, and these follow immediately one after another without being interrupted by exhortations, as was the case in the preceding section.[1] This time the exhortations are placed at the beginning (5:11 - 6:20) and at the end (10:19-39), leaving all the central portion of the text (7:1 - 10:18) to the three doctrinal sections, which thus take on a greater emphasis.

More striking than the difference in arrangement, is the difference in point of view. The author passes from the relationship of resemblance, demonstrated in the preceding section, to the relationships of difference and of surpassing excellence. His aim is to shed light on the specific characteristics of the priesthood of Christ. He is not satisfied with having proved that we Christians "have a high priest;"[2] he now wants to explain what kind of high priest we have.[3]

This concern starts from a penetrating insight into the conditions of the fulfillment of the plan of God. The relationship of continuity between the realization achieved by Christ and the preparations for it in the Old Testament have formed, as we have seen, an indispensable foundation that enables us to speak of fulfillment. But although this relationship is fundamental, it is not enough. A simple repetition of ancient realities could never be considered as the full realization of the promises of God. If the only relationship between the priesthood of Christ and that of Aaron were one of resemblance, the religious situation of mankind would not have progressed. As the successor of Aaron after so many others, Christ would only have occupied a place of inferior rank in the history of humanity and his priesthood would hardly merit our attention.

But this is not the case. Quite the opposite! Christ is high priest in a radically new way. As well as a profound continuity—one so profound, in fact, that it is not apparent at first glance—the priesthood of Christ presents, in relation to the Old Testament priesthood, certain aspects of discontinuity which show clearly that it is situated on a different level. Of course, it is not a matter of ruptures which would conflict with the essential aims of the priesthood—for this would destroy the argument—but neither is it a question of mere superficial variations, like the ones to be observed within the Old Testament. Examples of these, none of them significant, are the numerous differences that we see between the Temple of Solomon and the Temple after the Exile. After the Exile, as before it, the Temple of Jerusalem was a material building, and the differences that could have been noted, far from showing signs of progress, led rather to disappointment, as the prophet Haggai gives us to understand (Hag 2:1-3). It was not possible, therefore, to discover here the definitive fulfillment of God's expressed intention to dwell in the midst of his people.

For there to be an authentic fulfillment, it is necessary that the differences introduced constitute a decisive advance. Old limitations and imperfections must disappear to leave room for a perfect reality bearing the mark of God's creative intervention. One must pass from the inferior level of prefigurations, with their inevitable inadequacies, to the higher level of divine realization. This is precisely what the author demonstrates for us in the case of the priesthood of Christ.

His spiritual insight is here revealed in an astonishing way. He shows himself capable of extracting in succession, from the same concrete data, the arguments he needs to prove opposing relationships. The oracle of Psalm 110:4, which he has already used in 5:6, 10 to prove a fundamental resemblance between Christ and Aaron, is now used in Chapter 7 to prove, on the contrary, that the priesthood of Christ differs from that of Aaron and is superior to it. One could cry sophism, but this would be a mistake. The author's dialectical skill does not involve any deceit. In the first instance, he takes the oracle as a whole, without any analysis of detail, and correctly shows therein the attestation that Christ has been proclaimed priest by God. Thus appears a relationship of similarity to Aaron. In the second instance, on the other hand, each statement of the oracle is subjected to careful analysis; this, without in any way questioning the fundamental resemblance, reveals significant differences which mark a change of level.

It is not only the oracle of Psalm 110, but all the final affirmations of Hebrews 5:9-10, which are presented under these two successive lights. When he declares that, as the result of his Passion, Christ

> having been made perfect
> has become for all those who obey him a cause of eternal salvation,
> proclaimed by God a high priest according to the order of Melchizedek (Heb 5:9-10),

the author intends, from all the evidence, to conclude the preceding section (3:1 - 5:10), which has proved the relationship of continuity: Christ, just like Aaron, has been named priest by God. But he wishes at the same time to announce the following section (5:11 - 10:39), which will underline the differences between the two priesthoods and will prove the superiority of Christ the high priest. He therefore chooses his words so as to effect a very skillful transition between his first and his second exposition on the priesthood.

His expression presents a threefold structure, which characterizes the central exposition. The three affirmations which it contains correspond to the three moments of priestly mediation, as we earlier described them.[4] The first affirmation represents the ascending movement, for it expresses the sacrificial transformation: Christ has been "made perfect" by his offering. The second corresponds to the descending movement, for it affirms the saving efficacy of the sacrifice: Christ reveals the ways of God to "those who obey him" and brings them "salvation." Finally, the third expresses the central moment: the admission of the priest to God's presence.

We thus pass from the twofold structure of the preceding exposition, which showed the necessity, for the mediator, of a double relationship, to a threefold structure, which marks the three phases of the mediating activity.

The author is careful to indicate at once that his choice of words truly constitutes the announcement of the new exposition that he is preparing to give: "On this matter," he declares, "we have much to say" (5:11). However, he does not begin immediately, but first of all sets about his task of preparing his readers by means of a powerful exhortation (5:11 - 6:20). It is only after this that he tackles the themes set out in his preliminary announcement. We should note that he does not take up these themes in the order in which he stated them, but expounds first (7:1-28) the one which he had mentioned last (5:10). This is his customary manner of proceeding.[5] He is transgressing the rules of Greco-Latin rhetoric,[6] but is conforming to the Old Testament taste for inversion, which has the advantage of facilitating transitions.

The author, moreover, has a very simple way of helping his listeners to follow the course of his exposition: before each of the three sections, he recalls one of the three affirmations of the declaration (5:9-10), and so indicates the precise point that he wishes to develop.

At the end of the preliminary exhortation (5:11 - 6:20) which precedes the first section of the exposition, the author recalls the third affirmation of 5:9-10 and that alone: Jesus has "become a high priest for ever after the order of Melchizedek" (6:20). The section that begins immediately after this is entirely concerned with this subject (7:1-28). At its conclusion, the author indicates, by his choice of the final word of the last sentence, the theme of the following section: this theme will be that of the sacrificial transformation of Christ, expressed in 7:28 by the same verb as in 5:9a, "made perfect." The beginning of the second section (8:1) refers to this qualification and expressly confirms that the author wishes to treat this subject, and that it is "the chief point of the present exposition." The very length of this section is proof of this: with its 41 verses (8:1 - 9:28) it is the longest in the whole Epistle. After it, there remains only one last theme to be developed, that of the saving value of the offering of Christ. To recall it to the minds of his listeners, the author uses the same procedure for the third time: he places a word taken from the announcing sentence (5:9b) right at the end of the section (9:28). This time the word is "salvation." In this way, the third and last section of the whole exposition is introduced. It will contrast the powerlessness of the Old Testament priesthood with the perfect effectiveness of the unique sacrifice of Christ (10:1-18).

Each section, as we can see, has its clearly distinct theme: the personal position of the priest in 7:1-28, his sacrificial activity in 8:1 - 9:28, the fruits of this activity in 10:1-18. But when he is treating one theme, the author never loses sight of the other two. On the contrary, he shows the close connections of the three themes with one another and in this way constructs a firmly structured whole, which gives a very coherent vision of the specific characteristics of the priesthood of Christ.

1. The Figure of Melchizedek (Heb 7:1-10)

The introduction of Melchizedek,[7] with which the exposition begins, is bound to disconcert the modern reader. This personage, who is mentioned only in two very brief texts of the Old Testament,[8] is described by our author in a way that makes him appear a mysterious being: "without father, without mother, without genealogy, whose days have no beginning and whose life has no end"; "he remains a priest for ever" (7:3). Already, in the story of Genesis, the unexpected character of the appearance of Melchizedek raises numerous questions and encourages more or less problematical speculations. A manuscript fragment, found in Grotto XI at Qumran, presents Melchizedek as a heavenly being to whom belongs the power of eliminating "Belial and his assistant spirits" and of carrying out God's judgments.[9] This manuscript, we should note, says nothing about the priesthood of Melchizedek and therefore adopts a very different slant from that of the Epistle to the Hebrews. But it shows that the figure of Melchizedek exercised a real fascination at the time. Far from diminishing, this fascination increased among certain Christians who read our text. Melchizedek was made an eternal being, a "great supernatural power," a first incarnation of the Word of God, or even a divine being superior to Christ, or again, an apparition of the Holy Spirit.[10]

a) *The starting point and the view point*
Such interpretations stem from an error of perspective in the reading of the Epistle and, more precisely, from a lapse of memory concerning the earlier context. They take the first phrases of Chapter 7 as if they were an absolute beginning and as if they constituted the basis of the author's doctrine. By naively following the order of the chapter, they imagine that the author is starting from the text of Genesis 14:18-20 and is making it, in itself, an object of study;[11] they think that he then examines the oracle of Psalm 110:4 and that finally he meditates on the figure of Christ the high priest. When one approaches the text in this way, the person of Melchizedek takes on an exaggerated importance and the most risky speculations become possible. But to think this way is to be totally mistaken about the manner in which the author's thought is moving. In reality, its movement is just the opposite. The author did not start with the contemplation of Melchizedek so as to next become interested in Psalm 110, and finally to come to Christ. On the contrary, he started with the contemplation of Christ, in whom he saw the fulfillment of Psalm 110; he then considered the oracle of the psalm, and was led, finally, to go back from the psalm to the story of Genesis. That this was the real sequence of his thought is

proved by the earlier context: in contemplating Christ the high priest,[12] the author was led to quote Psalm 110:4, and it is only after repeating three times the words of this oracle, in which he finds the name of Melchizedek,[13] that he goes back to the story in Genesis in order to compare its data with that of the psalm.

The last phrase of Chapter 6, which immediately precedes the introduction of Melchizedek, retraces this perspective in a very precise fashion. This phrase affirms that henceforth our hope penetrates "within the veil," that is to say, into the heavenly sanctuary,

> there, where Jesus, who has become high priest after the order of Melchizedek, has entered on our behalf, as our precursor, for eternity. (Heb 6:20)

The starting point is therefore Jesus, and Jesus glorified. His glory is defined by Psalm 110 as a priestly glory of a particular kind. It is specified in two expressions: "after the order of Melchizedek" and "for eternity." The believers are therefore invited to consider the biblical personage of Melchizedek in order to recognize in him a prefiguration of the glorified Christ, high priest for eternity. Once this perspective has been grasped, there is no risk of wandering off into inconsistent interpretations.

b) *The image of the eternal priest*

The author proceeds, as always, in an orderly and methodical fashion. In the first paragraph (7:1-10) he directs his attention to Melchizedek himself and comments on the text of Genesis.

An initial subdivision (7:1-3) presents Melchizedek, briefly recalling all the information provided by Genesis 14:18-20—that is to say, the titles attributed to this personage and the facts concerning him—and commenting at once on the titles mentioned, while the commentary on the facts is reserved for the following subdivision.

> This Melchizedek, indeed, king of Salem, priest of the Most High God, who met Abraham on his return from the defeat of the kings and blessed him, to whom specifically Abraham paid the tithe on everything, who is first called "king of justice," then king of Salem, that is "king of peace," without father, without mother, without genealogy, having neither beginning of days nor end of life, but having been made like to the Son of God, remains a priest for all time. (Heb 7:1-3)

There is one observation about the grammar that is important here for the interpretation. These three verses form one single sentence, the subject of which is at the beginning and the verb at the end. Reduced to its principal elements, the sentence says: "This Melchizedek indeed . . . remains a priest for all time." All the intervening elements serve simply to prepare for the final affirmation. The conjunction *gar* ("indeed") relates this sentence to the conclusion of Chapter 6, which proclaimed the eternal priesthood of Jesus. We perceive here the movement of the author's thought, which is indeed that which we have just described: in order to comment on the verses of Genesis, he has compared them with the oracle of Psalm 110 and has discovered that the two texts throw light on each other. The two affirmations of the oracle, "for eternity" and "after the order of Melchizedek," in some way find their basis in the text of Genesis. The priest "after the order of Melchizedek" must be a priest "for eternity" (6:20), for (*gar*) Melchizedek, in Genesis, is presented as "priest for all time" (7:1-3). A parallelism of position underlines the connection between the statement of 6:20 and that of 7:3; both are found at the end of a sentence. The attribution "for eternity," taken from Psalm 110 and applied in 6:20 to the priesthood of the glorified Jesus, is echoed in 7:3, in the qualification "for all time," based on the text of Genesis and applied to the priesthood of Melchizedek. The two attributions, however, are not identical; the one concerning Melchizedek (*eis to dienekes*) is weaker; it does not express eternity, but only the absence of interruption. This difference reveals that in the eyes of the author, Melchizedek was only a prefiguration of the eternal priest, a sketch which represented him in a suggestive, but imperfect, fashion. Another expression that immediately precedes this clearly demonstrates this point of view: Melchizedek "has been *made like to* the Son of God." He was not the Son of God, but the text of Genesis has described him in such a way that his figure suggests the person of the Son of God.

In speaking of the "Son of God," the author goes beyond the limits not only of the text of Genesis 14 but also of Psalm 110, and he again indicates his real point of departure: the contemplation of the "eminent high priest who has passed through the heavens, *Jesus the Son of God*."[14] Between the three successive stages of Revelation (Gen 14; Ps 110; the glorification of Christ), he discerns a perfect coherence: only Christ the Son of God could really become the "high priest for eternity" proclaimed by Psalm 110, and he alone could present himself, at the same time, as the one who had been prefigured in a mysterious fashion in Genesis 14 in the portrayal of Melchizedek.

This having been said, we must now look more closely at the way in which the author sets about finding in the Melchizedek of Genesis 14 a biblical prefiguration of the glorified Christ, the Son of God and the eternal priest.

The examination of the name and titles of Melchizedek is enough to show that this personage represents Christ, Messiah-king and priest. The name of Melchizedek can, in fact, be translated "king of Justice," and his title "king of Salem" can be understood as "king of peace." The same symbolical renderings are found in the writings of Philo.[15] Justice and peace were the gifts expected of the Messiah-king.[16] If one adds the other title of Melchizedek, "priest of the Most High God," one obtains the union of the priesthood with the royal authority, which corresponds exactly with the position of the glorified Christ, proclaimed "high priest," that is to say, both king and priest. Our author suggests all these connections, but he does not insist here on the authority which Christ possesses, for this aspect has been sufficiently developed in an earlier section (3:1-6). At this moment, the specific traits of the priesthood of the glorified Christ are what hold his attention: the eternal priesthood of the Son of God.

But how can one discover these traits in the text of Genesis 14, which says nothing like this? The answer is simple: instead of examining the words of the inspired text, we must consider its silences. We then ascertain that the Scripture fails to include, with respect to Melchizedek, several details which would be of primary importance since we are dealing with a priest. Normally, a priest must take into account his genealogy, to prove that he belongs to a priestly line. The Book of Ezra relates that, on the return from the Exile, a certain number of Jewish priests who were unable to rediscover their family tree, found themselves excluded for this reason from exercising priestly functions.[17] Now Melchizedek is presented in Genesis 14 without the least mention of his family origins: he appears "without father, without mother, without genealogy" (Gen 7:3), and yet the inspired text declares him to be a priest. This paradoxical situation suggests a special priesthood, one very different from that envisaged by the Law of Moses. Furthermore, nothing is said about either his birth or his death: "his days have no beginning, his life has no end." These omissions have the effect of "making him like the Son of God," whose existence is eternal.[18]

It is clear that, if the author had been content to study this text of

Genesis 14 by itself, he would not have discovered so much illumination. He would more likely have ended up in bewilderment and perplexity, similar to that which we find in the Jewish discussions on the subject of Melchizedek. In these, they question his origin, they invent a genealogy for him, they argue about his manner of blessing Abraham. But when compared with Psalm 110 and the glorification of Christ, even the anomalies of the text become significant. The way in which the Bible presents Melchizedek makes him the image of a priest who is at the same time the Son of God. The divine Sonship is shown negatively by two omissions which support each other: the absence of a human genealogy, and the absence of temporal limits. If there had been a human genealogy, there would also, of course, have been a limit in time. The text proves to be coherent even in its silences.

The figure of an eternal priesthood is delineated by these two features, to which our author will continue to return, a figure which clearly departs from the traditional notion of priesthood, such as is expressed elsewhere in the Old Testament, where one foresees, naturally enough, the death of the high priest and his replacement by one of his descendants.

c) *Priesthood and divine Sonship*
The decisive point here is the connection between priesthood and divine Sonship, for the eternity of the priesthood results from the divine Sonship. This connection is not new in this Epistle. The author has already discussed it several times. From the beginning of his first exposition on the priesthood of Christ, he has linked to the divine Sonship the first fundamental quality of our high priest: it is "as Son" that Christ is "worthy of faith" for relations with God (3:5). Later, when concluding this section which demonstrates the authority of Christ the high priest, the author has again drawn attention to his dignity as "Son of God" (4:14). The following section (4:15 - 5:10), whose theme—that of solidarity with mankind—has no direct connection with that of divine Sonship, does however recall in two places that Christ is Son of God.[19] The same insistence is found again in the section that we are in the process of studying. The divine Sonship here occupies two key positions, one at the beginning (7:3) to throw light on the figure of Melchizedek, and the other at the end (7:28) to define the priesthood of Christ.

We must therefore clarify the relationship which the author establishes between sonship and priesthood, if we wish to have a correct idea of his teaching. The first question is: when the author declares that Melchizedek has "been made like the Son of God," is he thinking of the Son of God in his eternal pre-existence, or in his human existence, or again in his glorification won as a result of his Passion?

At first sight, the insistence on the indefinite prolongation of the priesthood would incline one toward a connection with the Son of God in his eternal pre-existence. In this case, Melchizedek would represent the priesthood of the Word of God as, for example, Philo conceives it. The Logos is the mediator between God and creation. Our author has, in fact, presented the Son as the one "through whom God made the worlds" (Heb 1:2). The priesthood would have belonged to Christ even before the Incarnation. Nevertheless, this interpretation is not in accordance with the doctrine expressed in other passages of the Epistle, according to which Christ has *become* high priest.[20] He has always been the Son; the author never says that he has "become" Son; but he does say repeatedly that he had to "become" high priest. There is therefore no immediate link between the divine Sonship and the priesthood. The latter is not to be confused with the role of the Son with respect to the creation.

We should note that the actual phrase of 7:3, which underlines the resemblance between Melchizedek and the Son of God, includes a qualification which excludes the application of this text to the Son in his pre-existence. We cannot say of the pre-existing Son of God that he is "without father." Indeed, he has God for his Father! The qualification makes sense only in respect to the Son of God incarnate, who has no earthly father. But can one say that the king-priest Melchizedek represents the incarnate Son in his earthly life? This is equally out of the question, for other qualifications are not applicable to him in this stage of his existence. How can it be maintained that Jesus, on earth, was "without mother" and "without genealogy"? Some verses later, our author will affirm the opposite. He will observe that "Our Lord is sprung from Judah" (7:14); he therefore has a genealogy. And it must be acknowledged that his earthly life had a beginning and an end.

The only interpretation that fits is the one which applies the text to the glorified Christ. Here, indeed, he reveals himself as both new man and eternal Son of God. One can say of the risen Christ that he is a man "without father, without mother, without genealogy," for his resurrection was a new begetting of his human nature, in which neither human father nor human mother intervened, and which made of him a "first-born" (Heb 1:6) without genealogy. If St. Peter can say of Christians that they have been "born again by the resurrection of Christ" (1 Pet 1:3), the same affirmation is still more valid for the Risen One himself. Our author will evoke the same mystery in other words when he will speak of the "greater and more perfect tent" which has permitted Christ to enter into the presence of God (9:11). He explains that this tent, in which one recognizes a symbolic designation of the human nature of the Risen Lord, is "not made by human hand, that is to say, it is not of this creation."[21] These negative definitions correspond, in another sphere, to those which the author attributes in 7:3 to Melchizedek, when describing him as a prefiguration of the Son of God, and they confirm that he intends to speak there of the glorified Christ. That he ought also to be recognized as the eternal Son of God is asserted very clearly by our Epistle in other passages, especially when it proclaims that Christ, enthroned as a result of his struggle for justice, is the person who has created heaven and earth, and who remains when everything perishes.[22]

This, then, is the perspective in which the description of Melchizedek is situated. It is exactly the same, we should remember, as that fixed by the author at the end of Chapter 6, just before beginning his exposition. The priest whom Melchizedek prefigures is neither the Son of God in his pre-existence nor Jesus in his earthly life, but he is Christ, the Son of God, glorified as the result of his Passion.

In our author's view, it was not enough for Christ to be the Son of God in order by the same token to possess the eternal priesthood. Nor was it enough to be the Son of God incarnate. A transformation of his humanity was necessary, a priestly consecration of a new kind which made him "perfect." When the author, at the end of the chapter, again takes up the title of "Son," he takes care to attach to it the mention of this transformation: the one who has been established eternal high priest is, indeed, the Son, but the Son "made perfect."[23]

If this consecration was necessary for him, why then all this insistence on his divine Sonship whenever his priesthood is mentioned? For the very simple reason that the divine Sonship brings to the priesthood of Christ a specific determination that makes it a priesthood without peer. Since the priesthood is a mediation, it requires, as we have repeatedly stated, the union of two relationships in the person of the priest: the relationship with God and the relationship with mankind. The value of the priesthood depends on the quality of these two relationships. The divine Sonship obviously concerns the relationship with God; it constitutes the closest conceivable bond between God and another person. It therefore assures to Christ the best possible position for fulfilling, on this side, the role of mediator. What other priest could possibly be compared with him in this respect? How could one be better qualified to present himself before God? What greater authority could one have for speaking in the name of God? We understand why our author insists on the divine Sonship of Christ, when he wishes to prove the inimitable value of his priesthood.

d) *Melchizedek and the Levitical priesthood*

After having shown a relationship of resemblance between Melchizedek and the glorified Christ, the author directs his attention to the differences that exist between the priesthood of Melchizedek and that of the Jewish priests. This is the topic of a second subdivision (7:4-10), the function of which is, obviously, to prepare for the comparison between the Levitical priesthood and the priesthood of Christ. If Melchizedek is shown to be different from the Jewish priests and superior to them, then Christ, a "priest after the order of Melchizedek," will also be in the same position of difference and superiority, attested by the Old Testament itself.

The difficulty here consists in finding a common ground between two priesthoods which the Old Testament never puts in contact with each other. In the Bible story an interval of several centuries separates Melchizedek from the Levitical priests. How then does one establish a connection between them? With rabbinical skillfulness, our author succeeds in this attempt, by using the facts reported by the Bible in the story of the encounter between Melchizedek and Abraham.

The first event that he comments on is the payment of the tithe: Abraham the patriarch has brought to Melchizedek "the tithe of everything" (Gen 14:20). The author sees here his opportunity for a comparison with the Levitical priesthood, which also received tithes:

> Behold the grandeur of this person to whom Abraham the patriarch gave a tithe of the chosen spoils.
> And those of the sons of Levi who receive the priesthood have

authority from the Law to tithe the people, that is to say, their own brethren, who moreover are descended from Abraham. But this person, who is not of their genealogical descendency, has subjected Abraham to the tithe . . . . (Heb 7:4-6a)

The comparison leads to a reconsideration in succession of the two traits which, according to the preceding text, characterize the priest Melchizedek: the lack of any genealogy and an unlimited life-span (7:3). The question of the genealogy is raised first because, as it constitutes the link between the Levites and Abraham, it allows the separations of the two periods to be surmounted. The situation of the Levitical priests, who tithe the other Israelites, who like themselves are descendants of Abraham, is therefore compared with that of Melchizedek, who is able to tithe Abraham himself, even though he lacks this genealogy. The observable differences prove the possibility of a priesthood which is not tied to any genealogy and they already suggest that this priesthood is of a higher order.

Leaving this matter of receiving the tithe for a moment, the author turns to the other significant fact, that of the blessing, in order to confirm explicitly the relationship of superiority. Melchizedek

blessed the one who had the promises. Now without any question, it is the inferior who is blessed by the superior (Heb 7:6b-7).

Taken in the strong sense, blessing is a word which assures the transmission of a divine gift, and in particular the gift of a happy and fruitful life. Its movement is necessarily a descending one, for "every excellent endowment, every perfect gift comes from above" (Jam 1:17). Blessing is, in fact, granted by God himself or by the authorized representative of God, father of a family (Heb 11:20-21) or priest. By blessing Abraham, Melchizedek is therefore revealed as superior to Abraham, ancestor of the Levitical priests.

Having said this, the author now returns to the tithe, and to the relationship of difference, considering this time the second trait characteristic of Melchizedek's priesthood, namely his unlimited existence:

Here, those who receive the tithes are men who die, whereas there, we have one of whom it is affirmed that he is living. (Heb 7:8)

The contrast is forcibly expressed. It is based on the wording of the biblical text, which assigns no limit to the life of Melchizedek, although it expressly mentions the death of Aaron, mourned for thirty days, and assigns to the date of the decease of the high priests the role of legally limiting the validity of certain regulations.[24] Finally, the author succeeds, in a way, in putting the Levitical priests themselves into an attitude of submission in the presence of Melchizedek:

> One might even say that Levi himself, who receives tithes, has himself paid tithes through Abraham, for he was already in the loins of his ancestor when Melchizedek met him. (Heb 7:9-10)

Thus ends this intermediate stage of the demonstration. It has brought out relationships of difference and superiority between Melchizedek and the priests of Israel. The author has managed to find, in the text of the Bible itself, arguments capable of shattering the traditional conviction which attributed absolute value to the Levitical priesthood. He has shown that even before the birth of Levi, the Bible evoked the existence of a priesthood that was different from that of the Levites and superior to it. He has prepared, in a very skillful fashion, for the continuation of his argument.

2. The Priest According to the Order of Melchizedek (Heb 7:11-28)

The transition between the first paragraph and the second is made with the greatest of ease. The end of the first paragraph spoke of Levi (7:9-10); the beginning of the second speaks of the "Levitical priesthood" (7:11). A similar connection may likewise be observed for the other term of the comparison: the text moves from the personage of Melchizedek, as it appears in Genesis 14, to the "priest according to the order of Melchizedek" mentioned in Psalm 110.

a) *Difference and superiority*

Faithful to his method, the author establishes relationships of difference and superiority, and uses for this purpose the two characteristic traits already emphasized: lack of genealogy and life without limit. The argument now bases itself on the text of the psalm and goes boldly forward. The paragraph has two subdivisions.[25] The first (7:11-19) stresses the relationship of difference and exploits two phrases in Psalm 110: "in the line of Melchizedek," and "for eternity." The second (7:20-28) stresses the relationship of superiority and draws attention to God's oath mentioned in the psalm and, again, to the words "for eternity."

Here is the text of the first subdivision, which at first sight is not very clear:

If in truth a perfect consecration had been conferred by the Levitical priesthood—it was the foundation of the legislation given to the people—what need would there still have been for the raising up of a different priest *in the line of Melchizedek*, one who was not designated in *the line of Aaron*? For a change of priesthood necessarily requires a change of law. For the one to whom this text refers in fact belonged to a tribe from which no member was ever set apart for the service of the altar. Indeed, it is well known that our Lord is sprung from the tribe of Judah, a tribe about which Moses said nothing in his legislation on the priests. And the evidence is still stronger, if it is according to the likeness *to Melchizedek* that there has been raised up a different priest, who did not become one by virtue of a legal enactment of carnal descent, but in virtue of the power of an indestructible life. Indeed, he receives this affirmation: *Thou art a priest for eternity in the line of Melchizedek*. Thus there is, on the one hand, an abrogation of the preceding requirement, because of its powerlessness and futility—the Law, indeed, made nothing perfect—and, on the other hand, the introduction of a better hope, by means of which we approach God. (Heb 7:11-19)

In these verses the author twice introduces the appearance of a "different priest," whom he sees witnessed to in Psalm 110. He notes first that the psalm speaks of a priestly order which is not that of Aaron but that of Melchizedek. The Greek phrase *kata ten taxin*, which we have rendered here as "in the line of,"[26] in order to avoid the ambiguity of the word "order," in fact signifies more precisely "according to the order of," not in the sense of "command" but in that of "classification." The Hebrew text of the psalm uses here the expression *'al dibrati*, unique in the Old Testament, the most exact rendering of which would undoubtedly be "on the model of." The psalm therefore indicates a different order of priesthood. Our author clarifies this through the question of the genealogy, which was determinative for the priesthood "according to the order of Aaron," but which, on the contrary, played no part in the priesthood of Melchizedek. According to the Law of Moses, only the descendants of Aaron could have access to the dignity of the high priesthood. By placing the new priest in the line of Melchizedek, the oracle of the psalm freed him from this Old Testament prescription. In fact, our author comments here that the person to whom the oracle applies did not have a Levitical genealogy: "it is well known, indeed, that our Lord is sprung from the tribe of Judah," which was not a priestly tribe. His priesthood is not based on a genealogical relationship; we rediscover here the first characteristic emphasized in the introduction of Melchizedek (7:3,6).

The second trait follows immediately and confirms the relationship with Melchizedek, and at the same time, the difference from the Jewish priesthood: the psalm calls the new priesthood "eternal" (7:17). The first trait, being a negative one, was not enough to establish a solid link between the new priest and Melchizedek. Indeed, in itself the lack of a priestly genealogy obviously does not constitute a title to possess the priesthood! But the eternity of the priesthood is a positive trait, which effects the transition from a simple external classification—a priest who evokes Melchizedek—to a real fulfillment: a priest "according to the likeness of Melchizedek" (7:15). The change in terminology noted between 7:11 "in the line of," and 7:15 "according to the likeness of," is not a simple variation of style, as is sometimes said; it indicates a forward movement in the argument. Verse 16 clarifies the meaning by opposing the reality which serves as the basis for the new priesthood to the Old Testament norm of access to the priesthood. The Jewish priesthood had been governed by "the law of carnal descent," that is to say, by a law of hereditary transmission, which tied it to a genealogy and therefore also to the limitations of mortal existence. The new priesthood, on the contrary, is founded on "the power of an indestructible life"; the author is of course referring to the power of life which revealed itself in the resurrection of Christ and which made of him a "living" priest, "for eternity."[27] The difference here already appears quite clearly as a superiority. It allows the author to conclude this first subdivision by greeting the arrival of a "better hope" (7:19).

The second subdivision (7:20-28) continues in the same line. Observing that the affirmation of the new priesthood in the psalm is supported by God's oath, it deduces from this that "Jesus has become the pledge of a covenant of greater value." The divine oath, in fact, assures the priesthood and the mediation of Jesus a validity that will last forever:

And in the measure in which this was not realized without the taking of an oath—for whereas the others became priests without the taking of an oath, this one was addressed with an oath by him who says to him: *The Lord has sworn and will not go back on his word: Thou art a priest for ever*—in this measure, it is of a better covenant that Jesus has become the pledge. (Heb 7:20-22)

In order to make his argument more secure, the author again turns to the affirmation contained in the oracle of the psalm. He notes that we move from the multiplicity and the instability of the Old Testament priests, who tumbled one after the other into death, to the perfect stability of a unique priest,[28] "always living to intercede":

And whereas those who became priests were numerous, because death prevented them from continuing, this one, since he remains *for eternity*, possesses an inalienable priesthood. And that is why he is in a position to save in a definitive manner those who approach God through him, since he is always alive to intercede on their behalf. (Heb 7:23-25)

The exposition is then able to conclude with a description of the ideal high priest, recalling that this person, on all the evidence, surpasses the high priests of the Law of Moses:[29]

For it was fitting for us to have such a high priest, holy, blameless, unstained, separated from sinners and exalted above the heavens, who has no need, like the [other] high priests, to offer sacrifices daily, first for his own sins, then for those of the people. He did this once and for all by offering himself. Indeed, whereas the Law appoints as high priests men affected by weakness, the word of the oath-taking, which was later than the Law, [establishes as high priest] a Son, made perfect for eternity. (Heb 7:26-28)

What is really new in this whole paragraph is its polemical tone. The author is no longer content with peacefully setting forth his subject; he launches an offensive. From the first phrase (7:11) he attacks the Levitical priesthood. He questions its value and hints at its suppression: "If a perfect consecration had truly been conferred by the Levitical priesthood, . . . what need would there still have been to raise up a priest of another kind?" From the fact that the psalm refers to a priest belonging to a priestly order different from that of Aaron, the author draws conclusions unfavorable to the Levitical priesthood: he invites us to recognize that it was inadequate, that it was defective, that it had to be replaced. The difference attested by the oracle becomes a formidable argument.

This polemical orientation, however, was not imposed by the text of the psalm. The latter is susceptible to several interpretations, according to the actual context in which it is placed. Read in the context of Judaism, the oracle would not appear to require a devaluation of the Levitical priesthood, but by attributing a different priesthood to the king, it would be allowing, rather, the peaceful co-existence of the two priesthoods. Situated at another, more mysterious level, the priesthood of the king would not be taking the place of the other. The Levitical priests could and should continue to perform their liturgical functions in the place of worship, according to the requirements of Moses. But our author reads the oracle in the context defined by a new event, that of the glorification of Christ. In the light of this knowledge, the oracle takes on a less pacific meaning. It suggests a comparison that is unfavorable to the Levitical priesthood and implies that after the establishment of the perfect priesthood, the Old Testament priesthood has lost its whole reason for existence. In the future one will rightly be able to speak of "the abrogation of the former institution" and "the introduction of a better hope" (7:18-19).

b) *Critique of the Law*

The polemical orientation that we have just noted characterizes the rest of the exposition. We shall encounter it again in the second section (8:1 - 9:28) and in the third (10:1-18). It contributes greatly to revealing the originality of the priesthood of Christ, and not only its originality but also its exclusive value. The coming of Christ the high priest brings with it a radical change in the manner of understanding the priesthood.

In the present paragraph, the author immediately shows the enormous significance of the discussion by underlining the close connection that existed between the Old Testament priesthood and the totality of the Law of Moses. No sooner has he referred to the "Levitical priesthood" than he inserts a parenthesis to recall that it "was the basis of the legislation given to the people,"[30] and he takes care to explain at once that "a change in the priesthood entails of necessity a change of law." There is a mutual dependence between the Law and the priesthood: it is the Law that regulates the organization of the priesthood,[31] but, on the other hand, it is the priesthood that gives value to the Law. If the priesthood does not achieve its objective, the Law is seen to be powerless and can only be repealed.

It is clear that the author is not considering the Law of Moses simply from the sociological point of view, but rather from the religious standpoint. In the Bible, the Law is presented as the Law of the Covenant, which regulates the life of the people of God and is concerned primarily with the relationship of the people with God. The religious aspect is fundamental in the Law of Moses, which appears as an instrument of mediation. If the Law is shown to be incapable of guaranteeing a good relationship between the people and God, it has failed in its purpose and can no longer guarantee the unity of the people. In his polemic against the Law, the author here is at one with St. Paul. The point of view is the same—that of the value of the Law in the relationship of mankind with God—and the conclusions are no less radical (7:18). But the route followed is different. While Paul takes the Law in the aggregate and denies it any power in making a man just before God,[32] our author makes a more precise analysis. He observes that the Law is an institution of mediation and that, from this point of view, its most decisive role must be the organization of the priesthood, since the specific function of the priesthood is the exercise of mediation.[33] If we wish to determine the value of the Law we must then, before all else, confirm the efficacy of its priesthood.

c) *The question of the "teleiosis"*
The verification consists chiefly in seeing whether the institution of the priesthood succeeds in bringing about a true *teleiosis*. Such is the question posed by the author in 7:11. The Greek term that he uses has no exact equivalent in English and needs to be explained. That is why, for the moment, it is better simply to transcribe it. *Teleiosis* does not mean "perfection," the word for which is *teleiotes*, but signifies the "action of making perfect," the suffix -*sis* serving in Greek to form nouns of action. The *Nueva Biblia Española* has translated it as "transformation," which deals well with its active aspect without, however, defining the kind of transformation involved.

What exactly is the thinking of the author when he says in 7:11: "If truly there had been a *teleiosis* through the Levitical priesthood . . ."? The form of the phrase shows that our author had in view a current opinion, the validity of which he is calling into question. The opinion referred to is that, in the Old Testament, there was *teleiosis* thanks to the Levitical priesthood. It is enough to refer to the use of *teleiosis* in Leviticus to understand the allusion. The word is found there seven times, always in the same context, that of the consecration of the high priest.[34] It is applied to the sacrifice of priestly consecration. We observe the same phenomenon in the parallel passage of the Book of Exodus, where the word is found five times in the space of thirteen verses.[35] Outside of these chapters, *teleiosis* is not found even once in the whole Pentateuch. Its employment in the Greek version of the other books of the Old Testament is infrequent and scattered[36] and cannot enter into our reckoning here, since the author is speaking of *teleiosis* in connection with the "Levitical priesthood." In reading the texts of Exodus 29 and Leviticus 8, we readily conclude that Israel possessed a *teleiosis*: the consecration sacrifice of the high priest. It is this instinctive conclusion that the author has the audacity to challenge.

The implicit basis for his argument is as follows: he takes the term in its fundamental sense, "the action of making perfect," and at the same time he considers its technical usage, "the consecration sacrifice of a priest." He approves of the choice of the term for this technical usage, because it corresponds to a valid intuition. A true priestly consecration would, in fact, have to consist in a profound transformation of the future priest, which would make him really perfect, so that he would be worthy to enter into relationship with God. Without a radical transformation of his whole being, sinful man is incapable of approaching the all-holy God and thus, too, of exercising the priesthood. For him, a *teleiosis* is indispensable. Leviticus is perfectly correct in making it obligatory.

But the ritual provided does not meet the demands of the situation. It is ineffectual. The ceremonies prescribed by the Law of Moses in no way possessed the capacity of bringing about the interior transformation of the human being who was subjected to them. They were nothing more than sacrifices of animals, with the smearing of the blood of the sacrificed beast on the body of the man to be consecrated (Lev 8:22-28). Such exterior rites symbolized a transformation, but were powerless to bring it about. They did not make perfect. Therefore, they did not deserve their title of *teleiosis*, they were not "an action that made perfect." They remained at the superficial level of "the flesh," "without effect or usefulness," the level of the Old Law: "The Law," the author observes, "has not made anything perfect" (7:19); it was therefore incapable of effecting a true priestly consecration.

That is why it was necessary for a different priest to be "raised up," a priest set up by means of an authentic *teleiosis*, a real transformation of his flesh and blood nature. No longer an ineffectual ritual consecration, but a sacrifice which took over his whole being so as to open it up to the re-creative action of God, and which introduced his renewed humanity into eternal intimacy with God.

In short, it is the necessity for the Passion and Resurrection of Christ that appears again here. In order that another priest could be "raised up," it was necessary for Christ to submit himself to the transformation of his human self, achieved in his Passion and manifested in his Resurrection. The new priest "raised up" had to be a man "raised up again." By the Greek word that he chose and repeated (*anistasthai*: 7:11, 15), the author certainly intended to suggest this connection, for this verb can mean both "to raise up" and "to raise up again." The oracle of Psalm 110 agrees perfectly with this perspective, for it attests the participation of the new priest in eternity: "Thou art a priest for eternity." Read in the light of the glorified Christ, the oracle allows us to infer the insufficiency and the suppression of the Old Testament priesthood.

The last sentence of the section (7:28) is therefore able to express a complete contrast between the priesthood regulated by the Law and the one that the oracle affirms. "The Law establishes as high priests men affected by weakness." They were deficient before their consecration, weak men and sinners; they have remained the same afterwards and have therefore been deficient priests; the ritual consecration prescribed by the Law had not transformed them. They have never been in a position to raise themselves up to God and really to exercise mediation. "In contrast, the word of the oath"—that is to say, the oracle of Psalm 110, God's oath which is applied to the glorified Christ—this word institutes as high priest "a Son who has been made perfect for eternity." His priesthood is defined by the union of three terms, the first of which expresses his Sonship, "a Son," and the third his transformation, *teteleiomenon*. This third term is understood simultaneously in its general sense of "being made perfect" and in its technical sense of being "consecrated as priest," for, in the case of Christ, his priestly consecration was truly effected by means of a real transformation of his being as man,[37] which made him into the perfect man, that is to say, the man recreated according to God's plan, perfectly united to God and totally open to his brethren. Only a priestly consecration of this kind could establish a true priest.

The union of these terms, we must remember, was not self-evident. It is not in his capacity as Son of God that Christ was "made perfect." How could the "splendor of the divine glory" (1:3) be "perfected"? The transformation to which Christ submitted himself did not affect the Son of God in him, but the man of flesh and blood. The author has clarified this in the text of 5:7-9, to which he now returns. There he did not hesitate to assert that, in order to be proclaimed high priest, Christ had to travel a road that did not accord with his dignity as Son: "although he was Son, he learned obedience through what he suffered and [was] rendered perfect . . . ." We therefore find here in 7:28 the twofold implication of priesthood, relationship with God and relationship with mankind, expressed in an extremely dense formula.

Between the first term (a "Son") and the third ("made perfect"), the author has inserted the expression which, in the oracle of Psalm 110, characterizes the new priest: "for eternity." This expression is to be related closely with the two terms that frame it. On the one hand, it defines the value of the priestly consecration received by Christ: he has been consecrated high priest "for eternity." His priesthood is definitive. This is a great novelty. On the other hand, the phrase expresses the relationship between this aspect of the priesthood and Sonship. If Jesus has been able to be consecrated high priest for eternity, it is because he was the Son of God.

Thus ends the first section of the central exposition. Its purpose has been to specify the level achieved by the priesthood of Christ. Building on the Old Testament itself, it has demonstrated that the personal position of Christ the high priest is incomparably superior to that of the priesthood of the Old Testament, to the point of taking away its very reason for existence. The decisive point in the chain of reasoning is the attribution to Christ of a priesthood which lasts "for eternity." In interpreting this phrase of Psalm 110 in the light of the Paschal glorification of Christ, the author has given it its fullest possible meaning, and has been able, as a result, to show that it implies a break with the priesthood of Israel, which was transmitted by genealogical succession to men who were certain to die. On the other hand, he has shown that the way in which Genesis 14 presents Melchizedek allows us to discover a prefiguration of the definitive priest in this biblical personage. The convergence observed between Genesis 14, the oracle of Psalm 110:4, and the position of the glorified Christ lends a great deal of strength to the argument.

We should notice, in closing, how different the point of view adopted in this section appears to be from that of Chapter 5. There, the author described a parallelism between the priesthood of Christ and that of Aaron. Here, on the contrary, he emphasizes the distances that separate them. There, he described in poignant fashion, Christ's participation in human frailty and he mentioned his painful offering, the road to his priestly consecration. Here, on the contrary, he shows the grandeur of the new priest once consecrated. Unlike the Old Testament priests, he has not remained mired in a condition of frailty, but has been able to overcome this and arrive at perfection—we know from other earlier texts[38] that the means utilized has been the frailty itself; he therefore has no need to offer sacrifices in the future. He stands before our eyes in his imposing stature as priest Son of God, established for ever in the priesthood. This position obviously consti- tutes for him an extraordinary personal glorification, but it would be a mistake to stop at this aspect alone. It is necessary to see also and above all that it gives to Christ a priestly qualification without prece- dent: it puts him "in a position to save completely those who, through him, draw near to God, because he is always living to intercede on their behalf" (7:25).

Notes

[1]The two brief paragraphs of doctrinal exposition (3:1-6 and 5:1-10) are separated, as we have seen, by a long series of exhortations (3:7 - 4:14 and 4:15-16).

[2]Heb 4:14 and 4:15.

[3]Cf. 7:26-28: "It is *such* a high priest who was fitting for us" and 8:1f: "It is *such* a high priest that we have."

[4]Cf. above, Ch.II, 3 c.

[5]Thus the theme of "the high priest worthy of trust," last presented in 2:17, is at once developed in 3:1-6, preceding the theme of mercy (4:15 - 5:10). Furthermore, the theme of "belief," presented in 10:38f, is immediately developed in 11:1-40, preceding the theme of "endurance" (10:36; 12:1-13).

[6]According to Quintilian, "it is a grave defect not to follow, in the exposition, the

order adopted at the announcement of the topic" (*Inst. Orat.*, v. IV, ch. 5).

[7]"Melchizedek" is the transcription of the name as it is spelled out in Greek in the Epistle. The transcription corresponding to the Hebrew would be: "Melkizedeq."

[8]Gen 14:18-20 and Ps 110:4.

[9]Cf. M. de Jonge - A.S. van der Woude, "11Q Melchizedek and the the N.T.," *NTS* 12 (1965-66), pp. 301-326.

[10]There are many references to this question in Spicq's commentary, v. II, pp. 205-206. Recently, A.T. Hanson has defended once more the opinion according to which "Melchizedek *was* the pre-existent Christ," (*Jesus Christ in the Old Testament*, London, 1965, pp. 65-72).

[11]Such a commentator affirms, somewhat hastily, that the whole chapter is nothing but a midrash of Gen 14:18-20.

[12]Heb 2:17f; 3:1-6; 4:14-16.

[13]Heb 5:6, 10; 6:20.

[14]Heb 4:14; cf. 3:6; 1:2-5.

[15]*Leg. Alleg.* III, 79-82.

[16]Cf. Is 9:5-6; 11:1-9; Mic 5:4; Ps 45:8, cited in Heb 1:9; Ps 72:7.

[17]Ezr 2:61-63.

[18]Cf. Heb 1:8, 10, 12.

[19]"My son, it is thou": Heb 5:15; "although he was the Son": Heb 5:8.

[20]Heb 2:17; 5:5; 6:20.

[21]Heb 9:11; cf. Mk 14:58; 2 Cor 5:17.

[22]Heb 1:10-12; cf. also 4:14.

[23]Heb 7:28, last word; cf. 2:10; 5:8f.

[24]Death of Aaron: Num 20:24-29; death of high priests: Num 35:25, 28, 32.

[25]The limits of the subdivisions are marked by verbal repetitions which form "inclusions." Cf. *La Structure littéraire*, pp. 128-136.

[26]This is the translation of the *TOB* in 7:11 (twice), but not in 7:17, where nonetheless the expression is the same. In 7:17 the *TOB* has "in the manner of," another possible rendering of *kata ten taxin*, which I have myself employed above in Heb 5:6, 10 and 6:20, while knowing that it is only an approximation. Here it is not correct to translate as "manner," because the author is distinguishing "order" and "resemblance"; "manner" mixes up these two notions.

[27]Cf. Heb 7:8, 17. With regard to the "power" deployed in the resurrection of Christ, cf. Eph 1:19f.

[28]To describe the priesthood of the eternal priest, the author uses an adjective whose meaning is hard to determine: *aparabatos*. This adjective is a derivative of the verb *parabainein*, which means "to walk at the side of" and "to transgress"; it is normally used to qualify a command and signifies "untransgressable," "inviolable." As this meaning is not suitable here, the translators are faced with the necessity of finding another. The Jerusalem Bible translates "immutable"; the *TOB* "exclusive"; while I have used "inalienable." None of these translations can be offered as certain.

[29]In this conclusion the author returns to the title of "high priest" (7:26, 27, 28), which he had abandoned in favor of "priest" on account of literal faithfulness to the two texts that he was commenting on (Gen 14:18; Ps 110:4). These texts reflected the usage of earlier periods. In the language contemporary with the Epistle, the two texts are in fact speaking of high priests, since they are concerned with priests who are at the same time kings.

[30]7:11. P. Andriessen and A. Lenglet propose a slightly different interpretation in which the connection is directly between "Law" and "*teleiosis;*" the connection between Law and priesthood is not however thereby suppressed, cf. art. cit. *Bib* 51 (1970), p. 215.

[31]Cf. Ex 28 - 29; Lev 8 - 10; etc.; Heb 7:5, 16, 28; 8:4; 10:1-3, 8.

[32]Cf. Gal 2:16; Rom 3:20.

[33]Cf. above, Ch. II, 3 d.

[34]Lev 7:37; 8:22, 26, 28, 29, 31, 33.

[35]Ex 29:22, 26, 27, 31, 34.

[36]2 Chr 29:35; Jdt 10:9; Sir 31 (34):8; Jer 2:2; 2 Mac 2:9.

[37]Cf. Heb 2:10; 5:8f.

[38]Heb 2:17f.; 4:15; 5:7-9.

CHAPTER VIII

The Decisive Priestly Action

In beginning the second section (8:1 - 9:28) of his great central exposition, the author announces that he has arrived at the "capital point" of his sermon. The Greek term that he uses (*kephalaion*) does not merely designate the most important point, but also the one that makes it possible to recapitulate everything. What exactly is this point? It is a little difficult to define it precisely because of the recapitulatory character of this section, which appears as a kind of synthesis. In it the author speaks of sitting at the right hand of God and of liturgy, of an offering and of promises, of a new covenant and of purification of consciences, of bloodshed and of an eternal inheritance, and on all these points he compares the Old Testament situation with the one instituted by Christ. Among such an abundance of themes, how does one discern the one which characterizes the section, the one around which all the others are organized?

1. The Specific Theme and the Overall Structure (Heb 8:1 - 9:28)

At first sight, the introductory sentence does not shed much light, for it seems to be no more than a resumption of the theme of the preceding section. This had ended with the description of the ideal priest, established for eternity in his more than celestial glory (7:26-28). The author is now proclaiming that we have such a high priest:

> Now the chief point of our exposition is that we have such a high priest, who has taken his seat at the right hand of the throne of the Majesty in heaven, minister of the sanctuary and of the true tent, the one which the Lord set up, not a man. (Heb 8:1-2)

In speaking of sitting at the right hand, the author is confirming and completing the application he has just made to the glorified Christ of the priestly oracle of Psalm 110. The image of sitting at the right hand of God is, as is well-known, inspired by another oracle of the same psalm. It would seem that the point of view is not changing but is remaining static.

But a closer scrutiny reveals that in reality it is on the way to becoming dynamic. Indeed, the verb used to speak of sitting does not describe an acquired state, but an action. The verb is not one that indicates a state, "being seated," (*kathemai*) as in Psalm 110 or in other christological texts,[1] but is a verb of action (*kathizo*), and it is employed in a tense, the aorist, which reinforces the aspect of action. To bring out the nuance expressed, one might translate it "a high priest who *has taken his seat* at the right hand of the Majesty . . . ." The title given to Christ immediately afterwards continues in the same dynamic sense, for it suggests activity, not repose: Christ is named *leitourgos* ("celebrant"), a word derived from *ergon* ("work"). This title enables us to understand the manner in which Christ has taken his seat at the right hand of God: by accomplishing an act of worship, a liturgy. The following sentence provides a new clarification by speaking of an offering to be presented:

> Every high priest is established in order to offer gifts and sacrifices: whence the necessity for him too to have something to offer. (Heb 8:3)

The last verb of this sentence, we should observe, is again an aorist (*prosenegke*), in contrast to the present (*prospherein*) applied to "every high priest." What is therefore asserted is the necessity for Christ where he now resides to make an act of offering. It was through an act of offering that he arrived at the right hand of God.

The perspective is defined gradually and more sharply in this way. The specific theme of this section is the act of offering accomplished by Christ. We have passed from a static contemplation to a dynamic orientation. This offers more than one advantage. It is at the same time more stimulating and more enlightening. It has to be admitted that the argument of Chapter 7 remained rather abstract. The glorious position of the ideal priest certainly arouses our admiration, but it risks appearing rather removed from ordinary human existence. To correct this impression, it was essential to show the dynamism that explains the glorification and defines its concrete significance. This is what the author does in this section. Instead of contenting himself with a description of the glorified Christ, he sets out to bring to light the path followed by Christ, the transformation effected in him, a path which we shall then be invited to follow, a transformation which will be transmitted to us. This is the "essential point" of the exposition. In the scheme of priestly mediation, it corresponds to the ascending phase, which in reality governs all the rest.

We should now recall that, in preparation for this section, the author has used in 5:9, and repeated in 7:28, a verb that is pregnant with meaning, the verb *teleiousthai*, "to be made perfect," which in the Pentateuch serves to describe the consecration of the high priest. This verb exactly defines the way in which the author conceives his subject.

In the preceding section, he has rejected the Old Testament ritual's claim to confer a true priestly consecration. He has declared that the Law is powerless truly to transform a man so as to make him a priest. In conclusion, he has asserted that, on the contrary, the Son, proclaimed a priest by Psalm 110, has obtained this transformation.[2] He now has to expand his assertion and explain more fully the various aspects of the *teleiosis* of Christ, this action which, by making him perfect, has made him a high priest.

It is true that certain aspects of this theme have already been set out in preceding texts. In 2:10 the author has revealed that it was a question of a profound transformation, brought about by God "by means of suffering." In 5:7-9 he has shown that this transformation was the fruit of a suppliant offering and of a painful education in the course of which Christ "learned obedience." Assuming that these fundamental presuppositions are still present in the minds of his listeners, the author does not pause to repeat them; he is more concerned to throw light upon the other dimensions of the decisive event.

With this in mind, he compares the mystery of the Passion and of the glorification of Christ with the movement of the Old Testament cult. The general structure of the section clearly reveals this line of thought. After the introductory statement, we can identify two major paragraphs, the first of which (8:3 - 9:10) is concerned primarily with the Old Testament cult, and the second (9:11-28) with the mystery of Christ. An expression marks the limits of the first paragraph: "to offer gifts and sacrifices" (8:3; 9:9); it characterizes the Old Testament worship by the multiplicity and exteriority of its offerings. In the second section, there is an analogous expression corresponding to the first, but with an element of opposition to it: "to offer himself" (9:14, 25); it characterizes the unique and personal offering of Christ. In itself, the contrast of the two expressions is already significant. It shows that the author remains faithful to the point of view adopted in the preceding section: he is bringing out the difference between the priesthood of Christ and the Old Testament priesthood.

Each of these two paragraphs consists of three subdivisions, the limits of which are carefully marked by the device known as "inclusion." The changes of theme are sufficient, moreover, to indicate the arrangement of the whole. In fact, the central portion of each paragraph is a subdivision that treats the theme of the Covenant and as such is clearly distinguished from the two other subdivisions. The general scheme is as follows:

	(A. Level of the worship	8:3–6
I	(B. *Question of the Covenant*	8:7–13
	(C. Description of the Old Testament worship	9:1–10
	(C′ Description of the worship of Christ	9:11–14
II	(B′ *Foundation of the Covenant*	9:15–23
	(A′ Final level of the worship	9:24–28

In the middle of the first paragraph, the author raises the question of the Covenant (B). He criticizes the first Covenant on the basis of Jeremiah's proclamation of a new Covenant. In the middle of the second paragraph (B′), a corresponding development proclaims Christ "the mediator of a new Covenant," and parallels the foundation of this new Covenant with the rite performed by Moses in founding that of Sinai.

On each side of these developments concerning covenant, the other subdivisions take as their theme the organization of the cult. The fact is especially clear for subdivision C of the first paragraph, which is entirely devoted to the description of the Old Testament worship. Here the author first speaks of the sanctuary and of its division into two parts (9:2-5), he then recalls the legislation for the Old Testament rites (9:6-7) and he concludes with a critical evaluation (9:8-10).

A contrast is immediately set out in the following sub-division (C′), the first of the second section. This solemnly describes the decisive intervention of Christ, which it presents as a new liturgy, each element of which stands in contrast, respectively, with the corresponding element of the preceding organization.

At the center of the whole, we have then two antithetical subdivisions, C and C', which have as their common theme the act of worship. This confirms the fact that the perspective adopted is dynamic and not static. Attention is focused primarily on an action, the sacrificial offering of Christ.

The initial and final subdivisions, A and A', also develop the theme of worship: their vocabulary is evidence of this. The verb *prospherein*, "to offer," is repeated three times in the former and twice in the latter subdivision, and other terms lead in the same direction: "gifts" (8:3, 4) and "sacrifices" (8:3; 9:26), "tent" (8:5) and "sanctuary" (9:24, 25), "render worship" (8:5) and "liturgy" (8:6). How is this perspective different from that of the central subdivisions C and C'? One can discover this by noting the presence of terms which do not appear elsewhere: the author speaks of "earth" (8:4) and of "heaven" (8:5; 9:23-24) and he describes the relationship between "model" (*typos*: 8:5) and "reproduction" (*antitypos*: 9:24), between "heavenly realities" (8:5; 9:23) and "figure" (*hypodeigma*: 8:5; 9:23) or "sketch" (*skia*: 8:5). In these two subdivisions our attention is therefore more specifically directed to the level on which the cult is situated: earthly and figurative on the one side (A), it is heavenly and authentic, and consequently definitive, on the other (A').

These first observations help us to grasp the arrangement of this section (8:1 - 9:28) in its entirety. The author has adopted a concentric structure, which enables him to emphasize, at the center, the theme on which all the rest depends: the decisive priestly action, the sacrifice. The contrast described between the traditional sacrifices (C) and the sacrifice of Christ (C') serves to throw into relief the original and definitive value of the fulfillment effected by Christ. The other subdivisions which precede and follow show the relationships which bind the other aspects of the priesthood to the sacrificial act. The initial (A) and final (A') subdivisions direct the attention to the level attained in the celebration of the worship and they are therefore closely related to the theme of the priest's position with respect to God. As this was the theme of the preceding section (7:1-28), the transition between the end of Chapter 7 and the beginning of Chapter 8 is made very easily. As to the intermediate subdivisions, B and B', their role is to describe the ties that exist between the cult and the Covenant. For this reason, they suggest the benefits which the sacrifice brings to the people of God. This point corresponds to the third moment of the priestly mediation, the descending phase. This will be the theme of the following section (10:1-18); we shall therefore not be surprised at seeing the prophetic oracle of Jeremiah quoted in B taken up again in 10:16-17. The complexity of this central section is thus made clear and its synthetic character revealed. The author, wishing to throw full light on the essential importance of the sacrificial action, was striving to show all its repercussions, and he was thus led into recalling the various aspects of priestly mediation in organic fashion.

2. Critique of the Old Testament Cult (Heb 8:3 - 9:10)

In the first paragraph of the section we again find the polemical orientation already present in 7:11-28. At first this does not appear clearly, because the author must first of all introduce his subject by a general affirmation on the necessity of sacrifices (8:3a) and its application to Christ (8:3b). But the polemical aspect quickly becomes apparent and takes on more and more strength until it achieves its climax in the last lines of the section (9:9-10).

It is important to keep this fact very much in mind if one wishes to avoid becoming the victim of a kind of optical illusion. A superficial reading of the Epistle to the Hebrews can give the impression that the author remains very attached to ritual cult. Indeed, he does not cease—especially in this section—referring to this worship and employing its vocabulary. He seems to be carrying his readers backwards and bringing them back to the ancient institutions. But this impression does not correspond with reality. The author, is in no way moving backward; rather he is inviting his listeners to go forward. His purpose in speaking of the Old Testament ritual worship is only to submit it to a methodical criticism and to set forth a new and profound concept, which requires a change of mentality, or rather, a conversion.

Natural religious sensibility moves spontaneously in the direction of ritual worship and inclines one to live one's religion at this level. The observance of the rites is felt to be essential. One gains a certain feeling of security from them in connection with relationships with the divine world, as well as the satisfaction of mystical tendencies. But does not ritualism constitute an escape from real existence? We may ask ourselves what position the New Testament takes on this subject and, in particular, what teaching is given here by the Epistle to the Hebrews, which directly addresses the question.

a) *The worship that prefigures what is to come*
The author begins, as we have said, by considering the level

achieved in the celebration of the cult. After recalling that priests were appointed to offer sacrifices and that our priest, Christ, had therefore to present an offering, he immediately calls our attention to this precise point: on what level is the priesthood of Christ situated? And he begins by excluding one possibility: it is not possible for Christ to be an earthly priest:

> Every high priest, in fact, is appointed to offer gifts and sacrifices; whence the necessity for him also to have something to offer. Of course, if he were on earth, he would not even be a priest, for there are those who offer gifts according to the Law. (Heb 8:3-4)

The earthly priesthood is regulated by the prescriptions of the Law and these do not leave room for a priest without a genealogy. But what is the value of the priesthood of the Law? By underlining here again, as he has already done at 7:11-12, the ties which unite the Old Testament priesthood and the Old Law, the author is now in a position to submit them both to the fire of his criticism:

> These persons perform worship that is a rudimentary representation of the heavenly realities, as Moses was warned when he was about to construct the Tent:
> "See," he says, "you shall make everything according to the model that was shown you on the mountain." (Heb 8:5)

The priests of the Law are earthly. They are on the earth before their consecration and they are still there afterwards. The cult they celebrate is earthly. It consists in sacrifices which do not succeed in really rising up to God. They amount to nothing more than impotent rites. The victim is destroyed and the priest remains where he is. Christ's case is quite different. The author lets this be clearly understood without, however, giving any explanations. To obtain positive information, it is necessary to wait for the corresponding subdivision of the second section, that is to say, the end of Chapter 9. The commentators who, having failed to perceive the overall structure of the section, try to supply the conclusion at once, lose their way in false interpretations. Some imagine a totally heavenly liturgical activity for Christ, a ceremony that takes place in heaven, such as the offering of blood. In fact, the author has no desire to transport us to the plane of mythological imagination; he wishes to get us to penetrate into the reality of the events that Christ lived. We do not need to picture to ourselves Christ imitating in heaven the liturgy of the earthly sanctuaries. This is not the sense in which he is a heavenly priest (cf. 10:11-13): he is so in the sense that his Passion has truly raised him up to God's level. At the beginning of his offering, Christ was on the earth like the other priests, but at its completion he has left this world. His offering has resulted in an effective transformation, which has transported him to another level of existence. It is not a question of a ceremony, but of an existential fulfillment.

The ceremonial aspect is left to the earthly worship. The author makes it the object of his criticism. He observes that the priests of the Law "perform the worship that is a rudimentary representation of the heavenly realities."[3] To confirm this interpretation, he cites the text of Exodus 25:40, where Moses receives the command to "make everything according to the model which was shown [him] on the mountain." In its original context, this phrase of Exodus was intended to guarantee the validity of Israelite cult, by affirming that the sanctuary set up by Moses corresponded to a model revealed by God himself. However, it also revealed the limits and the imperfections of the earthly worship, which could not go straight to the divine realities. It is this negative aspect that our author brings out. He already had it in mind in his introductory sentence, when he specified that our high priest is the "celebrant . . . of the true tent, the one that was set up by the Lord, *not by a man*" (8:2). The opposite has to be said about the tent fashioned by Moses: it was set up by a man and not by the Lord; it is therefore not the "true tent." It remains on the lower plane as an imperfect copy.

The words chosen by the author to define the level of the Old Testament worship appear as terribly polemical, if one compares them with texts where a similar expression is employed in the Old Testament. Indeed, the author employs the verb *latreuein* ("to perform worship") with a complement in the dative. The Old Testament very often uses this word to proclaim that worship is to be rendered only to God, and, on the other hand, to severely forbid the making and worshiping of images, including images "of that which is in heaven."[4] When he declares that the priests of the Law "are offering worship to a rudimentary representation of heavenly things," the author is suggesting nothing less than a comparison between Israelite cult and idolatry. This is almost incredible audacity. But it was not without precedent: in the Epistle to the Galatians, Paul speaks in the same sense when he likens submission to the Law to idolatrous practices, and in the Acts of the Apostles the discourse of Stephen adopts a similar point of view with reference to the Temple of Jerusalem.[5] This discourse, moreover, finds support in the Old Testament itself, which on this point as on many others, shows an astonishing capacity for self-criticism, for it did not refuse to receive and to perpetuate the attacks launched by the prophets against the ritualistic cult.

Daring as he is in his attack, our author takes care, nevertheless, not to be one-sided. Far from denying all merit to Old Testament institutions, he recognizes a twofold value in them. On the one hand, he admits that they constitute the human imitation of a pre-existent divine model. On the other hand, he concedes to them a prophetic function, that of prefiguring the realization of God's plan. The word *hypodeigma* expresses this second idea. Its meaning, in fact, is not "copy" as it is sometimes improperly translated here, but "outline" or "model," literally: "a mark placed underneath," a first provisional sketch which prepares for the definitive design. Later, the author will say that the Law possessed only "a rough sketch of the good things to come and not the actual expression of the realities" (10:1).

To avoid remaining in the abstract, let us say at once that the author will apply the first meaning of *hypodeigma* to the "sanctuary,"[6] or "Holy of Holies," of the Temple of Israel. The Holy of Holies is presented as an earthly image of the eternal dwelling of God, a human reproduction of the pre-existing heavenly sanctuary. On the other hand, the other meaning will be applied to the "first tent,"[7] that is to say, to the prior part of the Temple, that called the Holy Place, which preceded the Holy of Holies. In this "first tent," the author sees a rough sketch of the "new and living way" that Christ was to inaugurate (10:20), "a greater and more perfect tent" (9:11). We shall have occasion to return to this point.

The Old Testament institutions therefore had a value, but a limited one. They did not go beyond the stage of an earthly representation and were therefore incapable of effecting a true mediation. Christ himself did not remain at this level. In concluding the first subdivision, the author explains the difference:

> In fact, it is a very different liturgy that has fallen to him, for he is the mediator of a much better covenant, governed by better promises. (Heb 8:6)

This very significant sentence expresses the mediating function of the priest, and at the same time shows the ties which unite cult and covenant. The citation that immediately follows proves that the Greek word *diatheke* must be translated here as "covenant" and not as "testament," for it uses *diatheke* four times in this sense. But already in this same sentence the title of "mediator" (*mesites*) has tilted the balance to this side. In fact, it is not in order to draw up a will, but to seal a covenant that one resorts to the services of a mediator.

Our author rightly sees very close ties between cult and covenant. The value of a covenant depends directly on the act of worship which establishes it. A defective liturgy cannot bring about a valid covenant. Those who wish to establish an authentic covenant must first concern themselves with finding a liturgy of irreproachable quality. The reason for this is easily understood. The establishment of a covenant between two parties who are distant from each other can only be accomplished through an act of mediation and, when it is a question of mankind and God, the mediation has of necessity to be conducted through the cult. The great problem is therefore to find the act of worship that is capable of overcoming all the obstacles to union between mankind and God.

b) *A covenant that has to be replaced*
In speaking of a different cult for a better covenant, the author has allowed it to be understood that the ancient covenant left something to be desired. In the second subdivision (8:7-13), he openly states this controversial position and takes the trouble to justify it. His argument is exactly parallel to the one he used in 7:11 in connection with the priesthood. From a prophetic text which proclaims the establishment of another covenant (Jer 31:31-34) he draws the conclusion that the first covenant was defective. The desire to change is, in fact, a sign of dissatisfaction. When an organization is functioning perfectly, no one feels the need to look for another.

> In fact, if this first [covenant] had been irreproachable, there would have been no question of setting up a second. (Heb 8:7)

His case is stronger here than in 7:11, because (unlike the oracle of Psalm 110, which says nothing about the Levitical priesthood) the prophecy explicitly subjects the Covenant of Sinai to an unfavorable comparison. Jeremiah contrasts the covenant concluded at the time of the Exodus with a new covenant that God promises. This one, God says, "will not be on the model of the covenant I made with their

fathers . . . " (8:9). The contrast is then continued implicitly, when the
prophecy specifies that God will write his laws on their hearts (8:10);
everyone knew that at Sinai they had been written on stone.[8]
The positive part of the prophecy is undoubtedly more important
than the part that censures. Our author is aware of this, and will show
it later in taking up only the positive elements of the text of Jeremiah
(Heb 10:16-17). But here he is remaining within his polemical perspective. After quoting the oracle, instead of giving importance to the
marvelous promise of a personal relationship with God for each member of the people, he takes an argument from the qualification given
the promised covenant to reinforce his negative judgment:

> In saying "new," he made the first [covenant] obsolete; now, what
> becomes obsolete and has grown old soon disappears. (Heb 8:13)

The harshness of this judgment is all the more impressive in that the
person who has announced a "new" covenant and at the same time
vowed that the old one will disappear is, according to the text of
Jeremiah, God himself. The word of God has declared the first
covenant imperfect and provisional. The aspect of rupture that the
Christian fulfillment necessarily involves thus clearly comes to light.
Our author is particularly clear on this point. Already in 7:18 he has
not hesitated to proclaim "the abrogation of the former dispensation";
in 10:9 he will declare without ambiguity that Christ "suppresses the
first dispensation in order to establish the second." No room is left for
the compromises of an ambiguous pacifism.[9]

c) An ineffectual cult

With the third subdivision, we arrive at the decisive point. In order
to understand the fundamental reason for the imperfection of the old
covenant and the necessity of replacing it, we must examine *the cult
associated with this covenant*. This is what the author now does.

> The first therefore had its rites of worship and its holy place, which
> was of this world. (Heb 9:1)

The author, here as in 8:7 and 8:13, avoids using the word "covenant"
(*diatheke*) when referring to the ancient institutions and simply says
"the first." This reticence shows that in his eyes the dispensation
established at Sinai did not fully deserve the name *diatheke*, any more
than the consecration of the Levitical high priest deserved the name
teleiosis. The covenant of Sinai obviously possessed what it needed in

order to function: a "holy place," which in principle was a place for meeting with God, and "rites" which were intended to allow the priest to enter into contact with God. But what was the actual value of the worship thus defined? A preliminary comment already suggests the response: the holy place was "of this world" (*kosmikon*). Belonging to "the world" is certainly not the best qualification for what claims to be the sanctuary of God!

Without insisting on this point for the moment, the author briefly recalls how the holy place was furnished:

> In fact, a tent was set up, the first, called Holy, in which was the lampstand, the table and the Bread of the Presence, and after the second curtain, a tent called Most Holy, with a golden incense burner and the Ark of the Covenant covered all over with gold in which were a golden urn with the manna, the rod of Aaron which had blossomed and the tables of the Covenant; above the ark, the cherubim of glory overshadowing the mercy seat. Of these things there is no time to speak now in detail. (Heb 9:2-5)

Basing his description on the Law of Moses, the author speaks of a "tent" and not of the "temple" as in the time of Solomon. He shows himself particularly attentive in noting the system of ritual separations, which—as we have seen in Chapter II—in fact characterized Old Testament cult. The division of the Holy Place into two parts, one of which is called "holy" and the other "Most Holy" is not only mentioned but also accentuated, owing to a grammatical opportunity offered by the Greek language: instead of saying "the first part of the tent," the author literally says "the first tent" (9:2, 6) and he does the same for the other part, which is presented as a second tent.

He then comes to the regulation of the ceremonies:

> The things having been installed in this way, the priests who perform the acts of worship every time go into the first tent, but into the second, the high priest alone, only once a year, and not without the taking of blood which he offers for himself and for the failings of the people. (Heb 9:6-7)

The author here takes the same care to emphasize the separations. He clearly distinguishes the rites which the priests celebrate in "the first tent" and those which are reserved to the high priest alone and which are celebrated "in the second." In this way he comes to the most solemn act of worship of the Israelite liturgy: the entry of the high priest into the Holy of Holies, only once every year, on the great

Day of Atonement (Lev 16). Far from questioning the importance of this ceremony, he brings out its unique character, implying that this was the supreme moment toward which the whole ancient worship was tending and in which the whole system of ritual separations reached its climax.

But now comes the critical evaluation to bear on this act of worship. Of necessity, it applies to the whole system. It is a negative verdict, a statement of ineffectiveness and failure:

> By this the Holy Spirit was showing that the way into the sanctuary had not yet been made known, as long as the first tent was still standing. It was a symbol for the present time: gifts and sacrifices are offered which have no power to make inwardly perfect the one who performs the worship; as they are based only on food and drink and various ablutions, they are no more than carnal rites which last only until a time of renewal. (Heb 9:8-10)

The two successive evaluations correspond closely enough to the two parts of the earlier description. The first evaluation (9:8) more directly concerns the relationship between the first and second tent (9:2-5); the second evaluation (9:9-10) concerns the rites that are carried out in it (9:6-7).

In this division of the Holy Place into two parts, the author discerns a sign given by the Holy Spirit: a sign which "showed that the way to the sanctuary had not yet been made known, as long as the first tent remained standing." What does this mean? First of all, we find here the vocabulary already used in 8:2 to define the activity of Christ, "minister of the *sanctuary (ta hagia)*" and of the "true tent (*skene*)." But we may note a twofold difference: on the one hand, the author does not speak here of the "true tent," but of the "first tent," the first part of the Holy Place of the old covenant; on the other hand, the phrase expresses a relationship of mutual exclusion between the "way to the sanctuary" and the "first tent." It is easy to understand that the distinction between the "first tent" and the "sanctuary" corresponds in some way to the distinction in the preceding verses between "first tent" and "second tent." We say "in some way," because the expressions in 9:8 show that we must be careful not to confuse the second tent with the true sanctuary. In fact, the first tent was the way that led to the second, but it was by no means the way to the sanctuary. In principle, it had been arranged with this in mind. It was to serve as the entry way to the sanctuary, that is to say, to the divine dwelling. But in fact, as it was a human construction, it could give access only to another human construction, a second tent, which was not truly God's dwelling place. "The Most High does not, in fact, dwell in human constructions."[10] And so, "as long as the first tent remained standing," its presence showed that the way to the true sanctuary was not yet known.

The author did not simply write, as he is sometimes misunderstood to have said, that "the way to the sanctuary *was not opened up*," which could lead one to believe that the way was known, but forbidden. He wrote that this way "had not yet been made known"; God had not yet revealed it. The furnishings of the Holy Place and the rites performed there offered, as it were, a proof of non-revelation. A tent which leads to another tent is obviously not the way to the true sanctuary. But no other way was known. The rites themselves confirmed this situation of ignorance in their own way. In fact, if on the solemn Day of Atonement, the high priest had started out on the right path and had arrived in God's presence, then his attempt at mediation would have been successful, and in consequence the preceding prohibitions would have had to be abolished. But what was in fact experienced was the very opposite. When the ceremony was over, one found oneself at exactly the same point as before it had begun: the people had always been forbidden to enter the sacred precincts, the priests were able to go no further than the Holy Place, and the high priest himself had to wait a whole year before being authorized to re-enter the Holy of Holies. All these prohibitions proved that mediation had not been established and that the road had come to a dead end. Since the liturgical laws formed part of the very text of the Bible, inspired by the Holy Spirit, our author is correct in saying that it was "the Holy Spirit" who demonstrated in this way that the road to the sanctuary had not yet been made known. The system of ritual separations had proved to be ineffective.

Carrying this analysis further, the author then tries to account for this failure. The Old Testament ritual, he says, constitutes "a parable," a symbolic representation, which applies to "the present time." He obviously does not mean by this expression the time inaugurated by Christ but, on the contrary, the time of the world before its redemption, the time that St. Paul calls "the present wicked age" (Gal 1:4). Christ has inaugurated the time "to come,"[11] that of the new creation. The present time, however, continues to unfold in a provisional manner. It corresponds to an imperfect level of existence, of which the ancient worship reveals the limitations: "gifts and sacrifices are offered which are incapable of making inwardly perfect the one who performs the worship"; it is, indeed, "only a matter of carnal rites, such as food and drink and various ablutions, which last only until the time of renewal."

In spite of some difficulties of detail, which it would take too long to discuss here, the meaning of this text is clear. The question of *teleiosis* reappears here, in a negative phrase as in 7:19. We notice, however, an advance in the thinking. In 7:19, the sentence simply stated a fact and that concerned the Law: "the Law has made nothing perfect." Here, the phrase affirms an impossibility; it therefore goes much further. Then too, it defines the means used: "gifts and sacrifices," as well as the goal that must be reached: a profound transformation of the person, who must be "made perfect in his conscience."

In this way the author opens up original perspectives regarding the finality of the sacrificial offering. One understands sacrifice spontaneously as a means of pleasing God and obtaining his good graces. It is a "gift," a present, from mankind to God. Some even think that they will be able to make use of it to bribe God, as they corrupt judges with bribes.[12] The author's expression suggests an entirely different orientation. It implies that the result of a sacrifice ought above all to be the transformation of the one who makes the offering. There was already some idea of such a transformation in the Old Testament for a particular type of sacrifice, that of the consecration of the high priest. Our author makes us understand that every sacrifice ought to be sacrifice of priestly consecration, of *teleiosis*, for its purpose is always to make a man worthy to present himself before God. But for this, the ancient rites proved unsatisfactory. In fact, they could only confer an external ritual transformation which, according to the expression used by the Septuagint, was limited to the hands: they sought "to make the hands perfect."[13] In order to approach God, is it enough to have one's hands consecrated by a rite? Obviously not. A transformation of the conscience is necessary. On this level, the Old Testament worship did not provide any effective mediation. The victim offered certainly underwent a transformation, but only in the sense of a destruction. As for the one who made the offering, he inevitably remained outside the sacrifice: how could the immolation of an animal make perfect the conscience of a man? Consequently, one is bound to admit the powerlessness of the Old Testament worship and its radical ineffectiveness.

In his analysis, as we can see, the author has used in turn two modes of expression. Adopting first, in 9:8, a terminology of space and movement he shows that there was a need to find the true road to arrive at God's dwelling place. Then in 9:9, adopting a terminology of personal transformation, he shows the necessity of an efficacious act of worship at this level. He will take up these two ideas in the positive paragraph (9:11-14) and will then show the very close relationship that they have with each other. Transformed by his sacrifice, Christ has himself become the true way which the believer follows when he in turn allows himself to be transformed.

But before dealing with this revealing text, we must first look back at the paragraph which we have just studied. In three successive stages, the author has directed his attention to the worship as it was practiced "according to the Law." He has defined the level of this worship (8:3-5), he has examined the covenant which corresponded to it (8:7-13), and he has described its Holy Place and its rites (9:1-10). On each occasion he has made a critical judgment: the level of the Old Testament worship was earthly and figurative; its covenant, imperfect and provisional; the Holy Place, inauthentic; and its rites, inefficacious. But it must be noted that on each occasion too his judgment is based on the Old Testament itself: an oracle received by Moses (8:5), a prophecy of Jeremiah (8:8-12), the inspired witness of the ritual (9:8). We learn from this that the author does not take an entirely negative position with respect to the Old Testament. He acknowledges, on the contrary, a permanent revelation value in it, and it is precisely here that he looks for light. It is this faith-guided procedure itself which leads him to observe that the Old Testament, as revelation, announces the end of the Old Testament, as institution. This was also Paul's position.[14] True fidelity to the Old Testament leads one, therefore, to pass beyond it to welcome its fulfillment in Christ. Such is the movement of the thought. The objective is not to criticize but to arrive at definitive values. The introduction was already aware of this when it established a positive direction for the whole section. This orientation was never lost sight of[15] and one recognizes it in the last words of this paragraph, which open up the prospect of a "time of renewal."

3. The Sacrificial Act of Christ (Heb 9:11-28)

It is with Christ that the situation is put right. His name is also the first word of the positive section (9:11-28) and it recurs four times. It defines the structure of the paragraph, marking the limits of the first subdivision (9:11-14) and those of the third (9:24-28). We have already noted above that the first subdivision forms an antithesis with the one that precedes it, the last of the preceding section. It is made up of two long sentences, which are constructed with particular care. Another high priest, another tent, other blood, another entrance: such are the components of the first sentence (9:11-12). They take up again, in contradistinction, the elements of verses 7-8. The second sentence (9:13-14) has a more complex construction, for it begins with some supplementary allusions to Old Testament cult and takes the form of an argument *a fortiori*. However, when it comes to speak of Christ (9:14) it adopts the same antithetical perspective as the preceding sentence, this time applying it to the data of verses 9-10: in the case of Christ, it is a question of another offering, which was not a "carnal rite," but an act accomplished under the impulsion of the "eternal Spirit," and one which, because it is effective on the level of "conscience," opens the way to an authentic "cult."[16] Because of this correspondence, we again find here two successive ways of describing the sacrificial action, the first by means of a terminology of space and movement (9:11-12), the second by means of the terminology of offering and of personal transformation (9:14). The distinction between them, however, is not complete: the two sentences have in common the mention of blood, which leads us to understand that the movement affirmed in the first sentence has been possible only because of the sacrificial transformation described in the second. A correspondence between "more perfect" (9:11) and "to make perfect" (9:9) directs the thought in the same direction: whereas the Old Testament sacrifices had appeared to be "incapable of making perfect" (9:9), Christ had at his disposal a "more perfect" tent (9:11). Is this not an allusion to a successful sacrificial transformation? To answer this question, we must now examine the sentence as a whole more closely.

a) *The sacrificial process and the more perfect tent*
The best way to approach the interpretation is undoubtedly to begin by providing a really faithful translation of the text, one that respects its literary disposition:

> But Christ, having appeared as high priest of the good things
> to come,
>   by the greater and more perfect tent,
>   not made with hands, that is to say, not of this creation,
>   and not by the blood of goats and calves,
>   but by his own blood
>   entered once and for all into the Holy Place,
>   having found an eternal redemption. (Heb 9:11-12)

This sentence presents a concentric structure. At the beginning the person who is intervening is named, "Christ," and at the end, the action that he has carried out, "entered into the Holy Place." A title qualifies Christ: "high priest . . ."; the participle "having found" explains the result of the action achieved, "eternal redemption." With regard to the exact wording of the title, the textual tradition is uncertain: some manuscripts say "high priest of the good things to come," and others "high priest of the good things that have come." Since in any case the complement of the final participle determines the meaning of the phrase, the author intended to refer to "eternal redemption" whether he wrote "to come" or "that have come." One may apply either qualification to "eternal redemption," according to one's point of view. Because Christ has found it, redemption "has come," but because it is also eternal, it belongs to the world "to come."

The central part of the clause is reserved for two additional elements, the "tent" and the "blood," both introduced by the preposition *dia* ("by") repeated three times. The author insists on these elements. He describes the "tent," first positively and then negatively, and then the "blood," first negatively and then positively. This arrangement establishes the closest possible literary connection between the tent and the blood. As to the "sanctuary," it is only named, without being either described or qualified. (It is in the third subdivision [9:24] that the author will give some clarifications in its regard.) Here his attention is concentrated not so much on the end to be achieved as on the way to be followed and the means employed: the tent and the blood. The blood comes second. (It will be examined more closely in the following sentence.) Placed first and described at greater length, the tent attracts more attention. It is not possible to regard it as a secondary element in this sentence.

For the author it is a question of a well defined reality, which he supposes is known to his listeners. He has already described it in 8:2

as "the true tent, which the Lord set up, not a man." Here he says, again with the article: "the greater and more perfect tent, not made by human hand . . .," and his phrasing shows that this tent is, together with the blood of Christ, the means employed to enter into the sanctuary. The meaning of the phrase must have been clear to the Christians of the first century, but it is no longer so for twentieth century exegetes, who offer various interpretations.[17] All, of course, recognize that the author speaks here in an imaginative style, inspired by the Israelite liturgy which he has just described. In 9:8 he has ruled out the possibility that the "first tent" might be "the way to the sanctuary." Now he declares that Christ has made use of another "tent" and that this one is the right way, for by means of it Christ has truly "entered in to the sanctuary." But what is the reality to which the metaphor refers?

It is here that the opinions diverge. Some exegetes think that our author is simply transfering the image of the earthly temple to heaven, and imagining a celestial temple divided into two parts, the first of which would correspond to the "Holy Place" and would be called here "the greater and more perfect tent."[18] This interpretation, which is in material harmony with the letter of the text, is extremely poor in doctrinal content and throws little light on the insistence of the author on the role of the tent, and even less on the parallelism that he establishes between the tent and the blood.

The same difficulty also counts against the cosmological interpretation proposed by some other commentators.[19] According to them, the tent represents the lower heavens which Christ had to pass through in order to reach the divine heaven. That Christ has "passed through the heavens" is explicitly stated in the Epistle.[20] But the question is to know if the author in this phrase had this imagery in view. A qualification he gives suggests the opposite. He states that "the greater tent" is "not of this creation": now, in two other texts, he says that the heavens are part of this creation and that they will perish with it.[21] Therefore the "tent" cannot be identified here with the heavens.

To avoid this objection, Michel and, after him, Andriessen[22] make use of a more subtle distinction: between the cosmic heaven, which belongs to this creation, and the divine heaven, where God dwells, there would be an intermediate heaven, neither cosmic nor divine, and it is this heaven which our author would be referring to as "the tent . . . which is not of this creation." Andriessen specifies that it is the heaven of the angels that is in question, and he looks for support for this distinction in certain traditional Jewish texts. The "most profound meaning" of Hebrews 9:11 would then be that "Christ, in passing through the heaven of the angels, has made of it an area of life and worship for all the children of God."[23] The proposed distinction of an angelic heaven that is neither cosmic nor divine is not clearly supported in any passage of the Epistle, nor does it appear anywhere in the New Testament. To have recourse at this point to Jewish traditions is contra-indicated, because the author has just said that "the road to the sanctuary *had not yet been made known*" in the Old Covenant. Jewish beliefs then are not the place to go to find light on this subject. Rather, we must inquire of the specifically Christian tradition. This tradition does not give any soteriological importance to the heaven of the angels, and our author less than any other, for he began his Epistle by attacking opinions that were too favorable to the angels.[24]

The close parallelism that the author established in this sentence between "the tent" and "the blood" points us toward another interpretation, which has, precisely, the advantage of being deeply rooted in the primitive catechesis. Because the blood is "the very blood" of Christ (9:12), is there not reason to think that the tent also has a special relationship with Christ, and why not a relationship of the same order? To specify this relationship, it must be remembered that the author is in the process of evoking the theme of the Temple in a context of destruction and of rebuilding.[25] This theme, which the Chronicler makes the central theme of sacred history, is carried forward in a new and most significant manner in the Gospel catechesis. There it is directly connected with the mystery of the Passion and Resurrection of Jesus, not only in the Gospel of John but also in the Synoptics.[26] Jesus predicted the destruction of the Temple of Jerusalem[27] and also announced that in three days he would raise up the sanctuary again; the Gospel tradition connects this prophecy with the Resurrection. This tradition predates the composition of the Gospels and there is therefore no anachronism in supposing that this part of the tradition was known to our author and his listeners.

A general acquaintance with the Gospel catechesis is explicitly attested in several places in the Epistle[28] and one of the definite affirmations of this catechesis, very close to the present theme, plays a fundamental role in the theology of our author. I am speaking of Christ's sitting at the right hand of God, solemnly foretold in both Mark and

Matthew immediately after the recalling of the theme of the Temple,[29] with which it has a strong biblical link: he who was to sit on the right hand of the Power is indeed the Messiah, Son of David and Son of God, whose task is to consist in building the Temple of God.[30] In the Epistle, the assertion about sitting at the right hand is recalled five times[31] and, in particular, at the beginning of the present section (8:1). The connection of the text on the tent with the Gospel tradition on the sanctuary becomes all the more probable. It becomes morally certain when we note that a qualification given to the "more perfect tent" exactly corresponds to the one that is given in Mark 14:58 to the temple that Jesus is to construct in three days: they are both said to be "not made by human hand."[32] It is true that the Gospel affirmation is contained within the context of a deposition of false testimony, but its tenor shows that the evangelist does not see falsehood in this part of the sentence, and a comparison with John 2:19 confirms that Jesus truly pronounced a prediction of this kind.

Read in this light, the sentence of Hebrews 9:11 takes on its full meaning. "The greater and more perfect tent" is the temple constructed in three days, "not made by human hand," but a divine work realized in the Passion and Resurrection of Jesus. We no longer need to be surprised at the importance attributed by the author, in the sacrificial act of Christ, to this new tent, nor at the position he gives it at the very center of this section (8:1 - 9:28), which is itself central in the section 5:11 - 10:39 and in the Epistle taken as a whole. The parallelism with the blood is easily explained, since the more perfect tent is none other than the glorified body of Christ, the new creation realized in three days thanks to the shedding of Christ's blood.

It may be objected that none of the terms used in this sentence make us think of the Resurrection of Christ, but it must be noted that the penultimate word of the preceding phrase, "rebuilding," suggests this aspect of the mystery; in addition, the author will later suggest a connection between the "redemption" and the "resurrection" (cf. 11:35), and finally he will conclude his discourse by closely connecting the Resurrection of Christ and the Blood of the Covenant: it is "in blood of an eternal covenant" that "the God of peace . . . has caused our Lord Jesus Christ . . . to rise from the dead" (13:20). In an analogous way, Hebrews 9:11-12 describes a close connection between the body of the risen Christ and the blood of his sacrifice.

Another possible objection comes from the spatial meaning instinctively given to the preposition *dia*. Is it not illogical to say that Christ passed through his own glorified body in order to enter into the sanctuary? But to stop short at this objection is to misunderstand the style of expression used: the author is using metaphorical language and he is playing with the flexibility of the terms that he employs. On the level of metaphor it is clear that *dia* is to be understood in a spatial sense; but nothing obliges us to stick rigidly to this meaning on the level of the reality that he is trying to convey. At this level, the author is taking *dia* in its instrumental sense: it is *by means of* his glorified body that Christ has gone to be with God. The parallelism with the blood makes this interpretation perfectly natural, since the same preposition *dia*, also used for the blood, clearly has the instrumental sense.

Nothing, therefore, prevents us from recognizing in Hebrews 9:11 an allusion to the Gospel tradition about the sanctuary constructed by Christ. On the contrary, everything invites us to adopt this interpretation. Having said this, it is advisable to note that our author is not satisfied with merely drawing on the tradition. He goes to the trouble of deepening it by introducing a distinction which advances the doctrinal reflection. The Gospels speak of the entire edifice of the temple; they use the word *naos*, which describes the building without distinguishing its different parts. Our author, however, distinguishes the "tent" (*skene*) and the "sanctuary" (*ta hagia*) and he thus focuses on the problem that was posed concerning the relationship of mankind to God. It was not a matter of building a "sanctuary," a dwelling for God, for such a sanctuary has always existed: it is God's own holiness which constitutes the only true sanctuary. To describe its transcendence, human language places it in heaven. The problem for human beings was rather to find a means of making contact with the holiness of God, or, to use a metaphor, to construct a vestibule which would introduce them to the divine sanctuary, in other words, a "tent." Obviously the tent would have to be proportioned to the divine sanctuary and fully suited to it, in order that by its means humanity would truly be able to enter into the intimacy of God. This was a problem that the Old Testament could not solve!

Of course, a "first tent" had been set up, but it was a human construction, a tent "made by human hands," which as we have already seen, could not lead into the true sanctuary "not made by human hands," but only into a second tent. Incapable of producing anything else, human beings had reached a dead end. They could not transport themselves into communion with God. The only solution was for God to give them the means, by replacing the "first tent" by another, that would be a divine creation and not a human construction (8:2). This is precisely what was accomplished in the Passion and Resurrection of Jesus, according to the testimony of the Gospels. There was a mysterious identification between the mortal body of Jesus and the Temple of Jerusalem. In condemning Jesus to death, the Jews condemned their Temple to destruction.[33] But Jesus, by transforming his own death into a perfect sacrifice, overcame the aspect of destruction that the event involved and made it result in the divine construction of a new temple "not made by human hands."

There is something greater and better here than a metaphor to describe the Resurrection of Jesus; it is a revelation of the nature and the scope of this Resurrection. This now appears not simply as the return to life of a man who had died, but as a transformation that radically changes the existential situation of all mankind and one which opens new possibilities for them. The Resurrection is to be seen as a complete renewal of the human being in Christ, a renewal so profound that one must speak of a "new creation" and of a "new man."[34] Its result is, more than anything else, to make humanity capable of perfect communion with God. Renewed human nature becomes a "tent" which leads into the "sanctuary," a "new and living way," which allows access to God. The first person to "inaugurate this new and living way" was Jesus himself. This is what our text affirms here, and again in 10:20.

Because it was "not made by human hands," the new tent is truly proportioned and adapted to the authentic sanctuary "not made by human hands" (9:24). This was not the case, before the Resurrection, for the nature of flesh and blood such as it had been assumed by the Son of God (2:14). "Flesh and blood cannot inherit the Kingdom of God" (1 Cor 15:50). A transformation was needed, a *teleiosis*. This was obtained thanks to the complete docility of Christ, in prayer and suffering (Heb 5:7-9). As a result of this *teleiosis*, the tent deserves the description "more perfect" (*teleioteras*, 9:11) and Christ that of "rendered perfect" (*teleiotheis*, 5:9).

The author adds the qualification "greater." In this way he describes another aspect of the mystery, that which concerns the relationship of the glorified Christ with humanity. The new tent, in fact, is not open only on the side of the divine sanctuary, but also on the people's side. Its capacity to welcome them is no longer subject to the narrow limitations which controlled entry into the Old Testament tent, to which only the priests and the high priest had access. All the faithful are now invited to go in.[35] By his Passion and his Resurrection Christ has acquired the capacity to reunite into one unique organism, which is his glorified body, all persons who are faithful to him. All become "participators of Christ" and form "his house."[36] He introduces them into the intimacy of God.[37] This is why one can and must affirm that he "has found an eternal redemption."

Understood in this way, the theme of the "tent" conceals inexhaustible doctrinal riches, and the place chosen by the author to speak of them is fully justified. At the center of the letter, the glorified humanity of Christ is given the role which belongs to it in the accomplishment of the redemptive sacrifice.

b) *The personal offering of Christ*
Immediately after the "tent," the author names the "blood" as another means that allows entry into the sanctuary. The following phrase accounts for the effectiveness of this means when it says that it is a question of the blood

of Christ, who through the Eternal Spirit offered himself spotless to God. (Heb 9:14)

It would be difficult to describe more fully and in so few words the specific traits of the offering of Christ and its marvelous novelty.

The first novelty is the personal character of the offering. Christ did not imitate the Jewish high priests, who offered external "gifts and sacrifices" and shed "the blood of goats and calves," but "he offered himself" and made use of "his own blood." This daring assertion is not made without preparation. Indeed, it relies on the earlier description of the Passion of Christ (5:7-8), while clearly going beyond it. In 5:7 the author already stated that Christ had "offered," but he limited the content of the offering to "prayers and supplications." Nevertheless, his expression led us to understand that the whole human person of Christ had been involved in this suppliant offering, which was made in a spirit of profound respect for God (*eulabeia*), and that the result of it had been his submission through his suffering to the transforming action of God. The same events can therefore be presented as an offering of one's self to God.

This shorter and stronger expression has the advantage of bringing out more clearly the relationships of resemblance and of difference which exist between the sacrificial activity of the Jewish high priests and that of Jesus. On one side as on the other, there is sacrifice and bloody sacrifice, but in the case of Christ it is a matter of a personal, existential sacrifice and not a ritual sacrifice. Christ "has offered himself": in this affirmation, the author combines two elements of the catechesis of the New Testament, on the one hand the presentation of Christ as a sacrificial victim,[38] and on the other the aspect of voluntary commitment which characterizes the Passion of Jesus. This aspect is revealed by words and by acts, in particular by the institution of the Eucharist and the attitude of Jesus at Gethsemani.[39] The substance of the affirmation is therefore not new, but the expression "to offer oneself" is our author's creation.[40] To speak of the gift of himself that Jesus made, neither the Gospels nor Paul use the ritual verbs *prospherein* or *anapherein*. They used the verbs "to give" or "to lay down" or "to deliver."[41] As for the Old Testament ritual, in which the verb "to offer" occurs very frequently, the expression "to offer oneself" is never found, for in that context it would have suggested a ritual suicide, an idea completely outside of the perspective of Israelite worship. In the Epistle to the Hebrews, such an interpretation is not possible, since the readers know only too well the circumstances in which the voluntary offering of Christ took place. It is obvious that Christ did not kill himself: he was condemned and executed. For him, the event of Calvary contained first of all an element of passivity; the word "passion" indicates this clearly enough, as does the verb "to suffer" and the passive verbs "to be abased," "to be tested," "to be made perfect."[42] Passivity, however, paradoxically enough became the occasion of the most effective activity possible: by the way in which he bore suffering and death, Christ was extremely active in his Passion and carried out a work of positive transformation which surpasses the first creation in value. This work is a "sacrifice" in the full sense of the word, that is to say, a transformation through establishing a relationship with God. We have already said that to sacrifice means "to make sacred," "to permeate with the sanctity of God."

Christ sacrificed himself. He was at one and the same time active and passive, the one who is offered and the one who offers, victim and priest. The Old Testament ritual never dreamed of this possibility; it demanded that the distinction be maintained. The priests of Israel were not worthy to offer themselves, for they were sinners and had to present sacrifices for their own sins. Nor were they capable of a perfect personal sacrifice; their generosity did not reach this level. Christ, on the contrary, was a "victim" worthy of God, for he was "spotless" (*amomos*: Heb 9:14). The Epistle to the Hebrews, like the First Epistle of Peter, borrows this adjective from the Pentateuch, where it describes the requirement governing the choice of the victims to be immolated.[43] Since in this case one would be dealing with animals, *amomos* was understood to mean the absence of all physical defect. In the case of Christ, the meaning is clearly more profound. It extends to the absence of all sin and of all complicity with evil.[44] Being "spotless" Jesus had no need to look beyond himself for a sacrificial victim, nor to make use of the blood of goats and calves. He was able to present himself in his own person with the certainty of being accepted.

But it is not enough to have a victim worthy to be offered to God, the passive aspect of sacrifice. There must also be a priest capable of making the offering, that is to say, of raising the victim up to God, the active aspect of sacrifice. Christ was this competent priest, because he had "the eternal Spirit" in him,[45] which, if we could put it this way, gave him the necessary upward strength to raise himself up to God. Here again the author uses the preposition *dia* ("through") as in 9:11-12, for he wishes to indicate the efficient cause of the sacrifice. In our text, the eternal Spirit takes the place of "the fire from heaven" or "the fire of the Lord" in Old Testament sacrifices.[46] According to the Old Testament understanding, this fire was indispensable for the accomplishment of the sacrifices. It had come down on the altar at the time of the inauguration of the priesthood and the dedication of the Temple, and had been maintained there continuously.[47] The conviction indeed prevailed that only fire from heaven could raise the victims to heaven where God dwelt. Beneath this symbolism there was a profound intuition: a true "sacrifice" is an accomplishment that surpasses human powers, it requires God's intervention, for it involves transforming a creature by imparting to it the divine holiness.

This intuition takes on its full meaning in the sacrifice of Christ, effected "thanks to an intervention of the eternal Spirit." In fact, the true fire of God is obviously neither the lightning that flashes from the clouds nor any similar material phenomenon, rather, it is the Holy Spirit, who alone is capable of bringing about sacrificial transformation. The way in which his action was inserted into the Passion of Christ has been described in Hebrews 5:7-8. The dramatic circumstances were confronted in prayer. Supported and guided by the Spirit, prayer opened the human condition of Jesus to the action of God who, through the Spirit, gave him the victory through painful obedience. According to the context of Hebrews 5:7-8 and other related passages, the power of the Spirit was shown in two closely connected ways: by inspiring a perfect conformity to the will of God[48] and by maintaining his fraternal solidarity with humanity even to the point of death.[49] We find here, in an original formulation, the two dimensions of evangelical charity, love of God and love of humanity, and we can conclude that Christ was a competent priest because he was filled with the power of the Holy Spirit, the power of a love without the least shadow of egoism. It was because he was burning with love that Christ transformed himself into a sacrifice pleasing to God.

Unlike Old Testament sacrifices, that of Christ was not external to himself but personal. It was not a "carnal rite" (9:10), but a spiritual work. It does not follow that this sacrifice was less real than the sacrificial offerings of the Old Testament cult. Quite the contrary! Christ shed "his own blood" (9:12); he made an offering of his own death (9:15).

The union of the two loves is so dominant a characteristic of this offering that the author cannot keep himself from expressing it in each of his sentences. At this point in his exposition, it is the way of Christ to God that he has especially in mind. The question of the efficacy of the sacrifice on behalf of mankind should not be dealt with until later.[50] But it is impossible to maintain a rigid distinction between the two points of view. From the end of the first sentence (9:11-12), the efficacy of the sacrifice is affirmed: Christ has "found an eternal redemption." And the second sentence (9:13-14) is concerned with accounting for this efficacy and defining its scope: the spiritual dimension of the offering of Christ insures that his blood will have the power to act in mankind at the deepest level, by purifying the conscience and so establishing authentic communication with God. It is not possible to distinguish two successive times, the first being that of the personal glorification of Jesus and the second that of his intervention in our favor, for the glorification of Jesus is indissolubly linked with his intervention on our behalf. It results from his Passion, an act that unites him with us,[51] and it consists for him in becoming our high priest, mediator of the new covenant.

c) *The blood of the Covenant*
In fact, after having affirmed the efficacy of Christ's sacrifice by saying that

> the blood of Christ who, through the eternal Spirit, offered himself spotless to God, will purify our conscience of dead works in view of the worship of the living God, (Heb 9:14)

the author connects it at once with the theme of the covenant and declares:

> That is why he is the mediator of a new covenant. (Heb 9:15)

In speaking of a "new covenant," he is clearly referring to the prophecy of Jeremiah which he has cited in 8:8-12, in the introductory paragraph. He is proclaiming its fulfillment. In his manner of treating this theme, the author faithfully follows Jeremiah on one point and complements him in an original way on other points, proving once again his powerful capacity for synthesis.

The prophecy of Jeremiah had already effected a first synthesis by merging two kinds of relationships between God and men: pardon for sin and covenant. The story of the conclusion of the first covenant, which our author will recall later (9:19-21), made no mention either of faults to be expiated or pardon to be obtained. The covenant sacrifice here did not reveal any connection with a sacrifice "for sin." There is nothing surprising in this: since it was precisely a question of instituting a first covenant between the people and God, there was no reason to be concerned with making amends for possible violations of a non-existent former covenant. But after the conclusion of the Sinai Covenant and the gift of the Law, the question of transgressions continually arose and their expiation was seen to be indispensable for the restoration of good relationships between the people and God. The oracle of Jeremiah clearly describes this situation. It is because of the breaking of the Covenant of Sinai[52] that God again takes the initiative; the new covenant that he announces includes the promise of pardon for sins: "I will pardon their iniquities and I will not remember their sins any more."[53] Faithful to this point of view, which characterized the spirituality of the Jews after the Exile,[54] our author ties expiation and covenant closely together. His statement about the covenant is tied to the preceding affirmation about the purification of consciences through a "that is why . . ." (*dia touto*), which is very significant: it is precisely because his blood "will purify consciences from dead works" that Christ "is mediator of a new covenant." The same connection is stated a second time immediately afterwards, when the author specifies that

A death has intervened for the redemption of the transgressions of the first covenant. (Heb 9:15)

Later, he directly connects the sacrifice that founds the Covenant of Sinai (9:19-21) with the principles which regulate purification and remission (9:22-23). In this he shows a realistic view of mankind's situation before God. It is an illusion to imagine that men can enter into the divine covenant on an equal footing like honorable partners. A work of restoration must first of all be accomplished for them and in them. The covenant is a gift of redeeming love. The prophets were profoundly aware of this. The author of the Epistle receives and transmits their message.

But he is not satisfied with citing their texts. He goes further than they do. In foretelling the new covenant, Jeremiah did not think of specifying how it would be established. Our author shows himself attentive to this aspect of the question which is, in fact, decisive. There cannot be a truly new covenant without a new foundation. The men of Qumran had the desire to enter into the new covenant, but not having informed themselves about the foundation that it must have, they tended to strive for a mere restoration of the old covenant through greater fidelity to the Law of Moses. The author of the Epistle does not remain at this unsatisfactory stage. He observes that, according to the Old Testament, a covenant between God and mankind is based on a bloody sacrifice.[55] He observes that the event of Calvary has fulfilled this requirement. The new covenant, therefore, has its proper foundation, which is seen to be different from, and clearly superior to, that of the first covenant. This is the real basis for its stability. It cannot be thought of as simply a prolongation of the

Covenant of Sinai nor even as its perfect restoration. It belongs to another order.

Because it sets the blood of Christ in relationship to the covenant sacrifice, our text adopts a point of view which is that of the account of the Last Supper, where Jesus offers his blood as the blood of the covenant. We have every reason to believe that the author was, in fact, inspired by this Gospel event. Indeed, outside the Epistle, the words "blood" and "covenant" are to be found together in the New Testament only in the formula of the institution of the Eucharist.[56] Several details reinforce the connection here. In Hebrews 9:20, when the author recalls the foundation of the Covenant of Sinai, he appears to be influenced by the words of the Last Supper, for instead of saying with Exodus 24:8, "Behold (*idou*) the blood of the covenant . . .", he begins the sentence with "This is" (*touto*) which is invariably found at the beginning of the formulas of the Institution. Subsequently he will twice speak of the blood of Christ as "the blood of the covenant."[57] Moreover, the union of the aspects of covenant and remission of sin, which we have just noted in Hebrews 9:15-23, constitutes a point in common with the formulation in the Gospel of Matthew: "This is my blood of the *covenant*, shed for many for the *remission* of sins" (Mt 26:28). Better still, all the words of this sentence of Matthew are found again in our text.[58] The author, however, refrains from making an explicit reference to the Sacrament. He is interested in the event itself, from which the Sacrament draws its value.

This event is, in actuality, a death. Our author does not fail to say so.[59] His reflections are directed to this point and, for that reason, they surpass the perspectives of ritual worship to include the harsh reality of existence. To declare, as he does, that "a death has intervened for the redemption from transgressions," is to speak no longer in ritual language—the ritual never speaks of the death of the victims offered in sacrifice, but simply defines the rites of the ceremony of offering—but rather to use the categories of penal law. The way in which the author, a little later (9:22), describes the necessity for the shedding of blood in order to obtain forgiveness also tends to suggest the case of criminals and not only ritual practices.[60]

Moreover, the word employed in the Greek Bible to describe the covenant, *diatheke*, gives him the opportunity to recall still another actual situation and to present another dimension of the death of Christ: its connection with an inheritance to be made available to all.

Diatheke, the general meaning of which is "disposition," had in fact taken on in the language of the period the technical sense of "testament." Far from feeling bound to adopt one sense to the exclusion of the other, our author exploits them both simultaneously when he writes:

> And that is why he is the mediator of a new covenant-testament, so that, [his] death having intervened for the redemption of transgressions committed under the first covenant-testament, those who have been called may have access to the promised eternal inheritance. For where there is a testament, it is necessary for the death of the testator to be registered. For a testament becomes valid only in the case of decease; it remains without effect while the testator is alive. (Heb 9:15-17)

The implicit principle that underlies the thought is that a word applied in the Bible to a divine institution cannot have, in this instance, a weaker sense than when it applies to a human institution. The divine covenant, called *diatheke*, must therefore have possessed all the value of a testament or will, and it was necessary that like a testament it should be founded on the only irreversible event, death.

The author sees a confirmation of this necessity in the manner in which the first covenant had been set up: blood had been employed, "the blood of calves and goats," offered in sacrifice.

> Hence it happens that even the first covenant was not inaugurated without the use of blood. When Moses had promulgated for all the people each commandment in conformity with the Law, he took the blood of calves and goats together with water, scarlet wool and hyssop, and with it sprinkled both the book itself and all the people, saying:
> "This is the blood of the covenant-testament which God has ordained for you,"
> and he likewise sprinkled with the blood both the tent and all the vessels used for worship. (Heb 9:19-21)

All this was a prefiguration of the event which was to be the basis of the definitive covenant-testament, the one which was to have an eternal value (13:20), for it would open the way to "the eternal inheritance." Logically, this event had to be a death.

But the author also joins another aspect to the testamentary one; he observes that the shedding of blood was equally necessary for purification:

> And it is with blood that, according to the Law, almost everything is purified, and without the shedding of blood there is no forgiveness. (Heb 9:22)

This shows to what a depth this purification would one day have to penetrate. Because he was a sinner, man needed a complete remodeling of his being, which could only come about through death. It was also necessary for this death to take on a positive meaning and serve to establish a new relationship between mankind and God, as well as a new solidarity among men. It was precisely this which was accomplished in the death of Christ, who was transformed into a self-oblation to God for the salvation of mankind.

In these lines on the covenant, we see that our author presents the death of Christ under a double and even a triple light: simultaneously as expiatory suffering, as covenant sacrifice and as condition for validating a testamant. Certain biblical texts in a remote way prepared for this astonishing coalescence for, as we have seen, they combined covenant and expiation on the one hand, and on the other they connected the promise of the "inheritance" with the covenant.[61] But these were no more than tentative gropings. In the Epistle, the synthesis is stated with full confidence, because Christ has effectively realized it. His generous death has abolished the obstacle of sin, which prevented the existence of a genuine covenant. As an act of total obedience to God and of complete identification with mankind, it introduces humanity into definitive communion with God. At the same time, it fully reveals the scope of the covenant and its testamentary character, which until then had scarcely been glimpsed: the purpose of covenant is permanent communion with God, and this is an eternal inheritance, the possession of which had, of necessity, to be founded upon death, for it could only be reached beyond death.

The entrance into the eternal inheritance clearly required a sacrificial offering of a greater value than those which earthly cult had at its disposal. This is what the author says in conclusion:

> It was necessary therefore, if the figures of the heavenly things are purified by these rites, that the heavenly realities themselves be purified by means of more effective sacrifices than those. (Heb 9:23)

This sentence, which announces the topic of the last subdivision

(9:24-28), seems rather strange, for it states the need for a purification of the heavenly realities. Some exegetes imagine here a ceremony of expiation that would take place in heaven itself. In reality, the parallelism indicated by the author between the heavenly realities of the new covenant and their "figures" (*hypodeigmata*) in the old covenant suggests a more satisfactory interpretation. According to the preceding context (9:19-21), the "figures" purified with the blood of animals were "the book and all the people," as well as "the tent and all the vessels used for worship." To determine exactly what are the realities which have had to be purified by the blood of Christ, we need only look for those which, in the new covenant, correspond to these Old Testament "figures." The answer is simple: it concerns the Christian Gospel and the Church, the "more perfect tent" and the Christian sacraments. These new realities are "heavenly," not in the sense that they have always existed in Heaven, but in the sense that they are defined by their relationship with Heaven and that they find their perfect fulfillment in Heaven.

The basic example is that of the "more perfect tent," the heavenly reality *par excellence* since it stands in direct relationship to the heavenly presence of God. We have seen that this tent is none other than the glorified body of Christ, and we can therefore easily understand that the author is able to affirm the necessity of sacrifice for this heavenly reality. The body of Jesus, which to begin with was a body of flesh and blood in solidarity with sinful humanity,[62] needed a sacrificial transformation to be raised up to the right hand of God and be able to fulfill its heavenly role.

Between the "more perfect tent" and the body of believers, another reality which must be considered, there is a close connection verging on identification (Heb 3:6). The believers, however, are not heavenly beings in the ordinary sense of the expression. They live on the earth. But they "have a share in a heavenly vocation" (3:1) and already taste "the heavenly gift" (6:4). The People of God to which they belong is a heavenly reality which needed to be purified by a more than ritual sacrifice in order to achieve its full growth: "Jesus suffered outside the gate in order to sanctify the people with his own blood."[63]

Still another point: the sacrifice of the old covenant had brought together the people and the book; the latter contained materially "all the laws of the Lord" (Ex 24:4). The new covenant brings a revelation that is both more transcendent and more intimate, a word which comes from Heaven and which is inscribed in people's hearts, the Word of Christ.[64] But this word also required sacrificial purification if it was to take on all its heavenly power. It is the glorifying Passion of Jesus which has given to his words—and to the whole of Scripture— their definitive meaning and their power to save. Henceforth, the voice which comes from Heaven is that of the blood of Jesus, "the sprinkled blood which speaks louder than that of Abel" (12:24).

In addition to the preaching of the Gospel, the new covenant includes, for the believers, other means of union with Christ, to which the term sacrament has subsequently been given. They too merit the qualification "heavenly," but each is subject to the condition stated in Hebrews 9:23: each of them draws its value from the sacrificial offering of Christ.

Interpreted in this way, the author's affirmation becomes perfectly coherent. There is no need to weaken the terms, as is done by the exegetes who think they have to apply them to Heaven itself.[65] On the contrary, it can be given its full meaning, for it is only an extension, through a comparison with Old Testament worship, of the principle revealed in the Gospels: "Was it not necessary for Christ to suffer in this way and so to enter into his glory?" (Lk 24:26).

d) *The most real level*

Having reached this point, the author concludes this "capital" section of his exposition by calling attention to the level reached by Christ in his act of offering. This level is the most real one possible. While Old Testament worship had not gone beyond a stage of unsubstantial imagery (8:5), Christ followed a path which establishes an effective relationship between mankind and God:

It is not, in fact, into a sanctuary made by human hands, a mere copy of the true one, that Christ has entered, but into Heaven itself, in order to appear now on our behalf before the face of God. (Heb 9:24)

In this way fulfillment is at last given to the deepest aspirations of the seekers after God, which is described in the Bible and elsewhere: "My soul is thirsting for God, the God of life: when shall I go and appear before the face of God?" (Ps 42:3). Christ reveals himself here as truly priest, for the role of the priest is to open up this possibility of an authentic encounter with God by becoming man of the sanctuary, who "stands in the presence of God" (Dt 18:5).

To indicate still better the reality that we must recognize in the sacrificial act of Christ, the author underlines its decisive and definitive aspect. Because Christ has reached his objective, he does not need to repeat the process, as was the case until then with the high priests, who each year renewed their attempt (9:25). His offering is not set in some cyclical system, where the same processes recur periodically (9:26a) and where transformations are more illusory that real: "What was, will be; what has been done, will recur; and there is nothing new under the sun" (Eccl 1:9). On the contrary, it is presented as a unique and irreversible event, which frees mankind from the perpetual return of things. With it come "the end of time" and "the abolition of sin" (9:26b). It is therefore an eschatological event, which introduces a radical change into human existence. It has a close connection with men's death, a unique and irreversible event for each of them (9:27), but—and here is an essential difference—it opens to mankind the prospect of salvation (9:28).

Having reached the end of this particularly important section (8:1 - 9:28), we are in a position to see more clearly what the author has set out to do. The point which he wished to develop was the sacrificial value of what we call the Passover of Christ, by which is meant the two aspects of the event, passion and glorification, for they form an indissoluble unity. A comparison with the Old Testament liturgy leads to a twofold conclusion. On the one hand, it must be recognized that the passion and glorification of Christ have constituted an authentic sacrifice, for they have corresponded exactly to what the ancient sacrifices endeavored to achieve: an offering made by mankind to God to overcome the obstacle of sin, to render to God a worship worthy of him, and to establish a covenant which opens up for the whole people the possibility of joyous entry into communion with God. It must also be recognized, on the other hand, that the passion and glorification of Christ have so clearly surpassed the Old Testament sacrifices in their own fundamental objective that these can no longer be regarded as valid sacrifices. Whether it is a question of the consecration of the priest, the atonement for sins, the establishment of a covenant or of access to the good things promised by God, the Old Testament sacrifices are revealed as ineffective attempts, empty forms, mere prefigurations of the true sacrifice.

What is special about the priestly action of Christ is, in fact, the fullness of its reality. Christ has surpassed the stage of external rites that cannot purify consciences (9:1-10), and has offered himself in the impulse given by the Spirit; he has poured out his own blood and so has won the sacrificial transformation of his humanity, which has become the "more perfect tent," fit for the true sanctuary (9:11-14). In the same action, by surpassing the level of the first covenant, which was both imperfect and provisional precisely because of the impotence of its rites (8:7-13), Christ, thanks to the irreversible efficacy of his death, has become the mediator of a covenant-testament which is totally and eternally valid (9:15-23). Finally, by surpassing the level of the earthly worship which was no more than that of figure (8:3-5), Christ has truly established perfect and definitive communication between mankind and God (9:24-28). It is in this way that he has become the perfect high priest.

In this closely argued and very rich doctrinal exposition, the author shows us all the dimensions of Christian "fulfillment." It is not simply a question of the realization of prophetic sayings, but also of the replacement of ancient institutions by a new reality which fulfills their functions better than they. The author acknowledges an important value in the institutions of the Old Testament, that of revealing in a concrete way the requirements of the situation and of trying to respond to them. The institution of the priesthood revealed by its repeated actions the need that men felt, in order to respond fully to their vocation, to find the right relationship with God. But this institution was powerless to satisfy the aspiration which it expressed. It was unable truly to fill with reality either the actions performed or, in consequence, the formulas used. "To offer to God," "to purify," "to make perfect," to establish a "covenant-testament," "to enter into the sanctuary," "to appear before God": so many words which, like oversized garments, float pitifully around a body for which they were not made. The intervention of Christ, on the contrary—that is to say, the manner in which, through his passion, he established himself in a new relationship with God and with mankind—all of this intervention has effectively achieved all that the Old Testament sacrifices aspired to do. It has, at the same time, filled the words with a substantial plenitude of content. This is why the action of Christ must be recognized as priestly and must be called a "sacrifice."

For this reason, one must be careful not to say that the author of the

Epistle is using "metaphors" when he applies the title of high priest to Christ and the name of "sacrifice" to his glorifying passion. His viewpoint is exactly the opposite: it is in the Old Testament that priesthood and sacrifice were taken in the metaphorical sense, as they are there applied to an impotent and symbolic figuration, while in the mystery of Christ these words have at last obtained their real meaning,[66] with an unsurpassable completeness.

Notes

[1]Lk 22:69 and Col 3:1, inspired by Ps 110:1.
[2]Heb 7:28; cf. 7:11, 18f.
[3]"Rudimentary figuration" is the correct translation of the *hendiadys hypodeigma kai skia*, literally "figuration and sketch."
[4]*Latreuein Theo* or *Kyrio*, and equivalent formulas: Ex 23:25; Dt 6:13; 10:12, 20; 11:13; etc. Prohibition to worship (*latreuein*) images: Ex 20:4f; Dt 4:15-19; 5:8f.
[5]Gal 4:3, 9f; Ac 7:47-50.
[6]*Ta hagia*, cf. 9:24.
[7]*He prote skene*, cf. 9:2, 8, 11.
[8]Cf. Ex 24:12; 31:18; 34:28; Dt 4:13, etc.
[9]In this connection one may recall the discussions that took place in 1973 between French and Egyptian bishops. In a declaration on the attitude of Christians toward Judaism, a French episcopal commission had written: "The first Covenant, in effect, has not been rendered obsolete by the new" (V.a). The bishops of Egypt then recalled the existence of the text of Heb 8:6, 13 and some other similar texts in the N.T. Cf. *Documentation catholique*, 1973, pp. 419-422, and 785-788.
[10]Ac 7:48; cf. 1 Kg 8:27.
[11]Cf. Heb 6:5; 9:11; 10:1.
[12]Sir 35:11; Is 1:23.
[13]*Teleioun tas cheiras*: Ex 29:9, 29, etc. Cf. above, Ch. VII 2 c.
[14]Cf. Rom 3:21; Gal 4:21-31.
[15]Cf. Heb 8:3b, 6, and 8:10-12.
[16]The antithesis is continual: between offering of gifts and sacrifices (9:9), and offering of oneself (9:14), between rites of flesh (9:10) and offering "by the Spirit" (9:14), between ineffectiveness at the level of the conscience (9:9) and purification of consciences (9:14).
[17]For more detail the reader is referred to my article: "Par la tente plus grande et plus parfaite . . . (Heb 9:11)," *Bib* 46 (1965), p. 128, completed in 1976 in a note of *La Structure littéraire* . . . , p. 267-268.
[18]W. Michaelis, "*skene*", *TWNT* 7, 1964, p. 378.

[19]C. Spicq, v. II p. 256, and many other authors.

[20]Cf. Heb 4:14; 7:26.

[21]Cf. Heb 1:10-12; 12:26f.

[22]O. Michel, *Der Brief an die Hebräer*, Gottingen, 1966, pp. 311-312; P. Andriessen, "Das grössere und vollkommende Zelt (Heb 9:11)," *BZ* 15 (1971) pp. 76-92.

[23]Andriessen, *op. cit.*, p. 91.

[24]Heb 1:5-13; 2:5, 16.

[25]Cf. *aphanismos*, "disappearance," in 8:13; and *diorthosis*, "renewal," in 9:10.

[26]Mk 14:58; 15:29, 38; Mt 26:61; 27:40, 51; Jn 2:19-22.

[27]Mt 24:1f. and par.

[28]Heb 2:3; 4:2; 5:12.

[29]Cf. Mk 14:58, 62; Mt 26:61, 64.

[30]Cf. 2 Sam 7:12-14; 1 Chr 17:11-14, etc.

[31]Heb 1:3, 13; 8:1; 10:12; 12:2.

[32]In Greek *acheiropoietos* (Mk 14:58), or *oucheiropoietos* (Heb 9:11), literally: "not made by hand."

[33]Cf. Mt 23:38; Lk 19:44; Mt 27:51 and par.; Jn 2:19.

[34]Cf. 2 Cor 5:17; Gal 6:15; Eph 2:15; 4:24; Col 3:10.

[35]Cf. Heb 5:9; 6:20; 10:19-22.

[36]Heb 3:6, 14.

[37]Cf. Heb 4:3, 16; 7:19, 25; 13:15.

[38]Cf. 1 Cor 5:17; 1 Pet 1:19.

[39]Cf. Mk 10:45; Jn 10:18; Mt 26:26-28 and par.; Mt 26:36-56 and par.; Jn 18:1-11.

[40]Heb 7:27; 9:14, 25.

[41]"To give": Mk 10:45; Mt 20:28; Gal 1:4; 1 Tim 2:6; Tit 2:14. "To lay down": Jn 10:15-18; 15:13. "To deliver": Gal 2:20; Eph 5:2, 25.

[42]"Passion": Heb 2:9, 10. "To suffer": 2:18; 5:8; 9:26; 13:12. "To be abased": 2:9. "To be tested": 2:18; 4:15. "To be made perfect": 5:9; 7:28.

[43]1 Pet 1:19; cf. Ex 29:1; Lev 1:3, 10, etc.

[44]Cf. Heb 4:15; 7:26. *Amomos* has a moral sense in Ps 15:2; 18:24, etc.

[45]This expression is unique in the Bible and its precise meaning is therefore difficult to determine. But it cannot be doubted that "the eternal Spirit" is the Spirit of God, the Holy Spirit. Why did the author say "eternal" rather than "holy"? No doubt in order to emphasize the relationship with "eternal redemption" (9:12) and "the eternal inheritance" (9:15) obtained through the Holy Spirit, and in order to express the relationship with the eternal priesthood (cf. 7:16-17). Is the absence of the article significant? It is not certain that it is, especially after a preposition (cf. M. Zerwick, *Graecitas Biblica*, Rome, 1960, no. 182); but if it is, the nuance is certainly not that we are dealing with *one* eternal spirit among others, but that what is involved is *a* communication of *the* eternal Spirit (cf. 2:4; 6:4); for the latter can only be one and the same.

[46]Cf. Lev 9:24; 1 Kg 18:38; 2 Chr 7:1; 2 Mac 2:10.

[47]Cf. Lev 6:5f; 2 Mac 1:18-22; 2:10.

[48]Cf. Heb 5:8; 10:4-10.

[49]Cf. Heb 2:14-18; 4:15.

[50]In the third and final section (10:1-18) of this central exposition (7:1 - 10:18).

[51]This aspect appears at the first mention of the glorifying passion of Jesus in 2:9 ("in

favor of all mankind") and comes back insistently in the following verses (2:10-18) as well as in 4:15 - 5:10.

⁵²Cf. Jer 31:32; Heb 8:9.

⁵³Jer 31:34; Heb 8:12.

⁵⁴Cf. Ezr 9:6-15; Neh 9:16f.; Bar 1:15 - 3:18; Dan 9:5-19.

⁵⁵Ex 24:3-8; Heb 9:18-21.

⁵⁶Mt 26:28; Mk 14:24; Lk 22:20; 1 Cor 11:25.

⁵⁷Heb 10:29; 13:20.

⁵⁸Here are the details of the contacts between Mt 26:28 and Heb 9:12-28. The words of Matthew are cited first, without brackets; then the reference to the parallel text in Hebrews is given, with its actual wording if this is not totally identical with that of Matthew: *touto* (Heb 9:20); *to haima . . . tes diathekes* (9:20); *to haima mou (to haima tou Christou:* 9:14; *tou idiou haimatos:* 9:12); *haima . . . ekchynnomenon (haimat-ekchysias:* 9:22); *eis aphesin (aphesis:* 9:22); *peri pollon . . . eis aphesin hamartion (eis to pollon anenegkein hamartias:* 9:28; *eis athetesin tes hamartias:* 9:26). The relationships are therefore extremely close.

⁵⁹Heb 9:15, 16, 17.

⁶⁰Cf. Num 35:31-33. I have emphasized this aspect in "Mundatio per sanguinem (Heb 9:22, 23)" *Verbum Domini*, 44 (1966), pp. 178-182.

⁶¹Cf. A. Jaubert, *La Notion d'alliance dans le judaïsme aux abords de l'ère chrétienne*, Seuil, 1963, pp. 311-315.

⁶²Cf. Heb 2:14; Rom 8:3.

⁶³Heb 13:12; cf. Eph 5:25-27.

⁶⁴Cf. Heb 12:25; 8:10; 10:16.

⁶⁵For example, J. Bonsirven, (see Ch. VI, note 21), *op. cit.* p. 411: "Here purification signifies dedication." C. Spicq, v. II, p. 267: "The idea of prior impurity is a non-sense for the heavenly sanctuary. It is only inaugurated and consecrated." But if so, why are bloody sacrifices necessary?

⁶⁶On this point one could criticize the position taken by J. Smith in his suggestive work, *A Priest for Ever*, London/Sydney, 1969. This author tends to reduce the affirmations of the Epistle concerning the priesthood and the sacrifice of Christ to a metaphorical sense. J. Delorme, though in a more qualified manner, in "Sacrifice, sacerdoce consécration," *RSR* 63 (1975), pp. 343-366, does not seem to me to take sufficiently into consideration the specific point of view of the author of Hebrews.

CHAPTER IX

An Efficacious Sacrifice

Transformed into a perfect offering, the sufferings and death of Jesus have won for him personally entrance into the true sanctuary where he appears before the face of God, who crowns him with glory and honor. But this event, as we have already said, cannot be reduced to a personal success—in which case it would not be priestly—on the contrary, its decisive consequences extend to the life of all mankind. It is this aspect that the author intends to emphasize in the section that concludes his great exposition (10:1-18). Faithful to his method in the earlier sections, he here proceeds by the effect of contrast. To the inefficacy of Old Testament sacrifices he opposes the perfect efficacy of Christ's offering. Once more, his demonstration relies on texts of the Old Testament itself: Psalm 40 in Hebrews 10:5-9, Psalm 110 in Hebrews 10:12-13, and the prophecy of Jeremiah in Hebrews 10:16-17. The Old Testament as revelation here again signals its own end as institution.

1. The Question of Efficacy (Heb 10:1-18)

The inefficacy of the Old Testament institutions is declared three times in the space of eleven verses. The author is not content to state it here as a fact;[1] he presents it as inevitable. It is a radical and definitive powerlessness: "The Law . . . *is forever incapable* of making perfect those who come to take part in the worship . . . for it is *impossible* for the blood of bulls and goats to take away sins" (10:1, 4). Whatever their number, the Old Testament sacrifices "*are forever incapable* of doing away with sins" (10:11).

It is precisely this powerlessness that brought about the coming of Christ and his sacrificial offering: "That is why, as he comes into the world, he says: Here I am!" (10:5-7). The situation then changes completely, for the offering of Christ is perfectly efficacious; two sentences proclaim this, using the Greek perfect tense, which expresses the lasting result of a past action, *"We have been sanctified* by the offering of the body of Jesus Christ, once and for all . . . . By a unique offering, *he has made perfect* for ever those who receive holiness" (10:10, 14).

Here, as in 9:9, the objective assigned to sacrificial worship is the transformation of men, their *teleiosis*. All those "who come," all those "who render worship," should in principle obtain this transformation,[2] which would allow them to approach God in full security. This obviously implies that the *teleiosis* reaches into their conscience and eliminates sin from it, and with sin the obstacle to communion with God. We are therefore not surprised to see our author insisting strongly here on sin: he mentions it nine times in these eighteen verses. This insistence makes clear a significant difference between the transformation of mankind and that of Christ. When the author spoke of the *teleiosis* of Christ in 2:10 and 5:9, it did not occur to him to include the elimination of sin. The reason for this omission is clear: Christ was always "without sin."[3] But now that he is speaking of the *teleiosis* to be communicated to mankind, the author returns constantly to the problem of faults to be effaced.

Sacrificial worship is the means prescribed by the Law of Moses for obtaining pardon for sins. The author observes the unfolding of this worship. He notes the multiplicity of the sacrifices (10:1) and the unceasing liturgical activity of the Jewish priests (10:11). A superficial reading could find cause for admiration here. This is, for instance, the reaction of the Jewish historian Josephus, who goes into ecstasies when he recalls the number of animals sacrificed at Jerusalem. Our author proves to be much more perceptive. He sees in all the apparent abundance the sign of failure. If one goes on indefinitely "offering sacrifices," it is because the intended goal is never achieved. These sacrifices do not liberate consciences; they only recall the persistent presence of sins (10:3). They are like so many failing attempts, which oblige one to go on endlessly repeating the effort. The sacrifice of Christ, on the contrary, does not have to be repeated: it has been offered "once and for all"; it is a "unique sacrifice," a "unique offering."[4] And this uniqueness is the sign of its effectiveness: after his unique sacrifice, Christ can henceforth remain seated at the right hand of God, because this unique sacrifice has obtained everything expected of it. It has brought about the transformation of the faithful.[5]

As already suggested above,[6] the reason for the contrast is here more precisely explained. The Old Testament sacrifices did not succeed in being effective because they were characterized by an inevitable exteriority. As he could not offer himself, the priest had to turn to the "blood of bulls and goats." But what relationship can really be established between the blood of a slaughtered animal and the conscience of a man?

It is impossible for the blood of bulls and goats to take away sins. (Heb 10:4)

On the other hand, what possibility is there for communion between a dead beast and God? The Old Testament itself had already described God's own disgust at these ritual massacres. The texts are not hard to find; our author has only too many to choose from.[7] He selects a passage from Psalm 40, which, taking the trouble to list four kinds of sacrifices, casts aside the whole of the traditional sacrificial worship and replaces it with a personal offering. Our author recognizes in the words of the psalm a prophecy which has found its fulfillment in the life of Christ:

On entering into the world, he says:
"Sacrifice and offering you did not desire,
But you fashioned for me a body;
Holocausts and sacrifices for sin did not please you.
Therefore I said: Here I am. I have come
—in the roll of the book it is written of me—
O God, to do your will." (Heb 10:5-7 - Ps 40:7-9)

In fact, Christ's offering corresponds perfectly with the viewpoint expressed by the psalmist. It is not an external rite, but a personal obedience: "Here I am, I have come to do your will."[8] Unlike the ritual sacrifices, which "God did not wish," an offering of this kind could not fail to be accepted by God, since it consisted precisely in "doing what God willed." Its consequence is the heavenly enthronement of Christ, who, from now on, sits at the right hand of God (10:12). A perfect communion with God has thus been achieved.

This offering, by its very nature, has a profound connection with the conscience of Mankind. As a personal obedience, it has consisted of a human act, conscious and free, and in addition it has been offered "for the sins" of mankind,[9] in conformity with the will of God. It is from this that its efficacy for our sanctification results: "In this will, we have been sanctified by the offering of the body of Jesus Christ once for all" (10:10).

2. Critique of the Law

Compared with the criticism of the cult such as the prophets expressed it, the position of our author is seen to be both more radical and less negative. It is more radical because it not only takes issue with the ritual worship, but at the same time takes aim at the whole system of the Law, which the prophets could not do. It is less negative because it has another sacrificial mediation to offer, which the prophets lacked.

The polemic against the Law begins with the first words of the first sentence, which closely associate "Law" with "shadow" (*skia*):

> What the Law offers is but a shadow of the good things to come, and not the true form of the realities. (Heb 10:1)

The perspective is not that of Platonic philosophy, which distinguishes the eternal "ideas" (*idea*) and their material "images" (*eikon*) or "shadows" (*skia*).[10] According to Plato, who is followed on this point by Philo,[11] the idea, which exists prior to the corporeal entity, always remains superior to it in perfection. Our author adopts a different perspective, which is that of the fulfillment of God's plan according to the Bible. He distinguishes between imperfect foreshadowing (*skia*) and definitive expression (*eikon*) of "the good things to come." Instead of coming at the beginning, the highest degree of reality comes at the end, in the eschatological realizations.[12] The Law which came before Christ is not superior to him, but inferior. It offers no more than rough outlines.

This first unfavorable evaluation prepares the way for a second, which constitutes the principal affirmation of the sentence and which we have already presented: since it only offers outlines, the Law is "for ever incapable of effecting the transformation (*teleiosai*)" which mankind needs (10:1). As the system is fundamentally ineffective, it has no right to continue indefinitely. In fact, the author is not slow to pronounce its recision. To this end, when he comments on Psalm 40—which in fact says nothing against the Law, but only criticizes the ritual sacrifices—he takes the initiative by noting the connection between these sacrifices and the Law:

> These are the offerings prescribed by the Law. (Heb 10:8)

This observation, the accuracy of which cannot be denied, allows him to include the Law in the criticism which is directed at the sacrifices.

God's objections to the Old Testament sacrifices touch the Law at the same time. Even better, in contrasting the ritual sacrifices prescribed by the Law with the offering of Christ which fulfills God's will, our author uses the psalm to support an opposition—astonishing to be sure—between the Law and the will of God. He does not stop there, but goes on immediately to describe the practical consequence, by declaring that Christ

> suppresses the first [state of things] in order to establish the second. (Heb 10:9)

According to the context, the first state of things refers to both the ritual worship and the Old Testament Law, which is of a piece with it: cult and Law are suppressed to be replaced by the offering of Christ and the will of God.

The prophets, obviously, could not go as far as this. When, in God's name, they rejected the ritual sacrifices, they took good care to avoid attacking the Law. They were insisting, rather, on the duty of observing it and they were denouncing Israel's contempt for the Law.[13] Consequently, one could not take their declarations about the rejection of the sacrifices literally, since the Law formally required this kind of worship. One was led to the conclusion that their chief criticism was not against the rites themselves but against the absence of the required dispositions in those who participated in them. The right attitude therefore seemed to be to continue to offer ritual sacrifices, but to try to have interior dispositions worthy of God.[14]

In our author's view, this is no solution. What is the use, in fact, of the sacrificial worship if it is first necessary to find other means— what means?—to create in oneself dispositions pleasing to God? It is clear that in this case the sacrifices have been deprived of all their efficacy. They can transform nothing. Now, a sacrifice ought to be an intervention that enables a man to change the state of his conscience and therefore his relationship with God. Where is a true sacrifice to be found?

The solution is provided by Christ and by him alone. It involves the total rejection of all ritual sacrifices, since they have no power of transformation, nor, in consequence, any true mediation value.[15] But one cannot remain at this negative stage. What will be the positive stage? A doctrine that would spiritualize worship, inviting everyone to unite himself inwardly with God? This would amount to an illusion because it would suppose the problem could be solved without anything having been done to resolve it. Where will sinful man find the wherewithal to free himself from his sin, which is the indispensable condition for union with God? And this would be, moreover, a regression on this side of the Law of Moses, which at least had the merit of being aware of the necessity of some sacrificial mediation. The Law cannot be purely and simply suppressed; it must be "fulfilled." The rejection of ritual sacrifices is not acceptable unless one is in a position to offer mankind in exchange an act of efficacious mediation. Christ has accomplished this act of mediation, true sacrifice, transformation of humanity through a sanctifying death which establishes a new relationship with God. Our author can therefore accept quite literally the prophets' rejection of ritual sacrifices, without in any way breaking the fundamental requirement of the Law regarding sacrificial mediation. This is fulfilled "through the offering of the body of Jesus Christ, once for all."

3. The Work of Christ (Heb 10:14)

In order to describe the work of Christ and to contrast it with the impotence of the Law, the author again uses, in 10:14, the verb *teleioun*, "to make perfect." Whereas the Law was "for ever incapable of making perfect" (10:1), Christ "has made perfect for ever those who receive holiness" (10:14). This last use of the verb *teleioun* marks an important stage in the doctrinal exposition concerning the priesthood.

Until now, this verb has been employed three times with reference to Christ, always in affirmative statements,[16] and three times with reference to the Law and the Old Testament worship, always in negative statements.[17] The three texts concerning Christ have added progressive clarifications, but they have all presented Christ in the role of recipient, as one subjected to a process of transformation of his humanity. According to 2:10, the one who was to bring about the transformation expressed by the verb "to make perfect" was God himself, and he was to bring it about "by means of suffering." In 5:9, the verb is in the passive: Christ has been "made perfect." The context puts this transformation into direct relationship with sufferings, as in 2:10, but it expresses more fully Christ's reactions under trial, and it shows, on the other hand, the connection of the event with the proclamation of the priesthood (5:10). We are thus led to understand that the painful education to which Christ submitted himself constituted for him a sacrifice of priestly consecration, not a ritual but an existential sacrifice, a profound transformation of his humanity. In 7:28, the verb is again found in the passive, and its context puts it into still more obvious relationship with the priesthood, for the sentence speaks of "establishing high priests." The sufferings are no longer mentioned in this passage, although they are evoked indirectly, thanks to a sacrificial statement: "having offered himself" (7:27). This expression is not in the passive like the participle "made perfect" (7:28), but in the active or, more correctly, in the reflexive mood. It reveals the personal role which Christ took in his own sacrificial transformation and so completes the coordinates of the event.

a) *A consecration that is communicated*
Hebrews 10:14 goes still further: it attributes the very action of "making perfect" to Christ, by giving this action a new area of application: "those who receive holiness." While thus far Christ has been presented as one who receives perfection ("having been made perfect," 5:9; 7:28), the author now says that he communicates it or, better still, that from this time on he has communicated it ("he has made perfect," 10:14). To the aspect of passivity is now joined an aspect of activity, and this in the same event, for "it is by a unique offering that he has made perfect for ever those who receive holiness." The glorifying passion of Christ has produced a double effect: it has transformed Christ, and has allowed him to transform his brethren, mankind. The transformation of Christ is a priestly consecration, a *teleiosis*; the transformation worked by Christ in his brethren is also a *teleiosis*, a participation in his own consecration.

We observe here a striking difference from the Old Testament *teleiosis*. In the Old Testament it was well understood that consecration to the priesthood benefited only the person who received it; he alone became high priest. After the sacrifices of his consecration, he alone was entitled to penetrate within the Sanctuary; nobody else could follow him (Lev 16:17). In the case of Christ, on the contrary, one unique sacrifice served both for the priest and for all the people. In one and the same act of offering, Christ receives the priesthood and closely associates the faithful with it.

The explanation of this unexpected novelty is found in the very different nature of the sacrifice of consecration. For the Old Testament priests, what was involved was an act of sanctification through ritual separation.[18] For Christ it was a question of an act which united him at the same time to God and to his brothers; indeed, the passion of Christ is at once an act of obedience to God and one of extreme solidarity with mankind.[19] For this reason, the transformation acquired applies not only to Christ but also, thanks to him, to all mankind.[20] To benefit from it, it is enough to follow Christ in the obedience of faith (5:9).

In 10:14 the participation of all believers in the priesthood of Christ is therefore affirmed. The author does not actually use the expression "the priesthood of the faithful"; he is not as explicit on this point as is the First Letter of Peter or Revelation, but the doctrine that he expounds clearly tends in this direction; it marks a complete change in the religious situation of mankind.

In this association of believers with the priesthood of Christ, our author sees the fulfillment of the prophecy of Jeremiah about the new covenant:

> By a unique offering, he has "made perfect" forever those who receive holiness. This is what the Holy Spirit himself also witnesses to us. For, after having said:
> "This is the covenant that I will make with them after those days,"
> the Lord says:
> "I will put my laws on their hearts, and write them on their minds, and I will no longer remember their sins and their iniquities." (Heb 10:14-17; Jer 31:33-34)

b) *The fulfillment of the new covenant*

In order to grasp how profoundly the author has understood the fulfillment of the divine promise, it is necessary to recall what he said earlier about the priestly offering of Christ.[21] There are close connections between these different texts. According to Jeremiah, the new covenant was to be characterized by an action of God within men's hearts. The tragic history of the Old Testament had, in fact, clearly demonstrated the necessity of a transformation of hearts (Jer 18:11-12). When the heart is evil, the best laws are of no avail. But how can men change their own hearts? At the very most they could present themselves before God with a "broken, contrite heart," and beg God "to create in them a pure heart."[22] God had therefore promised to intervene personally and "to write his law in their hearts."[23] It is easy to miss the real implications of this suggestive formula and never to get beyond a superficial interpretation, as if what is implied were nothing more than an emotional experience. But the word "heart" is used in the Bible in a very strong sense. It means the very deepest reality of a person's being. A gentle emotional experience, therefore, could not be sufficient to inscribe the Law of God in the hearts of man. A terrible struggle was necessary, a kind of fight with God, like that of Jacob (Gen 32:25-32), in which man's whole being had to be at stake. There would have to be a striving in which death would be confronted and in which it would be finally transformed into an occasion of supreme obedience and of love, in such a way that the human heart itself would emerge transformed.

Where could a man be found capable of confronting such a recasting of his being in the "devouring fire" of the divine holiness? For sinful man it was impossible. But Jesus offered to take on himself the trial which no son of Adam was in any condition to endure. Saying to God, "Here I am, I have come to do your will," he agreed to submit, in his human nature, to the necessary sufferings. He set out upon the path of the suppliant offering and of the painful learning process. In this way "he offered himself to God through the Eternal Spirit, a victim without spot." In doing the will of God even to the point of making an oblation of his body, "he learned obedience through his sufferings."[24] Henceforth, therefore, a new man exists, formed in perfect adherence to the will of God. Having learned obedience, he has the law of God inscribed in the depths of his being. A "new heart" exists,[25] a human heart transformed, "made perfect," totally united to God and to his brethren.[26] And this heart, created for us,[27] is at our disposal. In order that it may become effectively ours, "making us perfect" in our turn, it is sufficient for us to be among those "who receive holiness" (Heb 10:14) by following Christ in faith. In this way—and only in this way—can we enter into the new covenant (10:16) and have the law of God inscribed in our heart.

Faith makes the believer "a sharer with Christ" (3:14) and it unites him to his priesthood. Between Christ's consecration as priest and the participation of believers in this same priesthood, however, there is a difference which is of some importance. While Christ obtained his consecration directly, without the intervention of any mediator, the consecration of the faithful is totally dependent on the intervention of Christ. In the priesthood two aspects must therefore be distinguished, that of the worship rendered to God, and that of mediation. The first aspect is communicated to the faithful; those who, thanks to Christ, now have the opportunity to enter into the sanctuary and present their offerings to God.[28] But the other aspect, that of mediation, is reserved solely to Christ.[29] No one can bypass Christ and arrive at God;[30] *a fortiori*, nobody can claim to act as a substitute for Christ to lead other men to God. As mediation is the most specific characteristic of the priesthood, it is easy to see why the author has not given the title "priest" to Christians. The only priest, in the full sense of the term, is Christ himself. This is the great Christian innovation.

4. The Christian Situation (Heb 10:19-25)

The fullness of Christ's priesthood is revealed in the changed situation that he brings to mankind. Having completed his great doctrinal exposition (7:1 - 10:18), the author draws attention to this change and invites Christians to conform to it in their whole life. As we cannot here comment on all that he says on this subject, we will content ourselves with presenting its most important elements. These are summed up in the long sentence of 10:19-25, which expresses a strong connection between the priestly work of Christ and Christian life. The first three verses describe the religious situation created by Christ; the last four invite us to adopt corresponding attitudes.

a) *Abolition of the separations*
The sentence begins on a triumphal note, for the new situation is a privileged one. The word which characterizes it is the Greek word *parresia*, which originally meant "liberty to say everything" and expresses not only a feeling of confidence but also an acknowledged right. The right which Christians henceforth enjoy is the right to approach God himself in full confidence.

Therefore, brothers, we have the recognized right to enter into the sanctuary. (Heb 10:19)

An unprecedented novelty: between the Christians and God the barriers are suppressed, the passage is clear. By implication, the author is making here a complete contrast between the condition of Christians and that of the Old Covenant, as it was previously described. The system of ritual separations was then in control, the impotence of which the author has demonstrated.[31] The hoped-for sanctification remained out of reach. No valid mediation had been established between the people and God. The only effective product of this system was the establishment of separations. The people remained separated from the priests, for they were never authorized to enter into the temple building. And the priests could not follow the high priest, who alone could penetrate into the Holy of Holies. Separation also existed between the priest and the victim; the priest could not offer himself and the victim was powerless to free the priest from his sins, for it too was unable to really enter into communion with God. In short, there were obstacles everywhere. A viable route was simply unknown (9:8).

With Christ, all is changed. The separations are abolished; a "new and living" way is inaugurated (10:20). The separation that existed between the victim offered and God is now abolished, for Jesus, the victim "without blemish," who received the transforming action of God's Spirit with total docility, has been fully accepted by God and has entered into Heaven itself (9:24). The separation between the priest and the victim is also abolished; in the offering of Christ priest and victim are now one, since Christ "has offered himself." His sacrifice has at one and the same time sanctified him as victim and consecrated him as priest. The last separation, also, is abolished, that which had prevented the people from joining with the priest, for the passion of Christ is an act of complete assimilation with his brethren, an act which establishes a new solidarity, closer than ever, between him and them. Christ is a priest who unites the people with his priesthood (10:14).

The old barriers, therefore, no longer exist. All are now invited to approach God without fear. All believers "possess the acknowledged right to enter into the sanctuary" (10:19), though this right had formerly been reserved to the high priest alone and limited, even in his case, to a single annual ceremony.

b) *The Christian sacrifices*
Other passages of the Epistle show that the believers also enjoy the other priestly privilege, that of presenting sacrificial offerings to God. This comes as no surprise. It is clear that entrance into the sanctuary and the sacrificial offering are two activities closely bound together or, to state it better, two different ways of describing the same existential

reality, that is, the personal act which introduces man into the divine communion. The believers who approach God are therefore invited to offer their "sacrifices" to God. What will these sacrifices be? In what will Christian worship consist? Obviously, it will not consist in ritual sacrifices of the kind prescribed in the Old Testament. Christian worship must model itself on the sacrifice of Christ and will therefore differ radically from the Old Testament ritual worship: it must consist in *a transformation of human existence itself by means of divine love*, the true "fire from Heaven."

The sacrifice of Christ presents two inseparable aspects, each being realized by means of the other. One concerns the relationship with God: this is the aspect of obedience, of personal faithfulness to the divine will.[32] The other concerns the relationship with mankind: this is the aspect of fraternal solidarity, carried even to the total gift of oneself.[33] Instead of "aspects," one could say "dimensions," and so we could speak of the vertical dimension and the horizontal dimension which come together to form the cross of Christ. The union of these two dimensions characterizes in a similar way the Christian worship, the Christian transformation of human existence. The same expression "to do the will of God," which first defined the sacrifice of Christ,[34] now defines the Christian vocation;[35] it is as applicable to the attitude of the believer under trial (10:36) as it is to his positive activity (13:21). On the other hand, the desire to do what is pleasing to God moves Christians, as it did Christ, to devote themselves to others:

> Do not neglect to do good and to share what you have, for such sacrifices are pleasing to God. (Heb 13:16)

In this verse, the author employs the technical term for "sacrifice," (*thysia*) and he applies it to the life of fraternal charity. In an earlier verse he has rejected the Old Testament understanding of worship, which gave fundamental importance to exterior observances, in particular to rules concerning food.[36] Henceforth, worship can no longer be situated alongside of a life considered profane; life itself must be taken and transformed into a generous offering of obedience to God and of fraternal dedication.

c) *Christ's mediation*

But one essential point must never be forgotten: such a transformation of existence is possible only through the priestly mediation of Christ, who communicates to believers the purifying and renewing power of the Spirit. That is why the life of charity is always situated in an atmosphere of thanksgiving. Receiving everything through Christ, the faithful are invited to "offer through him at all times a sacrifice of praise to God" (13:15). This is the other essential aspect of Christian "sacrifices."

To claim to transform life without passing through Christ is to fall into the illusion of human pride and to commit oneself to failure. The words of 10:19-25 are particularly clear on this point. The verse begins by showing that a triple condition is imposed upon mankind's ability to approach God, and affirms that this triple condition is realized for them only in Christ.

To be admitted into God's presence, human beings need first of all "the right of entry," which allows them to advance without fear; next, they need a way leading them to the true sanctuary; and finally and above all, they need a priest to usher them into God's presence.

> Having thus, brothers, the acknowledged right of entry into the sanctuary by means of the blood of Jesus, [having] a new and living way which he inaugurated through the veil, that is, through his flesh, [having] an eminent priest established over the house of God, let us approach . . . . (Heb 10:19-22)

Jesus is the one who procures the right of way, for by entering into the sanctuary "through his own blood" he has "found an eternal redemption" (9:12). The right of way has therefore been given to the believers "in the blood of Jesus," which has been made fully effective by his death. Transformed into a perfect offering, the death of Jesus has in fact surmounted on behalf of human beings all the obstacles which prevent their communion with God.

The road leading into the sanctuary is likewise found in Jesus. He himself "inaugurated it for us through the veil." In specifying that this way is "new and living" and that it has a relationship with the "flesh" of Jesus,[37] the author helps his readers to understand that here, as in 9:11, he is referring to the mystery of the resurrection of Christ. The new and living way is none other than the glorified humanity of Christ, now become for all mankind the sole means of access to God. In 9:11 this glorified humanity was presented as "the greater and more perfect tent" which leads to the authentic sanctuary. One should not be surprised to hear it now called "the road," for in 9:11—and already in 9:8—the author has made it clear that the role of the tent consisted in being a means of access.

"Road" and "acknowledged right" are impersonal expressions. Because of this, they do not elucidate the most important aspect of mediation: the personal intervention of the mediator. The author is fully aware of this and it is for this reason that he takes care to add that we also have "an eminent priest over the house of God." In our movement toward God we are not alone; we have an experienced guide, "the pioneer of [our] salvation" (2:10). When we come before God, we have, to introduce us to him, a great high priest, who has been fully accredited, "the guarantor of a better covenant" (7:22). By specifying that this priest is set "over the house of God," the author recalls the theme developed at the beginning of his first exposition,[38] and with the same expression: the priest is the man of the sanctuary and he is "worthy of faith"; he has authority to speak in the name of God to those who make up "his house."

d) *Faith, hope, love*
In this way the second part of the development is introduced, in which the author invites Christians to adopt attitudes appropriate to the new situation created by the priesthood of Christ:

> Let us approach with a sincere heart in fullness of faith, having our hearts purified from every evil inclination, and our bodies washed with pure water. Let us maintain without fail the confession of our hope—for he who promised is faithful—and let us consider how to stir up one another to love and good works, not neglecting to meet together, as is the habit of some, but encouraging one another, and this all the more as you see the Day approaching. (Heb 10:22-25)

The fundamental attitude consists in following Christ the priest *in faith*. Enthroned with God, Christ is for us "a great high priest, worthy of faith." The first condition for approaching God is therefore not the fulfillment of a law, but recourse in faith to the priestly mediation of Christ. Once again we meet here the Pauline doctrine, which rejects the claims of the Law and makes faith the foundation of everything, but this doctrine is illuminated by a new brightness, thanks to the reflection on the priesthood. The reason for rejecting the Law is its inability to establish a valid priesthood, an effective mediation between human beings and God. The ground of this appeal in faith is the unique efficacy of the sacrifice and of the priesthood of Christ, which truly introduces mankind into communion with God. In making us adhere to Christ the mediator, faith opens up the only authentic possibility of the transformation of human existence by means of divine charity. The effort of sinful man cannot, in fact, serve as the basis of salvation, because it comes from a tainted source. A man must first be transformed, and his conscience must be "purified from dead works" (9:14), and this is obtained through the mediation of Christ the priest. Therefore faith is and always remains the first Christian attitude.

The second attitude is *hope*, which is really only a specification of faith. The message received is not, in fact, the revelation of an abstract truth, but the manifestation of a person who is "way" and "cause of salvation." It is therefore dynamic invitation and promise. "Let us maintain without failing," the author says, "the profession of our hope, for he who has promised is faithful." What gives Christian hope all its steadfastness is the certainty that the objective aimed at has already been effectively reached by a "pioneer,"[39] Christ, who "through the greater and more perfect tent . . . has entered once for all into the sanctuary" (9:11-12). There can be no obstacle to hope, for the road marked out by Christ has consisted, precisely, in transforming the obstacles into means for going forward. When trials occur, they provide the opportunity for a more real union with the sacrifice of Christ. Following the example of Christ, who in his Passion "learned obedience" and "did the will of God," Christians who are tried by suffering submit themselves to the divine transforming action and do God's will.[40] Instead of causing discouragement, trials therefore reinforce hope.

The third attitude in which the adherence of the faithful to Christ the priest is expressed is an intense *love*. This is demonstrated in fraternal mutual assistance and in all kinds of "beautiful works," as the Greek text says literally. Christians are solicitous for one another. Far from being marked by individualism, their spiritual life intensifies their mutual relationships. How could it be otherwise, since faith unites them to a "compassionate high priest," who has manifested the greatest possible solidarity with his brethren?[41] Thanks to him, they make up all together the house of God (3:6). Desirous to live up to their heavenly vocation (3:1), they help one another to avoid the dangers that threaten them and encourage one another to advance toward God with confidence.[42] Their "fraternal love" (13:1) is also shown in a very concrete manner by the material aid which they generously bring to those in need: the sick or poverty-stricken, persecuted Christians or those looking for shelter.[43]

e) *Eucharistic context*

Faith, hope and love are then the three spiritual attitudes characteristic of Christians, attitudes which enable them to live united to Christ the priest and so to transform their existence. The author, however, is not content to speak only of spiritual attitudes; he also suggests concrete means of being tied to Christ's mediation. The logic of his exposition requires the existence of such means, for a mediation that is not concretely expressed is no longer a mediation. If the possibility for Christians to worship God remains always tied to the mediation of Christ, then this mediation must be offered to them in a tangible fashion. This is precisely what the author tries to convey. He speaks not only about faith, but also about what we call the sacraments of the faith. These are nothing other than the tangible expression of the actual mediation of Christ.

In 10:22 one easily recognizes an allusion to Baptism, under its twofold aspect of material rite—Christians have had their "bodies washed in pure water"[44]—and of spiritual efficacy—they have had their "hearts cleansed from the evil that soils their conscience." In the preceding verses, one may also recognize an allusion to the Eucharist, not simply because the author mentions the "flesh" and "blood of Jesus" (10:19-20) in two parts of parallel phrases, but because the entire sentence corresponds as closely as possible to the reality of a eucharistic celebration. We should recall in this connection that the Epistle to the Hebrews, except for a few lines added at the end,[45] does not have the appearance of a letter but of a sermon intended to be pronounced aloud in the course of a gathering of the Christian community. Our passage suggests that the author had in mind a gathering that included a eucharistic celebration.

This passage is, in any case, best explained in such a context. The author explicitly speaks of the gathering of the community (10:25) as an expression of mutual love and a means of making progress. To speak in this way is to situate oneself within the sacramental order, in view of the fact that from the beginning of the sentence there is this insistence on the mediation of Christ. And above all, when the author mentions the body and blood of Jesus, he refers to the possibility of actual availability: the Christians have at this moment the right to enter into the sanctuary thanks to the blood of Jesus, it is at this moment that they have at their disposal the living way which is his glorified body. On the other hand, Baptism appears only as a preliminary condition, already realized—the verbs which refer to it (10:22) are perfect participles. It permits participation in the liturgy of the community, in which the mediation of the body and blood of Christ is presently at work giving the assembled faithful access to God, in a joyous profusion of faith, of hope and of love. It would be difficult to find a more appropriate and more vibrant description of eucharistic worship, sign and source of the Christian transformation of existence.

That the author did not speak explicitly of the "cup of the Lord" and of the "Lord's table," but simply alluded to them is easily understood if, precisely, the concrete situation made the allusions obvious. At the end of his sermon, he proceeds in the same manner when he says that we Christians "have an altar from which those who perform the worship of the tent have no right to eat" (13:10). This expression declares that there is incompatibility between Christian worship and Old Testament worship, and it clearly implies that the Christians do have the right "to eat from their altar."[46]

Some exegetes have thought that the position taken by the author against the ancient ritual worship should have brought him to reject also sacramental worship.[47] But this is a mistake, for it ignores the fundamental difference that separates the second cult from the first. There is, of course, a certain external resemblance between the two: in both cases symbolic ceremonies are celebrated. But in the case of the ancient worship, these ceremonies had no relation to a perfect existential offering, for the good reason that such an offering did not exist. The rites were supposed to have value in themselves or by virtue of the good dispositions of those who participated in them. In reality, this worship, as the author has successfully shown, had no effective capacity of mediation. Christian sacraments, on the other hand, are instruments of Christ's mediation. They do not present themselves as ceremonies that have value in themselves. Their value comes solely from the existential offering of Christ, whose effective presence they serve only to actualize. Thus they give the faithful the opportunity of adhering fully, with body and soul, to this offering and of allowing themselves to be transformed by it.

f) *Relationship between the "leaders" and Christ the priest*
One last trait deserves to be emphasized in order to complete the picture of the Christian situation: in the community, the priestly mediation of Christ is not only manifested by means of sacramental rites,

but also through persons. Just before the conclusion of his sermon, in a passage in which he refers to the Eucharist and Christian sacrificial worship which effects the transformation of their very existence, the author shows that the Christians are not just an amorphous mass, but a structured community which has its "leaders." Two references to these leaders serve to frame the whole passage (13:7 and 13:17) and are for this reason all the more significant. In itself the title "leaders" has nothing priestly about it. It indicates only a position of authority.[48] Only here in the New Testament is it used to designate those responsible for a Christian community, but it is found subsequently in the Letter of Clement of Rome to the Church of Corinth. What is interesting for us is not so much the title itself but the attributes attached to it, for these attributes make the "leaders" of the community the representatives, for this community, of Christ the mediator.

As "high priest worthy of trust" (3:1-6), Christ is henceforth, as we have seen, the mediator of the word of God. But how is this mediation concretely exercised? According to 13:7, it is exercised by the "leaders"; it is they who have spoken "the word of God" to the Christians.

Christ is the priest established "over the house of God" (3:6; 10:21). How concretely does he exercise his priestly authority? Here again one must answer: through the ministry of the "leaders"; it is to them that the Christians are invited to show obedience: "Obey your leaders and be subject to them."[49]

The priestly authority of Christ has no other purpose than to communicate "salvation to all those who obey him," for Christ is a "merciful high priest as well as worthy of trust"[50] This other aspect of the priesthood of Christ is made present also in the ministry of the "leaders," for they are to devote themselves to the service of the faithful. "They remain to watch over you," writes the author, "for the good of your souls" (13:17).

The priestly mediation of Christ is founded on the decisive act which establishes the New Covenant: the "offering of his body" and the shedding of "his blood."[51] In the life of the faithful, this unique sacrificial act is made present, as we have seen, by means of the Eucharist. Have the "leaders" a special role in the celebration of the Eucharist? The author says nothing explicit on this matter, just as he does not speak about bread and wine. But his way of presenting things points fairly clearly in the direction of a positive response. It is, in fact, difficult to see as simply accidental the fact that the twofold mention of the "leaders" (13:7, 17) frames a passage which defines Christian worship and which irresistibly suggests the eucharistic celebration under its triple aspect of the sacrificial meal where only Christians have the right to eat (13:10), of "sacrifice of praise" which they raise up to God through Jesus Christ (13:15), and of unique opportunity for the expression of community love (13:16).[52] Named before and after, the "leaders" are in this way closely associated with the fundamental sacramental action of Christian worship. Is it not likely that this close association is somehow connected to their identity as "leaders"?

The other passage in the Epistle where we have noted an underlying eucharistic structure (10:19-25) leads to the same conclusion. It mentions three elements of the mediation of Christ as actually being at the disposal of the Christians: his blood, his flesh and his personal intervention.[53] If we must admit that the flesh and the blood of Christ are actually at their disposal because they are made present in the lives of Christians in a sacramental manner, the close union of the third element with the other two invites us to recognize that it too should normally have its sacramental expression. The actual person of Christ, "the high priest set up over the house of God," must therefore be represented among the faithful at the moment when he is giving them his body and blood. By whom will it be represented, if not by those whom Christ himself established as instruments of his priestly authority and mercy? It is true that the author says nothing explicit on this matter. His statement directly expresses only the realities that effect the mediation: the blood of Jesus, his flesh, his person as priest. What suggests a reference to the sacramental presence of these realities is simply the assertion of their actual availability for Christian worship. These reservations having been made, is it not in order to think that, when read in this actual context and related to the data furnished by Hebrews 13:7-13, the triad of 10:19-21 goes some way toward attributing to the "leaders" of the Christian community the function of representing Christ sacramentally in the celebration of the Eucharist? The elements which lead us in this direction are undoubtedly tenuous and problematical, but their cumulative effect is not entirely negligible.

To say this is not to exaggerate the importance of the "leaders." It is rather to put them in their proper place. They are not mediators who would substitute themselves for Christ, but are believers whom Christ the mediator makes use of. What they do "for the good of souls," they do knowing that "they will have to render an account" (13:17). This final remark shows clearly that they are neither the absolute masters of Christians nor are they simply delegates of the community, but they are under the orders of Christ the priest, charged by him to represent him to their brothers and sisters, by exercising his authority and showing his mercy, and being responsible before him for this mission. Christ alone is "the great shepherd of the sheep" (13:20); he alone is the "cause of salvation" (5:9); he alone is "the high priest." His priestly mediation is not confined to a past event—this would make it inoperative in the present. It has the power to express itself through the whole course of time, by means of the signs and persons employed in its effective exercise.

Conclusion

Having come to the end of the Epistle to the Hebrews, we see the great depth of the author's answers to the question the Christians of the first century had to face: is the Christian community a community without a priest? Does the priestly institution of the Old Covenant find its fulfillment in the mystery of Christ or not? The answer is in the affirmative, without a shadow of hesitation. But it is not superficial. Solidly founded on the events of the life of Christ, on the texts of inspired Scripture and on Christian experience, it demands a radical change of mentality. The author could have considered the problem at the level of externals and said to the faithful: "Do not regret the old worship and its splendors. We too can organize beautiful ceremonies!" But this idea did not occur to him. He went to the root of the problem. For him the new liturgy does not consist in ceremonies, but in a real event, the death of Christ, a death that was offered up, one which completely changes the religious situation of mankind, because it transforms man and introduces him into the intimacy of God. Christians are then invited to go beyond the old conception of cult and of priesthood. They have a priest, but of an entirely different kind. They have a sacrificial worship, but one without animal immolations. Their vocation does not lead them to put their trust in exterior rites, but to pass through the existential sacrifice of Christ and so to profit from his priestly mediation. By adhering through faith to Christ the priest, by allowing themselves to be purified by his blood and sanctified by the offering of his body, and by themselves entering into the movement of his sacrifice,[54] Christians become capable of rendering an authentic worship to God, one which consists in the transformation of their existence by divine charity. The response given is not only positive, but it is also exclusive. Not content with asserting that the death of Christ is a sacrifice, the author demonstrates that it is the only true sacrifice. The Old Testament rites were not true sacrifices: they were powerless endeavors, they did not in fact bring about the sacrificial transformation which leads to communion with God. They could not find at that time a sacrificial victim pleasing to God, nor a priest capable of raising it up to God. In the death of Christ, on the contrary, all the conditions of an authentic sacrifice are realized in a perfect way.[55]

What is true of sacrifice is no less true of priesthood: Christ not only possesses priesthood, but is the one and only true high priest, the only one who has carried the priestly mediation to its conclusion. The priests of the Old Law remained confined to the plane of ineffective symbolism. Being sinful men, they were incapable of bridging the gap that separated them from God or, as a result, of charting a way for the people. Christ, by his total and perfect personal offering, became in his own person "the new and living way." His priesthood is situated at the highest level of reality; it is in the hearts of human beings that he establishes the New Covenant with the heart of God. "A high priest, worthy of faith and merciful," Christ fills to perfection all the functions of the priesthood, whether it be the sacrificial offering, or the entry into the sanctuary, or the transmission of the graces of forgiveness, of light or of blessing. We have noticed in particular that the author does not forget, in the priesthood of Christ, the aspect of the Word nor that of authority, both of which are necessary to guide believers on their journey toward God. In his concept of the priesthood there is a fullness in which nothing is lacking.

This conception proves to be very open as well. It is important to stress this here so as to forestall possible misunderstandings that could be caused by what has just been said regarding the exclusiveness of Christ's priesthood. This exclusiveness is not to be understood as an obstacle to participation. We are not being asked to imagine a priesthood shut in on itself; this would be a contradiction in terms. On the contrary, one of the original traits of Christ's priesthood is that it is shared with all believers. The old separation of people and priest is abolished. All are invited to enter into the sanctuary and to offer their sacrifices. In this regard, it would be well however to distinguish once again between two aspects of the priesthood, the aspect of offering and that of mediation. The aspect in which all are able to participate is that of offering. It is from this point of view that the author does not hesitate to call the offerings of Christians "sacrifices" (13:15-16), although they are not to be situated on the same level as the unique sacrifice of Christ. These offerings are "sacrifices" only in the sense that they are acts which open up personal and social life to the dynamism of divine love: they are not acts of mediation. The words of 13:15 are clear proof of this, for they explain that these "sacrifices" of the Christians have to pass through the mediation of Christ ("through him"). The aspect of mediation belongs uniquely to the sacrifice of Christ and to his priesthood. This does not prevent it also being the object of a certain participation, but this will be of another kind. Although the power of "rendering worship to the living God" (9:14) is communicated to all the faithful in every aspect of their lives, the power of representing the mediation of Christ is given only to well-defined instruments, sacramental actions and the persons of the "leaders," and it is not a question, we stress again, of a power to exercise mediation in the place of Christ, but only of the power to manifest the mediation of Christ.

By explicitly bringing out the priestly character of the mystery of Christ, the Epistle to the Hebrews has thrown new light on the whole of Christology. The priestly categories are seen to have been divinely prepared to give a more precise and more profound understanding of the riches of Christ, which obviously surpass the limits of royal messianism. But the converse is also true: in the light of the mystery of Christ, the popular conception of the priesthood has been transformed and deepened in an astonishing manner. We must speak of a new synthesis. Starting from this, a whole sequence of other doctrinal developments has become possible.

Having re-worked the notion of "sacrifice," the author has made possible the sacrificial interpretation of many affirmations of the Christian faith which were not sacrificial in the old sense of the term.[56] The sacrificial understanding of the Eucharist, suggested by the words of institution and by the mode of argument employed by Paul in 1 Corinthians 10:14-22, finds a fuller confirmation. The new notion of sacrifice, which is not only far distant from Old Testament ritualism, but also equally distant from a "spiritualization" of a philosophical kind, provides a solid and sure foundation for the sacrificial concept of the Christian life, which Paul had already portrayed in Romans 12:1, and which the author of the Epistle takes up in his own way (Heb 13:15-16). The participation of all Christians in Christ's priestly worship is clearly expressed and the participation of the "leaders" in the priestly mediation of Christ appears in several ways. Neither for the Christians nor for their "leaders," however, does the author employ the term "priesthood," nor the title of "priest"; he is too conscious of the partial and subordinate character of these two forms of participation in the priesthood of Christ. When he speaks of the time of the New Covenant, he reserves to Christ alone the vocabulary of the priesthood (*hiereus, archiereus, hierosyne*), for Christ alone possesses the fullness of the priesthood and gives to all the opportunity to share in it.

Notes

[1]Cf. Heb 7:19.
[2]Cf. the verb *teleiosai* in Heb 10:1.
[3]Cf. Heb 4:15; 7:26; 9:14. Paul, more audaciously, does not shrink from using expressions which indicate a close relationship between Christ and sin, e.g., Rom 6:10: "In dying he died to sin once for all," and Rom 8:3: "God sent his own Son in a flesh like that of sin"; but it does not follow that Paul thinks Christ a sinner; for him, too, Christ is "he who has not known sin" (2 Cor 5:21). The situation of the Redeemer paradoxically unites a complete absence of personal sin with a profound identification, in the flesh, with sinful humanity.
[4]Cf. Heb 10:10, 12, 14.
[5]Cf. Heb 10:12, 14.
[6]In Heb 9:9-14.
[7]Cf. Is 1:11; Jer 6:20; 7:22; Hos 6:6; Amos 5:22, 25; Ps 40:7-9; 50:13-15; 51:18f.
[8]Heb 10:9; cf. 5:8; Mt 26:42; Jn 6:38; Phil 2:8.
[9]Heb 10:12; cf. 9:26, 28; 1 Cor 15:3, etc.
[10]Plato, *Republic*, VII, 514.

[11]Commenting on Gen 1 - 2, Philo explains that God first created the perfect idea of mankind, and in the second place only the earthly man, necessarily less perfect. *De Opif. mundi*, 134f. (Loeb Class. I, 1929, pp. 106-107).

[12]Cf. 1 Cor 15:46f. "What is first is not the spiritual being, but the living being; the spiritual being comes after."

[13]Cf. Is 1:17; Jer 6:19.

[14]Cf. Ps 51:21; Sir 35:3f.

[15]"Mediation" is understood here in the strong sense of an intervention which establishes a relationship while suppressing the obstacles opposed to it, and it is a matter of mediation between mankind and God.

[16]Heb 2:10; 5:9; 7:28.

[17]Heb 7:19; 9:9; 10:1.

[18]Cf. above, Ch. II 3, b, c.

[19]Cf. Heb 2:14-18; 4:15; 5:7-9.

[20]The first Encyclical of Pope John Paul II expresses this doctrine: "It is a question of each man, because each has been included in the mystery of the Redemption and Jesus Christ has united himself to each one, for ever, through this mystery" (*Redemptor hominis*, no. 13).

[21]Cf. Heb 10:9f; 9:14; 5:7-9.

[22]Ps 51:12, 19.

[23]Jer 31:33; Heb 8:10; 10:16.

[24]Cf. Heb 5:8; 9:14; 10:9f.

[25]Cf. Ez 36:26; Jer 24:7; 32:39.

[26]"The redemption of the world—this awesome mystery of love, in which creation is renewed—is, in its deepest roots, the fullness of justice in a human heart, in the Heart of the first-born Son, in order that it may be able to become the justice of the hearts of many men . . . ." (*Redemptor hominis*, no. 9).

[27]Cf. Ps 51:12.

[28]Cf. Heb 10:19; 9:14; 12:28; 13:15f. It is clear that the Christian worship differs radically from the Old Testament sacrificial worship; see below Ch. IX, 4, b, c.

[29]Cf. Heb 8:6; 9:15; 1 Tim 2:5.

[30]Cf. Heb 7:25; 10:19-21; 13:15, 21; Jn 14:6.

[31]Cf. Heb 7:18-19a; 8:9-10; 10:1-4.

[32]Cf. Heb 5:8; 10:7-10.

[33]Cf. Heb 2:14-18; 4:15.

[34]In Heb 10:7, 9.

[35]In Heb 10:36 and 13:21.

[36]Heb 13:9; cf. 9:10. Already the author of Sirac was likening acting virtuously to worship rendered to God, but he never dreamed of rejecting the Old Testament concept of the sacrificial worship, cf. Sir 35:1-10.

[37]The precise grammatical function of the words: "that is to say of his flesh" is hard to determine. It can be understood as an explanation of the word "veil," which immediately precedes it: "through the veil, that is to say his flesh." The flesh of Christ is in that case being compared to the veil of the Temple, through which one passed in order to enter the Holy of Holies. Or else one can attach the genitive "of his flesh" to the principal term of the proposition, "way," and understand: "the way of his flesh." For other hypotheses, cf. J. Jeremias, "Brachylogie und Inkonzinnität im Präpositionsge-

brauch" *ZNW* 62 (1971), p. 131; O. Hofius, *Der Vorhang vor dem Thron Gottes*, Tübingen, 1972, pp. 81-83.

It does not seem essential to have decided this disputed question in order to be in a position to identify the "way," for the most important qualifiers in its regard are that it is "new and living," which can only be properly understood of the risen humanity of Christ. The relationships between 10:20 and 9:11 confirm this interpretation.

[38] Heb 3:1-6.

[39] Cf. Heb 6:19f; 12:2.

[40] Cf. Heb 10:36; 12:2-13; 1 Pet 2:21.

[41] Cf. Heb 2:11-18; 4:15.

[42] Cf. Heb 3:12f; 4:1; 10:25; 12:15-17.

[43] Cf. Heb 10:33f; 13:1-3.

[44] The mention of "pure water" refers to Ez 36:25, where it accompanies the promise of a "new heart," an extension of Jer 31:31-34 cited a little earlier by Heb 10:16-17.

[45] Heb 13:18 and 13:22-25.

[46] The elliptical expression "to eat at the altar" is clarified by the expression of Paul: "Those who eat the sacrificed victims, do they not communicate with the altar?" (1 Cor 10:18). The context speaks explicitly of the Eucharist in a perspective of participation in a sacrifice.

[47] An anti-eucharistic interpretation of Heb 13:9-11 has been sustained by O. Holtzmann, "Die Hebräerbrief und das Abendmahl," *ZNW* 10 (1909), pp. 251-260 and taken up with diverse variations by F.J. Schierse, *Verheissung und Heilsvollendung*, Munich, 1955, F.V. Filson, *Yesterday*, London, 1967, G. Theissen, *Untersuchungen zum Hebräerbrief*, Gütersloh, 1969, as well as by F. Schröger, "Der Gottesdienst der Hebräerbriefgemeinde." *MUTZ*, 19 (1968), pp. 161-181. Other authors have refuted this position: the most recent are J. Thuren, *Das Lobopfer der Hebräer*, Abo, 1973, and P. Andriessen, "L'Eucharistie dans l'Épître aux Hébreux," *NRT*, 94 (1972), pp. 269-277.

[48] Cf. Lk 22:26. On the subject of the ministry of the "leaders," cf. Ch. Perrot, "L'épître aux Hébreux," in *Le Ministère et les ministères selon le N.T.* (ed. J. Delorme), Seuil, 1974, pp. 118-138.

[49] Heb 13:17. In Ac 7:10 with reference to Joseph in Egypt, the word "leader" (*hegoumenos*) is associated with the expression "over all his house," cf. Ps 105:21. The relationship between the words of Heb 13:17 on the "leaders" and those of Heb 3:6; 10:21 on the priest Christ established "over the house of God" is made still clearer.

[50] Heb 2:17; 4:15; 5:9.

[51] Cf. Heb 9:12, 14, 22f; 10:10.

[52] Proposing a eucharistic interpretation of Heb 13:10, J. Thuren, (cf. note 47), p. 204, supports it by underlining the relationship of the Eucharist with grace (13:9), with the Passion of Christ (13:12), and with the "sacrifice of praise" (13:15), all elements explicitly mentioned in the immediate context.

[53] "The blood of Jesus" (10:19), "his flesh" (10:20), he himself "high priest established over the house of God" (10:21).

[54] Heb 9:14; 10:10, 19-25.

[55] In *Des choses cachées*, Grasset, 1978, R. Girard presents as a deplorable regression the sacrificial christology of the Epistle to the Hebrews, which according to him is contrary to the Gospel (pp. 251-254). He takes vehement exception to "the error of the sacrificial reading" (pp. 302, 458). But Girard starts from a one-sided negative conception of

238 / Old Testament Priests and the New Priest

sacrifice. For him, sacrifice is the sacral, illusory transfiguration of a slaughter due to a mechanism of "antagonistic mimesis." Without denying that this explanation can account for much of the evidence from the history of religions, we could question whether it is really adequate as a definition of sacrifice. The latter includes profound aspects which are by no means illusory and which are brought out already in the Old Testament, which shows concern to foster these and to combat deviations. To define sacrifice without taking these facts into account is to lack objectivity and to falsify the meaning of words. Another observation: R. Girard pays no attention to the re-elaboration of the notion of sacrifice effected by the Epistle to the Hebrews. He speaks as if the author had simply taken the current expression and applied it arbitrarily to the Passion of Christ. We have just seen, on the contrary, that the author has accomplished a work of unprecedented discernment and profound analysis. He has submitted the old conception to a rigorous critique to eliminate its deficiencies; but he has been careful to avoid judging it in a unilaterally negative way; he has retained what was valid in the idea, and, in the light of the Calvary event, has risen to a new conception which fulfills and surpasses it. Far from constituting a regression, such a "sacrificial reading" is extremely enriching for faith and for life.

[56]For example, Gal 1:4: "Jesus Christ who gave himself for our sins, in order to rescue us from the present evil world, according to the will of our God and Father"; or Gal 2:20; Rom 4:25; 1 Cor 15:3-4; Mk 10:45, etc.

PART THREE

A Priestly People

A Priestly People

Examination of the vocabulary of the New Testament has shown that in addition to the Epistle to the Hebrews, two other writings apply priestly terminology in one form or another to the Christian reality. These are the First Epistle of Peter and the Apocalypse or Book of Revelation. Certainly the question of the priesthood is far from occupying the place in these two works that it holds in the Epistle to the Hebrews. It makes only brief appearances. These, however, are not without importance or originality. In fact, neither John's use of the title priest nor Peter's mention of priesthood are in reference to Christ, rather they serve to define the position of Christians. In this they both appear more daring than the Epistle to the Hebrews, which, as we have observed, refrains from calling Christians "priests." They do, nonetheless, have one point in common with Hebrews: they too base their teaching on a text of the Old Testament. The difference is in the choice of text: while the Epistle to the Hebrews argues from an oracle of Psalm 110 concerning the king of Israel, the First Epistle of Peter and Revelation rest their argument on a divine promise contained in the Book of Exodus and addressed to the people as a whole.

We have then a new and complementary point of view: after the priestly dimension of the mystery of Christ, we have the priestly characterization of the Christian people. To be more precise, one should speak of two new points of view and not of one, for Peter and John have not exploited the text of Exodus in the same way. Using the Greek translation of Exodus, Peter speaks of "priesthood" in the singular and emphasizes the union of Christians in priesthood. Drawing directly on the Hebrew text, John speaks of "priests" in the plural, and also pays greater attention to the relationship between priesthood and kingship. It will therefore be appropriate to treat the two writings separately, in order to appreciate better the special contribution of each. Chapter 10 is devoted to 1 Peter and Chapter 11 to Revelation.

Neither Peter nor John are concerned with defining the connections between Christian priesthood and the apostolic ministry. Peter, however, speaks specifically of "presbyters" and so provides the opportunity for considering this question. An expression of Paul's regarding his own ministry (Rom 15:16) contributes to its elucidation, for he employs cultic vocabulary. This phrase is examined in passing.

The analysis of these texts concludes our study. It shows the perspectives which the New Testament opens up for the Church on the question of the priesthood.

CHAPTER X

The Church of Christ
A Priestly Organism

[The text of 1 Peter 2:1-10]

In the First Epistle of Peter, it is to the community of believers that priesthood is attributed. The statement on this point is clear: it occurs twice in the course of an enthusiastic description of the Christian condition. Being the principal foundation of the doctrine of the priesthood of the faithful, this text has been the object of numerous controversies and is often incorrectly interpreted. It therefore deserves our attention.[1]

The text in question constitutes the final section (2:1-10) of the first part of the Epistle.[2] A number of commentators are of the opinion that it is taken in its entirety from a baptismal catechesis for, from the start, it recalls the new birth of Christians and continues throughout in the same perspective.[3] One expression in the text, "like newborn babes," provides this hypothesis with its most convincing support, for it is perfectly appropriate only for the newly baptized.[4] The sentence which contains it employs the language characteristic of Christian conversion. Intimately bound up with the process of new birth, the latter comprises two opposite and complementary aspects: rupture and adherence. The aspect of rupture is expressed by the metaphor of the "laying aside" of old garments, perhaps inspired by the baptismal ritual: before descending into the water, the catechumen would have to undress. In any case, the formula means that the sinner has rejected evil, as one gets rid of old and dirty garments.[5] The aspect of adherence follows immediately, but is expressed by means of a different image, that of newborn babes who wish to drink milk. Christians are invited to desire "spiritual milk," that is, as is clear from the context, they must desire to receive the Word of God.[6] The apostle has just reminded them that it is to this Word that they owe their birth (1:23). He remarks that, in order to grow, the children of God need this same Word which has brought them to birth. From the desire for the Word, he passes on to attachment to the person of the Lord, and then introduces the theme of priesthood. Here is the whole text:

> Having therefore rejected all malice and all guile, hypocrisies, jealousies and all kinds of slander, like newborn babes, desire the unadulterated spiritual milk, in order that by it you may grow up to salvation, if at least you have tasted that the Lord is good. Approaching him, the living stone, rejected by men but chosen and precious to God, you also, like living stones, are being built into a spiritual house for a holy priesthood, with a view to offering spiritual sacrifices acceptable to God through Jesus Christ.
>
> For it is written in the Scripture: "Behold I am laying in Sion a corner stone, chosen and precious, and he who believes in him will not be put to shame."
>
> To you, therefore, the believers, honor, but for the unbelievers "the stone which the builders rejected, the same has become the cornerstone, a stumbling block and a rock of scandal." They stumble on it, not being obedient to the Word: it is for this that they have been destined. But you, you are a chosen race, a royal priesthood, a holy nation, a people for salvation, to proclaim the wonderful deeds of Him who called you out of darkness into his marvelous light, you who were not a people, but now are God's people, a people without [God's] mercy now you have been helped by his mercy. (1 Pet 2:1-10)

Immediately after the mention of "the Lord" at the end of verse 3, the text reveals a clear change in tone, although the Greek sentence is not broken, but continues with a relative pronoun and says literally "to whom approaching . . . ." The apostle no longer speaks of the renunciation of wickedness nor of desire for the Word of God. He speaks of the movement of Christians toward Christ and the perspectives that thus open before them. These verses interest us more directly because they contain the affirmation regarding priesthood.

Two parts of very unequal length are easily distinguished here. The first part, concise and short (2:4-5), describes the Christians' profession of faith in the mystery of Christ and the situation that results from this. The second part, of broader rhythm (2:6-10), appears as the Scriptural proof which supports the doctrine set out in the two preceding verses. The texts cited here are numerous. They fall under two categories, which correspond to two biblical themes, first that of the Stone[7] and then that of the People.[8] Successive antitheses stamp the passage as a whole with a movement full of vitality: first the unbelievers are contrasted with the believers, then the believers with the unbelievers, and finally there is a double contrast between the old situation and the new situation of the pagans who have come to Christ.

Close connections are evident between the doctrinal part and the biblical demonstration. We could say that, to express his doctrine, the apostle has taken his terminology from the texts that he intends to quote. This is particularly the case with the term "priesthood," which helps in 2:5 to define the situation of Christians united to Christ, and which reappears in the course of the second part (2:9) in a series of expressions drawn from a sentence in Exodus in which God says to the Israelites:

You shall be for me a royal priesthood, a holy nation. (Ex 19:6)

It is obvious that the sequence of Peter's text, where the quotation from Exodus comes in the second place, does not correspond to that of his thought process. Peter did not discover the phrase in Exodus after having applied the term "priest" to the Christian situation, but before. It was this Old Testament verse that gave him his point of departure. We must therefore examine it first. It is not new to us, for we came across it already when studying the complex reality of the Old Testament priesthood.[9] But we must now consider it more closely.

1. The Priesthood Promised to the People of the Covenant (Ex 19:6)

The promise of priesthood made to the people of Israel occurs in an imposing context, that of the foundation of the first covenant at Sinai.[10] The text where this promise is found belongs, it seems, to the Elohistic tradition; it constituted a covenantal formula. But in the final redaction of the Book of Exodus, it is reduced to an introductory role (19:1-15). It precedes the account of the impressive theophany as well as the revelation of the Decalogue, and it has a parallel, beyond the "Covenant Code," in the episode of the conclusion of the Covenant by means of a sacrifice.[11] The parallelism is particularly exact between the two declarations of the people reported in 19:8 and 24:7: "All that Yahweh has said, we will put into practice." It is interesting to note that, in speaking of the sacrifice of Christ, the Epistle to the Hebrews explicitly recalls the conclusion of the Covenant,[12] while the First letter of Peter, in speaking of the priesthood of Christians, uses a sentence from the introduction.[13]

In the Hebrew text of Exodus 19:5-6, God charges Moses to promise in his name to the Israelites that, if they obey him and respect his Covenant, they will belong to him in an altogether special manner (they will be his *segullah*, his "special domain") and they will be for him a "kingdom of priests and a holy nation" (*mamleket kohanim wegoy qadôsh*). A marvelous promise of a privileged relationship with God himself, master of the entire world! The expression *mamleket kohanim*, however, is somewhat strange. Its exact interpretation triggers discussions[14] which will be worth reviewing briefly, especially since the same data will also be of use to us in the next chapter.

One could hesitate, first of all, between two grammatical constructions, because *mamleket* in Hebrew can be considered either as a construct form, requiring a complement—which would yield the translation "a kingdom of priests"—or as a noun in the absolute state, which does not introduce a complement—this would be translated "a kingdom, priests." The Aramean targums and the Greek versions of Symmachus and Theodotus have adopted the second interpretation (in Greek: *basileia hiereis*), as does Revelation, as we shall see in the next chapter. On the other hand, Aquila has adopted the former (in Greek: *basileia hiereon*), as do the majority of modern translations.[15] The case of the Septuagint is special: since its translation at this point is rather far in general from the Hebrew text, it is not possible to be certain of the grammatical construction the translators assigned to these words.

According to some exegetes, the expression means "a royal power exercised by priests."[16] It does not apply to the people as a whole, but only to the leaders. The people are defined by the expression: "a holy nation." The two statements have a reciprocal relationship: because authority is exercised by the priests, the people are a holy nation. This interpretation, however, does not appear in the Jewish tradition. The targums apply the expression to the whole people; they translate: "You will be kings and priests." The targum of Jerusalem I even makes the point emphatic with its expression: "crowned kings and celebrating priests."[17] This sense better corresponds to the movement of the text, which is addressed to all the children of Israel without distinction and says to them: "You will be . . . ."

Applied to the whole people, the expression generates questions. What meaning does it have with respect to the political and religious organization of the Israelites? How does it accord with the institution of the monarchy and the existence of a separate priesthood? Schüssler Fiorenza thinks that the text of Exodus 19:6 expresses an ideal of democratic theocracy, in implicit opposition to the institutional monarchy and priesthood. "Israel finds itself in an absolutely immediate contact with its God," and such a situation "does not involve any need for mediating institutions, whether royal or sacerdotal."[18] Stated in such categorical terms, this opinion corresponds poorly with the biblical data. There is nothing to support it in the context of Exodus 19:6, where we do not find the least trace of polemic against mediating institutions. What is emphasized is not the equality of all the Israelites among themselves, but the privileged position of Israel with respect to the other peoples. "You shall be my own possession," says Yahweh, "among all the peoples" (19:5). Compared with other nations, the Israelites will enjoy great advantages on account of their special relationship with Yahweh. Constituting as they do the kingdom of God, they will enjoy a position of superiority over the others from the political point of view. By celebrating the worship of the One God, they will be superior to the others from the religious point of view. The problem of the internal organization of the people of Israel is not under consideration.[19] It is true that other texts of the Old Testament express a polemical position against the institution of a monarchy in Israel. Alongside objections of an economic and political nature, they also contain an objection of the religious order: to desire a king is to reject Yahweh, to refuse his sovereignty.[20] Although it did not prevail, this anti-monarchical current kept alive in Israel the consciousness of a specific exigency: on account of their particular connection with Yahweh, the people of the Covenant cannot fall for the temptation, in their political life, to follow blindly the example of the pagan nations.

On the point that is of greater interest to us, that of the institution of the priesthood, the situation is very different, for in this area the Old Testament leaves no room whatever for criticism or dissent. Whereas at its beginning the monarchy is presented in an ambiguous context of human aspirations, the priesthood is seen from the start as due to a divine initiative;[21] all the details of its functioning are regulated by the Law of God, which is not the case with the monarchy. And God himself protects and guarantees the priesthood of Aaron.

When Korah stirs up a movement of protest against the privileges of the priests and declares: "All the congregation are holy, every one of them," his claim is rejected in the most forceful manner, by a crushing divine intervention.[22]

Even the context of Exodus 19:6 does not say anything about a direct contact between the people and God. On the contrary, it emphasizes the necessity of keeping the distances.[23] Deuteronomy, it is true, employs less negative language. Instead of insisting, with the Book of Exodus, on the distancing of the people, it notes that the Israelites drew near, and saw and heard God directly when he was promulgating the Decalogue.[24] However, terrified by the dangers of such contact, they begged Moses afterwards to intervene as a mediator.[25]

To return to the interpretation of Exodus 19:6, it would be well to clarify that Schüssler Fiorenza herself concludes her reflections by noting the conditional character of the divine declaration and by declaring that the ideal expressed in these suggestive formulas "never became a reality."[26] The later Jewish tradition is not so categorical on this subject. We find the two opposite opinions represented there. Certain texts suggest that the divine promise has been fulfilled: all Israelites are already, in some degree, priests of the Lord. Other texts assert the opposite: the disobedience of Israel has placed an obstacle to the realization of the promise; its fulfillment must now be considered an object of expectation for the Messianic times.[27] The evidence of the Old Testament clearly supports this second position.

2. The Meaning of the Word "Hierateuma"

The Epistle of Peter uses not the Hebrew text of Exodus 19:6 but the Greek version of the Septuagint. Instead of a literal translation of the expression *mamleket kohanim*, the Septuagint preferred a fairly free adaptation which replaces the plural "priests" (*hiereis*) by a singular *hierateuma*. It seems that this word is a creation of the Alexandrian translators. It is not attested in any text of Greek literature. We have no direct evidence then for determining its exact meaning, and we must therefore proceed in another way: analyze its formation, examine the meanings taken by words of like formation, and then try to see, among the possible senses, which one best corresponds with the context. This piece of research has been carefully carried out by several authors, whose works we shall make use of.[28]

It would be well, however, to underline one first point, which has escaped their attention and which concerns the meaning of the Greek suffix -*ma*. This suffix gives a concrete meaning to the words it helps to form. It indicates neither a quality nor a function, but the product resulting from an action or, in a more general sense, an ensemble of things or of persons in relation to this action: *ktisma* signifies "creature/creation," the tangible result of the action of "creating." Formed by means of the suffix -*ma*, the word *hierateuma* will therefore have a concrete meaning and will be able to represent neither a priest quality nor a priest function, which are expressed by other words.[29]

The complete analysis of the term calls attention to two other elements in its composition: the root *hier* -, which indicates the sphere of the "sacred," and the suffix -*eu*, which describes the connection with a function. From the etymological point of view, the word *hierateuma* therefore signifies "a certain concrete reality with relation to a sacred function."

Words with a like formation are numerous in Greek. Two hundred and twenty-four substantives in -*euma* have been noted. The contexts in which they are used confirm the analysis just made. It is not, strictly speaking, a matter of *nomina actionis*, as is often stated too facilely, but of terms which have a concrete meaning in connection with a given action or function. They could be classed in several categories, according to their different semantic specializations. One of these is particularly apt in throwing light on the meaning of *hierateuma*, as Cerfaux showed very well, and Elliott even better. This is the category of words which describe a group of persons exercising a certain function: *bouleuma*, group of senators, *techniteuma*, corporation of artisans, *politeuma*, collectivity of citizens. These words have a threefold connation: 1) they apply to persons; 2) not considering them as individuals but as forming a group; 3) this group is characterized by a specific function.

This "personal-corporate-functional" sense exactly corresponds to the context of Exodus 19:6, which applies *hierateuma* to the Israelites as a whole: "You will be for me," says God, "a *hierateuma*, a group of people exercising the priestly function." In choosing this translation, the Septuagint has then added to the Hebrew text a corporate aspect which did not appear in the simple plural *kohanim*, "priests"; or, more precisely, it has extended to the priesthood the corporate aspect which was expressed in Hebrew by the terms of the context, "kingdom" and "nation." Moreover, it was concerned to emphasize this divine promise, for it repeated the expression in Exodus 23:22, where the Hebrew text does not contain them.

To be complete, it must be added that the word *hierateuma* is not necessarily limited to only one meaning. The example of *bouleuma* is instructive on this matter. *Bouleuma* has two possible meanings: sometimes it designates the group formed by the senators; at other times it designates a session of the senate.[30] In both cases, the meaning is concrete, but in the first, the principal element is the group aspect, while in the second it is the aspect of their functioning, the concrete exercise of a function. In an analogous way, *hierateuma* can take on, according to the context in which it is employed, the sense of "priestly organism" or that of "priestly functioning." A sentence in the Second Book of Maccabees requires rather this second meaning. Alluding to the restoration of the Temple cult after the persecution of Antiochus, it declares that God has given his people the *hierateuma*.[31] Since it is a question of a gift granted to a group of persons, the word does not designate this group of persons, the people, as in Exodus 19:6; it could, strictly speaking, refer to another group, that of the Levitical priests, but it is not clear to what historical fact the phrase would then refer, while the sense of "functioning of the priesthood" fits exactly the events that we know of: after the profanation of the Temple and the interruption of the priestly activity, the victory of Judas Maccabeus had permitted the purification of the Temple and the resumption of worship.

3. The Priestly People (1 Pet 2:9)

The verse in which Peter draws more directly on the text of the Septuagint is that of 1 Peter 2:9. We shall therefore begin by analyzing this verse, and only then study the more complex formulation of 1 Peter 2:5.

A careful comparison of 1 Peter 2:9 with Exodus 19:6 (LXX) reveals a fundamental resemblance, together with several significant differences. The resemblance consists in the fact that the word *hierateuma* and the qualifiers associated with it serve to qualify a group of persons indicated by the pronoun "you" and opposed to another category of persons. In Greek, the two sentences have an identical beginning:

hymeis de, "but you," and contain the same titles: *basileion hierateuma* and *ethnos hagion*, "royal priesthood" and "holy nation." It follows that the term *hierateuma* has fundamentally the same meaning in 1 Peter 2:9 as in Exodus 19:6: it is applied to persons, since it qualifies a personal pronoun; it presents these persons as a collectivity endowed with a certain unity, since it is in the singular, and it indicates as a unifying element the common relationship to a sacred function.

On other points, the two texts diverge one from the other. A first difference may appear important: in Exodus 19:6 it is God who speaks; in 1 Peter 2:9 it is a man, an apostle. In reality, this difference has no real significance, for Peter is not speaking in his own name, he is conscious of being no more than the mouthpiece of God and this is precisely why he adopts the words of Exodus. What should rather engage our attention is the change in tense, the change of audience, and the change in conditions. The phrase in Exodus is in the future, it is addressed to the Israelites, whom it is contrasting to the pagan nations, and it is preceded by a conditional proposition. In Peter, the affirmation is applied to the present, it is addressed to people drawn from the pagan nations, and it is not conditional. The perspective is then radically transformed.

We pass from a promise: "You will be for me a royal priesthood . . ." to the proclamation of a fact: "But you, you are a royal priesthood . . . ." The promise is fulfilled; God's plan is realized. One can object, it is true, that in Peter the statement is not so explicit; in Greek it does not include a verb and so it appears as an acclamation ("But you, a royal priesthood!"), rather than as an affirmation ("You are . . ."). Its application to the present, however, is beyond all doubt. The following verse confirms this, for it contrasts the past situation of those to whom the Epistle is addressed (you . . . *formerly* a non-people) with their present situation (*now*, people of God).

To bring out even more this aspect of fulfillment, Peter expands the text of Exodus by adding to it several expressions drawn from a prophecy of Deutero-Isaiah. Announcing the wonders of a new Exodus, the prophet gave other glorious titles to the people of God:

> My chosen race, my people whom I have saved in order to declare my mighty deeds (Is 43:20-21, LXX).

Peter takes these titles adapting them somewhat to his expression, and by so doing obtains a more impressive series of laudatory titles, which exalt the dignity of the Christian people:

But you, a chosen race, a royal priesthood, a holy nation, a people destined for salvation, to proclaim the great deeds of him who called you out of darkness into his marvelous light. (1 Pet 2:9)

Peter obviously is not unaware that all this glory has nothing to do with human pride, it is the gift of a merciful love. He concludes:

Once you were no people but now you are God's people; once you had not received mercy but now you have received mercy. (1 Pet 2:10; cf. 1:3)

Situated in this context, the word *hierateuma* has its corporate aspect even more clearly accentuated than in the text of Exodus, for it is placed in parallel with a greater number of collective terms: "race" (*genos*), "nation" (*ethnos*), and "people" (*laos*). The sacred function with which it is connected is not clearly specified. Elliott thinks that the idea of priestly function is not really what holds Peter's attention and that "the significance of *hierateuma* lies not in its cultic connotations, but together with *basileion*, in its designation of the electedness and holiness of the Divine Regent's community."[32] Before accepting this position, we should first examine the data in the text more closely.

In the statement of 2:9, the attention of the exegetes is directed to the final proposition: "in order to proclaim the great deeds . . ," which describes a function of witness before the world. More than one commentator thinks he can discern here the sacred function that defines the priesthood.[33] This opinion deserves consideration, though it cannot be regarded as immediately decisive. The action of "proclaiming" is, in fact, the only one mentioned here, and, on the other hand, among the four titles attributed to the Christian community, that of *hierateuma* is the only one which directly implies an activity. One could, however, object that in this sentence the end described is not directly connected to the proclamation of the priesthood; it is separated from it by two other statements and has a closer connection with the second of these, for it too comes from the text of Isaiah 43:21, which does not speak of priesthood. Moreover, the Old Testament does not regard the act of proclaiming the good deeds of God as a priestly activity. In begging for divine assistance, any Israelite struggling with a distressing situation would bolster his request with a promise of public thanksgiving: "In the full assembly I will praise you" (Ps 22:23). The psalms of supplication regularly include this promise and the psalms of thanksgiving represent its realization: "Come, listen . . . I will tell you what God has done for me" (Ps 66:16). From this point of view the function of witness does not appear to be specific to the priesthood. But there is reason to inquire whether Peter has remained tied to the perspective of the Old Testament. To shed light on this, it is necessary to analyze the other passage in which Peter speaks of the priesthood (2:5).

But we must first complete the analysis of verse 9. A controversial detail must be briefly mentioned: the function and meaning, in Exodus 19:6 and 1 Peter 2:9, of the word that precedes *hierateuma* and which in Greek is *basileion*. When used as an adjective, this word means "royal"; as a substantive, it refers to a royal possession and has very varied meanings: kingdom, royal power, royal palace, the king's crown. In the Septuagint, the word is most often used as a substantive. In Exodus 19:6, however, the construction of the Greek phrase hardly permits us to consider it as a noun, for it is immediately followed by *hierateuma* and by a coordinating conjunction *kai*, which introduces another expression: *basileion hierateuma kai ethnos hagion*. In such a case, the normal translation is: "royal priesthood and holy nation." In order for *basileion* to appear as a substantive, it would have to be coordinated itself by a *kai* to the word *hierateuma*. In 1 Peter 2:9 the situation is less clear, for here we have an enumeration without any conjunction. It is therefore possible, grammatically speaking, to separate *basileion* from *hierateuma* and to consider it as a substantive. However, the disposition of the phrase rather suggests that it should be taken as an adjective qualifying *hierateuma*, for these two words are preceded and followed by pairs of analogous words; so one obtains a series of three parallel expressions: "chosen race, royal priesthood, holy nation," with a chiastic inversion (noun-adjective, adjective-noun, noun-adjective) frequently found in the biblical writings.

If one accepts this interpretation, the priestly organism formed by the Christian people is seen to be qualified by "royal." In the other hypothesis, one would have two distinct titles, "royal-possession" and "priestly-organism," both applied to the Christian community. The emphasis is then slightly less on the priesthood and a little stronger on the relationship with the divine king. This does not correspond well, in reality, with Peter's customary orientation in this Epistle, for nowhere else does he refer to the theme of the kingdom.

He prefers to speak of the divine "glory." If he has put the word *basileion* in 2:9 as also the word *ethnos* in the pair of words which follow, it would seem to be simply because he found these two words in the text that he was quoting. In 2:5 he uses neither one nor the other, but from each of the two pairs he retains only one term, *hierateuma* for the first, *hagion* for the second, and he combines them in a novel expression, *hierateuma hagion*, "a holy priesthood," which reveals what he wishes to emphasize.

God's promise in Exodus was conditional. Its realization was to depend on the obedience of the people and their fidelity to the Covenant (Ex 19:5). Unfortunately, in spite of the promises they made (19:8), these conditions were never observed. The prophets continued to reproach Israel unceasingly for its unfaithfulness and to point out the breaking of the Covenant (Hos 1:9). God, nevertheless, did not give up his plan; he promised a reversal of the situation:

I will love the Un-Loved and to that which is Not-My-People I will say: You are my people and they will say: My God. (Hos 2:25)

It is the fulfillment of this prediction that Peter is proclaiming. His words are therefore no longer conditional. Does this mean that no condition has been fulfilled and that the royal priesthood has been granted by God as if by force to disobedient and rebellious people? To understand it in this way would be to badly misinterpret Peter's text! But one would be equally mistaken in asserting that the requirement of Exodus 19:5 was fulfilled by mankind, who in this way have allowed God to succeed in his plan. The context shows that a condition has been fulfilled, but one different from the first: not the observance of the Law, but the following of Christ through faith. It is, in fact, to believers that Peter applies the glorious titles that had been promised to the people of Israel. The pronoun "you" of 2:9 takes up that of 2:7a and we can join these two texts: "To you therefore honor, you the believers . . . you, a chosen race, a royal priesthood . . . ." Faith is the new condition that allows human beings, imperfect as they are, to exercise sacred functions and to enter as priests into the service of God. The foundation of the priesthood is therefore not human merit, and conversely, human wretchedness no longer constitutes an obstacle to participation in the priesthood.

The change of conditions involves a change with regard to the audience addressed. If the sole requirement is faith, the promise of the priesthood is no longer reserved, as in Exodus, to Israelites only, but it is valid also for pagans who come to Christ. The contrast is no longer between Israel and the pagan nations, but between "believers" and "unbelievers." In this way, fulfillment takes on a universal extension for which the prophecy of Exodus made no provision but which had been anticipated by other prophetic texts. Had not God announced that his Servant would not be content with "bringing back the remnant of Israel," but that he would also become "the light of the pagan nations,"and that his house would be called "a house of prayer for all the nations"?[34] Peter's statement does not make any distinction. In itself it can apply to all Christians, whether they came from Judaism or from paganism. Other passages of the Epistle show that Peter is speaking especially to pagan converts.[35]

4. The Building of the Spiritual House (1 Pet 2:4-5)

The statement of 2:9 expresses a position acquired or, more exactly, a privilege received. It is illuminated by the previous context, which shows how this position was reached, how this privilege was received. The doctrine of the priesthood of believers appears here in all its admirable dynamism and in all its spiritual depth:

So come to him, our living Stone—the stone rejected by men but choice and precious in the sight of God. Come, and let yourselves be built, as living stones, into a spiritual temple; become a holy priesthood, (*hierateuma*), to offer spiritual sacrifices acceptable to God through Jesus Christ. (1 Pet 2:4-5)

To be completely literal, the translation should begin with the relative "*to whom* you approaching . . . " but this form is hardly tolerable in English. The Greek relative refers to the person of "the Lord," that is, of Christ, who is named at the end of the previous verse. As to the verb "you are being built," its Greek form *oikodomeisthe* does not allow us to determine whether it is an indicative or an imperative, for the form is identical in both instances. Some commentators, Spicq, for example, give it the value of the imperative here and so turn the sentence into an exhortation. Others, e.g. Selwyn, understand it as an indicative and see the sentence as an affirmation. This second interpretation seems better founded for several reasons: in the first place, because the verb is in the passive, and this passive, "to be built," can hardly be employed in the imperative; in any case, it is not so used anywhere else in the New Testament. Furthermore, this verb is introduced by a relative pronoun, which makes the imperative even more unlikely. Finally, from the doctrinal point of view, the nuance of exhortation should rather be attributed to the participle "you approaching," situated at the beginning of the sentence. Christians are implicitly being invited to approach Christ. If they approach him, they become part of the spiritual house that is under construction. Even if *oikodomeisthe* is taken as an imperative, the sentence does not attribute the construction of the house to human beings. This is a divine and not a human achievement.

The sentence clearly divides into two parts, the first of which is linked to the participle "you approaching" and describes adherence to Christ, while the second, which includes the principal verb, "you are being built," expresses the result of this adherence. This arrangement throws a vivid light on a fundamental trait of the doctrine of the priesthood of believers. It shows that the first point of this doctrine is the absolute necessity of the mediation of Christ and of continual union with him. It is only in the measure that they adhere to Christ that believers may become a priestly organism. There is reason here to challenge Elliott's position, according to which "there is no foundation for the common assumption that in 1 Peter the community is a body of priests by virtue of participation in the priesthood of Christ."[36] Certainly Peter, unlike the author of Hebrews, never gives Christ a priestly title. But this observation, although literally correct, is by no means sufficient to settle the question. In fact, the mention of priesthood in 2:4-5 is indissolubly united with the person and work of Christ. The priestly organism exists only by virtue of an adherence to Christ ("you, approaching him . . .") and it performs its function of "offering sacrifices" only by virtue of the mediation of Christ ("by Jesus Christ").

In addition, this reference to the priesthood is set in a context of assimilation with Christ: "in approaching him, the living stone," believers in their turn become "living stones," and it is in this way that they are able to be part of the priestly organism. Christ, who has been accepted by God as the foundation of the new building, transforms into his own image those who follow him and draws them along in the current of his own mystery. Peter's sentence clearly shows that the believers share in priesthood only through union with Christ. To imagine that the priestly organism is made up of believers alone, to the exclusion of Christ, would be to go completely against the sense of the text. We must recognize, rather, that for Peter, as for the author of Hebrews, only Christ possesses the priesthood in fullness, for he is the sole mediator. Here, as in Hebrews, the believers share in the priestly *worship*, but they do not exercise priestly *mediation*; they are, on the contrary, subject to it. Later in his exposition, Peter will return to this point when he says that "Christ died once for our sins, the just for the unjust, in order to give us access to God."[37]

To describe this adherence to Christ, Peter uses the verb "to approach" (*proserchomai*), which is also used several times in Hebrews. According to its context, the verb primarily applies to a spiritual advance, to an adhesion of faith, as in Hebrews 10:22 or in the Fourth Gospel, where "to come to" (*erchomai pros*) and "to believe in" are parallel expressions. But after baptism, the profession of faith is normally expressed by participation in the liturgical life of the Christian community: by coming regularly to listen to the Word of God, to take part in the prayers and in the Eucharist, and to practice brotherly love.[38] Here, as in Hebrews 10:22, the verb *proserchomai* may very well carry a connotation of this kind.

The believers' profession of faith is directed to the risen Christ. The qualification given to the "stone" suggests this specification when it says that it is a question of a "living stone."[39] But the apostle is careful to recall the path which has led Christ to his glorious life: before being "honored in the sight of God," the "living stone" was "rejected by men." Faith is, in fact, not just an acceptance of the person of Christ, it is also openness to the whole mystery of his Passion and Resurrection, conscious acceptance of the course that his life has traced out.[40]

To be still more precise, the believers' profession of faith applies to Christ in as much as he has become, by his Passion and Resurrection, the foundation of new relationships between people and the principle of a new solidarity. Christ, the "living stone," is henceforth the basis of a new construction, the bond of a new communion, which unites human beings with one another by placing them in relationship with God. The word *lithos*, which in Greek designates a stone that can be used in the construction of a building, is rich in all these connotations, which are then developed in the second half of the sentence (2:5).

This second half evokes, in fact, the construction of a house and it defines its nature and indicates its purpose. Without saying so, Peter follows the schema proposed by a verse of Psalm 118, which he will cite a little later.[41] The problem raised here is that of the choice of material for the construction of a building. The builders discard a stone which they regard as unusable. But, through the intervention of God, this rejected stone becomes the "cornerstone," which holds the building together. In this way, new significance is given to the perspective outlined by Peter in verse 4: the honor given by God to Christ, "the stone rejected by men," does not consist—at least, not entirely—in a heavenly glorification which exalts him personally, but it consists above all in making him the sole valid foundation by which the solidity of a construction can be assured. Having become the "living stone" by his Passion and Resurrection, Christ has acquired the capacity to join other stones to himself, and these stones are transformed by contact with him, receive his new life and are incorporated into an edifice which is held together solely by dependence on him.

This building is defined with the help of two expressions, the second of which particularly interests us: "spiritual house" and "holy priesthood" (*hierateuma hagion*). Their coupling prevents us from adopting a banal interpretation of the metaphor of the "house": on the contrary, we must see here, as in filigree, all the richness of the biblical theme of the house of God, with the developments conferred on it by the evangelical tradition. We have already had occasion to note the importance of this theme as well as its relationship with priesthood.[42] The Old Testament habitually calls the Temple of Jerusalem "house of Yahweh," or even just "the house." Similar expressions are found in the Gospels and in the Acts.[43] By using the word "house" (*oikos*) rather than "sanctuary" (*naos*), which Paul uses in analogous contexts,[44] our text has greater affinity with the current of Messianism which finds its origin in the oracle of Nathan (2 Sam 7). To David, who had conceived the grandiose project of building a temple worthy of God, the prophet brought the divine response: it would not be David who would build a "house" for God, but God who would build for David a royal "house," that is to say, a progeny who would reign after him. And this progeny, given by God to David, would build a "house" for God.

Of course, the prophecy of Nathan had found a first realization in Solomon, David's heir who reigned after him and who had built the first Temple. This, however, was only an initial stage which could not exhaust the scope of the prophetic word. The New Testament reveals that this word reached its perfect fulfillment only through the Resurrection of Christ. Son of David, enthroned with God for an eternal reign, the risen Christ is the "royal house" given by God to David. But—something even more unexpected—the glorified body of Christ is at the same time the "house" built for God by the Son of David, the true "sanctuary."

By adhering through faith to the risen Christ, believers are not only introduced into this sanctuary, but they become its "living stones." In fact, this is not a question of a physical building. No physical building could assure mankind of an authentic relationship with God, for "God is spirit" (Jn 4:24). It is a question of a "spiritual house," that is, a house that owes its construction and cohesion to the action of the sanctifying Spirit.[45] In order to become its cornerstone, Christ himself has been "put to death according to the flesh, and brought to life according to the Spirit" (1 Pet 3:18). His glorified humanity, entirely imbued with the Holy Spirit, gives to those who are united to him the opportunity to be transformed by the Spirit in such a way that they become house of God. This is the substance of the doctrine which Peter evokes in a few words. We find it again in more explicit terms (except with regard to its relationship to the Passion and Resurrection) in a passage in the letter to the Ephesians, which bears a striking resemblance to our present text: "In the Lord you yourselves are also built together into a dwelling of God in the Spirit" (Eph 2:22).

Since it is at the same time Temple of God and community of believers, the "spiritual house" appears as the perfect realization of the New Covenant, under its two inseparable aspects: communion with God and communion among human beings. The term "house," however, is too static to describe it completely. Peter has therefore completed it with another word, *hierateuma*, which in turn is explained by a verbal locution: "to offer sacrifices." We note here that the grammatical connection between the two expressions, "spiritual house" and "holy priesthood" is not the same in all manuscripts. In some there is a simple juxtaposition, so that the grammatical function is the same: the believers united to Christ become a "spiritual house, a holy priesthood." In others, there is a subordination by means of the preposition *eis*: the believers become a "spiritual house for a holy priesthood." Better attested, this second reading is preferred by the critical editions.

The divergence between the manuscripts probably comes from the difficulty presented by the word *hierateuma*. The suppression of the preposition *eis* is best explained by the desire to take *hierateuma* as a title applied directly to the community of believers and so give this word in 2:5 the identical meaning that it has in 2:9: "You are a *hierateuma*, a priestly organism," which would correspond with the promise in Exodus 19:6. The presence of the preposition *eis* obliges us, however, to give the word *hierateuma* a slightly different meaning, for it is no longer on the same footing with "spiritual house," and no longer directly qualifies the believers. Instead of explaining the nature of the spiritual house, it now indicates its purpose. The meaning that would now be appropriate is that of "priestly functioning," a possible meaning of *hierateuma*.[46] The verbal locution that follows, placed simply in apposition with *hierateuma*, specifies what kind of "functioning" is involved: "to offer spiritual sacrifices."

But is it normal to take the same word in two different senses in the same text, separated only by a few words? Elliott thinks not, and he tries to maintain in 2:5 the "personal-corporate-functional" meaning which he has established for Exodus 19:6 and 1 Peter 2:9. But in doing so he does not take into account the difference in formulation. To take an analogous example, the word "government" could quite easily be taken successively in its functional meaning ("To be charged with the government of a great country is a frightening responsibility"), and in its corporate sense ("The government is composed of ministers and secretaries of state"); the appropriate sense is determined by the formulation of the phrase itself and not by the meaning employed in another sentence, even a neighboring one. In our case, the formulation of 1 Peter 2:5 suggests that *hierateuma* should be understood in the sense of "priestly functioning," while that of 2:9 requires the sense "priestly organism." In the first text, the personal aspect and the corporate aspect are not by any means absent, but they are expressed by another word, "house." In the second text, in which "house" is not repeated, these two aspects must be carried by *hierateuma*. Read after the words of 2:5, the *hierateuma* of 2:9 appears indeed as equivalent to the entire expression which there defined the community of believers: "a spiritual house for a priestly functioning." This observation allows us now to respond to the question left unanswered in the preceding paragraph: Can one say with Elliott that "the significance of *hierateuma* is not to be situated in its cultic connotations"? The words of 2:5 leave no doubt on the matter; Peter has a priestly function very much in mind. He speaks explicitly of the offering of sacrifices. It is not possible to consider the cultic connotations of *hierateuma* as secondary in this context.[47]

5. The Christian Priesthood

In the introduction to his book, Elliott recalls Luther's use of the priestly text of 1 Peter; on a number of occasions the great reformer turned to this text as a basis for his argument against the ministerial priesthood of the Catholic Church and to support his assertion that all Christians have an equal claim to be priests, that all have the same powers with respect to the Word of God and to the sacraments, and that in consequence the priests and the bishops do not possess any particular power or any authority, except that which the faithful grant them.[48] The force of Luther's affirmation is such that it has left a lasting impression. Still in our time, the idea continues that Peter's words apply to Christians taken individually, affirming their equality in the priesthood, and that they have no connection with what was later called the priestly ministry of bishops and priests. Each of these points needs to be examined.

On the matter of the individualistic interpretation of the text, Elliott's study is particularly illuminating. A searching semantic analysis of the word *hierateuma* and of its use in Exodus 19:6 and 1 Peter 2:5, 9 leads this author to dispute radically the possibility of such an interpretation: "It is semantically inadmissible to attempt to reduce either of these words [*basileion* or *hierateuma*] to an individual-distributive classification."[49] Peter is speaking of a "new society," holy and chosen by God. "The predicates for this new elected society are collective and corporate, applicable only to *a people, a community*, and not to individuals. It is in this sense that they were used in 1 Peter 2:4-10."[50] On this important point Elliott is perfectly correct: *hierateuma* has a corporate sense and the context in which it is placed strongly underlines this aspect, both in verse 9 (with "race," "nation," "people") and even more in verse 5 (with "house"). By speaking of the construction of a "house," Peter clearly shows that he is not considering the believers as individuals standing side by side, each one a priest on his own account, but rather as persons set in relationship with one another so as to form together a single priestly organism. The condition to be fulfilled in order to share in the priesthood is to be integrated into the common construction, to be inserted into the organism. A believer who would refuse this condition and claim to go to God in an individualistic manner would exclude himself from the Christian priesthood. The idea of a priesthood exercised by individuals independently of the body as a whole does not in any way enter into Peter's perspective.

Does this mean that the Christian priesthood cannot be exercised except in community activities of the whole assembly of believers, as for example in the celebration of the Eucharist? In itself, Peter's text is too little developed to allow us to resolve this question; but the orientation of the whole Epistle does not favor restricting the perspective in this way for, in spite of the constant use of the plural, it always implies a personal engagement of each Christian in "his whole conduct" (1:15) and not simply a contribution to common activities. We must therefore distinguish between an individualistic claim to the priesthood and a personal participation in the common priesthood. The prayer and the priestly offering of a Christian can never be individualistic, but it does not follow from this that their only valid expression is one which is communal. The condition for being able to present an offering to God is always to accept being part of the "spiritual house" founded on Christ; there is no other "holy place" for meeting God. But it is not necessary to be physically in a Christian assembly to fulfill this condition. Even when all alone in a desert, a Christian worthy of the name is spiritually united to the Church and, in consequence, is truly participating in its priesthood.

As to the equality of all in the priesthood, Peter's text says absolutely nothing. To be sure, it describes the participation of all believers in the priesthood of the Church, but it does not speak of equality. In connecting "priestly organism" with "spiritual house," it rather suggests different levels of participation. In a building, in fact, all the stones form part of the edifice and are joined one to another, but they are not all on the same level nor do they all fulfill the same function. A house, of necessity, has a differentiated structure. The existence of a priestly hierarchy in the Church is in no way at variance with the idea of *hierateuma*, as Peter presents it in 2:4-5; on the contrary, it is implicitly contained therein.

This becomes clearer when one examines the way in which the Epistle to the Ephesians develops the theme of the construction of the Church. The assertion in Ephesians 2:22 is very similar to that in 1 Peter 2:4-5. A Synoptic presentation shows very close connections:

Ephesians 2:21–22	*1 Peter 2:3–5*
21 . . . in the Lord,	3 . . . the Lord,
22 in whom	4 you, approaching him . . .
you too	5 you also, like living stones,
you are being built together	you are built
into a dwelling of God	[into] a spiritual house.
in the Spirit.	

Now, the immediate context of Ephesians strongly indicates the existence of a structure in the building:

You are the members of the house of God, constructed as you are on the foundations of the apostles and the prophets, the cornerstone being Christ Jesus himself, in whom the whole construction is put right and grows to form a holy temple in the Lord. (Eph 2:19-21)

In the house of God, all do not have an identical position. Some have been placed as foundations of the building; the others cannot take part in the construction except by agreeing to rest upon them.

Later, taking up the subject in slightly different terms, the Epistle gives a more detailed list of the various functions that Christ confers upon the members of his body:

It is he who has placed some as apostles, others as prophets, others as evangelists, others as pastors and teachers, so as to organize the saints for the work of the ministry, in order to build the body of Christ . . . in order that . . . living in truth and love, we may grow in all respects toward him who is the head, Christ, from whom the whole body, joined and knit together by every joint with which it is supplied, according to the activity attributed to each of its organs, works out its growth and builds itself up in love. (Eph 4:11-12, 14-16)

In the Epistle to the Romans, the passage which invites all Christians to offer themselves as living sacrifices (Rom 12:1-2) is likewise followed by an expansion on the diversity of functions in the unity of the body of Christ (12:3-8). All these texts clearly show that in describing the Church as a "spiritual house destined for a priestly function," Peter has no intention, as some affirm, of advocating an egalitarianism with regard to priesthood.

His words are even sometimes presented as if, in the Church, he would reserve the qualification of "priest" (*hiereus*) only for the laity and would deny it to those who exercise the pastoral ministry. This is an obvious error. It is true that Peter does not speak explicitly in this passage either of apostles or of those in charge of communities. His allusion to the "newly born" suggests that he is speaking particularly to newly baptized Christians. But it would be absurd to maintain that what he is saying applies only to them and that Peter therefore excludes himself from the "priestly organism" at the same time as those in charge of the communities and the Christians who have been baptized for a long time! The "you" that he employs is not opposed to an implicit "us," but to a "they," referring to the unbelievers. The remainder of the clause states it clearly: "To you therefore the honor, to you the believers, but for the unbelievers the stone has become . . . a stumbling block." The meaning of the text is therefore that all the believers are united in the same priestly organism. Peter is proclaiming the priestly character of the entire Church, in so much as it forms a building founded on Christ. If the totality of the building is priestly, then its structure too must be recognized as priestly, as it cannot be separated from the whole, and priestly by a special right, for it has a special bond with Christ.[51]

6. Presbyters and Priesthood (1 Pet 5:1-4)

Toward the end of his letter Peter explicitly bears witness to the existence of a structure in the priestly organism formed by the Christian community. It is true that he does not use a priestly title at this point, but simply employs the title "presbyters," the word then in use to designate those in charge of the communities.

Since the Greek word which he uses, *presbyteros*, is the term which has given us our term "priest," it is appropriate to examine it more closely at this point. In the first century, *presbyteros* was not a priestly title. The first meaning of this word is "older person." In Jewish circles where Greek was spoken, it had been given a particular meaning: it served to translate the Hebrew *zeqenim* and to designate the members of the council charged with directing the community. In principle, this council was actually made up of "older" men. *Presbyteros* in this way became an authority title which could be rendered "elder." This designation passed from Jewish communities to Christian communities of Jewish origin and finally spread through all the Christian communities, where it became the term for an ordained ministry, characteristic of the structure of the Church in the following centuries.

The Gospels, which reflect the situation at the time of Jesus, quite often use the word *presbyteros*, but never in a priestly sense. Twice they take it in the general sense of "older person,"[52] using it sometimes to designate the master minds of the former generation,[53] but above all they use it in the technical Jewish sense: "the elders of the people" were one of the three well-known groups that constituted the Great Sanhedrin at Jerusalem. The two other groups were that of the *archiereis* and that of the *grammateis*. We encountered them in the course of Chapter I. It is intriguing to observe that, out of these three categories, the one whose Greek name is most closely related to the English "priest" is also the one most distant from it in meaning. The *presbyteroi* in the Great Council, in fact, represented the lay element. The religious authorities were represented by the *archiereis*, in charge of worship, and by the *grammateis*, experts in the interpretation of the Sacred Books. English translations usually translate *presbyteroi* as "elders" or "presbyters," *grammateis* as "scribes," and *archiereis* as "high priests." The theme of this work is the priesthood, and so we are not interested in the *presbyteroi* of the Gospels, but in the *hiereis* and the *archiereis*.

In the Acts of the Apostles, the situation changes perceptibly, for alongside the Jewish sense of the word we now find its Christian usage appearing.[54] On several occasions Luke mentions the existence of "elders" in the Church of Jerusalem; he reports that Paul and Barnabas "appointed elders" in the recently founded communities (Ac 14:23) and that Paul summoned "the elders of the Church of Ephesus" during his visit to Miletus (20:17). The word carries the same meaning in six Epistles of the New Testament,[55] which include the First Epistle of Peter. In this Christian usage, the word is sometimes translated as "presbyters," to distinguish it from its other uses.

As Christian reflection continued to explore the various aspects of the ministry of the "presbyters," the word designating them acquired, over the course of centuries, a greater richness of content. In particular, it acquired a more and more markedly priestly connotation. This is why its derivative, "priest," which has always been applied to a

Christian ministry, is at the same time the equivalent of the Greek *hiereus* and is therefore used also to designate the ministers of both Jewish and pagan ritual worship. This makes for an extremely complicated linguistic situation. It is not possible here to unravel all its aspects. Our problem is only to see whether the priestly connotation taken on by the term "presbyter" can or cannot find support in the New Testament.

The only writing which speaks at the same time of Christian priesthood and of Christian "presbyters" is the First Epistle of Peter. The connection which it establishes between the two realities is not easy to define, for he speaks of them in different contexts. Three chapters separate the exhortation addressed to the presbyters (5:1-4) from the passage which proclaims the priestly dignity of the believers (2:1-10). First observation: the two texts have no explicit connection. Peter does not mention the presbyters when he calls the Church a "priestly organism," and on the other hand, he does not refer to the priesthood when he addresses the presbyters. The latter do not receive the title *hiereis*. No connection is explicitly expressed between the priesthood of the Church and the ministry of the presbyters. This silence shows, first of all, that Peter took for granted the current designations for presbyters. It would have been surprising if he had not. When a name that describes a function comes into common use, it is not easily changed, even when the understanding of the function is considerably modified.[56] Another aspect is more significant: the absence of all reference to presbyters in 1 Peter 2:4-5 shows that the priesthood of the Church is not based on their ministry; its basis is elsewhere and the text indicates this: it is Christ, in the mystery of his Passion and Resurrection.

Once this essential point has been brought to light, we would do well not to stop with a one-sided insistence on the argument from silence, but open our eyes to the connections that can be found between the two passages. Here is the translation of the second:

> I therefore exhort the presbyters among you, I myself a presbyter too and a witness of the sufferings of Christ, and also an associate in the glory which is to be revealed;
> feed the flock of God, which has been entrusted to you, watching over it, not by constraint but willingly, according to God; not for shameful gain but devotedly, not domineering over those in your charge, but making yourselves models to the flock. And when the

chief shepherd appears, you will obtain the unfading crown of glory. (1 Pet 5:1-4)

One can pick out several contact points between this exhortation to the presbyters and the text on the priesthood of the Church. The beginning of each offers significant parallels, although the terms employed are different: they both evoke the Passion of Christ and his glory.[57] This parallelism suggests that the foundation of ministry is the same as that of priesthood. Secondly, the mention of the "flock of God" (5:2) corresponds to the idea of the construction of a "spiritual house" (2:5). It is evident that these two expressions define one and the same reality. The aspect that remains implicit in the first text becomes explicit in the second: it was not said that the spiritual house had a structure, but it is said that the flock has pastors or shepherds. In fact, the responsibility of "feeding the flock of God which has been entrusted" to them, and also of "watching over" them (*episkopountes*[58]), falls upon the presbyters. This charge constitutes a special participation in the relationship that Christ himself has with the flock; in an earlier sentence, in fact, Christ has been named "the shepherd and guardian of your souls;"[59] here he is called "chief shepherd," literally "arch-shepherd," a title which is not without a certain connection with that of *archi-hiereus*.[60] In 2:4-5, it will be remembered, Peter has strongly emphasized the mediation of Christ: in order to be integrated into the priestly organism, Christians must draw near to Christ and their sacrifices must pass through him. In presenting the charge of the presbyters as a realization of the very mission of Christ, Peter has initiated a priestly understanding of their role. He himself does not draw this conclusion, but he provides the elements that lead in that direction.

7. Apostle and Priesthood (Rom 15:16)

Before Peter, Paul had made a suggestive comparison between the priestly service of the Temple and the ministry of the Gospel:

Do you not know that those who perform the sacred rites draw their livelihood from the Temple, that those who serve the altar share with the altar? In the same way, the Lord has ordained that those who proclaim the Gospel are to live by the Gospel. (1 Cor 9:13-14)

The expressions: "those who perform the sacred rites" and "those who serve the altar," which are circumlocutions used in order better to emphasize the correspondence between the service performed and its recompense, actually designate the Jewish priests, for the verse refers to the role of the priests prescribed by the Law of Moses.[61] Paul therefore is likening the Christian apostolate to a priesthood.

It might be objected that we have here only a simple comparison and that care must be taken to avoid concluding too quickly that it offers a priestly understanding of the Christian apostolate. But another of Paul's expressions shows that he did indeed think of his own vocation in this way. Speaking to the Romans about "the grace given to him by God," he defines this grace by saying that it aims to make of him

> a minister of Christ Jesus for the pagans, one who fulfills the holy work of the Gospel of God, so that the offering of the pagans should be made acceptable, being sanctified in the Holy Spirit (Rom 15:16).

All the terms of this text make use of cultic categories and express a close relation between the ministry of the apostle and sacrificial worship. In itself, the word *leitourgos*, "minister," is not a term reserved either to the priesthood or to worship, any more than is its English equivalent, but it is susceptible of a cultic meaning and the context clearly gives it one here, by linking it to a sacred work, an oblation and a sanctification. In the Epistle to the Hebrews, the same title is applied to Christ in a cultic sense, and it is specified by complements which make it the equivalent not only of "priest" but of "high priest," "minister of the sanctuary," that is to say, of the Holy of Holies (Heb 8:2). By presenting himself as a "minister of Christ Jesus," Paul shows that he does not consider himself as a high priest, but as a functionary of subordinate rank.

The verb which follows, "fulfilling a sacred work" (*hierourgounta*) evokes more directly the priestly qualification (*hiereus*). A detailed study reveals, however, that this word does not necessarily refer to a priestly function, as is the case with the verb *hierateuéin*.[62] In contemporary Jewish texts, the verb *hierourgein* most often designates the action of offering a ritual sacrifice and it is therefore employed with reference to priests who offer these sacrifices, but one also finds it in cases where the rite is performed by persons who are not priests, for example Abraham or Saul. Some texts even use it to speak of lay persons making sacrificial offerings, through recourse to the ministry of priests. By itself, the usage of the verb does not allow us to decide whether Paul is likening himself to the priest who performs the truly sacrificial rites, to the Levite who assists the priest, or even to the layman who provides the victim for the sacrifice. What follows in the text, however, would seem to exclude this last interpretation when it mentions the "oblation of the pagans." In his study of *hierourgein*, Weiner has not noted this detail. Undoubtedly he has relied too much on the current translation, which gives the pagans only a passive role in the phrase: "so that the pagans may become an offering . . . ." But in fact Paul speaks of the "oblation of the pagans," and this expression must be understood in an active sense: the pagans furnish the victim of the sacrifice, even if this victim, from the point of view of Romans 12:1, is their own persons. Paul is then viewing himself as a celebrant, one who offers, and not as an ordinary believer. The opposite would have been surprising coming from him, since he hardly made a habit of minimizing his own vocation.

Having said this, it is important to note that even while presenting himself as a minister of sacrificial worship, Paul in no way likens himself to the Old Testament priests, for he is referring to a totally different idea of sacrifice. It is no longer a matter of putting the corpse of an animal on the fire of the altar and of "causing smoke to rise;"[63] it is a matter of sanctifying living people by communicating to them the fire of the Holy Spirit, and that is done by means of evangelization. It is from this that the whole difference between the ministry of Paul and the old ritual priesthood derives; this difference is enormous. It is clear enough then why Paul did not appropriate to himself the title *hiereus*, but went to the trouble of looking for circumlocutions that better define his ministry. Nevertheless these circumlocutions suggest a priestly interpretation. And truly, if one admits that the sacrificial transformation brought about by the Holy Spirit merits the name of sacrifice better than the ancient holocausts, one must also agree that the ministry of the Christian apostles deserves a priestly characterization much more than does the ancient cult.

8. Spiritual Sacrifices

Just as Paul speaks of "the oblation of the pagans," Peter mentions the "spiritual sacrifices" which the new converts are called to offer to God through Jesus Christ. It is this new kind of offering which characterizes the priesthood of the community of believers. Is it possible to determine what Peter means by "spiritual sacrifices"? Since the immediate context does not offer any clarification, the undertaking is difficult. One point at least is clear: the word "spiritual" contrasts the sacrifices of Christians with the "carnal rites" spoken of in the Epistle to the Hebrews (9:10), that is to say, with the animal sacrifices common to the Old Testament and the pagan cults. We must again emphasize that Peter does not take "spiritual" in the philosophical sense of a mental offering, but in the Christian sense of an offering made under the action of the Holy Spirit. From the beginning of his Epistle he has situated Christian existence "in the sanctifying action of the Spirit." In speaking of "spiritual sacrifices," he is at one with the perspective of the Epistle to the Hebrews on the sacrifice of Christ, which has been realized "thanks to the Eternal Spirit" (Heb 9:14), and with that of Paul, for whom an oblation can only be "pleasing" to God if it has been "sanctified in the Holy Spirit."[64]

But where, concretely, are we to situate the offering of spiritual sacrifices? Must we see an allusion to the Eucharist here? The exegetes are greatly divided on this point.[65] Windisch, for example, completely excludes this possibility, while Lohmeyer supports it. Cerfaux argues against a Eucharistic interpretation and sees here only "the sacrifices of interior worship . . . good works and sufferings in imitation of Christ." In his opinion, the word "sacrifice" and also the word "priesthood" are to be taken in a metaphorical sense.[66] It is clear that this author is concerned to reserve the term "sacrifice" in its proper sense to the Eucharistic celebration, and likewise, the term "priest" to ordained priests.[67] More recently another Catholic exegete, Dacquino, starting with the same presupposition, has come to the opposite conclusion.[68] The common assumption is that good deeds, patience under trial, the fulfillment of the will of God in day-to-day existence cannot constitute a sacrifice in the true sense, but only a "priestly activity in the metaphorical and improper sense."[69] Examining Peter's text, Dacquino arrives at the conviction that the apostle intends to speak of a "sacrificial worship in the true and proper sense," of a "true community liturgy," and he then concludes that he is indeed speaking of the Eucharist.

In this discussion the most questionable element is the common presupposition, that is to say the idea of sacrifice, which creates a problem in choosing between the existential and the Eucharistic interpretations, obliging one to choose one or the other. To reason in this way is to fail to take into account the Christian reworking of the idea of sacrifice, as it appears in many texts of the New Testament and as it is systematically set forth in the Epistle to the Hebrews. If it were true that the fulfillment of the will of God in day-to-day existence cannot constitute a sacrifice in the proper sense of the word, then one would also have to say that the death of Christ was not a sacrifice. In reality, from the Christian point of view, true sacrifices are existential sacrifices: they consist in the transformation of existence by the action of the Holy Spirit, in union with the sacrifice of Christ. These sacrifices have a very close connection with the Eucharist, the sacrament of Christ's sacrifice, because the condition for their possibility is union with the sacrifice of Christ. The driving force which moves the Christian to existential sacrifices comes from the sacrifice of Christ, made present in the Eucharist, and the fulfillment of existential sacrifices—their reaching God—is only possible through the mediation of the sacrifice of Christ, itself also made present in the Eucharist. The latter then is clearly indispensable for existential sacrifice.

Consequently, we must refuse to accept the dilemma. Peter's text in no way obliges us to choose between an existential and a Eucharistic interpretation. On the contrary, it permits the combination of the two aspects.[70] We have already noted that the expressions used can well apply to a Eucharistic liturgy (what better way have Christians for "approaching" Christ in the mystery of his humiliation and glorification in order to be established as a priestly community and carried along in a movement of offering to God?), but no one is compelled to adopt this meaning exclusively. The most direct references are not to the sacrament of the Eucharist but to the reality of the Passion and Glorification of Christ, "rejected by men, but chosen in honor by God." This suggests that the "spiritual sacrifices" of Christians are themselves to be situated in day-to-day life, to be modeled on the glorifying Passion of Christ. And in fact, as Feuillet has rightly emphasized,[71] the general context of the Epistle suggests the establishment of a close connection between the "spiritual sacrifices" of Christians and the imitation of the suffering Christ, the favorite theme of the apostle.[72] In this connection, we should especially note the verbal contact that exists between the expression "*spiritual* sacrifices" and the insistent assertion of 4:14: "Happy are you if you are reproached for the name of Christ, for *the Spirit of glory, the Spirit of God* rests upon you!" The times when the Spirit of God rests upon the believers are certainly those which put them in the best position to offer spiritual sacrifices. The perspective, however, need not be restricted to these moments. The whole Christian existence is to be transformed into a spiritual sacrifice; Peter invites the believers to "no longer conform to their former covetous desires" but "to become holy in all their conduct," by means, obviously, of the "sanctifying action of the Spirit." The connection between the wording of these three texts,[73] contributes to clarifying the thought of the apostle and to opening up its full scope. Union with the sacrifice of Christ—which is of course actualized in the Eucharistic celebration—enables the members of the Christian community to live their priesthood in the whole of their lives.

This is now the time to take up the question left in suspense a little earlier, regarding the connection between the priesthood of believers and their vocation of witness before the world.[74] If one were to retain only the Old Testament perspective, one would be unable to discover any direct link between these two aspects of the life of believers: in the Old Testament witness before the world did not form part of the priestly functions. But if one takes the Christian point of view, according to which true sacrificial worship consists in transforming human existence by means of the love which comes from God, one can then—and indeed one must—include in the "spiritual sacrifices" the activity of witness. This activity, in fact, forms an integral part in a life of love. When they "proclaim the mighty deeds of God," by their words (3:15) and by their manner of living (2:12; 3:2), the believers are transforming life around them by spreading the light of faith and the dynamism of love. And so they are exercising their priesthood. Understood in this way, the priesthood of the Christian people "fulfills" the promise described in Exodus 19:6 by going beyond the limits imposed on it by its first context. It is no longer simply a matter of the honor of rendering worship to God, but also—and inseparably — of a mission on behalf of all human beings.

Conclusion

The priestly text of the Epistle of Peter appears above all as an ecclesial text. Peter uses the term *hierateuma*, supplied by the Septuagint, to define the Church. The apostle proclaims the fulfillment, in the Church, of the promise addressed to the people of God in the Old Testament (Ex 19:6). The Church is truly a "priestly organism," thanks to its union with Christ. Peter goes even beyond the text of Exodus and explains that Christians are called to offer sacrificial worship to

God. But he clearly indicates the way in which this privileged vocation must be realized: it is thanks to their faithfulness to Christ in the mystery of his Passion and Glorification that Christians are integrated into the construction of a "spiritual house," destined for "priestly work." An individualistic and egalitarian interpretation of the priesthood of the baptized is therefore excluded.

On the other hand, the themes employed say nothing against the existence of a ministerial priesthood; rather, they imply one, for a house has to have a structure. Some Pauline texts make this point more clearly and reveal, also more explicitly, a priestly understanding of the apostolic ministry. The worship of Christians united to Christ is of a new kind, "spiritual": it consists in accepting the renewing and sanctifying action of the Holy Spirit into human life itself.

Unlike the Epistle to the Hebrews, Peter does not apply the title of priest directly to Christ. However, he does in fact attribute to him a priestly position, for he insists on the necessity of his mediation. The priestly organism neither exists without him nor is it separable from him. The priestly function exercised by Christians, which is that of "sacrificial" activity, is entirely conditioned by the still more priestly function of Christ's own mediation.

By adopting a different point of view, the First Epistle of Peter contributes, like the Epistle to the Hebrews, to the re-working of the notion of priesthood and to its employment for the better understanding of the Christian reality. What Peter brings out magnificently is the constructive dynamism that proceeds from the mystery of Christ, the movement of offering connected with it, and the eminent priestly dignity which results from it for the entire community of believers.

Notes

[1]Beside the commentaries which at times study the matter in detail (that of E.G. Selwyn, for example, devotes to it a "note" running 14 pages), the work of J.H. Elliott is entirely devoted to it: *The Elect and the Holy, An Exegetical Examination of 1 Peter 2:4-10, and the Phrase Basileion Hierateuma*, Leiden, 1966. In "Le sacerdoce royal des fidèles: un commentaire de 1 Pet, II, 4-10," in *Au service de la Parole de Dieu* (Mél. Charue), Gem-

bloux, 1969, pp. 61-75, J. Coppens provides an extensive bibliography.
[2]The composition has been methodically studied by M.-A. Chevallier, "1 Pierre 1:1 -
2:10, Structure littéraire et conséquences exégétiques," *RHPR* 51 (1971), pp. 129-142.
[3]Cf. 1 Pet 1:3, 23; 2:2.
[4]One must however note with Chevallier (cf. note 2), pp. 139-140, that in this first
part of the Epistle (1:1 - 2:10), Peter never mentions baptism explicitly; he names it only
in 3:21. What he is bringing out is the reality of the new birth. He affirms its connection
with the Resurrection of Christ (1:3) and shows its origin in the power of the word of
God (1:23-25).
[5]Cf. Rom 13:12; Eph 4:25; Col 3:8; James 1:21.
[6]In Greek, the connection is close between the adjective "spiritual" (*logikon*), which
here qualifies the "milk," and the word *logos*, which designates the Word. On the
connection between "milk" and "doctrine," cf. Heb 5:12.
[7]*Lithos*, "stone": Is 28:16; Ps 118:22; Is 8:14. *Petra*, "rock": Is 8:14.
[8]*Laos*, "people": Is 43:21; Ex 19:5; Hos 1:9; 2:3, 25. *Ethnos*, "nation": Ex 19:6. *Génos*,
"race": Is 43:20.
[9]Cf. above, Ch. II, 3 b.
[10]Ex 19 - 24.
[11]Ex 21 - 23; 24:1-8.
[12]Heb 9:18-21; cf. Ex 24:1-8.
[13]1 Pet 2:9; cf. Ex 19:6.
[14]E. Schüssler Fiorenza offers an in depth exposition of the theme: *Priester für Gott*,
Münster, 1972, pp. 78-155. It is to this work that we chiefly refer in what follows.
[15]Cf. Schüssler Fiorenza, *op. cit.*, pp. 79-80, 89, 117.
[16]W.L. Moran, "A Kingdom of Priests," in *The Bible in Current Catholic Thought*, (ed.
J.L. McKenzie), New York, 1962, pp. 7-20.
[17]Cf. Schüssler Fiorenza, *op. cit.* pp. 101, 151.
[18]*Ibid.*, p. 150.
[19]The same comment is made by E. Cothenet, "La première épître de Pierre," in *Le
Ministère et les ministères selon le Nouveau Testament*, (ed. J. Delorme), Seuil, 1974, p. 141.
[20]Cf. 1 Sam 8:7, 11-17.
[21]Ex 28:1; Lev 8:1-3.
[22]Num 16:3-35; 17:5.
[23]Ex 19:12, 21, 23f.
[24]Dt 4:10-14; 5:23f.
[25]Dt. 5:25-31; cf. Ex 20:18-21.
[26]Cf. Schüssler Fiorenza, *op. cit.*, p. 151.
[27]*Ibid.*, pp. 152-154. The texts which suggest a fulfillment during Messianic times are
read in Mekhilta at Ex 19:6 (71a); cf. Strack-Billerbeck, III, p. 789.
[28]L. Cerfaux, "Regale sacerdotium," *RSPT* 28 (1939), pp. 5-39 (*Recueil L. Cerfaux*,
Gembloux, 1954, v. II, pp. 283-315); J. Blinzler, "Hierateuma, Zur Exegese von 1 Petr 2:5
und 9," in *Episcopus* (Mél. Faulhaber), Regensburg, 1949, pp. 49-65; the publication
already cited of Elliott (cf. note 1), pp. 64-70, and of Schüssler Fiorenza (cf. note 14), pp.
82-85.
[29]The "quality" of priest is called *hierosyne* (Heb 7:11, 12, 24), the function of a priest
is called *hierateia* (Heb 7:5; Lk 1:9). It might be objected that the evolution of language
often causes a word to pass from one sense to another. But it must be observed that if

usage easily gives a concrete sense to an abstract noun, the opposite can hardly come about. "Charity," the name of an abstract quality, can take on the concrete sense of "alms," but "alms" never designates a quality. In Greek, *ktisis*, "the action of creating" is at times used in the sense of "a creature," but *ktisma*, "creature" never signifies the act of creating. It would therefore be abnormal to attribute an abstract sense to *hierateuma*.

³⁰Elliott, op. cit., p. 66, no. 4.
³¹2 Mac 2:17; cf. 1 Mac 4:36-59.
³²Elliott, *op. cit.*, p. 223. This is one of the principal theses of this work.
³³Cf. C. Spicq, "Les Épîtres de Saint Pierre," Gabalda, 1966, pp. 92-93. "So too, the royal priesthood is also a praiser of virtue; its liturgy consists in singing literally the divine *virtues*." L. Goppelt, *Der erste Petrusbrief*, Göttingen, 1978, p. 152: "Their service . . . can only be witness for all."
³⁴Cf. Is 49:6; 56:7; Mk 11:17.
³⁵1 Pet 1:14, 18; 4:3.
³⁶Elliott, *op. cit.*, p. 220.
³⁷1 Pet 3:18; cf. Heb 10:19.
³⁸Cf. Ac 2:41f.
³⁹Cf. Lk 24:5; Ac 25:19, etc.
⁴⁰Cf. 1 Pet 2:21; 3:17f; 4:1-2, 12-14.
⁴¹Ps 118:22; 1 Pet 2:7.
⁴²Cf. above Ch. III, 4 a; Ch. V, 3; Ch. VIII, 3 a.
⁴³"House of the Lord": Mt 12:4 and par.; 21:3 and par.; Jn 2:16f. "The House": Lk 11:51; Ac 7:47.
⁴⁴1 Cor 3:16f; 2 Cor 6:16.
⁴⁵The Christians, "a chosen race" (1 Pet 2:9), are "chosen . . . in the sanctifying action of the Spirit" (1 Pet 1:1f).
⁴⁶Cf. above, Ch. X, 2. Elliott, *op. cit.*, p. 67, has shown that one of the possible meanings of substantives in -*euma* is "the communal functioning of persons with a common charge." With this author, we say "functioning" and not "function" as do some commentators who base themselves too exclusively on the context and do not take enough account of the form of the word (F.J.A. Hort, *The First Epistle of St. Peter*, London, 1898, pp. 109-110; F.W. Beare, *The First Epistle of Peter*, Oxford, 1961, p. 66). "Function" is too abstract and this meaning would be expressed here by *hierateia*. "Functioning" must be understood in the concrete sense of the effective exercise of a function.
⁴⁷We rejoin here the criticism of Elliott made by Schüssler Fiorenza, *op. cit.*, pp. 83-84.
⁴⁸See for example *De Captivitate Babylonica*, Works of Luther, Weimar ed., v. VI, p. 564. Elliott gives many other references to texts of Luther that have the same implications, *op. cit.*, p. 3.
⁴⁹Elliott, *op. cit.*, p. 223.
⁵⁰*Ibid.* The italics are Elliott's.
⁵¹Nothing in the text of Peter permits us to maintain, as J. Moingt does, that "the significance" of the priestly vocabulary in Christianity is "negative": "to forbid some to reserve for themselves, by means of a monopoly, what is the prerogative of all." "Services et lieux d'Église (III)," *Etudes* 351 (1979), p. 381. On the contrary, Peter means to express in a positive way a privilege enjoyed by the Christians in contrast to the

unbelievers and his concern here is not at all to define the internal relationships within the Christian community. To be sure, if all the believers have a share in the priesthood, no individual can rightly monopolize it. But nothing prevents the existence of distinct modes of participation nor that of exclusively held positions: in a body, the nerve cells have certain exclusive functions; it does not follow that the others do not form part of the body.

[52]Parable of the Prodigal Son: "the older (*presbyteros*) of the two sons was in the fields" (Lk 15:25). In the episode of the woman taken in adultery, the accusers "went out one by one, beginning with the eldest (*presbyteros*)" (Jn 8:9).

[53]The Pharisees boasted that they followed in all things "the tradition of the ancients" (Mk 7:3).

[54]Cf. Cothenet, *op. cit.*, (note 19), p. 533, on the word "presbytre" (elder).

[55]1 Tim 5:17, 19; Tit 1:5; James 5:14; 1 Pet 5:1; 2 Jn 1; 3 Jn 1. The text of Tit 1:5 instructs Titus "to establish elders in every city."

[56]Thus, in French, the noun "chauffeur" is still in use, even when the world has moved on from the steam locomotive, whose chauffeur in fact fed a fire, to the internal combustion engine, which has no furnace to be attended to; the *Grand Larousse encyclopédique* (1968) gives as the first meaning for the word "chauffeur," "conducteur d'automobile."

[57]Compare "the sufferings of Christ" (5:1) and "rejected by men" (2:4); "the glory that is going to be revealed" (5:1) and "chosen, honored by God" (2:4).

[58]This participle "guarding," "watching over," is found in the majority of textual witnesses, in particular in the most ancient, a papyrus of the 3rd or 4th century, but is lacking in some important manuscripts, e.g. Vaticanus. Its presence in the original text is therefore not certain, but only probable.

[59]1 Pet 2:25. The relationships are close: the presbyters are invited to perform the actions (*poimanein, episkopein*: 5:2) which correspond exactly to the titles of Christ (*poimen, episkopos*: 2:25). The title of *episkopos* is given to Christ only here in the N.T. Elsewhere it always designates the leaders of communities, already in 1 Tim 3:2; Tit 1:7; Ac 20:28. A comparison between Ac 20:17, "elders," and Ac 20:28, "bishops," shows that these two appellations were considered equivalent at one time. They were subsequently differentiated and have marked the distinction between "priests" and "bishops."

[60]*Archiereus* is the only word in *archi-* that is frequent in the N.T. "Arch-shepherd" is unique in the whole Bible. The title that most nearly approaches it is that of "great shepherd of the sheep" applied to Christ at the solemn conclusion of the Epistle to the Hebrews (13:20), where it is clearly equivalent to *archiereus*—the context speaks of the "blood of the Covenant"—as well as to "high priest over the house of God" (Heb 10:21).

[61]Cf. Num 18:8-19; Dt 18:3.

[62]Cf. C. Wiener, "*Hierourgein* (Rom 15:16)" in *Studiorum Paulinorum Congressus*, Rome, 1963, v. II, pp. 399-404.

[63]Cf. Lev 1:9, 15, 17; 2:2, 9, etc.

[64]Cf. Rom 15:16. Peter's phrase has a rare word in common with this text: *euprosdektos*, "acceptable," "agreeable," and the allusion to the Spirit.

[65]Selwyn, *op. cit.*, pp. 294-295, gives a summary of the opinions.

[66]Cerfaux, *op. cit.*, (note 28), pp. 302-303.

[67]*Ibid.*, pp. 314-315. The same tendency is found in Blinzler, *op. cit.*, (note 28), p. 63.

[68] "Il sacerdozio del nuovo Popolo di Dio e la Prima Lettera di Pietro," in *Atti della XIX Settimana Biblica*, Brescia, 1967, pp. 291-317.

[69] *Ibid.*, p. 308; cf. also pp. 303-304.

[70] Selwyn, *op. cit.*, decides in favor of this meaning, p. 297, and more recently so does J.N.D. Kelly, *The Epistles of Peter and of Jude*, London, 1969, p. 92. This author is quoted and approved by Feuillet (cf. note 71).

[71] A. Feuillet, "Les sacrifices spirituels du sacerdoce royal des baptisés (1 Pet 2:5)", *NRT* 96 (1974), pp. 704-728, and esp. pp. 709-713.

[72] Cf. 1 Pet 2:20, 25; 3:17f; 4:1f.

[73] 1 Pet 1:2, 15; 2:5.

[74] Cf. above, Ch. X, 3.

CHAPTER XI

Christians, Kings and Priests

[The texts of Revelation 1:6; 5:10; 20:6]

Taking its inspiration, like 1 Peter, from the divine promise contained in Exodus 19:6, Revelation three times applies the title of "priest" (*hiereus*) to Christians. But it shows at least an equal interest in the affirmation of royalty, based on the same text of Exodus, while Peter scarcely delays over this other aspect. The constant association in Revelation of royal dignity with the priestly dignity throws a peculiar light on the latter and situates the Christian vocation in an original perspective. As a result, the contribution of the three passages from Revelation is not without importance for our subject.[1] It completes the New Testament's teaching on the priesthood.

The title "priest" makes its appearance at the very beginning of Revelation, and this position gives it that much greater importance. Preceded by the word "royalty," it is placed in a solemn context of doxology addressed to Christ, and it seems to express the culminating point of the work of the redeemer:

He made of us a kingdom, priests for his God and Father; to him the glory . . . . (Rev 1:6)

The second mention of priesthood confirms and augments the impression produced by the first, for it too occurs at a beginning, and its context is still more solemn: we refer to the great heavenly vision (Rev 4 - 5) which, coming after the series of letters to the seven Churches, constitutes the introduction to Revelation proper. Formulated in terms almost identical to those of the initial doxology, the affirmation of royalty and of priesthood constitutes in 5:10 the principal theme of a canticle of praise uttered by the twenty-four Ancients (5:9-10) and it marks the most important moment of the whole vision, when the

Lamb takes possession of the sealed Book (5:7). It would be difficult to give it greater prominence.

The third text (20:6), which is much less impressive in its scope and differs considerably from the first two, nevertheless deserves attention because the theme of the priesthood, again associated with that of royalty, serves here to define the privileged situation which will be enjoyed for the duration of a mysterious thousand years by those who have had a part in the "first resurrection."

In these diverse passages the title of "priest" fits very naturally into the Book's movement and design, for Revelation has a very decided cultic orientation throughout and makes free use of liturgical terminology. It often mentions the sanctuary and the altar;[2] it presents personages clothed in liturgical garments who pronounce acclamations or intone canticles, and it describes scenes of adoration.[3] However, it never speaks of the slaughter of victims or of sacrifices, but only of the burning of incense, a symbol of prayer.[4]

Paradoxically joined to this interest in the liturgy is a pronounced taste for recalling the dramatic events of human history: power struggles, wars, cataclysms, the race for power. The association of the theme of royalty with that of the priesthood appears as a faithful reflection of this twofold orientation. Could we not find here the key, or at least one of the keys, which will enable us to enter into the secret of Revelation?

1. Is Christ a Priestly Figure?

Before analyzing the texts which attribute royalty and priesthood to Christians, it will undoubtedly be useful to examine the place given to Christ himself. From the very beginning, Revelation proclaims most clearly that Christ possesses royal dignity; it names Jesus Christ "the ruler of the kings of the earth" (1:5). In its final visions, it bestows a still more glorious title on the Lamb: "Lord of Lords and King of Kings."[5] But nothing of the kind is affirmed in reference to priesthood. The titles "priest" and "high priest" do not figure in the terminology of Revelation, lavish as it is in the titles it confers on Christ.

In the absence of the title, is it not at least possible to find in this work some priestly description of Christ? Several commentators believe so, and they advance as proof a peculiarity of the description of the Son of Man in Revelation 1:13. The first thing said about him is that he was clothed in a "long robe" (in Greek, *poderes*: "which goes down to the feet"). This "long robe" is believed to suggest a characteristically priestly garment. How are we to evaluate this evidence? The word *poderes*, which is not found elsewhere in the New Testament, is employed twelve times in the Old Testament. There it translates four different Hebrew words, only one of which denotes an exclusively priestly garment.[6] As a result, the allusion in Revelation 1:13 remains uncertain. Statistically speaking, the priestly interpretation has the advantage because the word *poderes* is in fact used eight times out of twelve for the clothing of the high priest.[7] But if the connections between the texts are examined more closely, it would seem that the opposite view carries more weight, because the wording of Revelation 1:13 is closer to Ezekiel 9, which does not speak of a priest. To the similarity in wording is added, in this case, one of literary genre, which in Revelation 1:13-20 as in Ezekiel 9 is that of a vision. Furthermore, a three-way connection between Ezekiel 9:2, Daniel 10:5 and Revelation 1:13 leads to the same conclusion. It seems then improbable that John intended to represent the Son of Man as a priest.[8] The other traits in the description rather suggest the sense of royal (the golden girdle round his breast) and even divine dignity: the hair is similar to that of the vision of God in Daniel 7:9 and the title proclaimed is the one which, according to Isaiah 44:6, belongs exclusively to God: "I am the First and the Last" (Rev 1:17). This affirmation of the divine dignity of the glorified Christ will appear still more clearly later, when "the One who sits on the throne" and "the Lamb" will receive the same adoration and glory (5:13-14). If Christ is being represented as fully associated with God himself in receiving worship, it is easy to see why he is not called "priest," for the priest is the person who offers worship.

Another scene, however, raises the question of a connection between Christ and ritual sacrifices. In Revelation 5:6 there appears "a Lamb as it were slain," which is obviously Christ himself.[9] Is this not a sacrificial presentation of the mystery of Christ? The matter is not as simple as we might think. In fact, the expression taken in itself has no immediate ritual connotation. The noun which here designates the lamb is *arnion*, a word which we never find used in the biblical regulations concerning sacrifices, the term regularly used being *amnos*.[10] Futhermore, the verb "to slaughter" (*sphazein*) is not strictly speaking a sacrificial term, but belongs to non-sacral, every-day vocabulary. In

Revelation 6:4 it is used to describe mortal combats, and in Revelation 13:3 it is used with reference to the Beast, whose slaughter certainly has no sacrificial value. Neither of the two biblical texts with which the expression in Revelation 5:6 is most closely related—a phrase of Jeremiah for *arnion* and one of Isaiah for *sphazein*—suggests the offering of a sacrifice. Jeremiah, like Isaiah, is thinking of a scene of carnage, which is very different: "I, like an innocent lamb (*arnion*), led to the slaughter house . . . " (Jer 11:19); "Like a sheep, he was led to the slaughter (*sphagen*), like a lamb to the shearing . . ." (Is 53:7). In speaking of Christ as a "slaughtered lamb," Revelation is not employing ritual terminology and is not trying to liken Christ to a sacrificial victim.

This having been said, if one considers the entire context instead of examining only the expression employed, it is possible to discern here a sacrificial structure. The "slaughtered" lamb is, in fact, standing before the throne of God; it has therefore already arrived at the place to which the sacrifice endeavors to elevate the offered victim. Once this ascending phase has been achieved, the Lamb can then activate the descending functions of mediation; it is to him, in fact, that power belongs to "take the Book and to open its seals,"[11] that is to say, to control the course of historical events.

We conclude, therefore, that John has inserted a non-ritualistic expression (*arnion esphagmenon*) into a sacrificial structure. In this way he has described the Christian paradox: a death which had nothing to do with ritual—the death of Jesus, penal execution of an unjust sentence—has been transformed into a perfect sacrifice and so has become the most decisive event of human history. But John does not stop at this fundamental assertion. He immediately goes on to specify the place and the role of Christians in the redemptive work of Christ, and it is in this connection that he speaks of royalty and of priesthood (5:9-10). We shall return to this text again in the course of this chapter.

2. The Work of Christ and the Royal Priesthood of Christians (Rev 1:6)

The first royal and priestly text in Revelation is at the beginning of the Book, as we have said, in an introductory section (1:4-8) whose form seems disconcerting at first sight. It is observed, in fact, to contain several literary discontinuities, in particular the abrupt change from a greeting to a doxology. The greeting is addressed to "You":

"Grace to *you* . . ." while in the doxology what we find is an "us": "He who loves *us* . . . ." The structure proposed by Schüssler Fiorenza[12] does not take any account of this discontinuity, and is therefore without appeal. The same must be said of the attempts of a number of authors who wish to find a hymn in these verses; for example, Lohmeyer, who believes that six strophes may here be distinguished. Vanni, on the other hand, has thrown light on the composition of this section by characterizing its structure as that of liturgical dialogue.[13] To the greeting pronounced by a celebrant who transmits to the faithful "grace and peace," gifts of the eternal God, of the sevenfold Spirit and of Jesus Christ, the assembly responds by praising Christ. It is in the course of this praise response that the royalty and priesthood conferred on Christians are mentioned. The clause presents first of all a threefold structure, expressing the motifs of the praise of gratitude. Each of the three elements begins in the Greek with a verb, followed by the pronoun *hemas*, ("us"). The English translation cannot reproduce this order exactly:

> To him who loves us,
> and who has released us from our sins in his blood,
> and he has made of us a royalty, priests for his God and Father,

Then comes the formula of doxology:

> to him be glory and power for ever and ever. Amen. (Rev 1:5-6)

The syntax of this sentence is irregular:[14] two participles, translated above by relative clauses, are syntactically coordinated with a main clause, "and he has made," which makes the latter all the more striking. This main clause speaks of royalty and priesthood. The insistence on these themes is evident, all the more so because the rhythm is gradually amplifying, from the first brief element to the third very long one. The culminating point in the work of Christ, which demonstrates his love ("he who loves us") and which first of all has obtained our liberation from sin by the shedding of his blood ("and who has released us . . ."), is to have made of us "a royalty, priests for his God and Father"). This is then too our principal motive for rendering him glory.[15]

a) *Relationship with Exodus 19:6*

The expression "royalty, priests for God" is clearly inspired by the passage of Exodus where God is charging Moses to transmit this promise to the Israelites: "You will be for me a kingdom, priests . . . ."[16] The two Greek words of our text do not reproduce the Septuagint version, as did 1 Peter, but constitute a literal translation of the words of the Hebrew text, *mamleket kohanim*, taken as two juxtaposed nouns and not as a single expression. The same rendering is also found in the targums and in the versions of Symmachus and Theodotus. The specification, "for God," corresponds to "for me" in the divine promise.

The resemblance is therefore evident. But here, as in Peter's text, it includes *numerous differences*, which entirely change the perspective.

First, instead of concerning the "house of Jacob" or "the sons of Israel" (Ex 19:3), the two terms are applied to persons who are designated by the pronoun "us." To whom does this "us" refer? The beginning of the sentence shows that it refers to men and women who know that they are loved by Jesus Christ and freed from their sins by means of his blood. The preceding verse (1:4) indicates that they belong to churches. They are Christians. The promise made to the children of Israel is now being applied to the members of the Christian churches.

And from promise, it has now become reality. Instead of an announcement about the future, "You *will* be . . . ," the passage contains the proclamation of a fact henceforth accomplished, "He has made . . . ." Moreover, instead of a verb indicating a state, "to be," there is an action verb, "to make," and the subject of the action is Jesus Christ. The christological importance of this change deserves to be emphasized. Nothing in the text of Exodus prepared for it. It is a new revelation.

With a daring vigor of style, John reunites in a single proposition two affirmations of different character: Christ "has made us a royalty," Christ "has made us priests." In this way he suggests a very close bond between these two aspects of the work of Christ, but without giving any explanation on this point. On the subject of "royalty," he will be more explicit in the second text (5:10), and we will then have the opportunity to explore this theme. For the moment, let us consider the expression, "he has made us priests," which enters more directly into our subject.

Constructed, as it is here, with a double accusative, the verb *poiein* means to establish someone in a function or a dignity. In the Old

Testament, the expression "to make priests" (*poiein hiereis*) is found twice in connection with priests established at Bethel by Jeroboam. The latter "appointed priests taken from the common people, who were not sons of Levi."[17] The biblical text censures this initiative of Jeroboam and describes it as "wicked conduct," for this king had neither the right nor the capacity to "make priests." The institution of a priesthood is, in fact, a divine prerogative.[18] Revelation claims that Christ had the right and the capability to exercise this prerogative. It affirms a very close relationship between Christ and priesthood. Christ "has made priests." Such an action reveals that he is himself more than priest.

b) *Action of Christ*
In what did this action of Christ consist, in actual fact? By expressing it with a verb in the aorist, the text presents it as a well-defined action, accomplished in the past and completed. The parallelism of the sentence places it in relationship with our liberation from sin, effected by Christ by means of his own blood. If we refer to the ritual of the consecration of Aaron, as related in Leviticus, we are led to give a deep significance to this parallelism and to see in it the expression of a close bond between liberation from sin and priestly consecration. In fact, the first sacrificial rite performed by Moses at the time of this liturgy is the offering of a sacrifice for sin.[19] Christ, the new Moses, has released mankind from their sins, in order to confer priesthood on them. The difference is that he has not employed, as Moses did, the blood of a bull, but his own blood. Furthermore, though the ancient rite prescribed still other sacrifices, that of "the ram of the holocaust," and that of "the ram of priestly ordination"[20] in order to bring out the positive aspect of the consecration, the text of Revelation itself only mentions the blood of Christ once. In this way it gives us to understand that the priestly consecration of Christians has not necessitated multiple sacrifices. The transformation of the human being brought about by the death of Christ comprised at one and the same time the negative aspect of destruction of sins and the positive aspect of elevation to priestly relationship with God. We find here, in substance, the doctrine expressed in the Epistle to the Hebrews: the blood of Christ purifies our consciences and gives us the capacity to render worship to God; by his unique offering, Christ has "made perfect" those who receive sanctification. Though less explicit than the Epistle to the Hebrews concerning the link between the offering of Christ and the

transformation of mankind, Revelation affirms more clearly the priestly character of this transformation: "he has made us priests."

Schüssler Fiorenza situates this action of Christ at the moment of baptism because she views Revelation 1:6 as a fragment of a baptismal profession of faith.[21] This hypothesis remains very problematical, for the style of the passage, with its expressive irregularities, is characteristic of the author. Revelation does not mention baptism, but "the blood" of Christ (1:5), and later the slaughter of the Lamb (5:9). The victorious death of Christ is the decisive event. It is this which has made us "a royalty and priests." Baptism is only its sacramental application.

Another difference also appears between the passage of Revelation and the text of Exodus, one which was already observed in Peter's text: while God's promise in Exodus was conditional, the affirmation of Revelation is absolute. The context of Revelation 1:5-6 does not even suggest, as does that of 1 Peter 2:4-10, that a condition has been fulfilled, that of faith in Christ, but it indicates on the contrary that an obstacle existed: far from being able to claim that they had remained obedient to God, as Exodus 19:5 required, Christians acknowledge that they were slaves to sin. But Christ has overcome this obstacle: "he has released us from our sins by means of his blood." Their priestly consecration, therefore, appears all the more clearly as a manifestation of his love for them and thereby evokes an outburst of praise from them: "To him who loves us . . . glory and power."

The work of Christ, as described in Revelation 1:5-6, not only manifests his love for mankind but also his love for God. We should note, in fact, that the words "for his God and Father," which correspond as we have seen to the "for me" of the divine promise of Exodus, grow rich with new connotations in Revelation. They no longer refer only to persons who become a kingdom of priests ("You will be for me . . ."), but are also related to the action of the one who made them priests. Christ's action has been done "for God" and it finds its most profound explanation in the fact that God is also "his Father." It is a proof of filial love, for it clearly leads to the glory of God the Father. Priests are, in fact, people who are given the task of rendering worship to God. On the other hand, the allusion to the divine Sonship of Christ in the passage that speaks of priesthood recalls the constant union of the two themes in the Epistle to the Hebrews and suggests the same profound relationship. The work of Christ, which establishes a relationship between mankind and God, is a work of mediation, and if he has been able to accomplish it with such success, it is because he is "the Son of God" (Rev 2:18). Only the Son of God was in a position to bestow on mankind an authentic priesthood, by allowing them to share in his own relationship with "his God and Father."[22] What he did, he did therefore at the same time for God and for us. He has fulfilled God's promise for us.

c) *The priesthood of Christians*
In what sense is the promise of Exodus fulfilled? What kind of priesthood are Christians able to exercise? The extreme sobriety of the text makes an answer to this question difficult. It is therefore not surprising to find that commentators offer differing opinions.[23] A comparison with the text of 1 Peter reveals a difference in the term employed. Revelation does not employ a collective noun (*hierateuma*), but a concrete one in the plural: *hiereis*, "priests." Because of this, it goes further than the Epistle of Peter. It is not satisfied with affirming the participation of all Christians in one and the same "priestly organism" founded on Christ, but it also attributes the priestly dignity to each Christian individually. By saying together with all his redeemed brothers and sisters: "he has made us priests," each member of the Church is acknowledging that Christ has made him or her personally priest. There is not only a collective priesthood of Christians taken as a whole: there is a plurality of priests, each one of whom is to be capable of offering worship to God. Revelation therefore states more clearly a certain personal autonomy of each Christian in the priesthood, which does not appear in Peter's text.

It does not follow that what is supported here is a kind of individualistic dispersion. The overall orientation of the sentence rather tends in the opposite direction. Indeed it is a community that is here speaking, as the fourfold repetition of the pronoun "us" indicates. The tone is very different from that of the proclamations found in the following chapters which insist, in the singular, on the responsibility of each person: "He who has ears to hear, let him hear what the Spirit is saying to the Churches. To him who is victorious I will give . . . ."[24] Moreover, the title "priests" is closely tied in the passage to a collective noun in the singular, "kingdom," which is also an attribute of the pronoun "us": Christ "has made of us a kingdom, priests." This combination of words suggests for priesthood the aspect of function exercised in common, as in the case of kingdom.

To be sure, John is not concerned here with setting out the internal organization of the Christian priesthood, nor with defining its distinctions of rank or of function. This does not mean that he excludes them. We should note that in the text he is drawing on, the promise of the priesthood was not addressed to individuals independent of one another, but to an organized people: it was to "the elders of the people" that Moses, after having called them together, expounded all that the Lord had laid down to him (Ex 19:7). Moreover, the form of liturgical dialogue adopted in this introduction of Revelation suggests that Christian priesthood finds one of its modes of expression in liturgical celebrations, where an ecclesial structure is apparent: the acclamation of the people (1:5b-6) responds to the greeting of the celebrant (1:4b-5a).

Later in the same chapter, John may perhaps be suggesting that the rulers of the Churches are priests by a particular title. Such at least is the suggestion made with respect to the identification of the "seven stars," which according to Revelation 1:20 are "the angels of the seven Churches." If one views the title "stars" as an allusion to Daniel 12:3 which speaks of stars in connection with those who teach justice, and if, on the other hand, the title "angels" as an allusion to Malachi 2:7 which gives this title to the priest by reason of his teaching function, one is led to understand that the star-angels are the leaders of the Churches—this has for a long time been one of the accepted interpretations of this passage—and also to admit — this is a new insight—that these leaders, charged with passing on the Word of God, should here be seen as priests.[25] Though this suggestion cannot be put forward as certain, it merits attention because it is supported by biblical texts. It helps to complete the picture.

But to come back to the priesthood of all Christians. On this subject, Schüssler Fiorenza wonders whether the title "priests" (*hiereis*) in Revelation 1:6 is to be taken in the literal or the metaphorical sense. She correctly notes that for John the question was not posed in the same terms as for later theologians, when the title "priest" had become traditional in the Church as the designation for those who have received ordination. The tendency then developed to regard the common priesthood as metaphorical and to reserve the literal sense for the ministerial priesthood. In the first century, the situation was totally different and Schüssler Fiorenza is right in observing this. But she is not so well advised when she suggests that the meaning of the title in Revelation is the same as that accepted in the surrounding Jewish or pagan world, the only difference being that "this priesthood is not related to any one of the numerous gods of the syncretistic milieu of Asia Minor or with emperor worship, but is exclusively directed to the God who is the Father of Jesus Christ."[26] If this were the only difference, we should then have to affirm that John thought of the priestly worship of Christians as modeled on Jewish or pagan worship, where the principal role of the priests consisted in offering slaughtered animals to the divinity. Is it really to be understood in this way? In fact, Schüssler Fiorenza implicitly renounces this view and adopts another when, a hundred pages later, she remarks that the title "priest" is never given in Revelation to the worshipers of the Beast, but is reserved to Christians. She then notes that "the term is specified soteriologically and defined by the redemptive work of the Lamb."[27] This second position is the one which best corresponds with our text. When John took the word "priests," he transformed its meaning because he set it in the context of Christian redemption, in the same way that he transformed the meaning of "kingdom" by placing this term in the context of the same mystery.

The priestly relationship of Christians with God has been made possible by the fact that they have been freed from their sins thanks to the blood of Christ (1:5). The obstacle of sin no longer exists between God and themselves. No traditional priest, whether Jewish or pagan, had ever found himself in a like situation with truly free access to God. From this point of view, therefore, no one was so truly a priest as Christians are now. But for the same reason, the form of priesthood is radically altered. It would be absurd for men and women who have been redeemed by the blood of Christ to go back to animal sacrifices. John will never suggest this kind of priestly worship.

Does the priesthood proclaimed in Revelation 1:6 include some aspect of mediation? Some commentators think so; they hold that Christians are conscious of being priests for the benefit of all mankind, on whose behalf they approach God. But this opinion finds no support in the text which, in speaking of the blood of Christ, rather draws attention to the necessity of the mediation of Christ for all mankind. Neither did the passage of Exodus 19:6 in any way suggest the sense of a mediation; it underlined a privilege, which is very different. In the same way, Revelation describes the privileged situation of Christians due to the generosity of Christ. Yet, for all that, this privileged situation is not reserved to a *numerus clausus;* it is available to all human beings.

So then in Revelation 1:6 John is proclaiming the fulfillment of the divine promise contained in Exodus 19:6, and he is showing that it is really a matter of a Christian fulfillment, that is to say, of a work of Christ himself and of a realization which surpasses the limits of the Old Covenant. By means of his redemptive death, Christ has won for mankind a profound transformation, which introduces them into a relationship with God, his Father, that is free from all obstacles. This relationship, which is available to each and every one of the faithful, makes them "priests," that is to say, sanctified persons who are able to approach God in order to offer him worship. This priesthood, a gift of the redeeming love of the Son of God, clearly surpasses the traditional priesthoods. It is a marvelous reality which causes praise to burst forth.

3. The Reign of Christ and the Priestly Royalty of Christians (Rev 5:10)

The second royal and priestly text of Revelation (5:10) faithfully takes up the words of the first, but throws light on them in a different way by situating them in a new context. This context is formed by the great heavenly vision of Chapters 4 and 5, which introduce the rest of the Book. It is helpful to observe its orientation briefly.

a) *The vision*

Structured with obvious care, the vision divides clearly into two parts, the first of which concerns God (4:1-11) and the second the Lamb (5:1-14). The problem posed from the beginning is that of the unfolding of the history of the world: "that which must take place" (4:1). The first part describes the divine majesty and the acts of homage it receives in heaven, and concludes with the recognition of God's right to take the glory once and for all (4:11), that is to say, to determine the course of events in a positive way.[28] At the beginning of the second part (5:1-4) there then comes an episode of dramatic suspense: the Seer catches sight of a sealed book close to God, which no one is able to open, which creates a frustrating situation. This is clearly the book of God's interventions in history, which spells out concretely how God will "take the glory." If no one is able to open this book, the positive divine plan will not be set in motion and evil will continue to ravage the world with impunity. The agony does not go on indefinitely, because the silence is broken by the proclamation of the victory of the Lion of Judah, a victory which will enable him to open the sealed book (5:5). The conquering Lion then presents himself, paradoxically in the guise of a "Lamb standing as if slain," who comes forward and takes possession of the book, giving assurance to all that through him the divine plan will be accomplished. It is at this decisive moment that the four Living Creatures and the twenty-four Elders acclaim the Lamb and recall that he has redeemed men of every race and has made them "a kingdom and priests."

This is the context in which the theme of the royal and priestly dignity of Christians recurs. The position occupied by this double theme is all the more striking when we observe that the "new canticle" sung by the four Living Creatures and the twenty-four Elders (5:9-10) is placed in the center of a cleverly arranged series of five canticles or acclamations,[29] some addressed to God, others to the Lamb, and the last to both God and the Lamb together.

This is the arrangement of these five canticles:

a) to God:	his holiness is proclaimed by the four Living Creatures	4:8
a') to God:	his right to glory by virtue of the creation is proclaimed by the 24 Elders	4:11
b) to the Lamb:	his right over history, by virtue of the Redemption, is proclaimed by the 4 Living Creatures and the 24 Elders	5:9-10
b') to the Lamb:	his right to glory is proclaimed by multitudes of angels	5:12
c) to God and to the Lamb:	glory is given to them by absolutely all creatures	5:13

The vision as a whole is centered on what may be called the coming to power of the Lamb. It is not simply a question of heavenly glorification, but of the inauguration of a reign over history. Henceforth, divine sovereignty over the course of the world's history will be effectively exercised through the agency of the Lamb. The central canticle specifically proclaims that the Lamb is "worthy" to exercise this power, that he has the right to it: "You have the right to take the book and to open its seals."

Having said this, the most remarkable thing about this canticle is the way in which it establishes this right and proclaims its application, for at this point it brings in *redeemed mankind*, without saying that they are men, and assigns them a place of the highest importance, although no mention whatever was made of them in the four other canticles or in the other narrative parts of the vision, except for a fleeting allusion to "the prayers of the saints" (5:8).

Here, then, is the whole of this canticle showing its structure:

Worthy are you to receive the scroll
and break open its seals,
for you were slain.
With your blood you purchased for God
men of every race and tongue,
of every people and nation.
You made of them a kingdom,
and priests to serve our God,
and they shall reign on the earth. (Rev 5:9-10)[30]

At the beginning the principal proposition affirms the right of the Lamb; next, a causal proposition gives as the basis for this right what he has suffered and accomplished; finally, a proposition whose verb has another subject specifies one effect of the work of the Lamb: the redeemed will reign.

b) *Emphasis on the kingdom*

A *comparison* between this canticle and the initial doxology (1:6) reveals a close and fundamental relationship. In both, Christ is glorified and the motive for his glorification is his redemptive work, the end result of which consists in the granting of royal and priestly dignity to redeemed mankind.

There are a number of differences in detail between the two formulations. Some are clearly due to the fact that the canticle is sung by heavenly beings and not by the Christians themselves, as was the case with the doxology. The pronoun "our" (*hemon*), used in the expression "our God," no longer refers to Christians but to the four Living Creatures and to the twenty-four Elders. Christians are designated by a pronoun in the third person (*autous*) which appears only once: "You have made of *them* . . . ." Again, the canticle, addressed directly to the Lamb, names him in the second person: "You have the right . . . you were slain . . . etc." and not in the third person, as did the doxology. God is mentioned twice instead of once, the first time without qualification, "You have bought for God . . . ," the second time with a possessive pronoun which refers to the heavenly beings, who say: "You have made of them for *our* God a kingdom . . . ." On the other hand, the relationship of God with the Christ-Lamb is not specified and consequently the name "Father," which qualified God in 1:6, does not appear in the canticle.

Other more important differences merit more attention, as they concern the themes of royalty and priesthood. Whereas in the doxology the glory and power of Christ were only referred to at the end in a very general manner, in the canticle, on the contrary, the glorious position of the Lamb is affirmed from the beginning in a much more precise way. The expressions used refer to what the Lamb has just done and to what he is getting ready to do. The Lamb has just taken the book, an action which marks the inauguration of his reign in history, and he is preparing to open its seals, that is to say, to exercise his authority. At the beginning of their canticle, the heavenly beings expressly recognize his right to act in this way. This beginning throws a clear light on the theme of the lordship of Christ.

At the end of the canticle there is a supplementary note, which does not have a parallel in the doxology of 1:6, but which corresponds to this initial stress. The affirmation "and they will reign (*basileusousin*) over the earth," concludes the canticle by taking up again and commenting on the word "kingdom" (*basileia*) that was just applied to the redeemed. It specifies the meaning of this term which, in Revelation 1:6, remained open to another interpretation. It could, in fact, be taken in a passive sense: "to be a kingdom for God," that is to say, "to be governed by God." The codicil in 5:10 shows that the sense is active: "to be a royalty for God," that is to say, "to reign in the name of God."

The correspondence between the beginning and the end of the canticle clearly implies that the lordship of the Lamb will be manifested on earth by the royalty of Christians. Here we have an affirmation of faith that is not without daring, especially in a time of persecution such as when Revelation was written! But that is exactly the principal message of this vision.

A further supplementary note helps to orchestrate the affirmation of the lordship of Christ. It is found at the center of the motivations introduced by *hoti*, "because," and it describes the universal extension of the redemptive work. This has not been held up by any barrier, but has reached "every tribe, tongue, people and nation."

c) *The theme of the priesthood*

In view of these observations, the theme of the priesthood could seem quite secondary in this passage and to have been retained only through inertia, in order not to modify the statement of Exodus 19:6, which connects it with royalty. But careful examination of the text and its context shows that this impression is mistaken. For John, the priestly qualification retains its full importance, and what characterizes the position of Christians is not their royalty, but the union of royalty and priesthood.

We have already noted that the account of the vision sets the Lamb in a sacrificial structure. The canticle faithfully reflects this situation and thereby reinforces the theme of the priesthood. In fact it gives greater prominence, even than the doxology of 1:6, to the evocation of the Passion of Christ and the relationship established with God. The canticle, like the doxology, describes three motives for the glorification of Christ, but though in the doxology the first motive was that Christ "loves us," in the canticle it is that he was "slain." Such a motive has little connection with the theme of royalty. To say that the Lamb has the right to assume power because he was slain is almost violently paradoxical. The purpose of this paradox is obviously to impose a transformation in the conception of power, by linking it to a sacrificial structure. The mention of the blood in the second motive of 5:9 accentuates the same point of view and leads much more naturally to the affirmation of priesthood than it does to the affirmation of royalty. The repeated emphasis on the relationship with God implies the same orientation: the Lamb has "purchased for God" men of every race and has made them *for God* a kingdom and priests. The relationship with God is the most specific aspect of the priesthood.

It is true that the expressions used to evoke the Passion are not taken from sacrificial ritual. We have seen that this is true of the word "slain"; it is also true of "to purchase" (*agorazein*). The verb *agorazein* is never employed by the Septuagint when it is speaking of ritual sacrifices. The operation of "redemption," prescribed for the first-born,[31] is described by another verb, *lytrousthai*. Moreover, this "redemption" is itself a rite opposed to that of sacrifice. In principle, the first-born belong to God and therefore should have been reserved for the worship of God.[32] They are bought back so that they will no longer belong to God and so will be capable of being put to profane uses. That is why every first-born ass's colt is redeemed by means of a lamb, which is offered in sacrifice as a substitute. The first-born of the Israelites are likewise bought back, in order to be dispensed from devoting themselves exclusively to the worship of God. The Levites replace them in these functions.[33] But in quite startling contrast, the Lamb of Revelation has bought men of every nation with his own blood so that they may belong to God and be able to devote themselves to the worship of God. John therefore is transforming not only the concept of royalty but also the concept of sacrificial worship and of priesthood. Christ's Passion is not a sacrifice of substitution in the old sense of the term. It certainly includes an aspect of substitution, in the sense that Christ did in our place what none of us was capable of doing—he has transformed human death into a means of a universal redemption (Rev 5:9)—but the principal aspect of the Passion is that of communion: by means of the death that he offered, Christ has brought about a sacrificial transformation of mankind which opens up to all men and to all women the possibility of a priestly relationship with God (5:10).

d) *Royalty and priesthood*
Christian royalty is a consequence of the priesthood. Defining the relationship of Christians with the world, it corresponds to the descending phase of the priestly function. The relationship with God is incomparably more important; the final vision of Revelation clearly shows this when it describes the New Jerusalem, "the dwelling of God with men."[34] The relationship with God is the sole fundamental relationship. Everything depends on it. In fact, the Book which controls the unfolding of history is found at God's right hand (5:1). In order to obtain a power which is not doomed to ruin, it is therefore essential to be admitted to God's presence (5:7). This is the explanation of the close union in Revelation between the theme of royalty and that of priesthood. John therefore does not accept the idea of a history of the world which would take its course independently of the relationship of Christians with God. For him, the determining element of history is precisely this relationship, which makes all Christians priests. However disconcerting or scandalous the course of events may appear, John maintains this conviction of faith and makes it a source of invincible perseverance and strength of spirit. He boldly affirms, even in the midst of persecutions, that the reign of God is being realized and will be realized upon earth thanks to the Christians, God's priests: "they will reign over the earth."

Conversely, the close link between royalty and priesthood stamps the priestly worship of Christians with its peculiar quality. Thus this worship cannot be confined to one narrow sector of human life. It has to do with the totality of human beings and with the immense movement of their history. Nowhere does Revelation place a limit. The very originality of its language shows the interpenetration of various domains. The passage of 5:9 is significant in this respect, for by way of describing the event which has put human beings into authentic relationship with God, it uses terms from the slaughter house, from commercial dealings, and from the most diverse sociological categories. The remainder of the Book, beginning with the successive opening of the seven seals, will show the connection between the actions performed in the heavenly sanctuary and the dramatic vicissitudes of earthly history.

e) *Exercise of the priesthood*

But in what way exactly do Christians exercise their royal priesthood? The canticle does not say. The context provides a little light when it mentions the "prayers of the saints" (5:8), which have their place in the heavenly liturgy, represented as they are by perfumes contained in golden cups. A little later, in 8:3-5, the role of these prayers is specified: they are associated with the perfumes offered by an angel on a golden altar, and their smoke ascends to God. After this ascending movement of worship there comes the descending movement: the angel takes fire from the heavenly altar and casts it in the direction of the earth. Then follow peals of thunder, lightning and a commotion that marks the unleashing of important events. Indeed, the angels with the seven trumpets begin right after this to give the signal for the apocalyptic plagues which signal the victory of God. This symbolical scene expresses the relationship between the prayer of Christians and the course of history: their prayer mounts up to God and has a decisive influence on the course of events.

John does not, however, appear to be systematic in his descriptions. In 8:3-5 the priestly dignity of the "saints," that is to say, of the Christians,[35] does not appear. Addressing prayers to God is not a priestly prerogative. In this scene, the one who acts as priest is in fact the angel, for it is he who, by means of the smoke of the incense, brings the prayers up to God. The image conforms with the concepts of the contemporary Jewish tradition. The Testament of Levi, for example, declares that the Angels of the Presence "offer to the Lord an agreeable spiritual perfume and an unbloody oblation."[36] The difference is that in Revelation the angels are at the service of Christ and render homage to his divine glory (Rev 5:11-13). Their intervention is subordinated to the initiative of the Lamb, who opens the seals. Another text is, without doubt, more significant with regard to the priestly position of Christians. It speaks of the sanctuary (*naos*) and says:

> Rise up and measure the sanctuary of God and the altar and those who are there in adoration. As to the court outside the sanctuary, leave it aside and do not measure it, for it has been given to the pagans . . . (Rev 11:1-2)

In this text the reference is clearly to the earthly sanctuary and not to the heavenly one. Those who are found there are the Christians; being priests, they have the privilege of entering into the sanctuary of God and of performing there their cult of adoration. A special protection is assured them. They will not fall under the power of the pagans. This guarantee of immunity can be considered as an aspect of their royalty, directly connected with their priesthood.

f) *Sacrificial structure*
Revelation, however, does not allow us to suppose that the Christians will possess an immunity that will shelter them from all suffering or a triumph that will be gained without effort. Their royalty is not of this easy kind. On the contrary, it goes side by side with endurance in tribulation. The second use of the word "royalty" in Revelation is significant in this respect:[37] "royalty" is here placed, precisely, between "tribulation" and "endurance." John presents himself to the Christians of Asia as their

> companion in tribulation, royalty and endurance in Jesus. (Rev 1:9)

Christian royalty is therefore in no way incompatible with a situation of trials and sufferings; it shows itself rather by the capacity to endure them. The vocation of the Christian is to be a victor, not by opposing violence with violence, but by an unyielding refusal to give way to evil and by remaining faithful until death:

> Do not fear the sufferings that await you; the devil is going to cast some of you into prison, in order that you may be put to the test, and for ten days you will have tribulation. Be faithful unto death and I will give you the crown of life. (Rev 2:10)

The victory gained in this way looks, on the surface, like a defeat. John declares that the Beast

has been given [power] to make war against the saints and to vanquish them. (Rev 13:7)

The fate of Christians appears miserable:

He who is destined for captivity, goes into captivity; he who is to be killed by the sword, is killed by the sword. (Rev 13:10)

But in this way they arrive at the true victory over the Accuser:

They have conquered him thanks to the blood of the Lamb and thanks to the word of their witness and they are detached from the love of their own life, until death. (Rev 12:11)

We see that the triumph of the Christians has a double connection with the victorious Passion of Christ: John notes first of all that this is in fact its foundation; it has made this triumph possible; if the Christians are conquerors it is "thanks to the blood of the Lamb." John then lets us glimpse a certain relationship of resemblance: in the image of Christ, "the faithful witness" who let himself be put to death, the Christians maintain "the word of their witness" and detach themselves from the love of their life "unto death." Through this double relationship, their royalty is set in the same sacrificial structure as the lordship of the Lamb and clearly shows its close connection with the priesthood.

The affirmation made in 5:9-10 about the priestly royalty of redeemed mankind therefore throws a very strong light on the situation of Christians and on their relationship with the mystery of Christ. In this text, the theme of royalty is more to the fore than in the doxology of 1:6, because the context proclaims the lordship of the Lamb over history. However, it remains clear that it is the priesthood which is the foundation of the royalty and determines its specific qualities, for it defines the privileged relationship of Christians with God. The priestly royalty of Christians is presented as the principal outcome of the redemptive work of Christ and, even better, as the reason for his enthronement. It is "because" the Lamb has made mankind, taken from all places, "royalty and priests" that he was found "worthy to take the book and to open its seals." And it is through their priestly royalty that his lordship is to be manifested on earth. It would be difficult to give this theme a greater importance.

4. The Priesthood and Reign of the Saints (Rev 20:6)

Very far from the first two texts, because it is found in the final series of visions of Revelation, the third passage that we should analyze has a very different tenor. This is what it sounds like:

Blessed and holy is he who has a share in the first resurrection!
Over them the second death has no power,
but they will be priests of God and of Christ
and they will reign with him for a thousand years. (Rev 20:6)

In this text, instead of being inserted in a doxology (1:6) or in a canticle addressed to the Redeemer (5:10), the references to the priesthood and to the reign are linked to a "beatitude," the purpose of which is clearly, as with the evangelical beatitudes, to encourage the Christians in their trials.[38] The concern, therefore, is no longer to recall the work already accomplished by Christ ("and he has made of us a royalty, priests . . ."), but a proclamation concerning the future: "they will be priests . . . they will reign . . . ." This new point of view presents a particular concern, but several expressions of the passage are disconcerting to the reader. What are we to understand by the "first resurrection"? And by "the second death"? And what is this "reign of a thousand years"?

These expressions are clarified, at least to a certain extent, by the preceding context. The "beatitude" comes, in fact, as the conclusion of a vision which describes a "first resurrection" (20:4-5). To be quite truthful, this account is very sketchy. A judgment scene is summarily sketched and the resurrection is affirmed. The only point that is explained is that this resurrection is not the general one; it is limited to the martyrs and to the Christians who have not submitted to the Beast. The rest of the dead are explicitly excluded. This specification allows us to understand the meaning of the beatitude: the first resurrection constitutes a privilege. It is to be obtained only by an unshakable attachment to the "witness of Jesus" and to "the Word of God"—even if it means "decapitation"—and by an obstinate refusal to adore the Beast and to receive his mark. Pronounced in a time of persecution, the beatitude of Revelation 20:6 is intended to help Christians to develop in themselves an attitude of intransigent fidelity, and with this in mind it opens up before their eyes the prospect of a great hope.

a) *Victory over death*

But what exactly is this hope? It is the hope of a victory over death, obtained well before the general resurrection—the latter will not take place until "a thousand years" later[39]—and which comprises three aspects. The first is a negative one: to be beyond the reach of the "second death"; the two others are positive: to be priests and to reign with Christ.

The "second death" has already been mentioned at the beginning of the Book, in the letter to the Church of Smyrna, which evokes a similar situation and point of view:

> Remain faithful until death and I will give you the crown of life . . . The conqueror does not risk being touched by the second death. (Rev 2:10, 11)

The second death is to be understood as total perdition without remedy, a fate to which Satan's accomplices are condemned. In fact, it is later identified with the "lake of fire," with "the burning lake of fire and sulphur," into which all who practice falsehood are finally cast.[40] Anyone who participates in the first resurrection escapes this dreadful fate. The second death can no longer affect him. He enjoys complete and definitive security, something which he could not possess before, so long as he had not given, in dying, the irrevocable witness of his fidelity.

This aspect of liberation is therefore new in the situation of the Christian who profits from the first resurrection. But can one say the same of the other two aspects of the promised beatitude: "to be priests," and "to reign"? Is it not rather astonishing to find again here, this time with verbs in the future—"they will be priests . . . they will reign"—privileges already possessed by all the faithful before they died? If the Christians who attend the liturgical assembly are already entitled to proclaim themselves kings and priests by virtue of the blood of Christ (1:6), how is it possible for the priesthood and royalty to constitute a special reward attached to the first resurrection? Does this not disclose a lack of coherence in the successive affirmations of Revelation?

After careful reflection, it becomes clear that a negative answer must be given to this last question. In fact, even supposing that the priestly and royal dignity promised to the Christians after their resurrection were not different in any way from the dignity possessed by all Christians through their baptism, it would still be an astounding innovation to find it to have endured beyond death. It must not be forgotten that death normally renders impossible the exercise of power,[41] and particularly that of the priesthood. A dead man cannot render worship to the God of life.[42] The Old Testament, fully conscious of this impossibility, ordered priests to avoid all contact with death (Lev 21:10-11). And the Epistle to the Hebrews expressly notes the difference between the Old Testament priests, whose ministry was suspended by death, and Christ the priest, who "being always alive," is able to exercise his priestly intercession uninterruptedly (Heb 7:23-25). Revelation therefore is not lacking in logic when it presents as new motives of blessedness the exercise of priesthood and that of royalty on the other side of death and when it relates this to a first resurrection. In order to be priests and to reign, one must first live again.

b) *Fulfillment of the priesthood*
But there is more. The priesthood of those who are the first to rise must not be thought of as a simple resumption of the former priesthood. In reality, it represents a much closer connection with God and with Christ. Two earlier passages in Revelation have emphasized this point, and this dispenses the author from having to develop it in 20:6. In 7:9-17, John has seen an immense crowd of people clothed in white, standing before the throne and before the Lamb, and acclaiming God and the Lamb. These people have a priestly position that could not be more prominent, for they are not only admitted "into the sanctuary" (*naos*), which is a priestly prerogative, but they are before the very throne of God, and they remain there "day and night" to offer their worship to God (7:15), something which had not been allowed to anyone, even to the high priest. How have they arrived at this position? One of the Elders explains:

> They come from the great tribulation and have washed their robe and made it white in the blood of the Lamb. (Rev 7:14)

This statement is parallel to the still more realistic statement in our text:

> they have been beheaded on account of their witness to Jesus and for the sake of the Word of God. (Rev 20:4)

In both instances, it is martyrdom that leads to a prominent priestly position. The martyrs have passed from the first level of the priesthood, the one common to all the baptized, to a higher level. The first level is based on the redemptive death of Christ, who "has freed us

302 / Old Testament Priests and the New Priest

from our sins" and has made us "priests for his God and Father."[43]
This first level is obviously not the term of the Christian life, but its
beginning. It constitutes the point of departure of a vocation which
leads to a more perfect realization of the priesthood, thanks to a
personal participation in the destiny of the slain Lamb. Revelation
never wearies of emphasizing this vocation. The martyrs fulfill it to
perfection.

Another text, closely connected with the preceding one, presents
one hundred and forty-four thousand persons who also enjoy a privileged relationship with God and with the Lamb.[44] These people, in
fact, are singing before the throne a new canticle which no one else
can learn (14:3). The reason for this privilege, as described in the
following verses, places them to some extent in parallel with the
second category of Christians mentioned in our text, "those who
refuse to adore the Beast and his image and to receive his mark on
their forehead and on their hand" (20:4). It is said of these one hundred and forty-four thousand, in fact, that "they are virgins," that
"their mouth has never known the lie" and that they are "without
stain" (14:4-5). Moreover, instead of the mark of the Beast, they have
written on their foreheads the name of the Lamb and the name of his
Father (14:1).
The death of the martyrs and the uncompromising fidelity of the
other faithful constitute therefore the means of entry to a more perfect
fulfillment of the Christian priesthood, source of happiness and holiness: "Happy and holy . . . they will be priests of God and of Christ"
(20:6). In the formulation used here to describe the priesthood, we
also note a change. While the earlier texts spoke of being priests for
God, this one says: "priests of God and *of Christ*." A revealing addition! Up to this point, Christ had been situated at the origin of the
priesthood. This was proclaimed as his work: "He has made
us . . . priests" (1:6). In a certain sense this had already put him above
simple priests. But in another sense this proclamation also showed
that he had placed himself at the service of the priesthood, and even
more at the service of God, because he had shed his blood in order to
give "to his God and Father" a great number of priests consecrated to
his worship. A very different situation is now attributed to Christ: he
is fully associated with God himself, even as the object of priestly
worship. The martyrs and the saints are therefore "Christian" priests

in a twofold sense: because they owe their priesthood to Christ and because they are devoted to the worship of Christ at the same time as to that of God.

That this is the true meaning of the text is clearly proved from other passages of Revelation, which describe precisely a worship of adoration offered at the same time to God and to the Lamb. The great vision of Chapters 4 and 5 concludes with a doxology which all creatures address jointly "to the One who sits on the throne and to the Lamb," and this doxology is followed by an adoration (5:13-14). In 7:9-17 the immense crowd of martyrs, of whom we have just spoken, combine in the same homage, without any distinction, "the One who sits on the throne and the Lamb" (7:10). In a document as concerned as is Revelation to fight against possible deviations in worship,[45] these testimonies to the divinity of Christ are all the more impressive. The ideal of happiness and holiness offered to the aspirations of Christians consists in becoming "priests of God and of Christ."

Royalty is added to the priesthood. For the first time this word does not precede the priesthood, but follows it. In this, John shows himself less dependent than before on the text of Exodus 19:6. But he takes care not to omit the aspect of royalty. He had already mentioned it in the vision, at the end of 20:4, with the two attributes that we find again in 20:6: to reign "with Christ," and to reign "for a thousand years." The former emphasizes the union with Christ in glory, which corresponds to the fidelity maintained toward him during their trial. It is "because of their witness to Jesus" that the martyrs have been beheaded (20:4); it is "because of the blood of the Lamb" that they have fought victoriously (12:11). As they have shared in his Passion, so they have a share in his power. This association with the Messianic reign was already promised at the conclusion of the letter to Thyatira:

> He who is victorious and who keeps my works to the end, to him I will give power over the nations . . . as I myself have also received it from my Father. (Rev 2:26, 28)

c) *Reign of a thousand years*
In our text (20:6), a new qualification which specifies the duration of this power causes perplexity. Those first resurrected will reign with Christ "for a thousand years." What does this mean? According to what has been said in the earlier verses, these "thousand years"

represent the length of a period of remission, which constitutes the penultimate phase of the eschatological events. Once the fate of the Beast and of the False Prophet has been settled—that is to say, the totalitarian power and the ideology which claims to justify it—an angel overpowers the Dragon, that is to say Satan, and chains him up for a thousand years. At the end of this period, the Dragon "is to be released for a short time." Then will come the final battle, which will end in his definitive defeat, and will be followed by the Last Judgment and the inauguration of the New Jerusalem.[46]

The interpretation to be given to the "thousand years" has of course been the object of interminable discussions. It would be outside the scope of this work to attempt to review and examine these opinions in depth. Many ancient authors, taking the visions of Revelation literally, believed the passage to contain a form of "millenarianism," a theory inspired both by Jewish Messianic speculations and by universal human dreams: before the general resurrection, Christ would return to the earth to reign there for ten centuries and he would unite with himself in this reign the most meritorious Christians, who would first of all be resurrected. This would be a period of extraordinary earthly happiness, the description of which gives rein to unbridled fantasies. This type of interpretation does not take account of the fact that Revelation always expresses itself in symbolic language. To interpret it as if it were communicating precise factual information is to guarantee falling into error. Moreover, millenarianism adds many elements to the text which it does not in fact contain. In this passage (20:4-5) John affirms neither a return of Christ nor a kingdom on earth.

The Augustinian interpretation, reacting against millenarianism, adopts a very broad point of view. The reign of a thousand years is considered to be a symbolic representation of the time of the Church, from the Resurrection to the end of the world. The "first resurrection" is understood as the rebirth of believers, effected through baptism. After their baptism, Christians are already kings with Christ. This second interpretation assimilates the text of 20:6 with the other two (1:6; 5:10), which in fact affirm the priestly royalty of the baptized. But it forgets that this time the context gives very different specifications. According to the words of 20:4, the first to be resurrected are first and foremost Christians who have been beheaded on account of their faith. It is therefore not simply a matter of baptized people in general.

It is undoubtedly better to see in Revelation 20:4-5 the forceful expression of a certitude often described in the New Testament:

> If we die with him, we shall live with him; if we hold fast, we shall reign with him. (2 Tim 2:11-12)[47]

John is not satisfied with repeating this general principle; his faith perspective discerns a more concrete application in the case of the martyrs and the other exemplary Christians: since they have participated more intensely in the Passion of Christ they have, without waiting, an effective participation in his reign. The martyrs and the saints "live" (20:5) already with Christ and just as the fruitfulness of the Passion of Christ has been manifested not only by his heavenly glory but also by the extension of his spiritual reign upon the earth so, in the same way, the martyrs and saints will enjoy power upon the earth in union with him. Their victory will procure for the Church a very long period of peace and will assure a new vitality. It seems therefore that this is the best way to understand the affirmation of a reign of martyrs and saints with Christ, lasting a "thousand years" before the general resurrection. And this reign is closely connected with their priesthood, that is to say, with the privileged relationship which they henceforth enjoy with Christ and with God. And so in this passage of Revelation we are entitled to recognize not only one of the first testimonies to the veneration which the Church has, from a very early date, accorded to its martyrs and saints, but also the foundation for the piety which has led Christians from the earliest centuries to turn to them for their intercession. If they are priests with Christ and reign with him, it is certainly not useless to address ourselves to them.

Whatever interpretation we adopt for the reign of a "thousand years," it must be recognized that, in its astonishing originality, the third priestly text of Revelation unleashes a powerful dynamic. Instead of seeking, as the two preceding texts do, to arouse in the hearts of the faithful feelings of admiration and gratitude for the gift of priestly royalty already received, it undertakes to guide them to a higher fulfillment of their royal priesthood. It puts before their eyes the example of the martyrs and of other exemplary Christians and shows the happiness and holiness that their unfailing fidelity has gained for them. It is significant that the best description that John can find for this happiness and this holiness is the affirmation of a priestly relationship with God and with Christ, joined to a personal participation in his reign, even before the end of time.

d) *Final happiness*

After the final eschatological battle (20:7-15), the description of the final happiness to be enjoyed by all the elect contains no further explicit mention of the priestly dignity. What is promised is an even closer relationship with God, a filial relationship:

> The victor will receive this inheritance, and I will be his God and he will be my son. (Rev 21:7)

The theme of the priesthood remains, however, below the surface, for worship is still involved. In the New Jerusalem,

> there will be God's throne and the Lamb's, and his servants will worship him. (Rev 22:3)

Like the high priest who bore on his forehead a golden diadem with the inscription "Consecrated to the Lord," the elect will have "the name of God on their foreheads,"[48] but their intimacy with God will incomparably surpass anything the high priest could claim. It will fully realize the hope expressed in the ancient worship, but one that was impossible to satisfy, even in the liturgy of the Day of Atonement. His servants are now admitted into God's presence and "will see his face."[49] Revelation does not fail to join the fulfillment of royalty to this perfect fulfillment of the priesthood, when it adds these final words to the last of the visions:

> And they will reign for ever and ever. (Rev 22:5)

And so this Book remains faithful to the end to the orientation taken in the initial doxology (1:6).

Conclusion

The specific contribution of Revelation in the texts which have been studied has been the union of the royal dignity with the priestly dignity. This theme holds pride of place in the Book as a whole. At a time when Christians were made to appear as victims and criminals, John invites them to recognize with pride that they are in reality priests and kings, that is to say, that they have a privileged relationship with God and that this relationship plays a determining role in the history of the world. Their priestly royalty is presented as the culminating point of the redemptive work of Christ (1:6; 5:10). The full realization of this twofold dignity is presented as the summit of Christian joy and holiness (20:6); it is therefore worth attaining at the price of the greatest efforts, or to put it better, at the price of the closest possible association with the Passion of Christ. The theme is always evoked in a glorious context: that of the doxology in 1:6, of the canticle of praise in 5:10, of the beatitude in 20:6. But the prospect of the path of suffering which leads to this glory is never absent: the blood of Christ in 1:6 and in 5:9-10, the martyrdom of Christians in 20:4.

The union of the royalty and the priesthood corresponds to an essential characteristic of the perspective of Revelation, which consists in establishing a very strong connection between worship and life, between the heavenly liturgy and earthly history. In this way the profound conviction of the decisive importance that the relationship with God has for all dimensions of human existence finds proper expression. To explain the way in which the priesthood of Christians is exercised here below, Revelation does not use the vocabulary of sacrifice. As it does not say that Christ "has offered himself in sacrifice," it does not invite the believers "to offer themselves." It prefers a realistic vocabulary, which speaks of endurance and fidelity, of tribulation, of slaughter and decapitation, and above all of victory. In this way it demonstrates that it is in the reality of life that the priestly relationship of Christians with Christ must be concretely realized. But by its manner of referring to the heavenly liturgy, Revelation clearly shows that the faithful Christian finds first his inspiration and then his fulfillment in the liturgical encounter with the Lord.

Notes

[1]These texts have been the object of a thorough scientific investigation by E. Schüssler Fiorenza in her important work already cited, *Priester für Gott*, (1972) (see above, Chapter X, note 14); more recently, cf. A. Feuillet: "Les chrétiens prêtres et rois d'après l'Apocalypse," *R. Thom* 75 (1975), pp. 40-66.
[2]*Naos*: 16 times; *thysiasterion*: 8 times.
[3]Cf. Rev 4:8-11; 5:8-14; 6:11; 7:9-12; 11:15-18; 14:1-3; 15:2-4; 19:1-8.
[4]Rev 5:8; 8:3f.
[5]Rev 17:14; cf. 19:16.
[6]*Hoshen*, "pectoral": Ex 25:7; 35:9.

[7]Besides Ex 25:7; 35:9, already indicated, three texts must be added where *poderes* translates the Hebrew *me'il*, "cloak": Ex 28:4, 31; 29:5 — this garment is not necessarily a priestly one: cf. 1 Sam 18:4; 24:5, 12; 1 Chr 15:27, etc.—another text where it is translated *mahalasot*, "festive garments": Zech 3:4, and two Wisdom texts: Wis 18:24; Sir 45:8. The four references where it does not refer to a priest are: Ez 9:2, 3, 11 (Hebrew *baddim*, flax) and Sir 27:8.

[8]Cf. R.H. Charles, *The Revelation of St. John*, Edinburgh, 1920. v. I, p. 27. In his study of the symbolism of the seamless tunic in Jn 19:23, I. de la Potterie comes to a negative conclusion: "The seamless tunic, symbol of Christ the High Priest?" *Bib* 60 (1979) pp. 255-269.

[9]Cf. also Rev 5:12; 13:8.

[10]Ex 29:38-41; Lev 9:3, etc.

[11]Rev 5:9; 6:1, 3, 5, 7, 9, 12; 8:1.

[12]Schüssler Fiorenza, *op. cit*, p. 172.

[13]U. Vanni, "Un esempio di dialogo liturgico in Rev 1:4-8," *Bib* 57 (1976), pp. 453-467.

[14]The translations habitually suppress this expressive irregularity, which is characteristic of the style of Revelation. Some copyists soon replaced the indicative *epoiesen* by the participle *poiesanti*.

[15]Instead of "he made of *us* . . ." (*hemas* in the accusative), some witnesses read "he made *for us* . . ." (*hemin* in the dative); among them the very ancient P[18] and Alexandrinus, an uncial of great authority. This reading profoundly changes the meaning: the Christians no longer *are* priests, they just *have* priests. The critical examination concludes by preferring the reading with the accusative, and it is confirmed by the parallel text of 5:10, where there is no variant in the dative.   For further details, see Schüssler Fiorenza, *op. cit.* pp. 70-72.

[16]Ex 19:6. Cf. above, Ch X, 1.

[17]3 Kg 12:31; Greek text, cf. 13:33.

[18]Cf. Num 16:7; Sir 45:7, 18f; Heb 5:4.

[19]Lev 8:14-17.

[20]Lev 8:18-21, 22-29.

[21]Schüssler Fiorenza, *op. cit.* p. 210.

[22]Rev 1:6; cf. 3:12, 21.

[23]Schüssler Fiorenza gives a summary of these opinions, *op. cit.*, pp. 229-230.

[24]Rev 2:7, 11, 17.

[25]W.H. Brownlee, "The Priestly Character of the Church in the Apocalypse," *NTS* 5 (1958-59), pp. 224-225. E. Cothenet, "L'Apocalypse" in *Le Ministère et les ministères*, p. 275.

[26]Schüssler Fiorenza, *op. cit.*, p. 233.

[27]*Ibid.*, p. 343.

[28]In Rev 4:11 the Greek verb *lambanein* is in the aorist and therefore does not express a process that continues indefinitely, but a specific action. That is why I translate: "to take the glory once and for all."

[29]Only the central acclamation (5:9f) is specifically called a "canticle."

[30]The manuscripts present different variants. In one case only is the critics' decision difficult: is the verb "to reign," at the end, in the future or the present tense? See Schüssler Fiorenza, *op. cit.*, pp. 73-74.

[31]Cf. Ex 13:13; 34:20; Lev 27:27.

[32]Cf. Ex 13:2; 34:19.
[33]Cf. Num 3:12, 40-51; 8:16-19.
[34]Rev 21:3-4, 7, 22f.
[35]Cf. 13:7, 10; 17:6.
[36]*Test. Levi* 3:6.
[37]The first use is found in the doxology of Rev 1:6, analyzed above.
[38]Schüssler Fiorenza correctly emphasizes this orientation, *op. cit.*, p. 342.
[39]Cf. Rev 20:7, 12-15.
[40]Rev 20:14; 21:8.
[41]Cf. Is 14:9-11.
[42]Cf. Ps 6:6; 30:10; 88:12f; 115:17.
[43]Rev 1:5f; cf. 5:9f.
[44]Rev 14:1-5.
[45]Cf. Rev 14:9-11; 19:10; 22:9.
[46]Rev 20:2, 3, 10, 12-15; 21:1 - 22:5.
[47]Cf. Lk 22:28-30; Jn 12:26; Rom 8:17; etc.
[48]Rev 22:4; cf. Ex 28:36-38; 39:30f.
[49]Rev 22:4; cf. Ps 42:3; Ex 33:20, 23; Lev 16:2, 13.

Final Reflections

At the end of this study it is difficult not to experience a feeling of wonder at the way in which the New Testament has treated the question of the priesthood. At the beginning, the situation was burdened with inextricable ambiguities, since the Jewish high priests also exercised political power, from a theocratic point of view. Even worse, Christians found themselves up against a hostile attitude: the high priests, as members of the Sanhedrin, had declared themselves against Jesus and had handed him over to Pilate, and from that time on had been maintaining their active opposition to the young Christian Church.

A fundamental problem which could have appeared insoluble was added to this external conflict: what connection was it possible to establish between faith in Christ and the institution of the priesthood? Neither in his birth, nor in his ministry, nor in his death did Jesus have the appearance of a priest in the traditional meaning of the term. The primitive catechesis therefore had not presented him as a priest. Those whom he had charged with spreading his Gospel had not thought of taking this title for themselves either, for, according to the thinking of the time, their ministry was not a priesthood; it was not attached to a sacred building and did not involve animal sacrifices or other similar rites. A break therefore appeared between the new faith and the Old Testament priesthood. There was no attempt to conceal it. It was, indeed, important to note it well.

a) *Break and fulfillment*
But was it a total break? This was the problem. Did the Old Testament texts about the priesthood, texts inspired by the Spirit of God, any longer have meaning for Christians? Could they be considered, from this time on, as non-existent and could one state that the Christian communities had nothing to do with priesthood? The faith of the Church never took this direction of denial. It was prevented from

doing so by its fidelity to the principle laid down by Jesus himself, who said: "I am come not to destroy but to fulfill" (Mt 5:17), and on the other hand by the attention that had to be paid to precise evangelical data, the most important of which was the saying of Jesus regarding the blood of the New Covenant.[1] The sacrificial interpretation of the death of Christ appeared more and more indispensable to the faith, for it was revealed as necessary to express the profound significance of this event. But in reflecting on this, it became apparent that it involved a complete rethinking of the idea of sacrifice. Instead of a ritual ceremony, performed with the blood of an animal, what was involved was a terribly real event of human history, in which Jesus had engaged his whole human person on the path of obedience to God and of self-offering to his brethren, even to death. In such a "sacrifice," it was not an animal victim that had been ritually "sanctified," but it was man himself who, in Jesus, had been transformed in two ways at once: he had been raised to a new relationship with God in glory, and at the same time he had acquired a new capacity for communion with other men. In this way the New Covenant had been fulfilled.

b) Christian rethinking

The rethinking of the idea of sacrifice prepared the way for a new understanding of the priesthood. Since Jesus had offered himself as a perfect sacrifice—to God and for mankind—he had to be recognized as the perfect priest, the mediator of the New Covenant. It is the Epistle to the Hebrews which methodically developed this doctrinal discovery. There is no need to repeat here the conclusions already set out earlier after the study of this masterly writing.[2] We simply remark that in the whole New Testament there is not another exposition of christology that is comparable in extension or in systematic presentation, to the priestly christology of the Epistle to the Hebrews. It is true that the Epistle to the Romans contains a more ample doctrinal exposition, but precisely, it is not devoted so strictly or so methodically to christology alone; it includes other subjects.

c) Christ, the only new priest

By its imposing volume, the priestly christology of the Epistle to the Hebrews brings out very clearly the most important point of the Christian position in regard to the priesthood: there is only one priest in the full sense of the term and this priest is Christ. Christ alone has been able fulfill effectively the essential function of the priesthood, which is to establish a mediation between God and mankind. He is the sole mediator. To attain an authentic relationship with God, it is absolutely necessary to go through him and, more specifically, through his sacrifice. No human being can do without the mediation of Christ and no one can substitute for Christ in fulfilling this role with respect to other persons. A single new priest therefore succeeds to the multitude of Old Testament priests. This is what the title of the present work is meant to underline.

d) *The participation of Christians*

Nevertheless, it still remains possible and justifiable to speak of "priests" in the plural, provided that one does not do so to the detriment of this basic position. Revelation does so, relying on a promise in the Old Testament. It attributes the title of "priests" to all the baptized and promises it in a special manner to the Christians who have carried their faithfulness as far as martyrdom. But it explicitly declares that this priesthood depends on Christ; it is his own admirable work. The First Epistle of Peter employs a more nuanced expression and elaborates the doctrine of the common priesthood more precisely by showing clearly that it is possessed by all Christians as a single entity, thanks to their faithfulness to Christ and that they exercise it only through the mediation of Christ.

The communication of the priesthood to the Church as a whole, as a "priestly organism," reveals a characteristic aspect of the mediation of Christ, an aspect which is expressed in different forms in many of the New Testament writings, in particular in the theology of Paul and in that of John. What characterizes the mediation of Christ is that it surpasses what is ordinarily understood by mediation. Christ is not, in fact, an external mediator between mankind and God, who would endeavor by his good offices to re-establish a proper understanding between the two parties. He is the one who, *in his own person*, has brought about the complete union between mankind and God, for the benefit of all mankind. For this reason, the priesthood of Christ is fundamentally open to participation. Whoever is faithful to Christ is associated with his priesthood, for he finds in Christ an immediate relationship with God. In one sense, the external mediation of Christ is always necessary; one cannot go to the Father without passing through him (Jn 14:6), but this mediation does not remain external: believers are assimilated into Christ, they become members of his body, with him and in him they form the sanctuary of God and are priests of God. The Epistle to the Hebrews itself describes this aspect well, although it does not speak of priesthood for believers. Indeed, it proclaims that the religious situation of mankind has been radically transformed by the unique sacrifice of Christ. A system of sanctification by ritual separations has been replaced by a dynamic of participation and communion, set in motion by the priestly offering of Christ, with the result that now all are invited to approach God without fear and to offer him their whole existence, while at the same time placing this existence at the service of communion among human beings.

e) *The participation of apostles and pastors*
In this priestly dynamic of participation and communion, what is the place of those who have been called to the apostolic and pastoral ministry? Should the title of priest be attributed to them, or should it be denied?

From one point of view, it is perfectly clear that it must be attributed to them: insofar as they are believers who are faithful to Christ and allow themselves to be taken into the act of his offering, the ministers of the Church obviously form part of the "priestly organism" formed by the entirety of Christians. They too, like all their brothers in faith, are called "to offer spiritual sacrifices pleasing to God through Jesus Christ," "to raise unceasingly to God, through Christ, a sacrifice of praise" and "not to forget to do good and to practice mutual assistance, for such sacrifices are pleasing to God." They have the duty of "presenting themselves to God as a living and holy sacrifice which is pleasing to him,"[3] and in this way to realize the existential worship of Christians, which consists in the transformation of their entire lives through divine love.

But the point in question is more specifically the following: besides this priestly qualification common to all, is there reason to attribute a special priestly character to the ministers of the Church? The texts that have been studied yield a twofold answer: on the one hand, it can be argued that there is no text in the New Testament which gives the apostles or other ministers of the Church the explicit title of priest, but on the other hand, the doctrinal development observable within the

New Testament clearly points toward a priestly understanding of the ministry.

The absence of the priestly title certainly shows that in the beginning Christian ministries were not understood to be a continuation of the Old Testament priesthood. The first aspect discerned was that of difference, and this aspect must never be denied or lost sight of. Moreover, the fact that the interest directed later to the fulfillment of the priesthood did not have as an immediate consequence the adoption of priestly titles for the ministries, but resulted first in the development of a priestly christology (in Hebrews) and in the outline of a priestly ecclesiology (1 Peter), is not without significance. It indicates a profound change in the manner of understanding cult and priesthood; instead of putting ritual expression in the forefront, attention was turned first of all to existential achievements. The priesthood of Christ was not achieved in a ceremony, but in an event, the offering of his very life. The priesthood of the Church does not consist in carrying out ceremonies, but in transforming actual existence by opening it up to the action of the Holy Spirit and to the impulse of divine love. From this specifically Christian point of view, the ordained ministries are at the service of the common priesthood, and not the reverse.

Having said this, it is necessary to remember a distinction which appears in the New Testament between the two aspects of the priesthood of Christ: the aspect of existential offering and the aspect of mediation. Christ offered himself, that is to say, he put his whole human existence at the disposal of God for the salvation of his brethren, and this is the aspect of offering. By this sacrifice of himself he brought about in his own person the perfect covenant between mankind and God, so that through him and in him all human beings can enter into intimate relationship with God. And this is the aspect of mediation. The aspect of offering is found in the priesthood of all Christians, who are invited to approach God with full confidence and to offer their sacrifices, that is to say, we repeat, to open their whole personal and social lives to the transforming action of God. The aspect of mediation, in the proper sense described above, belongs exclusively to Christ: "God is one, one also the mediator of God and men, Christ Jesus, the man who gave himself as a ransom for us all."[4] The possibility of Christians opening up their lives to God without the priestly mediation of Christ is inconceivable; it remains forever bound to this mediation.

If, keeping this distinction in mind, we consider the texts of the New Testament which describe the characteristics of the apostolic or pastoral Christian ministry, we observe that these texts present the ministers of the Church as the living instruments of Christ the mediator and not as the delegates of priestly people. The Epistle to the Hebrews places the "leaders" of the community at the side of Christ the priest, in mentioning their ministry of the word, their charge of souls, their authority.[5] (Let us not forget that, according to the Epistle, one of the aspects of the priesthood of Christ is the power to speak in the name of God.) Peter also puts the "presbyters" at the side of Christ, charged in the name of the "arch-shepherd" to feed "the flock of God," which is at the same time a "spiritual house destined to the exercise of a priesthood."[6]

Paul, for his part, defines his ministry by a formula which, without confusing it with the functions of the Old Testament priests, clearly expresses its priestly character, while noting clearly its subordination to the activity of Christ.[7] The apostle gives himself a priestly role, that of intervening to make "the offering of the pagans" acceptable, by virtue of its transformation by the fire of the Spirit. It is evident, nevertheless, that Paul makes no claim to have the Holy Spirit at his disposal. It is Christ who uses Paul's ministry to communicate the Spirit to those who are reached by this ministry.

As long as the doctrine of the priesthood of Christ had not been elaborated—and this did not take place until one of the last Epistles of the New Testament—it was not possible for anyone to think of attributing a priestly character to the Christian ministries, for this would have likened them to the Old Testament priesthood, from which they differed radically. But once this doctrinal development had been achieved, their relationship with the new priesthood appeared, even in formulas which were not specifically priestly. For example, Paul defines the apostolic ministry as an ability of divine and not of human origin, which makes the apostles "ministers of a New Covenant" (2 Cor 3:6). In itself, this formula had nothing priestly about it, but after the Epistle to the Hebrews had shown that for Christ the priesthood consisted in becoming, by sanctifying himself, the "mediator of a New Covenant," this phrase of Paul's necessarily took on the meaning of an association with Christ's priesthood. One can say the same of the "ministry of reconciliation," entrusted to the apostles by God, in immediate connection with the work of reconciliation accomplished by the Cross of Christ (2 Cor 5:18).

f) *The Christian point of view*

These texts and others reveal that the apostolic and pastoral Christian ministry has as its specific function the manifestation of the active presence of Christ the mediator; in other words, of Christ the priest, in the life of believers, in order that they may explicitly welcome this mediation and by its means transform their whole existence. This ministry must therefore be acknowledged as priestly in this sense. Compared with the common priesthood,[8] it might be called more specifically priestly, because the mediation of Christ is made present through it and because the most specific element of the priesthood is the exercise of mediation between God and mankind. But, from another point of view, one may feel that it is less really priestly, because it does not itself bring about the mediation, while the common priesthood is a real transformation of existence. However, it is not a matter of the same aspect of the priesthood in the two cases: the common priesthood is a personal *offering*, the pastoral ministry is a tangible manifestation of the priestly *mediation* of Christ.

But one must be careful not to make this distinction too rigid, which would give a false idea of the structure of the Church. The shepherds are not separated from the flock, they form part of it, subject like the rest to all the exigencies of the Christian vocation. Their ministry does not make them a caste apart; on the contrary, it puts them at the service of communion among all. As to the common priesthood, to reduce it to the practice of individual worship would be to distort it; in reality, it is closely related to the exercise of a mediation. Since Christian worship consists in transforming the world by means of divine love, its principal task is to establish and promote communion. When the priestly people unites itself through a life of love with the action of Christ's offering, it releases a dynamic of love which spreads throughout the world and progressively transforms it. It is clear that this task has more connection with an act of mediation than with ritual offerings in the manner of the Old Testament worship. However, it can only be accomplished through the priestly mediation of Christ, and this can only be accepted when it is made visible. This is the reason for a ministry in which this mediation is rendered visible and efficacious.

These reflections certainly make no claim to exhausting the subject nor to solving all the problems. Their aim is more modest: to contribute to the discussion, starting from the data provided by the New Testament and in line with the living tradition of the Church. The points of view, in fact, are varied, as a result of different experiences. The utilization of priestly categories contains an obvious danger, that of an unconcious return to the ritual concept of worship of the Old Testament. In this way, one would make a new "Old Testament priest" out of the Christian priest. In the past this danger of regression has not always been avoided. At the present time, however, the opposite tendency seems to have become dominant, one that tends to reject the priestly expression of the Christian reality. Would this not be just another form of regression—where one has not taken the trouble to assimilate the new conception of priesthood, such as it is worked out in the New Testament, and continues, in discussing the question, to take for granted the Old Testament ideas of priestly worship, as if no other possibility existed?

An effort is constantly needed to maintain the authentic Christian orientation, which consists in never erecting a barrier between real life and relationship with God, nor between the relationship with God and real life, but in combining them as closely as possible, so as to transform the whole of human life, thanks to the mediation of Christ who communicates the fire of the Spirit, and to make of it a continual offering of filial obedience to God and of fraternal dedication to mankind.

Notes

[1] 1 Cor 11:25; Mt 26:28 and par.
[2] Cf. the conclusion of Ch. IX.
[3] Cf. 1 Pet 2:5; Heb 13:15f; Rom 12:1.
[4] 1 Tim 2:5.
[5] Heb 13:7, 17; cf. above Ch. IX, 4, f.
[6] 1 Pet 5:1-4; 2:5; cf. above, Ch. X, 6.
[7] Rom 15:16; cf. above Ch. X, 7.
[8] Cf. "Sacerdoce commun et sacerdoce ministériel. Distinction et rapports," *NRT* 97 (1975), pp. 193-207.

Table of Principal Biblical Citations

Analytical Index

Angels, 4, 98, 192, 288, 291, 296-297

Animals, sacrificial, 30, 35, 49, 115, 166, 198 205, 214-215, 285-286, 289, 311-312

Anointing, priestly, 29, 44-46, 79

Apostles, 15-16, 267-269, 272, 316
Jesus "apostle," 98

Archiereus, 8-9, 41, 79-80, 235, 265, 267

Assembly,
of Israel, 45, 55
Christian, 263-264, 283, 300
cf. Church; Community

Assimilation,
condition of the priesthood, 70-73
without sin, 113-114, 132
cf. Humility; Man; Mankind; Relationship; Sufferings

Authority,
of the Jewish priests, 4-5, 8-12, 15-17, 39-42, 46-47
of the word of Christ the priest, 96-99. 106-107, 142-143, 230, 233
of the "leaders," 229-231, 234-235, 266-267, 316
cf. Teaching
over the house of God, 99-106, 226, 231, 234

Baptism, 5, 228, 243, 286, 300, 304, 313
of Jesus, 55

Blessing, priestly, 20, 24, 25-26, 30, 34, 50-51, 55, 56, 159
cf. Functions of the priest

Blood,
and flesh, 85, 129, 205-206
of animals, 30, 35, 166, 198, 215
of the Covenant, 53-54, 201-202
of Christ, 68, 189-194, 196-197, 225, 233, 282-286, 289, 294, 298, 301, 302
Eucharistic, 228-229, 231-232

Break (rupture), 14, 42, 52, 116, 168, 183, 200, 311
cf. Difference between; Fulfillment

Christ, 76-77, 94, 153-154
king or priest, 86-87, 280-287
not an earthly priest, 67
become high priest, 120-143, 233-235, 272-273, 312-313
of the order of Melchizedek, 160-169
offered in sacrifice, 189-209
cause of salvation, 218-222, 224-226
and the House of God, 103-107, 255-259
adored as God, 291-292, 298, 302-303
and the priesthood of Christians, 255-258, 290-298, 299, 306-307
relationship with apostles and presbyters, 264-268, 314, 316
cf. Blood; Glorification; High priest; Jesus; Mediation; Messianism; Sonship

Church, 205, 262-264, 272-273, 314-316, 318
cf. Assembly; Community; House of God; Organism, priestly; People of God

Communion with God, 30-31, 131, 204, 207, 215, 224, 226-227, 259, 295, 314
cf. Mediation; Relationship

Community, 34, 99, 229, 243, 252, 262-263, 273

cf. Assembly; Church
Conscience, 200, 208, 214, 215, 217, 227, 228, 285
cf. Holy, to make; Perfect, to make
Consecration, priestly, necessity, 25, 26-27
Old Testament, ritual, 29-30, 56, 72, 138, 160-161, 187-188
new, existential, 74, 83, 132-133, 137, 157-158, 175, 219
which makes perfect, 165-169
communicated to Christians, 219-220, 285-286
cf. Holiness; Perfect, to make; *Teleiosis*
Continuity, 134-135, 147-149
cf. Fulfillment
Covenant,
Old Testament, 40, 53-54, 165, 176, 182-183, 245-246, 254, 290
New Testament, 54, 55, 162, 176 200-204, 208, 220-222, 233, 259, 312, 316
cf. Love; *Diatheke*; Mediation; Blood; Relationship; Testament
Criticism,
of messianism, 86-87
of the Law, 164-165, 216-218
of the Covenant, 182-183
of ritualism, 49
of the Old Testament worship, 178-182, 184-188, 214-215
cf. Difference between; Break; Opposition
Death,
incompatible with the Old Testament priesthood, 7, 72, 159-160, 162-163, 168, 299-301
does not limit the priesthod of Christ, 160, 162-163
does not limit of priesthood of all Christians, 299-301

Death of Jesus, 9, 75, 80
sacrifice?, 50-51, 53-55, 68-69, 281-282
act of identification, 85, 124
transformed and transforming, 130-131, 220-221, 285, 295
priestly offering, 124-128, 197-198, 218-219, 233, 312
Covenant—testament, 201-207
Death of Christians, 298, 304-305
Diatheke, 182, 202-203
Difference between,
Jesus and the Jewish priests, 48-51
Christ and the Old Testament high priests, 115-116, 134, 141, 142-143, 147-149, 154-155, 160-164
Melchizedek and the Levitical priesthood 158-160
sacrifice of Christ and the Old Testament worship, 189-209
the Christian situation and the Old Testament situation, 232-233, 250-252
apostolic ministry and the Old Testament priesthood, 268, 315
Divine love, see Love

Effectiveness, 187-188, 196, 199-200, 208, 213-222, 229
Elders,
of the Jewish people, 9-12, 13, 15-16
of the Church, 242, 264-267, 316
Eschatology, 45-46, 105-106, 207, 216
millenarianism, 304-305
Eternity,
of the priesthood, 44, 152-157, 159-163, 168-169
of salvation, 130, 190, 196, 203, 204
of the Covenant, 207-208

313-314
the martyrs and the saints, 299-
307, 313-314
cf. Priesthood
Prophets, 14, 28, 43-45, 48-49
See the Index of Biblical References, Isaiah and Malachi
Purity,
ritual, 5-6, 7, 25, 29, 40, 203-205
of conscience, 201, 214, 228, 285

Qumran, 45-46, 57, 104, 201

Reinterpretation,
of the Covenant, 220-222
of Christology, 86-87, 234-235
of messianism, 76-79, 289, 295
of the priesthood, 56, 234-235,
289, 295, 311-313, 318
of sacrifice, 189-190, 196-200,
233, 270-271, 294-295, 312
cf. Fulfillment; Difference between
Relationship,
with God, 4-5, 12, 26, 31-36, 83-
84, 114-115, 127-128, 131, 158,
167, 206, 218, 289-290, 294-296,
298, 301-302, 305, 306, 313, 318
with mankind, 32, 33, 85, 86, 116-
119, 139
union of two relationships in
Christ, 78, 84-85, 86-87, 112,
137, 142, 158, 168-169, 196, 199-
200, 204, 208, 219, 221, 287, 312
their union in Christians, 104-
105, 226-227, 259, 262, 307, 314
Resemblance between,
Christ and Moses, 96-97, 100-101
Christ and Aaron, 134-136, 148
Christ and Melchizedek, 152-155
the offering of Christ and the Old
Testament sacrifices, 135-136,
201-202
the baptized people and Israel,

245
cf. Fulfillment; Continuity
Resurrection, 11, 15, 68, 126, 157,
162, 167, 193-196, 258
first, 299-300
cf. Glorification
Ritual separations, 4, 27-30, 35-36,
72-73, 185, 220, 248
abolished by Christ, 48-49, 73-
74, 223, 314
Royalty,
of the Jewish people, 246-248,
253-254, 284
of Christ, 13, 280
of Christians, 253, 279, 282-285,
290-298
of the martyrs and saints, 299-307
cf. Messianism

Sacraments, 202, 205-206, 228-230,
234
cf. Baptism; Eucharist
Sacred, 7, 16, 20, 27, 34
Sacrifice,
ritual, 6-7, 20-21, 24-25, 30, 34,
40, 49-51, 53-55, 116-119, 140-
141, 163, 213-222, 268, 281
of Christ, 54, 68, 141-142, 149,
167, 189-209, 233, 281-282
of Christians, 224, 234, 269-273
cf. Worship; Offering, Rites
Salvation, 46, 70, 82, 128, 130-132,
136, 142, 149-150, 169, 207, 227,
252
Sanctuary,
its construction, 10, 101, 195,
255-264, 273
earthly, 3, 10-11, 29, 34-35, 40,
184-186
accessible to the priests, 23-24,
30, 92
destined for destruction, 52-53
spiritual, 194-195

Weakness, 72, 113, 118-119, 135,
139-140, 168-169
cf. Trial; Mercy; Sin; Temptation
Will of God, 21-22, 124, 128-130,
140, 215, 217, 221, 224, 227, 270,
305
cf. Obedience; Prayer; Victory;
Life
Witness, 5, 252, 272, 298, 300, 301,
303
Worship,
Old Testament, 4, 11, 22, 24-25,

40, 183-184, 289
criticized, 43-44, 49, 176-181,
185-187
distinguished from mediation, 31-
32, 257, 316
new, 176-178, 189-238, 269-272,
289, 295, 296-297, 301-305, 307
cf. Ceremonies; Offering; Prayer;
Priesthood; Sacrifice
Worship, ceremonies of, 3-4, 24-25,
133, 166, 179, 186, 230, 233, 315
cf. Rites

Bibliography

R.E. BROWN, *Priest and Bishop*. Biblical Reflections, Paramus/New York/Toronto, 1970

C. BRUTSCH, *Clarte de l'Apocalypse*. Geneva, 1970

J. CERFAUX - J. CAMBIER, *L'Apocalypse de saint Jean lue aux chretiens*, Cerf, 1955.

A. CODY, *A History of Old Testament Priesthood*, Rome, 1969.

J. DELORME (ed.), *Le Ministere et les ministeres selon le Nouveau Testament*, Seuil, 1974.

J.H. ELLIOTT, *The Elect and the Holy*. An Exegetical Examination of 1 Peter 2:4-10 and the Phrase *basileion hierateuma*, Leiden, 1966.

A. FEUILLET, *Le Sacerdoce du Christ et de ses ministres* d'apres la priere sacerdotale du IVe evangile et plusieurs donnees paralleles du Nouveau Testament, Ed. de Paris, 1972.

O. MICHEL, *Der Brief an die Hebraer*, Gottingen, 1966.

C. ROMANIUK, *Le Sacerdoce dans le Nouveau Testament*, Le Puy/Lyon, 1966.

L. SABOURIN, *Priesthood*. A Comparative Study, Leiden, 1973.

K.H. SCHELKLE, *Jungerschaft und Apostelamt*. Eine biblische Auslegung des priesterlichen Dienstes, Fribourg-en-B., 1961.

E. SCHUSSLER FIORENZA, *Priester fur Gott*. Studien zum Herrschaftsund Priestermotiv in der Apokalypse, Munster, 1972.

E.G. SELWYN, *The First Epistle of St. Peter*, London, 1947.

C. SPICQ, *L'Epitre aux Hebreux*, 2 vol., Gabalda, 1952-53.

C. SPICQ, *Les Epitres de saint Pierre*, Gabalda, 1966.

R. DE VAUX, *Les Institutions de l'Ancien Testament*, v.II, Cerf, 1960.

DATE DUE

MAY 1 9 '89		
JUN 1 2 '89		
July 11 '89		
Aug 9 '89		
Sept 6 89		
APR 17 1996		
NOV 29 1997		